THE RYAN GREEN TRUE CRIME COLLECTION

VOLUME 3

RYAN GREEN

Disclaimer

This book is about real people committing real crimes. The story has been constructed by facts but some of the scenes, dialogue and characters have been fictionalised.

Polite Note to the Reader

This book is written in British English except where fidelity to other languages or accents are appropriate. Some words and phrases may differ from US English.

Copyright © Ryan Green 2019

All rights reserved

ISBN: 9781078400756

For Helen, Harvey, Frankie and Dougie

CONTENTS

TORTURE MOM 9
    Introduction 10
    Gertrude Van Fossan 16
    Gertrude Baniszewski 23
    Gertrude Guthrie 28
    Gertrude Wright 32
    Paula Baniszewski 40
    The Likens Arrangement 45
    The Missed Payment 51
    The Hotdog 56
    Unfit for Chairs 67
    Petty Vengeance 74
    Turning Inward 81
    A Cure for Sticky Fingers 88
    The Cola Bottle 93
    The Basement 99
    Missed Opportunities 104
    The Freakshow 110
    I'm Going to Die 117
    Get Me Out 122
    The Trials of Gertrude Baniszewski 125

MAN-EATER 130
    Introduction 131
    The Sinners 138

Daddy's Girl 145
Life on the Borderline 153
For Whom the Wedding Bells Toll 163
Marital Bliss 177
Alone in the Dark 190
The Dark Knight Returns 212
The Last Survivor 222
The High Price of Living 229
The Last Supper 239
No Remorse 250

TRUST ME 256
Hear My Confession 257
The Son of a Whore 265
Growing Pains 276
The Dying Light 283
A Boy Named Sue 292
Making the Perfect Killer 300
A Match Made in Hell 312
The Grand Tour 317
The Child Bride 324
Abandonment Issues 331
Alone at Last 341
The Downward Spiral 350
Anything You Say 357
Fruit of the Poisoned Tree 365
The Perfect Liars 373

BLACK WIDOW **375**
    Domestic Goddess 376
    Far from Arcadia 382
    Forbidden Love 389
    First Down the Aisle 395
    Mother Knows Best 400
    The Practicalities 408
    Hope Springs Eternal 416
    The Talk of Cedartown 422
    Brief Lives 427
    The War at Home 437
    Roaming Hearts 448
    The Price of a Life 459
    The Diamond Circle Club 468
    Wife of a Preacher 475
    The Last Supper 484
    The Giggling Granny 489
ABOUT THE AUTHOR **496**
MORE BOOKS BY RYAN GREEN **497**
FREE TRUE CRIME AUDIOBOOK **499**

TORTURE MOM

A Chilling True Story of Confinement,
Mutilation and Murder

Introduction

Jenny lay on the heap of dirty clothes that was meant to be her bed and stared up at the blue smoke curling across the ceiling. Here in the bedroom, it wasn't too suffocating but if she crawled out into the hallway then it was as thick as fog. The smoke wasn't keeping her awake. She had gotten used to the smoke in this house—she had accepted that it was going to stain anything white to yellow and make her clothes, her hair and even her skin reek like an ashtray.

From down the hallway, she could hear the chatter of voices and the warbling of one of Stephanie's records. There was never a moment when the kids from the neighbourhood weren't lingering around the house, smoking and sharing their snide little secrets. There wasn't enough money for food, but they always had cigarettes: the visitors, the children of the house and 'Mother'. Jenny strained to listen for the old woman's voice underneath all the hubbub. It was shrill and nasal. It would cut through what the children were saying with ease. Jenny couldn't hear it.

There were no doors in the house. Privacy was an invitation to sin. The old woman stalked around whenever she could be bothered to move, peering into every dark corner to make sure that none of the girls were straying from purity. If she had been speaking, then Jenny was sure that she would hear it. But if the old woman wasn't spitting poison through there, then it meant that she could be standing over Jenny right at that moment.

Looking back on them now, the beatings hadn't been too bad. The violence and the cruelty had been the worst that Jenny had ever experienced in her life—the welts that had been left across the backs of her legs had burned and stung every time that she moved—but compared to the evil that she now knew was lurking just under the surface in every single person she met, Jenny understood that a few whacks with a stick was far from the worst thing to happen to a person. She closed her eyes and tried to look like she was asleep. Maybe the old woman would just pass her by if she came in and Jenny was sleeping.

The nasal whine raised hairs on the back of her neck when Jenny finally picked it out, a high-pitched wheeze that she was pretty sure only dogs should have been able to hear. It was the old woman's snoring. She must have fallen asleep in her chair. Jenny's eyes popped open and she gasped with relief. The danger wasn't completely past: any one of the monsters in the other room could still torture her at the drop of a hat, but there were limits to how much they would be willing to do without permission. The old woman may have just seemed like a skeleton stuffed in a skin suit, but with a look or a word, she could bring any one of the children to their knees. Nothing happened without her permission, whether it was explicit, or implied.

For a little while, Jenny just lay there, feeling the fear start to ebb out of her body. She had never really known fear before she came to this house, not the bone-deep dread that followed her everywhere that she went now. Knowing the specifics of what could and probably would happen to her was worse than anything that her imagination could have manufactured. She would not have been able to imagine what burning human flesh smelled like before tonight, and a year ago she would not have been able to imagine being so hungry that it would smell appetising. The fear had burrowed so deeply into her heart that it had changed her in ways that were so insidious she hadn't even noticed to begin with.

It started innocently enough, one of the girls would make a mean comment and Jenny would laugh along even though it wasn't funny because it was easier to fit in than to stand out. Going against any of them came with dangers, but while the boys might shove her or kick her crutches away, the girls went whispering back to the old woman. Jenny barely ate as it was. She couldn't afford to lose any more meals. The real proof of how far she had fallen was when the social worker came. She repeated every vile lie that the old woman had hissed into her ear without flinching. Just the hint of a threat was enough to leave her numb and quaking for days. Just the simple words, 'Do you want to go to the basement?'

When Jenny started to cry she was careful to muffle it with her sleeve. It wouldn't be good for one of the children to hear her. It would be even worse if the old woman was disturbed. Jenny would do anything to avoid the awful weight of that woman's attention. The children weren't safe by any stretch of the imagination. Jenny pictured them as hyenas wearing human clothes most of the time, braying and just waiting for the opportunity to tear into her flesh the moment that she seemed defenceless. But the old woman held their leash, and as long as she didn't decide to set them on Jenny, she would be safe. She kept telling herself that she would be safe soon. As if this nightmare had an expiry date already decided. In a way, it did. The thing in the basement would determine how much more of this misery Jenny had to endure before all of this family's dark intent was focused exclusively on her. She struggled to get her breathing under control, to turn her gasps and sobs into the quiet breathing of a girl asleep. The old woman might not be able to see her, but a sniffle at the wrong moment could unravel all of her hard work pretending to be one of the pack.

If she thought about the basement for too long, Jenny started to feel sick. She couldn't afford to lose her appetite any more than she could afford to lose a meal as punishment. She could feel her bones pressing up under her skin when she ran her hands over herself. Not that she dared to even touch herself over her clothes anymore. Not after the lecture on sin and self-pollution that the old woman had inflicted on them after the last time she caught one of the boys adjusting himself.

When she was afraid, Jenny didn't even dare to think about the basement—far too keenly aware that she might end up there. But in these brief moments when the tide of dread was out, she refused to think about it, more often than not, because thinking about it hurt, and she was hurting too much these days. When polio had ravaged her, she knew that there were going to be aches and pains for the rest of her life, but she couldn't recall them ever being so intense as when she had come to this house. She was beaten very rarely, even compared to the old woman's own children, but with nothing to eat, she sometimes thought that her body was quietly consuming itself.

This night was different. The sharp pangs of terror that the basement usually brought on had been drowned out with anticipation. Tension had been thrumming in the air ever since the gruesome display earlier on. Even if it had gone back down to a simmer now, it was soon going to boil over. She told herself that everything was going to be okay. She told herself that she didn't really believe time was running out. That the thing in the basement was still going to be there for years to come. Tears started to prick at the corners of her eyes again. Everything was going to be fine. Nothing was going to go wrong. Everything was going to be fine. Jenny had always been a terrible liar.

She pulled herself up to sitting and strained to hear any hint of movement from the other room. The laughter had turned raucous, the old woman was snoring steadily, there was never going to be a safer time for her to move. There was never going to be another chance to take this risk. Her crutches were propped in the corner, and they made such a racket that there was no possibility of sneaking around if she used them, so instead Jenny dragged herself slowly across the dust-caked floor to peer out into the hall. Through the blue fog, she could see the silhouettes in the living room. The shadows in the shape of people that she could have mistaken for human beings if she didn't remember what she had seen that day. The old woman was out of sight, but the trilling of her snores was unmistakable. Jenny could do this. Everything was going to be fine.

She dragged herself along the hallway, letting her weak legs take only a portion of her weight in case she needed them rested for a mad rush back to bed if there were any sign of trouble. It took longer than it should have to travel down the short hall, swerving to avoid mounds of trash or heaps of empty cola bottles. She made it to the kitchen unnoticed, but when the door to the basement stood before her, she froze.

It had been a long time since she had last willingly gone down those stairs, and back then the possibility of being locked down there in the basement hadn't even occurred to Jenny. She could already smell the thing down in the basement. Even from up here with the door closed the stench of it wafted up. The sickly sweetness of ammonia undercutting the farmyard stench of excrement. Jenny started breathing through her mouth. She could do this. Everything was going to be fine. The door creaked as she pressed it open and it was all that she could do to keep herself from scrambling back to bed. For another dreadful moment, she held herself still, kneeling on the kitchen floor and feeling the weight of it all pressing down on her. She strained for any sign from the living room that she had been heard, but after a moment another ripple of laughter assured her that she had gone unnoticed. With a brush of her fingertips, the door swung open the rest of the way and Jenny looked down into the abyss.

Beyond the reach of the light from the bare bulb hanging in the kitchen was a darkness so complete that Jenny could barely understand it. As if the stairs led down to a solid black wall with nothing beyond that point. All of the fear that she had quashed came rushing back. How could anyone live in that total darkness? How could you open your eyes to nothingness when you woke up and close your eyes on it when you tried to fall asleep? She stared into that darkness and tried to will her body forward. She was vulnerable kneeling out here in the open. If she went down the stairs, then she would be safer. That lie was so big that she couldn't even get through telling it to herself before rejecting it. Just as she was about to turn tail and flee back to bed, she heard a sound from beneath her.

Down in the basement, the thing had heard her coming. Jenny could hear it even now, scratching around on the packed dirt of the floor. It knew that she was here. Somehow it knew. She heard something like a sob echoing up from the darkness, and that was enough to strengthen her resolve. She crab-walked down the stairs, lowering herself carefully to stay silent and not even flinching when she pushed the door shut behind her, blocking out the last of the light. In that deep darkness, she felt her way forward, step by step, muscles aching from the effort, heart hammering in her chest. This could be her life. If she was caught coming down here, this would be her life.

She almost ran again when her foot brushed against dirt instead of another step, but instead, she forced herself upright. Down here in the hot darkness the smell was almost overpowering. Every breath was a struggle not to gag. It was like stepping inside a septic tank. She staggered forward a couple of steps before her foot brushed against something unmistakable. Bare human flesh. With quaking hands, Jenny bent down and touched her sister's arm. Following the emaciated lines of it down to where her hand was curled into a claw. She wasn't sure when she had started crying, but now it wouldn't stop. A whisper croaked out of the darkness. 'Jenny?'

'I'm here. I'm here now. Everything is going to be okay.'

Sylvia's breath came out like a rattle, but there was no fear in her voice when she answered.

'I'm going to die.'

Gertrude Van Fossan

In the late September of 1929, America was about to plummet from a precipice. In less than a month the Wall Street Stock Exchange would crash, plunging the country into the Great Depression. The working class of America would struggle and die by the thousands as the intermittently prosperous nation experienced its worst economic collapse in history. Homes would be repossessed, businesses would collapse and the boom following World War I that many had hoped would continue forever would instead drag the whole nation to the verge of collapse.

At this time of great upheaval and impending doom, a baby girl was born. Gertrude Van Fossan was the third of an eventual six children in the Van Fossan family. The Van Fossans were of mixed ancestry, combining a long line of Polish immigrants on her mother's side with a better established Dutch family on the other. Very little is known about the early years of her life, except that she was quite firmly a daddy's girl, spending every moment that she could with her father, who doted on her. In tough times, attention was the only currency that the Van Fossan family really had to spend, so it was unsurprising that the other members of the family soon came to resent how close that relationship had become. The elder children tolerated it well because the youngest was always going to be the centre of parental attention, but even after new babies were born into the family, Gert still got the lion's share of affection.

Her mother perceived the closeness of the relationship as a threat when her daughter was only a toddler and did all that she could to separate her from her father, but it did no good. Swiftly, this 'concern' transformed into a coldness that bordered on hatred. When her father was out of the house, Gert lived in a frosty silence, with her mother barking instructions but otherwise ignoring her entirely. Viewed in contrast to the relationships that her mother had with the other children, this only made her poor treatment more pronounced. The other five children in the house behaved exactly as one would expect. They saw Gert as different—an outsider—and they isolated her.

This only exacerbated the problem. With only one source of affection in her life, Gert clung to her father ever more desperately. While he did not understand the situation that he was abandoning her to when he left the house, he did recognise that desperation and he responded as any kind and loving father would: by lavishing even more attention on her than his other children. It took very little work for Gert's mother to turn the other children against her completely, and even when she attended school she was bullied, both by friends of the other Van Fossan children and others who merely preyed on the isolated girl. Her schooling was inconsistent in those early years, partly because of the complete lack of interest from her mother in ensuring that she attended, but also because Gert chose to avoid situations where she would be at a disadvantage.

The family did not weather the Great Depression well, nor did their hometown of Indianapolis. Gert's father went through several jobs and took to drinking when he could afford it. Her mother blamed Gert for all of her father's failings and most of the other troubles that befell the family, but as Gert was her father's favourite there was nothing that could be said or done against her without reprisals. While she wasn't having a healthy and happy childhood, her father saw to it that Gert wasn't entirely devoid of joy, and just the mention of him was enough to bring a smile to her face. As long as he was around, she had hope for a better future.

Daddy had been home for a couple of hours and dinner was over. It had been another 'tight' week, so dinner hadn't been much more than soup and Daddy hadn't had a thing to drink. Instead, he had shooed mother and the other children out of the kitchen and was now sitting there in his chair by the oven listening to Gert practicing her reading. She didn't read well, and she knew it. She wasn't stupid just because she was ten. But for Daddy she was willing to put in the effort, to struggle through each tangle of letters and get it right, because when she did she could see that smile creeping over his face. It made her feel warm even when the wind was howling and the windows popped out of their frames a little. When she got to the end of the page he actually clapped his hands together and it was all that she could do to resist bouncing up and down on the spot. That smile. She would remember that smile every day for the rest of her life. Daddy made some joke about the already forgotten page that she had just read and she laughed along just like she was meant to. She could tell it was a joke by the little crinkles by his eyes; they were a dead giveaway every time he was being funny with her. When she laughed, he laughed along with her, so in about a second they were both laughing about nothing and it was the best part of Gert's day. In the other room she could hear mother snapping at the little ones, outside she could hear the wind whipping by, but here in this kitchen, everything was warm and perfect. When Daddy made a silly face, her giggles got even more pronounced. The crinkles disappeared from beside his eyes, but that silly face kept her laughing. It was as if he had seen a ghost. His eyes were bulging like they would pop out of his head. She kept laughing as he toppled forward off his chair. His face bounced off the corner of the table on his way to the floor. Her fit of giggles turned into a strangled shriek. 'Daddy?!'

She scrambled down onto the floor beside him. Blood was oozing lazily from his forehead and pooling underneath him, but his eyes were still bulging wide open. 'Daddy!' He jerked and bucked on the floor like he was wrestling with some unseen force. Whatever he was trying to throw off was overpowering him easily. He let out a groan so deep that it barely sounded human. Gert had her hands full of his shirt and she was screaming. 'Daddy. Stop it! Daddy!'

Mother came barrelling into the room and let out a matching wail when she saw her husband lying there. She shoved Gert aside and started bellowing his name. Shaking him. She reared up and slapped him in the face, still screaming. The other children peered in through the door, curiosity and horror vying for a place on their vacant little faces. Gert tried to get back to her father, but her mother stopped her with a jab of her finger. She hissed, 'What did you do to him?!'

Gert couldn't get a breath in between her sobs. 'He was... He was laughing. Then he just fell. He just fell over!'

Mother's eyes narrowed. 'Get out.'

Gert scrambled back, eyes darting between Daddy and the woman hanging over him like a vulture. She couldn't do as she was told. It was like there was an elastic cord stretching from her heart to her daddy and every step away from him put more strain on it. 'Should... Should I get the doctor?'

Mother's voice cracked. 'Do you have doctor money? I don't.'

One of the other children cried from the doorway. 'What should we do, mommy?'

In an instant, their mother sprang into action, gathering up the children and shooing them away from the door. All the kindness that she denied Gert rolled off her in waves, calming the other children. Gert slipped back into her place by her father's side. In the other room, her mother was telling the children some lie about Daddy going to heaven. He wasn't going anywhere. He was right here on the kitchen floor. She burrowed into him, letting the ebbing warmth of his body surround her and straining to hear the beating of his heart. She didn't hear a thing.

If Gert had hoped that her relationship with her mother was going to improve with the death of her father, she was sorely mistaken. In addition to being irrationally blamed for her father's death, she reacted badly to the trauma of the event itself. She began to experience night terrors and without her father to act as counterbalance, her mother's cruelty escalated again and she began to beat Gert for disturbing the sleep of the other children.

The next three years were a living hell for Gert. She was treated worse than an animal at home, completely ignored by her mother and carefully ostracised by her siblings to avoid any taint from associating with her. In the mythology of the household, she was the root of all evil. Whenever something was wrong with a household item, Gert had been the last to use it. Whenever there wasn't enough food to go around, it was because Gert had taken more than her fair share. It got to the point of a running joke that the other children would bark out Gert's name whenever they so much as stubbed their toe.

In school, her social life remained desolate for another three years, but then something amazing happened. By the age of fourteen, Gert had abandoned all hope of female friendship. Her mother had poisoned that well early on in her life, and the constant spreading of rumours by the girls in her class regarding Gert's status as a pariah had left her soured to the very idea of spending time with other women. Boys were her only real option, but she didn't dare to defy her mother enough to be considered a tomboy, and without some common ground she just wasn't interesting to the preteens. The sudden onset of puberty and the associated rush of hormones changed all of that. Suddenly boys were interested in Gert again and she revelled in all of the attention. Her mother heard rumours early on and screeched at her daughter for the impropriety of her behaviour, but up until that point, Gert wasn't even aware that anything 'wrong' was going on. She was aware of sex in an abstract way. When her father had been alive she would often hear unusual sounds coming from her parents' bedroom and was always dismayed the next morning to discover that her father would take sides with her mother in any ongoing arguments. She could not connect those sounds and the very gentle flirting that she was experiencing with the boys at school. She did not understand why her mother was so furious at her, but she was past the point of caring. Any punishment that could be inflicted on Gert already had been. There was nothing more that her mother could do to make her life miserable. Drawn by the promise of the attention that she had been so desperately craving, it was no wonder that Gert made the choices that she did.

The other girls may have been shyer to start with, but soon Gert was in competition with every single one of them for the affection and attention of the boys in school. Gert could charitably be described as average looking, and her personality had never had the opportunity to flourish with no social outlet. She began to push past her own boundaries of comfort and decency to keep the boys' attention. She would let them touch her in places that she knew she shouldn't. She would touch them back. The rumour mill went into overdrive, spreading malicious whispers about her antics around the whole town and it was widely considered to be just a matter of time before she got knocked up. For the first time, Gert felt like the whisper network of girls was actually helping her. Every boy in the school was suddenly interested in her, and plenty of boys who she had never even heard of started to come calling for her, too.

To her mother's absolute horror, Gert began dating in earnest by the time that she was fifteen, moving on from the little kisses and fumbles that she had dealt out to her schoolboy friends to the pursuit of real relationships. In her entire life up until that point, Gert had had only one successful relationship, the one with her father, so it was hardly surprising that she was drawn to older men. She was courted by a succession of men between two and eight years her senior, almost all of them pursuing her because of the sordid reputation that she had developed about the town. At the age of sixteen, she finally escaped from her horrible home life through the only mechanism that was available to women at that time. She dropped out of school, packed up the few meagre possessions that could be considered hers and left her mother's shadow, never to return.

Gertrude Baniszewski

Gert married John Baniszewski only a few months after they had begun dating. He was an eighteen-year-old police deputy with a good career ahead of him. The wedding was a fairly subdued affair, with only John's family in attendance. Gert didn't have any friends of her own, her mother loudly disapproved of her relationship with John to anyone who would listen, and she had no intention of involving any of her siblings in her life from that day forward. It was as if Gert's mother's wish had finally come true: her daughter vanished.

Even though John wasn't earning much, the local bank was happy to help out an officer of the law, and the two of them settled into a modest house on the edge of suburbia immediately after their brief honeymoon in Ohio. John had little control over his work schedule in those early days, so the young lovers took whatever time that they could get together, with Gert often popping down to the station to deliver a bagged lunch around the middle of John's shift. Sandwiches were pretty much the only thing that Gert knew how to prepare at that point in her life. Her mother had thrust many chores on her but never trusted her in the kitchen, and almost immediately her atrocious cooking put a strain on the new relationship. John had been drawn in by rumours about Gert's sexual expertise, but after spending some time with her he had realised that she would fulfil the role of wife perfectly well. She wasn't just content with the idea of playing house and raising children for the rest of her days; she was also sharp enough that he felt like he could trust her to handle the running of his household. As was often the case with young men living alone, he felt the need not only for companionship and romance but also for a replacement for his mother.

He had assumed that he was going to get a submissive and obedient servant out of the deal, but he was sorely mistaken. Gert kept the house as tidy as she could manage, nagging at John for making a mess when he was at home. She was frugal with the household budget, often chastising John for his spending too much when he went out drinking with his buddies after work. All of her virtues soon turned into vices. John had expected her cooking to improve with time, but by the end of their first year together she still wasn't capable of doing much more than John himself could. Worse still, the one area of marital life where John had expected her to excel—in the bedroom—was where she disappointed him even worse than everywhere else. To Gert, sex was a mortal sin; it was a painful, distasteful chore that she had to endure to pay for this life that she had so desperately wanted. While her clumsy fumblings had been more than enough to satisfy boys her own age, John had some experience with women and he felt like he had been defrauded. When it became clear that she had no idea what she was doing he let his disappointment show, and that only led to her becoming even more withdrawn and distant. The problem escalated, with Gert becoming almost catatonic during their lovemaking and John becoming ever more violent until eventually, that violence bore fruit.

Over the course of the first decade of their marriage, Gert was pregnant more often than not, and they eventually had four children. Gert's entire personality shifted once she became pregnant for the first time. Every part of the home had to be spotless, well beyond her usual slack standards, after she had learned about the risks of infection to her unborn child. Her cooking finally began to improve as she heard from doctors about the importance of nutrition and began to pick up hints and tips from the other young mothers who attended clinics. She never formed friendships with any of these women, but she had finally come to recognise that other people were a resource that she could exploit.

Initially, John was pleased with the change that had come over Gert. Even if she wouldn't willingly let him touch her—'to protect the baby'—she was finally growing into the wife that he had always expected her to be. Once the baby was born, that contentment turned back into frustration. Where before she had been obsessively attentive to John's needs, she had now found a new centre for her life. She could not make John into a man like her father. She would never have the close, intense relationship that she so desperately craved with him, so she had switched her focus to her children: tiny little people who she could mould into the perfect partners to accompany her through life. Everything that she couldn't be bothered to do for John, she did for the children willingly. Every moment of her time was devoted to them, and the same jealousy that had blighted Gert's childhood home soon started to rear its ugly head again.

It isn't clear exactly when John started to beat Gert. It didn't happen during any of her pregnancies or immediately after she had given birth, but the rest of the time seemed to be open season. The reason given for the sometimes-brutal bouts of domestic violence was that Gert was annoying him. She made no attempt to escape from the situation at the time, believing that it was just another unpleasant experience that she had to endure to have the life that she wanted. Sometimes the annoyance was that she was making too much noise. Other times it was simply that he didn't like the way that she looked at him. She was never hospitalised by the beatings, although on several occasions she probably should have been. John realised that going too far might damage his standing in the community and jeopardise his job, so he was careful in his abuse—

using Gert as a punching bag but making sure not to lose control. He had years of experience dealing with beaten wives by that point in his career and he knew what triggered investigations. He was well liked around the station, so even if she had made a report it would have gotten lost, but he preferred to be careful.

During that decade, Gert suffered repeated injuries to the head, sometimes leaving her dizzy and disoriented for days afterwards and sometimes leaving her too bruised to venture out to the minimarket to buy food for the week. She got better at cooking, more inventive, able to stretch leftovers out over an extra day when she needed to. She got better with her makeup, too. Her mother had never taught her how to put it on. Such a thing would have been shameful on a little girl —whorish—but Gert learned by watching other women in public bathrooms. The first time she saw someone powdering on foundation it was like a revelation, and suddenly the waiting time between a beating and venturing outside again was halved.

The revelation of foundation was nothing compared to the day that Gert learned about divorce. It had always been a topic only spoken of in hushed tones when she was growing up. As a child, she had known that it was something so wrong that they weren't supposed to speak about it, but not what it actually entailed. By the time she had four children she wasn't quite that naïve anymore, but it was still an abstract concept, a punishment for truly terrible wives who didn't submit to their husband's whims. It was only when she caught a whisper of the local gossip about a woman in her own neighbourhood divorcing her husband that she truly realised that it was a possibility. She was almost overwhelmed by the idea. The word 'divorce' hung heavy in her head all through the rest of the week. The next time that she annoyed John, he lifted a hand to smack her and it slipped out from between her lips like a mantra. He had frozen, fist clenched, eyes bulging, and in that moment she realised just how impotent he had become. By the next week, she had the paperwork filed and the courts had awarded her full custody of the children. John didn't even try to contest it.

Gertrude Guthrie

It was only a few short months later that Gert found herself a new husband in Edward Guthrie. Gert's second wedding somehow managed to provide even less of a pleasant experience for her than the first, with the entire Guthrie clan of Indianapolis in attendance and drinking heavily throughout the night.

She was still young, and as pretty as she had ever been, and Eddie seemed charming compared to her brute of an ex-husband. He was unemployed when he met Gert and it was quite possible that a big part of her appeal was that she came with child support payments attached. While John had been a social drinker, wasting his paycheques down at the bar with the other policemen, Eddie was more serious in his pursuit of oblivion. He would pilfer each cheque as it came through the door and spend at least half of it on liquor before Gert even knew that it existed. They weren't drastically worse off than when she was married to John. The children still got fed, clothed and sent off to school. She still doted on them like only a mother would. They wanted for nothing, and if Gert had to patch and darn some of her own clothes then it was hardly the end of the world. She had made it through the Great Depression without a complaint. If she had to do a little bit of stitching and wash the neighbours' laundry for some extra money, then it was hardly the worst thing to happen.

Eddie didn't much care for the children. To begin with, he was awkward in their company, but as time dragged on he became actively hostile towards them. The first time that he hit one of the kids while drunk he woke up in the gutter outside with a nasty lump on the back of his head. He kept his hands to himself from that point forward, but he always felt Gert's watchful eye on him, even when he was in a stupor. He hated the way that she doted on the kids, loathed the way she would chat with them as though they were her friends rather than the nasty little leeches on her time that they really were. If he could have had Gert, and the child-support cheques, without the children then Eddie would probably have been a very content man. As it was, he spent every moment in their company sullen.

For all of his other faults, Eddie was at least good company. When he was sober and alone with Gert he was attentive and affectionate. For the first time in her adult life, Gert came to understand that sex wasn't just a misery that women had to endure, but something that she might actually enjoy. The actual act was still something that she forced herself to play-act through, but when she did, Eddie was like putty in her hands. Men had always been dangerous to her; even when her father was still around he was as likely to shout at her as to defend her, and she had always treated the boys who she was dating like barely domesticated animals, waiting for them to turn feral at any given moment—another holdover from her mother's education on the desires of young men. It was only now that she was coming to realise that men could be tamed using exactly the same thing that her mother had always warned her they were after. She had seen a glimmer of that when she was courting attention as a teenager, but now that she was fully grown she was finally realising the potential. She managed to keep Eddie pliant and pleasant for almost three months with the cunning application of a little bit of flirtation. With a little bit more than flirtation, she managed to get him to stop drinking and get back out into the world to look for work.

Once he had an income of his own and some better prospects, he filed for divorce without even speaking to Gert about it. When they met in court his given reason for leaving her was that "the children annoyed him" and in the face of such utter lack of empathy and no counter-arguments from the stunned and furious Gert, the judge granted the divorce without any complications. The entire relationship from meeting to divorce lasted less than a year.

The child support cheques from John were still coming through intermittently, and now that they weren't being intercepted by anyone, Gert found that she could afford everything that the family needed with ease, provided that she remained thrifty. Still, there was a great deal of shame attached to being a single mother, and she found herself growing lonely in the long evenings when the children were settled in their beds. At the same time, after the humiliation of the divorce from Eddie, her confidence was too beaten to attempt another round of dating.

She bumped into John one day when he was out on patrol in the neighbourhood, entirely by accident, and the two of them immediately fell back into their old familiar rhythms of conversation. She hadn't meant to invite him over for dinner, but when there was a lull in the conversation it had felt like the appropriate thing to do. When he'd shown up on her doorstep the kids had gone into a frenzy of excitement that their father was home. Gert could remember that excitement when her own father came home. She could remember the pain of separation so acutely that it might as well have been yesterday. After dinner she plied John with a bottle of Eddie's leftover liquor until the kids were all settled and snoring in their beds, then she plied him with the new skills that she had developed in their time apart. If the kids had been delighted to see their father at dinner time, they were even happier when he was still there for breakfast. Within a few weeks, everything was settled and John had moved back in.

Their second wedding was a low-key affair, attended by only a few close family members and conducted without much ceremony. Both Gert and John seemed considerably more relaxed this time around. That sense of calm followed them back to their home, too. Finally feeling like he had the wife that he deserved, John became a better husband. Finally feeling like she had him under her thumb, Gert became a better wife.

All of that tranquillity lasted about a year before Gert became pregnant again. She had almost carried the baby to term before she miscarried. It wasn't the first time that this had happened to her, but it was the first time that it had happened so late, and she sunk into a deep depression. The house fell into disrepair, the meals became dull and tasteless, and then eventually stopped appearing on the table at all. Their love life shrivelled up and died, and every complaint that Gert ever had about her first marriage to John came back around again to haunt him. He started to hit her again, at first just to snap her out of hysterical episodes, but soon just because he felt like she deserved it. It seems that she felt the same way because she made no attempt to stop him, even needling him to the point of violence on more than a few occasions. She continued her descent into darkness until she discovered that she was pregnant once again, at which point she snapped back to her old self. John had been on the verge of leaving the house again before she got the news, and he was so pleased by the sudden change in her behaviour and demeanour that his violence immediately stopped, adding further credence in her mind to the theory that she deserved whatever punishment he had been dishing out for her being a 'bad wife.' Over the course of the next seven years, this pattern would repeat itself over and over. She would miscarry and fall into a depressive slump, then she would become pregnant again and recover. By the end of their second marriage, Gert had given birth to two healthy children. The rest had died before they could come to term. After seven years of this emotional rollercoaster, John was the one to file for their second divorce. Once again, Gert was left with full custody of all six of her children, uncontested.

Gertrude Wright

At 37 years old, Gert was an unstable single mother with six children and no income beyond what she received from her ex-husband in child support. After relying so heavily on John for financial support during their second marriage, and with the gradual degeneration of her faculties, Gert found herself unable to cover the mortgage payments on the home that she had shared with her husbands and children throughout their lives and was on the verge of eviction when she latched on to Dennis Wright as a possible saviour. Dennis was already married to someone else when she met him, and she was ten years his senior. Gert leveraged both of those power imbalances for all that they were worth, using sexual favours as a reward whenever Dennis pleased her in other ways. She moved into his home the day after his wife moved out and brought her whole brood along with her. Young Dennis was not a particularly well-adjusted individual himself, prone to self-destructive bouts of drinking that may have explained his impaired decision making when it came to his new living arrangements. Whatever power Gert had over him seemed to be effective—he shouldered the financial burdens of his suddenly expansive family without a complaint.

Gert's instability did not vanish just because she had managed to snare herself a new lover. His lovely home on East New York

Street was soon caked in filth as she refused to clean up after herself or her children. She dumped food and rubbish onto the floor as she lost interest in it and on more than one occasion one of the younger children almost choked on a discarded piece of filth. Dennis was quietly horrified by the creature that he had invited into his home, but Gert's sexual domination over him wouldn't let him escape.

Dennis had spent almost a month planning his escape from Gert's clutches. He knew that if she was in the room with him—if she could lay those hands on him—then all was lost. So he planned around it; he knew that he was most pliant just after one of their 'date nights', so he waited until she had scheduled one so that his exit would be just before it. He wasn't proud of the idea of sneaking out on a household full of kids and a woman who had clearly been through too much, but this was all getting too real for him too quickly. He didn't even know if he wanted kids, let alone six of the wailing little bastards. He hadn't had any with his wife, so he certainly wasn't ready to dive into it with some woman he barely knew. He didn't have to endure for much longer, he just had to wait for Gert to start making some advances so that he knew she was in the mood, then he could pack a bag and get out of dodge. Then the rancid house, the screaming kids and she would just be a distant memory. He had family out of state, he could find a job anywhere, he didn't have to stay and suffer through a lifetime of misery with that hag just because she could lick her lips and make his knees weak.

He was ready for the usual cacophony as he walked up to the door, ready to trip over discarded soda bottles and smell the sharp tang of soaked diapers, but instead, the house was almost silent. He pushed open the door tentatively and almost gasped when he realised that he could see the carpet in the hallway again. All of the mail, newspapers and assorted crap that had formed a thick patina over the hallway had been peeled off. The base of the walls where muddy boots had splattered was now scrubbed clean and the mound of coats by the door had been squirreled away into some closet. He closed the door quietly, scared that if he made too much noise it would burst this bubble of peace that had somehow formed in his house. It actually felt like his house again—not a warren of screeching feral children or a garbage heap. He wondered for a moment if he had come in the wrong door. Then he wondered if he had gone deaf. Both worries vanished when he heard Gert in the kitchen, her voice lilting in song like something out of a Disney movie. He paced softly along the corridor, admiring the clean floors, the clean walls, the clean everything. He hadn't even realised how oppressive the filth had gotten until it was gone, and now it was like a weight had been lifted off his chest and he could breathe again. He did, drawing in lungsful of fresh, clean air and the faintest hint of bleach.

He was grinning by the time that he reached the kitchen and the warm aromas of a homecooked dinner joined the mix. Gert was by the stove, singing away to the children gathered around the table and lounging around the counters. Judging by the state of their faces they had already eaten before he arrived, which was lucky because Gert turned to him with a startlingly bright smile. She looked like a different person. The sunken eyes, the sneer, it was all gone. The woman that she pretended to be in those moments when they were tumbling in the sheets and he was losing control of his life, that was the woman who was standing in his kitchen right now, cooking him his dinner and looking like the perfect picture of a pristine housewife. He would never have known that until yesterday her clothes were filthy and crusted with sweat. He couldn't have even guessed at the horrific state of his house before today if he looked at it now. But of course, he wasn't looking at it because he only had eyes for Gert. She drifted over and planted a soft kiss on his lips and he couldn't even stop smiling long enough for that. 'Welcome home, Dennis. Dinner will be ready in just a moment. Why don't you grab a seat.'

She shooed the kids away with a wave of her hand and they all filed out, with a few of them casting resentful looks back. He was pretty sure he could smell peach cobbler in the oven, so he could understand that jealousy.

The meal was delicious, but it was nothing compared to the way that Gert was looking at him, or just the way that she looked. It was like somebody had turned the clock back on her sad life and she was back to being young and beautiful again. She smiled easily and batted her eyelids whenever he complimented her, and he found that he just couldn't stop complimenting her because everything was so sweet in that moment. She came around to sit on his lap after he was finished eating and wiped at the corner of his mouth with a napkin. 'I'm sorry I haven't been treating you right, Dennis, but I promise that all that is changing now.'

'Yeah?' He grinned.

Her hands slipped over his chest and up around the back of his neck. Her eyes filled up his vision, huge and heavy-lidded like a cow's. He wet his lips. 'Oh yeah.'

'I've been dreadful to you, and I want to start making it up to you tonight.' She shifted slightly on his lap and with a shiver, he realised just what making it up to him might look like. In the back of his mind, a little voice was screaming that he had a plan—that he was getting out—but he quashed it without a second thought. That was before she changed. Now everything was going to be all right.

Hours later he fell back onto his side of the bed, slick with sweat and aching with effort. It was a good pain, the kind of pain that leaves you well aware of just how alive you are. In the moonlight he could see Gert stretched out across the bed, her skin shimmering in the blue tint. Her laugh came out in a throaty rumble and his was so low it was almost a growl. 'You starting to forgive me yet?'

He let out a noise that could only be described as a giggle. 'I just might, at that. I just might.'

She leaned over and the little sheet that was covering her fell away. He felt a familiar stirring at the bottom of his stomach. Her eyes widened when she noticed him twitching. 'Again, already? Are you trying to wear me out?'

'Takes more than two tumbles to put you to sleep.' He smirked back.

'Not so fast now, we've got some things to discuss first.'

He rolled over and started to crawl towards her. 'Better discuss them fast, because here I come.'

'Well, there is a certain order to things. First comes love, then comes marriage...'

He stopped crawling and his good mood started to cool just as quickly as the sweat on his back. 'You know I can't up and marry you. I'd need to get my papers in to the courthouse first and that takes time and lawyer money.'

She wiggled across the bed in a very distracting fashion until they were close enough to kiss. 'I just think that we should get it settled sooner rather than later is all. Because... you never know what might happen.'

The cold had settled into Dennis' bones by now. 'What is that supposed to mean?'

'I just mean... well you do know where babies come from, right? You aren't that young.'

His stomach turned over and in an instant, all of the dull dread he had been pushing to the back of his mind came bursting back in like an unwelcome house guest. 'I don't want any babies, Gert.'

She shrugged, setting things jiggling and distracting him all over again. 'Well, life doesn't much care about what we want, Dennis. We get what the Lord gives us, and we have to make do. You know that I love every one of my babies, but I didn't want a single one of them after the first. And here I am anyway.'

He was staring at her now, trying to look past the sheen of sweat and the distracting flesh and focus on the woman behind it all. He met her eyes and tried to push all her tricks to one side. His eyes darted down to her stomach. Was it looking fuller than before? Was it just the filling meal that they had shared? Was she... His fist had clenched before he had time to think. 'Are you telling me something?'

'Well, I'd hoped that we could talk about our plans—'

'Have you got a baby in your gut?' He growled over her whispers. 'Have you?'

For a moment that calm confidence on her face wavered and he could see the sunken-eyed hag staring out at him again. The nightmare that had ruined his house, ruined his life and had plans to ruin his future too. A baby. There would be no coming back from that. She would have her hooks in him forever if she had a baby. He had seen what she had done to the cop that she had been running around with before. He would be paying out of his nose until the day he died. He would never be able to escape. A state over or the other side of the country. It wouldn't matter once his name was on that birth certificate. He reared back from Gert like she was a venomous snake. 'I don't want any babies!'

She smiled at him indulgently and rubbed a hand over her stretch-marks. 'Maybe should have thought of that before you—'

His fist caught her in the cheek, hard enough to draw blood. She didn't even cry out. She had too much experience at taking beatings for that; he had seen her scars. Instead, she just looked surprised. A little bit disappointed. He hit her again, this time in the eye, which snapped her head back with a satisfying thump.

He was not going to have a baby. She was not going to get her hooks in him. He was going to get free. He rained blows down on her and she lifted her bare arms up to fend the worst off from her face. He almost took delight in driving his fists into her chest, watching the gentle curves of her body darken and bruise under his assault.

It was only when he started to hammer his knuckles down into her stomach that anything like a rational thought even crossed his mind. He didn't have to have a baby. She couldn't do this to him. He wouldn't let her do this to him. He hit her there, again and again, at some point she had started to scream and cry. Now she was begging him. 'Not the baby. Please. Anything but the baby.'

He almost left the bed as he drew his fists up and hammered

them down again. And again. There was blood on his hands and there was blood on the sheets, but it wasn't enough. He wanted the baby out of her. He wanted it broken and gone. He didn't care if it was a baby. He didn't care if it was right or wrong. He wasn't going to let her do this to him.

The blood didn't come until later, and it wasn't as much as Gert had been expecting. The pregnancy was too early for it to be much, but it was still a sure sign that Dennis had gotten his way. She lost the baby in the early hours of the next morning while Dennis lay snoring contentedly in their bed. She sat there on the toilet, hollow-eyed, and felt all of the joy and life draining out of her body.

The relationship limped on after that. Gert unwilling to give up her claim on him and Dennis too weak-willed to wrench himself free from her dubious charms. She'd kept up appearances since the pregnancy. Kept the house spotless and the children well behaved. He had a hot meal on the table every night when he got in from work and she was more than willing to leap into bed with him at a moment's notice. It should have made him suspicious, but he just wasn't that smart. She didn't let him know that she was pregnant until he managed to work it out for himself and this time he accepted it with dull complacency. Gert genuinely believed that she had won him over, body and soul.

When the baby came she named it Dennis Junior. When she returned home from the hospital the father had vanished into the night.

Of all the degradations and embarrassments that Gert had suffered in her life, this one was the most brutal. There was no trace of Dennis left behind, not even his name. She claimed to anyone who would listen that Dennis had married her before he left. That the baby wasn't a bastard. That she was a widow. She rattled through different lies so quickly that she often switched stories in the midst of a conversation with a single neighbour. Whatever had rooted Gert in reality before had now come untethered. She stopped eating and only drank when one of the older children put a bottle of soda into her hand. Doctors came by to visit her frequently, and the talk of the neighbourhood was that she was suffering from chronic illnesses. She went from looking like a relatively pretty middle-aged woman to looking skeletal within a few weeks as if Dennis Junior were sucking the very life out of her.

The rumours circulated quickly enough, and once again in her life that network of whispers among the women nearby actually served to help Gert. She was asked to babysit on many occasions and paid generously for her efforts. Women who had managed their household workloads effortlessly throughout their adult lives suddenly needed to pass some of their washing to her to clean and iron because they just couldn't manage anymore, and she was such a dear for helping them out. More cash changed hands. John's child support payments were few and far between. He had learned about Dennis, about the comfortable home that Gert was nesting in, and he had decided that she didn't need his hard-earned money anymore. There was rent to pay on the house and children to feed and clothe, so she went through the motions despite it all meaning nothing to her.

Paula Baniszewski

While Gert was going through all of her various dramas and traumas, time had not stood still for her children. Her eldest daughter Paula had been forced into the role of friend and confidant to her mother since a very young age, learning all of the gruesome details of her one constant parental figure's life second-hand, after Gert had applied her own peculiar lens to events. She grew up with a fairly warped understanding of the world, with her understanding of romantic relationships being heavily coloured by the way that her mother interacted with men, which Paula of course saw as perfectly normal. Her teenage dating life had been less successful than Gert's. In part, this was because the sexual revolution had arrived by the time she was a teen, and as such every other girl her age was considerably more willing to be wooed. She also lacked the desperation that her mother had experienced at that age. She didn't need attention and affection. She received plenty of that from her mother, even if it came in the form of a far too familiar friendship rather than a normal parental relationship.

When Gert had her breakdown following her abandonment by Dennis, that support system vanished for all of her children, and for the first time, Paula found herself looking outside of her family for love. This began with befriending all of the neighbourhood children and school mates that she could get close to. With her mother completely checked out of reality, Paula found herself the de facto head of the household, and she used the extremely limited resources that provided to her fullest advantage. The 'Wright' house became a local hotspot for the teenagers, where they were free to smoke, listen to music and lounge around without fear of parental supervision. On the few occasions that Gert resurfaced from her room, she played along with the laidback attitude that Paula had painted her with. Gert remained unable to distinguish what was appropriate for adults to say and do around teenagers, trapped in a constant state of arrested development since her own teenage years by the isolation of her abusive relationships. Still, Paula's friendships and the expansive social network that she was growing wasn't enough for her.

Paula's date was only a year younger than her, and while she normally wouldn't have bothered with a kid like that, she couldn't deny that he had a boyish charm to him. A record was still playing in the living room and the chatter of the usual crowd almost drowned it out. She wasn't worried about anyone spotting her kissing a boy. They were all too wrapped up in their own melodramas to give her a second thought, even if she was ostensibly the hostess. When his hands slipped down to squeeze her backside Paula jumped as if she had touched a hot stove, then she pressed back into it and returned his open-mouthed mauling with the same. Every time he squeezed her, she could feel her heart thumping harder. With a giggle, she broke away and with one last nervous glance towards the living room, she took him by the hand and dragged him into her bedroom. Technically she had to share it with the other girls, but they were all chattering away in the other room. No prying eyes or hoots and hollers were going to be coming their way.

They stumbled over some old worn out shoes and nearly fell into a heap of old broken toys, but they made it to Paula's bed without any further incident. She had seen her mother with men often enough to know how this was meant to go. She guided the boy's hands up to her chest and moaned as loudly as she dared, even though it mainly hurt when the boy got too excited and mashed her breasts in his blunt fingers. She struggled out of her blouse and he was fiddling with his belt, eyes wide and mouth hanging open in anticipation. She leaned in to kiss him again with half of her buttons undone and it only took him a second to remember what he was meant to be doing. Paula was starting to feel warm. The sounds from the other room were fading away until all that she could hear was the boy's panting breath and the thunder of her own heartbeat in her ears. The door creaked open, but Paula was so lost in the moment that she didn't even realise anyone else was in the room when the screech began. 'Sinners!'

Paula leapt off the boy and tried to scramble away but her mother caught her by her hair and dragged her back. 'You filthy whore. In my house. My house!'

With a jerk of her arm, she drew a strangled yelp out of Paula and drove her to her knees. 'And you! Don't ever let me see you sniffing around my girls again. You hear me, you piece of trash. Get yourself out of this house before I do something I'll regret.'

The last few weeks had not been kind to Gert. Her hair had begun to recede and the lack of nutrition had made her eyes sink even deeper into the skull-like mask of her face. She looked like a nightmare made flesh at the best of times, but here in the deep shadows with her voice shrieking, it was lucky that Paula's date didn't wet himself as he scrambled to escape without even granting her a sympathetic glance back. Gert stormed out after him, screaming at the top of her lungs, banishing the children from her house with one long tirade of vile insults and curses. Paula was left kneeling in the darkness with tears streaming down her face and any joy from her first kiss long forgotten in the tide of terror that had just swept through her life.

Any attempt by Paula to date was met with similar outbursts and disruptions to her social routine. After the first incident, Gert removed every internal door in the house and had the older boys chop them up for firewood. The next time that she saw Paula talking with a boy alone, her happy-go-lucky façade slipped once again and she dragged the girl inside for a long lecture about how she was going to ruin her life, getting knocked up outside of marriage, destroying her prospects. When that lecture didn't work, and Paula was caught coming in late with her lips pink and swollen from kissing, Gert began crafting rules for the family for the first time in her life. Every Sunday they would attend church and for the rest of the week, it infused her lectures with new hellfire and brimstone. It wasn't enough that Paula was going to ruin her life, but she was going to tarnish her immortal soul, too. The lectures became infrequent before long, then Gert slipped back into her old habits. None of the kids had dared to confront her with the truth of her own sinful behaviour. She still called herself Mrs Wright to deflect any suggestions of impropriety, but everyone in the neighbourhood knew the truth, which meant that all of their kids knew the truth, too. None of them were willing to insult Gert by talking about them, whether because of her wild temper, because they pitied her or because they appreciated the things that she did for them – but they all knew her shame and she loathed them for it.

For Paula's part, she moved her dating life out of the line of fire with as much subtlety as a teenager can manage. She knew that like her mother her only real hope for a comfortable life was to marry well, but like her mother her taste was questionable and her patience was extremely finite. Rather than waiting for a boy her own age to establish himself and ask her out, Paula started sneaking out in the evenings and frequenting the local bars, where rumours of her presence were less likely to trickle back to her mother. It didn't take her long to snare a successful local business owner, and if he were thirty years older than her that hardly mattered in the grand scheme of things. He took her to motels and they slept together regularly for about a month before she broached the subject of marriage, since he didn't seem inclined to talk about it. That was when he took his wedding ring out of his pocket and slipped it back onto his finger. Paula may not have been taught much in the way of morals from her mother, but she had some sense of personal pride. She told him what she thought of him and left him alone in that motel room without a backwards glance.

It only took a month or two for her to realise that something was wrong, and despite all of the troubles that she had gone through with her mother since she started trying to date there was never any question in her mind that Gert was the only one that could help her. They took the bus to the doctor's office while one of the neighbourhood mothers watched the young ones and the rest of the kids were off to school and a quick blood test confirmed what they already knew—Paula was pregnant.

It was the final straw for Gert. Already close to breaking point, seeing her daughter repeating exactly the same mistakes that she had made was enough to push her over the edge into full mania. With the work of all the older children the house had been kept liveable up until that point, and through a silent agreement they had forced enough food into their mother to keep her from dying, but now Gert went beyond her usual catatonic state into viciousness. If she caught the children doing housework she would chase them out. If they tried to feed her, she would scream at them until they gave up. Where before, she would put up with any amount of silliness and roughhousing in her living room, now she actively encouraged it, spreading rumours amongst the neighbourhood children with a delight and viciousness that startled even the most hardened of the usual snide commentators. Where before she had lived in squalor because she was too lost to the world to do anything about it, now she revelled in the gruesome state of her hovel and the depths of misery that she had sunk to.

The Likens Arrangement

Paula pressed on with her life as though her mother weren't in the midst of a complete nervous breakdown. Her dating life ground to a halt with the pregnancy but she had managed to keep it a secret from the neighbourhood kids and even most of her brothers and sisters, so her social life didn't suffer. Their house had become the social hub for all the teenagers in the neighbourhood long before this latest collapse in standards, but now it was the only place to be. Teenagers were not perturbed by the mess, and the fact that Gert not only let them do whatever they wanted but actively joined in with their petty squabbles was amazingly entertaining to the kids.

Still, even Paula needed a break from being in that house sometimes, and even though the majority of her friends congregated there every day after school, occasionally she managed to slip out and visit one of the ones who had decided not to. Darlene McGuire was from an Irish family who were just slightly on the wrong side of respectable and Gert had treated her to a few searing comments as a result. She would still come around the house fairly often, but it wasn't a daily occurrence for her as it was for so many of the others.

Darlene was a nice girl with a mess of curly black hair, and Paula didn't have enough nice in her life. If there was a nasty rumour going around town, you wouldn't hear it from her, and if the church was doing a charity drive Darlene would give her last penny because she wanted to help, not just because she was trying to keep up appearances like all the rest of them. Her only bad habit was taking in strays. Her mother had to forcibly evict several cats and dogs over the years, along with a handful of birds and, on one memorable occasion, a possum. The latest pair of strays that she had picked up were introduced to Paula as Sylvia and Jenny Likens. Sylvia looked to be about Paula's age, as pretty as anyone Paula had ever met, soft-spoken but friendly. Jenny was a little bit younger and lot more awkward than her sister. She had leg braces strapped on over her clothes, a reminder of a bout of childhood Polio that she had never quite recovered from. Darlene had found them wandering around town and dragged them home with her when it became clear that they had nowhere to go.

With a little bit of wheedling and cajoling, all four girls headed back to Paula's house. They settled in her room to listen to some records and drink soda while the older girls smoked and tried to pry the story out of the younger two. It all came out after an hour or so, with each of the Likens girls contributing her share reluctantly.

In the middle of the night, Betty had shaken her daughters awake. She had a bag packed for each of them. A crazed look shimmered in her eyes and there was a bruise around one of them. She spoke in hissing whispers. 'Come on girls, we're getting out of here. I'll not spend another night under the same roof as that bastard.'

They had stumbled around in the dark getting into their clothes, and after a couple of attempts, Betty managed to get Jenny's braces snapped into place without nipping her. Together they all snuck out into the dimly lit street, and for a brief moment when the cold night air hit her face, Sylvia wondered when this strange dream was going to end. They made it to the bus station before the reality of it had started to sink in, and Sylvia was wondering if she could make a break for it back to her father. Lester wasn't a particularly terrible father any more than Betty was a terrible mother—they were just intensely and deeply self-involved. Their relationship had taken centre stage throughout their entire lives. Their daughters were just set dressing.

If Sylvia had run back to him he would have continued to be a thoroughly average father and Betty would vanish into the night just like she had planned. Life could stay the same, more or less, if she just found the courage to stand up and run home. Jenny met her eyes. She was perched on the edge of the row of plastic bucket seats opposite Sylvia and she looked like she was ready to cry. Sylvia could have abandoned her mother to whatever bizarre adventure she had planned, but she couldn't leave Jenny to suffer through it alone. She just couldn't. Together, grasping tightly to their sparse luggage and each other's hands, the girls boarded a bus to Indianapolis and hoped for the best.

The bus smelled faintly of urine, and the only other people on it were frankly terrifying to Sylvia. A wild-eyed man with a bushy beard occupied the back seat, surrounded by empty beer cans. An old lady who didn't seem to be breathing had her head resting against the window near to the front. The sisters slipped into a seat together behind their mother, and Sylvia didn't complain once even though Jenny seemed to be doing her level best to crush every bone in her hand. As the bus rumbled along, the sharp pangs of terror started to dull and the realisation that it was still the middle of the night settled on them heavily. Jenny was the first to drift off, her snores a gentle whisper in Sylvia's hair. Next, her mother slumped forward over her overstuffed purse and started to drool. Sylvia was the last to fall asleep, nervousness jerking her back to attention every time that the bus rattled but exhaustion dragging her back down again just as quickly.

They arrived in Indianapolis before the sun came up, gathered their cases from beneath the bus and headed out into the town with 'fresh hope in their hearts'—according to Betty. Unfortunately, the fresh hope in their hearts was not matched by cash in their purses.

Betty had spent everything that she had with her on the bus tickets and now their grand adventure was coming to an abrupt end before it had even begun. Sylvia was stoic, but it didn't take Jenny long to complain about missing breakfast. Betty's eyes had lighted up with misguided romantic notions about caring for her babies now that they were all alone in the world, and a few minutes later the girls were waiting outside of a minimarket while their mother went in to steal them something to eat. Sylvia was practically vibrating with tension, even before the police car pulled up in front of the building. When Betty was led out in cuffs, Sylvia had to drag Jenny away so that she didn't give them away and have them all dragged off to jail. The girls had spent the rest of the day rambling around the city aimlessly until Darlene had found them and taken them home.

Paula was rather taken with all of the drama in the story, and while she had now come to find Jenny to be dull as dishwater, Sylvia seemed like she could be a friend. It was with that friendship in mind that she walked down the hallway to her mother's room where she lay like a corpse, unmoving in her bed, and asked if the two girls could stay the night, paraphrasing the story of their escape from an abusive husband in the hopes of stirring some empathy in the dead-eyed woman. Gert crept through to meet the girls with a grin plastered over her face that made Jenny shiver. 'You lovely girls are welcome to stay the night. Of course you are. Don't you worry, we will take good care of you and in the morning we will find out where your mother has gotten to. Don't you worry about a thing."

There was so much warmth forced into those words that even the ever-sceptical Sylvia didn't doubt them. She thanked "Mrs Wright" profusely until the woman stopped her with a giggle. 'Just call me Mom dear, everybody does. All the little boys and girls who come through that door.'

The Likens girls slept in Paula's bed that night after Darlene had gone home, and after the exhausting ordeal of the previous day, they slept through until almost lunchtime when a hammering on the door woke everyone in the house. Gert slunk through in her nightgown and jerked the door open, expecting some fool of a door-to-door salesman. Instead, she came face to face with Lester Likens, and just behind him Darlene McGuire.

Darlene had met Lester roaming the streets searching for his daughters. He had been called when his wife was put into the county jail and the subject of bail came up. All of the paperwork was already being processed and Betty would be released before the end of the day. Their brief separation and the anguish that they had both felt was enough to drive them to reconcile, and through the plate glass of the visiting room at the jail the two had renewed their pledges of love and loyalty to one another and started to make plans for the future. Plans that once again centred their romantic notions and left their daughters on the periphery.

Lester gave Gert a gap-toothed grin and started to explain. He had friends who were working the touring carnival circuit and making really good money, and both Betty and Lester had been offered a place with one that was just about to head south. Unfortunately, there was no room for kids in the carnival. The girls had rushed out to greet their father once they knew that he had arrived, and they were relieved to hear that his problems with Betty were, at least temporarily, at an end. They were a little taken aback at his plan to abandon them, however. He switched immediately to the wheedling voice that he usually used when he had angered their mother. Talking about what a great opportunity it was for them. About how it would let them save up for a better future for the girls. They were unconvinced, but they weren't the one that Lester's pleading was meant to convince. In the end, he turned to Gert and outright asked her if she would keep the girls for him. Giving them room and board in exchange for twenty dollars a week. Twenty dollars a week would keep Gert in cigarettes for the rest of her life, and regular, guaranteed money was a rarity in her house. She took very little convincing before she agreed to take the girls on. With the number of children already in her house, she joked that she probably wouldn't even notice a couple more.

With everything agreed on her doorstep, Lester shook hands with Gert and went off to make arrangements for the rest of the girls' belongings to be passed along. Not once did he step inside and see the horrific state of disrepair in the house. Nor did he cast a glance around for long enough to realise that there were half as many beds as there were people living there. He was just delighted that he was going to be able to rush off into the sunset with his darling wife once more. Inside the house, Paula made a show of being happy that the new girls were moving in, telling Sylvia that now they were going to be like sisters, but already she was uncomfortable having these strangers living with her. In normal circumstances, she probably would have genuinely embraced these two lost souls, but circumstances were anything but normal, and she had a massive secret that she was trying to keep under wraps. One that would be almost impossible to conceal from a pair of girls her own age who were going to be sharing her living space.

The Missed Payment

For the first week of their strange new tenancy, the Likens girls were bemused by the strangeness of 'Mom' and the packed household of neighbourhood children. In a way, it seemed almost like a teenage utopia with no rules except the ones that they chose to abide by themselves. Sadly, like so many periods of anarchy throughout history, this resulted in a horrible hierarchy of social Darwinism where the strong preyed on the weak. The Baniszewski kids all held some measure of power in the circle by virtue of it being their home, with the older girls Paula and Stephanie holding the lion's share. Whichever boy seemed to have their preference at any given moment also gained a measure of respect and power, with Stephanie's sporadic boyfriends leaping to the head of the pack. Gert oversaw all the infighting with an impartial eye, only intervening if it looked like the situation might turn against her children, and even then, only when she felt like things were getting out of control. Even in this chaos, there were certain rituals that she still forced the family to observe. They attended the church every Sunday, and if there were other events being held there through the week she scrubbed every child down and sent them along. She was aware of how tentative her grasp on respectability was and had long ago discovered that having the church vouch for her was a good way to avoid having to actually make any personal improvements.

The Likens girls had perfect attendance at the local school, once again enforced by Gert with the same quiet fury that she used to keep everyone attending church. Even when Jenny was in pain because of her legs, she still attended without fail. Truancy was another sign of impropriety which Gert would not tolerate. She was desperate to keep her personal situation hidden, even though so many people had already learned about it through the whisper mill of neighbourhood gossip. The Likens girls seemed to get on well in school, achieving academically and making friends easily. The Baniszewski clan had considerable sway within the school, and the fact that Paula was willing to vouch for the new girls went a long way towards establishing their social credibility.

It was after a pleasant day of school that the Likens girls returned home to find the place bizarrely quiet. All of the usual after school crowd were absent, with only the Baniszewski kids themselves still lingering around. Thinking that they had stumbled onto some new family ritual that they knew nothing about, they tried to make themselves scarce until they could ask Paula what was going on. In the room that the four girls shared, Paula was waiting, but so was Gert. Without a word, the two women seized a hold of Sylvia and forced her face-down onto the pallet of dirty clothes that she had been forced to use as a bed. Gert was roaring and screaming. 'I took care of you two little bitches for nothing! Lie down there! Lie down.'

She scrambled on top of Sylvia and hauled down her skirt and her underwear while Paula giggled, then she hefted a stirring stick from the kitchen and began to beat Sylvia's bare backside, the girl screaming the whole time. Jenny was frozen with terror, trapped in a moment of indecision between running for her life and trying to help her sister. She didn't get a chance to make the choice. Paula grabbed her and threw her down on the makeshift bed beside Sylvia, wrestling to get her underwear and her skirts down and getting them hopelessly tangled in Jenny's leg braces. Gert rained blows down on Jenny's backside too, then started beating her way down the girl's already aching thighs, drawing wails of anguish out of the girl.

'Your no-good lying rat of a father promised me that he would pay his way. It's been a week and I ain't seen a God damned penny from him. I've been feeding you and washing you and putting a roof over your head and raising you right and that bastard hasn't even sent me a measly dollar. Twenty dollars a week. That is what we agreed. Twenty dollars. A pittance. To keep his darling daughters safe and well. Well, you ain't going to be safe and well. Not if I ain't going to get my twenty dollars! Do you bitches hear me? If he don't pay, you get beat!'

The blows continued to rain down on the girls and it seemed like the more that they cried out, the more excitable Gert became. On a backswing, she smashed a mirror, and when Paula stepped forward with a cry of dismay she caught the stick across her knuckles, too. 'Mom!'

Gert slowed and stopped, trailing the tip of the stick over the curve of Sylvia's red raw backside with visible delight. Gert's breathing was as ragged as the sobs that were still slipping out of Sylvia. She leaned down close and hissed into the teenager's ear. 'If your daddy hasn't paid what he is meant to by tomorrow you're going to get it again. If he hasn't paid by the end of the week then I am renting you girls out at a dollar a ride until I make my money. You hear me, whores?'

Sylvia moaned out, 'Yes!' and that seemed to be enough to satisfy Gert. She stalked out of the room with a sneer still on her face. Paula left a moment later, pushing through the crowd of her younger brothers who had gathered in the doorway to get their first good look at what a girl looked like with no clothes on.

The humiliation stung the girls almost as badly as the beating that they had just taken. The next day, Sylvia had to help Jenny limp into school with every step drawing a tear to their eyes. Paula strolled on ahead of them with a superior smirk still on her face.

Lester's cheque arrived that same morning, accidentally delayed by the postal service as it crossed state lines.

There was never much to eat in the house. Gert kept the cupboards bare, sending one of the older kids out to fetch in something simple when she herself got hungry enough, which was rarely. It didn't take long before the Likens girls went foraging to help supplement the occasional meals that they were receiving. They had discovered that they could trade discarded Cola bottles in at the local store for credit, so one day after school they went out foraging and after scouring the nearby streets, they had gathered enough to buy themselves some candy. They ate a fair portion of it on their walk back to the house, but Sylvia insisted that they save some for the Baniszewski children, whom she still felt a great deal of sympathy for, despite the way that they had revelled in her humiliation.

Gert caught them handing the sweets out and immediately another fury overtook her. She accused the girls of stealing the candy, and when Sylvia tried to explain how they had earned the money to buy it, she was dragged back through to her bedroom and thrown down for another beating. This time Jenny had the good sense to stay silent and out of the way, but Paula and Stephanie both came in to watch the show as Sylvia's underwear was hauled off again and she was paddled with a wooden spoon while Gert chanted, 'Thief! Liar! Thief! Liar!' over and over. She pinned Jenny in place with a stare. 'Are you going to lie to me too, little thief? Here I am, doing everything for you and this is how you repay me? Well, little liar? Where are your lies? What's your story? Come on, little thief, tell us your story!'

With every outburst, she unleashed another searing strike across the back of Sylvia's thighs. Each sneering demand was punctuated by another scream. 'Answer me, you lying little bitch! Tell me the truth!'

Jenny could hardly speak through her sobbing, at least until Paula grabbed her ponytail and jerked her head back. 'It's... it's like you said. We stole the candy. We stole it. Please... please stop.'

Gert hammered the spoon into Sylvia's back with a squeal of victory. 'I knew it! I knew you were a nasty little liar.'

She grabbed the back of Sylvia's hair and dragged her face up so that she could see the tears streaming down the girl's face and the terror in her eyes. 'If you ever lie to me again it will be the last time. Do you hear me, you filthy little bitch? Do you hear me?!'

Sylvia hissed out between her gritted teeth, 'Yes.'

Just as suddenly as all the madness had begun, it was over. Gert stormed back out of the room with Paula trailing out behind her, shaking her head in mock shame as she left. Jenny rushed to her sister's side and cradled her as Sylvia sobbed pitifully. Only her sister heard her whispering. 'I just wanted to do something nice.'

The Hotdog

Sylvia and Jenny were on their best behaviour from that moment forward. Which meant that they tried to fade into the background and go completely unnoticed. All of Sylvia's friends at school watched as she drew away from them and became quiet. The neighbourhood kids who had initially taken such an interest in her now judged her to be just as dull as her sister, and they were sidelined. The girls avoided Gert as completely as possible, realising that the only way to be safe from her bizarre accusations was to stay out of sight. But even that proved insufficient to protect them from Gert's ever-deepening madness.

One night after school the church had a raffle that the Baniszewski children were all sent to attend while their mother lay in bed—to maintain her presence in the community without her having to move. It was a dull affair as usual, but the Likens sisters were secretly delighted. Reverend Julian was a simpering man, quite unlike the fire and brimstone preachers that they had encountered on the road with their parents, but he seemed to genuinely care for the wellbeing of all of his parishioners, which meant that he could be relied on to sneak them a little bit of food as charity every time he saw them. He had watched their weight loss over the course of the last few months, and he had been informed through the grapevine that even though money was tight in the Baniszewski household, kindly Gertrude had invited these orphans to live with them. It was the least that he could do to provide them with a small share of the buffet meal that he had laid on from the edible donations.

It had been three days since the Likens girls had eaten, and they were shaky and weak. Sylvia had to stop her sister from stuffing her face on several occasions. Painfully aware of the pitying looks that the other attendees were giving them and determined not to draw any attention to them, she limited herself to sandwiches spaced out over the course of the low-key event. That and one little chocolate cake slice that Reverend Julian slipped into her hand when he was saying goodbye. She held onto her sister's arm on the way home, helping to support her when the usual weakness in her legs combined with the malnutrition to drag her to a halt.

Once they were back to the house, Sylvia tucked Jenny into bed and tried to settle her before the usual ruckus from the living room got so loud that it woke her up. Gert didn't seem to object to the girls sleeping. Anything that kept them out of sight seemed to please the old woman. Sylvia took a long hard look at her own "bed." If she stayed here then there would be no barbed comments, and no chance for 'Mom' to punish her from some new imagined slight. But the music and laughter in the living room sounded just a little too tempting. Sylvia decided that she deserved some good things in her life, even if she could only have them from the periphery.

When she came out into the hall, the living room fell silent. With dull dread she plodded through to see Gert sitting in the midst of the children, holding court. 'And here comes the little piggy now.'

There weren't many of the neighbourhood kids lounging around tonight. The church social hadn't been quite cool enough for most of them, and with the Baniszewski house empty except for Gert they felt a little awkward. Gert's kids were enough to fill the small room to bursting all on their own, of course. The little ones started making little oinking noises until Gert silenced them with a glare. "I hear that you're out bringing shame on me again."

Sylvia wondered if she could run back to her room, but it wouldn't help—there were no doors. The crowd could just come pouring in and drag her back out to stand trial. 'I don't know what you mean... Mom.'

She couldn't often bring herself to use the title that Gert had chosen for herself, but it always seemed to make the matriarch of this wretched clan happy when she did.

Sylvia could tell from the predatory stares that she was getting from Paula and Stephanie that she needed all the help she could get right now. Gert's face was still and hard as stone. 'Why are you so disgusting?'

The little ones started to giggle at that. Sylvia had no idea what to say to that, so she stared down at the scuffed tops of her shoes.

'Did you think that nobody was going to notice you stuffing your face, pig? Did you think that my beautiful children had no eyes in their heads? Did you think that the whole neighbourhood wasn't talking about how you took all of the food that was meant for everyone and stuffed it down your filthy throat? Do you know what they're whispering now? They're whispering that old Gert doesn't take care of those children. That I starve you. Why do you want to shame me so badly? Why would you do that? Were you raised by animals? Did you grow up in a pigsty, nursing from a sow?'

Sylvia could already feel tears pricking at her eyes. Her stomach ached with hunger, even after the extra treat that the reverend had slipped her. She was always hungry now. Hunger and fear took turns to make her stomach ache, but the pain was constant. It made her do stupid things, such as answering back. 'I didn't... I wouldn't.'

Gert jerked upright in the chair. 'So my babies are all liars now are they? And all the good people at the church too, you're calling them all liars? When I have the Reverend come around my door banging and wailing about the sin of gluttony and how vile and debased you were, shovelling the scraps that the church provides him to eat down your maw, I am meant to believe you? I am meant to believe a filthy liar like you over a priest? Over the word of God himself, we are meant to listen to the gospel of Sylvia Likens the filthy little liar?'

'I didn't say—'

'You didn't have time to say a damned thing when you were stuffing your face with everything. You disgust me. Are you hungry Sylvie? Are you so hungry you need to shame yourself? Shame us all?'

The tears that she had been holding back began to flood down Sylvia's cheeks, but that just seemed to excite 'Mom' even more. She was straining forward in her seat and making a dreadful croaking sound, somewhere between a gasp and a laugh. Sylvia's treacherous stomach chose that moment to let out a dreadful grumble and Gert rocked back in her chair. 'Well it might not be fine dining like you are used to, but I was going to cook you something tonight. Have you still got room or have you stuffed yourself too full?!'

Sylvia shook her head again. Not ever sure what she was answering to anymore, just wanting to deny the whole situation was happening.

When she looked up Gert was out of her chair and moving. She caught Sylvia by her hair and dragged her wailing along the corridor to the filthy kitchen. She tossed her into the one chair that still had all of its legs and went to the cupboards. Gert plucked a stale bun out of one cupboard, a jar of hotdogs from another and a ragged-edged knife from a drawer. She didn't take her eyes off of Sylvia for a single moment as she sawed into the bun, shoved the cold, dripping sausage into it and marched over. 'Can't have you going hungry now, can we? Wouldn't want the whole neighbourhood to hear about how hungry poor, put-upon Sylvie is. Never working a day in her life. Wasting the best years of her life hanging around in some poor old woman's house and taking advantage of her kindness in every single way.'

'I'm sorry.'

'You're what? You're hungry? Well don't worry, dear, I've got something for you right here. Oh, wait. Wait. I can't just give you something as plain as this. That isn't good enough for little miss Sylvie. It needs to be fancy! Let's make it fancy!'

Gert pulled open the bare cupboards and dug around until she found mustard and ketchup, then she emptied almost the whole bottle of each onto the bun in her hand until it was pouring over the top and running off onto the floor. 'That is more like it. A meal fit for the fancy little princess. The poor starving Sylvia. Go on. Eat up.'

'I don't want... I can't...'

Gert rammed it into her half-closed lips and screeched. 'Eat it, you little bitch! I made it for you. You are so hungry you have to shame us all. Now eat it.'

Sylvia choked on the squirt of mustard that had made it past her closing lips and started coughing. Gert took her opportunity. She rammed the whole hotdog and bun into the girl's mouth, screaming, 'Eat it, you bitch. Eat every last bite!'

Sylvia was scrambling to get away, but Gert pushed forward until the chair hit the wall and kept ramming the hotdog in and out of the teenager's mouth, her eyes alight with some dark passion that Sylvia couldn't even begin to understand. The hotdog hit the back of her throat and she gagged, giving Gert another chance to ram it in. All the while, the woman was ranting and raving. 'Why did you do it, Sylvie? Why are you ruining that tight little body? No man is going to want you if you're fat. Nobody will ever want you if you're fat. You'll end up all alone. You are going to end up all alone in a house full of ungrateful little bastards that shame you every chance that they get. You are going to be hideous and bloated. You are going to be so fat that people laugh at you when they see you waddling down the street. Is that what you want, you rancid little bitch? You want to ruin your perfect little body by stuffing your face?"

Sylvia had no opportunity to answer. All that she could do was try to chew the mush of bread and condiments in her mouth and try not to choke on the rubbery lumps of cold hotdog before Gert pried her jaws open again to ram in some more. She had made it through half of the hotdog before nausea overtook her. The slimy ketchup was running down her face, the bright stinging taste of the mustard was burning down her throat. Her eyes were streaming with tears. What had started as an emotional breakdown had been carried on by the sharp vinegary stench of the mustard and the constant gagging. When Gert's filthy fingers went into her mouth to try to force down the latest mouthful it was too much. Sylvia choked and then retched up the noxious concoction that had just been forced into her. Gert leapt back out of the way and stared on in obvious disgust as both the hotdog and everything else that Sylvia had managed to eat that night was sprayed across the kitchen floor.

When the girl finally stopped throwing up, Gert patted her gently on the back and placed the surviving half of the hotdog in her hand. 'Just eat the rest, then you're done.'

Sylvia looked up at her with tears still streaming down her face, but whatever glimmer of empathy she hoped to find in Gert's sunken eyes just wasn't there. With shaking hands, she lifted the hotdog to her mouth and took a tentative bite. Almost immediately the foul mix of flavours—bile and mustard and sickly-sweet ketchup—had her retching again. She forced the first morsel down her throat, breathing heavily through her nose and trying to keep calm. Then she leaned forward and took another bite of the squelching mess, gulping it down despite her whole body trying to force it back out. She could do it. She could finish it. She was strong. That was what she kept on whispering to herself, in her mind. Gert looked on with barely disguised lust on her face, watching every lump sliding down Sylvia's slender neck with fearsome attention. Her fascination turned to frustration as Sylvia chewed her way through the whole gruesome meal. The girl stared up at her as she swallowed the last bite, beaming and victorious. 'I finished it!'

Gert's mouth was twisted into a comforting smile, but she shook her head. 'You did great, sweetheart, but you haven't finished yet. I told you to eat the rest.'

She gestured expansively to the spattering of vomit across the floor. Amidst the sour-smelling partially digested food it was almost too easy to pick out the pink lumps of hot dog scattered across the floor. Even without the vomit, the floor was so filthy that just the thought of eating off it was vile. Sylvia's mind just rebelled at the idea of what Gert was asking her to do. She sat in the chair, staring at the vomit and trying her hardest not to start laughing hysterically. It had to be a joke. Nobody could actually expect her to eat that. Gert tipped her out of the chair onto her hands and knees. 'Eat it, you little bitch. Eat it.'

She put her foot on Sylvia's back, between her shoulder blades, and forced her face down into the yellow tainted slime. 'Eat it!'

Sylvia closed her eyes and opened her mouth. This wasn't happening. This could not be happening. She felt something brush against her lips and it took all her strength not to retch all over again. If she was sick again then she would just have more to eat. She would have to do this all over again every time she was sick. She couldn't do it again. She kept her eyes shut and lapped at the foul-tasting fluids like she was a dog. There was so much mustard that she could hardly taste anything else. All that she had to endure was the texture and the sliminess. There was a bark of wild laughter from the doorway but Sylvia kept her eyes shut. Of course, the Baniszewski kids were watching her suffer. Of course, they were laughing. She wouldn't have expected anything less from this living nightmare. Gert had her fingers tangled in Sylvia's hair and she was leading her along the floor like a pet. Guiding her mouth to each patch of vomit. A constant litany was hissing in her ear. Gert was hunched over so close that Sylvia could feel her dry lips on the back of her neck. 'Eat every last bite. Get fat. Get so fat that nobody will ever want you. Go on, piggy. Gobble it all up. You were so pretty. You were such a pretty girl but you had to go and ruin it all. You ruined it all and now nobody wants you. You are going to be alone forever.'

Sylvia kept her eyes screwed shut tightly and tried to imagine that she was anywhere else. Doing anything else. Tasting anything else in the world. Anything except for the bitterness of bile and mustard. Even that wasn't the worst of it. The worst were the strange crunchy morsels that scratched over the roof of her mouth. The things that couldn't have been food. The things that were clearly splinters or filth that had been crusted onto the floor for months or years. Each one of those made her shudder and struggle to keep the contents of her churning stomach down, but she couldn't do this again, so she kept it all inside. Without warning it was over. Gert hauled her to her feet and stroked her hair. She smeared the mustard and ketchup off the girl's cheek with her sleeve and let out a mournful sigh. 'I only punish you because I care. You know that. If you would just be good, we could avoid all this nastiness. You've learned your lesson now, haven't you? You're never going to shame me like that again, are you? You're going to be a good girl from now on, and I'm never going to have to punish you. Wouldn't your parents be so ashamed of you if they knew what you just did? If they knew why you had to do it? They would hate you for it, wouldn't they? They wouldn't be kind to you like I am, trying to teach you a lesson so that you don't ruin your whole life.'

Paralysed with fear at what new hell Gert might inflict on her next, Sylvia nodded along with the cascade of lies as it went on and on. Like a timid lamb, she let Gert lead her to the kitchen sink and wash the filth from her face. Like someone who had been stripped of all dignity, she let Gert guide her through to the heap of dirty clothes that was now her bed and stroke her hair gently until she fell asleep, with tears running down her cheeks because it was the only thing resembling kindness she had experienced in her whole time in the Baniszewski house.

A week later—once the weight of shame and self-loathing had settled in properly—Sylvia met with her parents. Gert arranged things so that when Lester and Betty came to visit they didn't see the inside of her house. She couldn't tolerate any adult visitors, particularly when those visitors might go spreading nasty rumours around. The teenagers and the children were manageable, she had leverage over them. If they wanted to use her home as their little clubhouse then they needed to keep their nasty little mouths shut about the state of it. Since Dennis Wright abandoned her, Gert had lost any interest in men, so there was no risk of one of her dates letting her secret slip. The few neighbourhood women who used to come around to drop off their laundry or a child to be babysat now had their teenage neighbours carry it along when they were heading to visit anyway. There were no unpleasant rumours about Gert in the neighbourhood. The same pity that had always hung over her was still present, but her strange relationships with the teenagers wasn't ever subjected to scrutiny. After all, most of the parents were just relieved that they didn't have a horde of stinking teens occupying their homes.

Instead of a home visit, the Baniszewski family filled up one side of a public bus and rode to meet the Likens at Garfield Park. The meeting started off poorly. Betty was shocked at how skinny her daughters had gotten, but Gert had anticipated this line of questioning and launched into a ready-made story—explaining that the girls had both decided to go onto a diet in solidarity with her oldest daughter Paula, who had been putting on too much weight recently. As Gert lied to the Likens, one petty deception after another—painting herself as a saint—she made direct eye contact with Sylvia. She was daring the girl to challenge her. After the humiliation of the hotdog incident, the week of constant mockery at the hands of the Baniszewski children, and seeing how readily her parents were lapping up Gert's lies, Sylvia found that she couldn't. She couldn't find it in herself to fight each of these petty battles. She couldn't bear for her parents to find out what she had done, crawling around on all-fours.

Lester and Betty were delighted by the stories that Gert was telling them about their daughters, in particular about the good work that they were doing with the local church charities and the way that they were collecting cola bottles from the neighbourhood trash to make donations. Once again Sylvia received a pointed stare and nodded along glumly, flashing her mother a nervous smile when eyes turned her way. When the conversation turned to the special diet that Sylvia had been on, straying dangerously close to the awful truth of the last week, tears started to prick at her eyes and her face flushed dangerously red. Lester was mostly oblivious to the emotional lives of their daughters, but Betty saw and grabbed onto her daughter's hand. 'What is wrong, honey?'

Sylvia's tears threatened to escape. She had been doing so well. She had been keeping up appearances just like 'Mom' wanted her to and now her stupid face was going to give it all away. Luckily Gert wasn't so easily shaken. She leaned over to whisper to Betty.

'Our Sylvia is just feeling bashful because her new trim figure has been getting her a lot of attention from the gentlemen.'

Sylvia was absolutely scandalised, and the ensuing blush was intense enough to wipe any concern from her mother's mind. She fell completely silent for the rest of her parent's visit, dreading the tales that would be spun to cover up any other mistakes that she made. Jenny had missed out on the worst abuses and had been so mortified at the spanking she had received that she didn't dare to speak of it.

At the end of the visit, Betty embraced her daughters while Lester handed over an envelope of cash as an advance for the rest of the month. The carnival circuit was apparently paying well and keeping the two of them stimulated enough that they were happy together once again. Sylvia had tears in her eyes when her mother left, but even then Gert swept in to wrap an arm around her shoulders and spin a story about what a good daughter they had to miss them so much, and about how happy Sylvia was when their letters came. Neither girl had ever seen these letters but neither of them had the courage to ask.

On the bus ride home, Sylvia was seated next to 'Mom.' Gert pulled her in close and stroked her hair. Whispering softly into her ear that she had been a good girl. Petting her like she was a dog that had behaved itself well in company. 'I knew that you could be a good girl with the right discipline. I was so proud of you today. You did such a good job. You and me are going to be the best of friends now, you will see. A pretty little thing like you, why you remind me of me at that age. I had all the boys chasing after my tail too. Don't you worry though. I won't let them get you. I won't let them ruin you. Not a good girl like you.'

Being made into Gert's accomplice should have been enough to turn Sylvia's stomach, but it wasn't the most upsetting part of the day by far. The worst part was that she leaned into that touch and forced herself to believe the lies she was being told because the alternative was too horrible to contemplate.

Unfit for Chairs

The next few weeks lulled the Likens girls into a false sense of security. Gert didn't suddenly become their best friend overnight—not by any stretch of the imagination—but her outright hostility to them seemed to have ceased after they had shown that they could be trusted to uphold the lies that were the foundations of her life. With that new acceptance came a better relationship with the eldest Baniszewski girls, Paula and Stephanie. They were adept at reading their mother's moods and, for that reason, began to cosy up to the Likens girls again, starting to refer to them in casual conversations as being their adoptive sisters rather than homeless orphans. Jenny was taken in by the new overtures of friendship and became a part of their social group, on the fringes but still included in the daily activities of the hive of teens that centred around the house. Sylvia wasn't so quick to accept the girls' behaviour at face value. The abuse that she had suffered made her reluctant to join in with their casual chatter, scared of the way that her words might be twisted against her at a moment's notice, but eventually, even she succumbed to the draw of a social life and became a sitting member of the living room crowd.

Increasingly, the older girls were talking about their love lives, with Stephanie practically salivating over the thought of her new boyfriend Coy Hubbard, a fifteen-year-old regular of the Baniszewski house whom she thought was dreamy. Paula was a little more careful, talking only in the past tense about her affairs, and carefully avoiding any mention of the sexual escapades that had driven her mother over the brink into outright madness. Her pregnancy remained a secret from the Likens girls and the neighbourhood at large, but the Baniszewski kids were well aware of her delicate condition and ran interference for her, both with the boys that were interested in her and with their mother, who was particularly sensitive to the subject, preferring absolute denial to dealing with the realities of having a pregnant teenager around the house.

Jenny had admitted early on to having almost no experience with boys due to the problems that she had with her legs, leading to many of the boys in attendance offering up their services before a growl from the dozing Gert warded them off. When pressed, she mentioned that she had kissed a boy once before they moved to Indianapolis, but she couldn't even remember his name anymore. There was hooting and cheering from around the room and Sylvia found herself joining in despite herself. It was nice to have this little bit of normalcy after the craziness of the last month. Just having people she could call friends and a place where she could talk again felt like freedom. It felt like being a teenager again. She found herself appreciating Gert for giving her that back, for giving it to all of these kids—as if the bitter and twisted woman weren't the reason it had been taken from Sylvia to begin with.

Sylvia joined in with the conversation shyly at first but with a great deal of appreciation from the boys in the audience. Many of them had been extremely interested when Sylvia first came into their social circle, as she put the plain-faced Baniszewskis to shame and lacked the sharp tongue and potential ostracization that was a known danger of dating them. With more than a small amount of giggling on all sides, Sylvia talked about going steady with a boy before they had moved to Indianapolis. When pressed she admitted that they had kissed pretty often, leading to another round of whooping and cheering. With a bright smile on her lips and a flush on her cheeks, she leaned forward and stage-whispered, 'I even let him feel me up over my sweater once.'

There was rapturous applause from the boys in the audience and Paula nodded approvingly, trying to keep the smile on her face from being too obvious. Sylvia had never felt so accepted since the moment that she set foot in the "Wright" house. She turned her shy smile towards Gert, expecting the old woman to be grinning along with the rest of them, but the old woman's face was contorted into a rictus of fury and her eyes were glazed.

Gert rose up from her seat and thrust an accusatory finger at Sylvia's face. As she rose she let out a blood-curdling wail. 'Whore!'

She slapped Sylvia around the face and launched into one of her rants, eyes unseeing, spittle bubbling from her lips. 'To think that I let filth like you into my home. There is nothing in this world more detestable than a whore. That's what the Bible says. You're lower than the lowest worm. Fornicating and spreading your slime all over. All over my beautiful house. You've spoiled everything. Your life is ruined. Everyone knows you're a whore now. A filthy, filthy prostitute. How many men have you laid down with, whore? How many?'

In her panic, Sylvia forgot the lessons that her time in the Baniszewski house had taught her. She forgot to stay silent and take the abuse. She'd forgotten to let it wash over her. 'What? I've never even—'

Gert pushed her so suddenly she didn't have a chance to save herself. Her chair toppled over backwards. Before she hit the floor, her head smacked against the plaster of the wall, showering her in white dust. Gert ripped the chair out from under her and loomed, still screaming at the top of her lungs. 'Everybody knows now! You're a prostitute! A filthy whore. Everybody knows that you let a boy touch you. Why didn't you listen? I was trying to save you. Now you're never going to be anything more than a whore for all the rest of your days. You've sullied yourself. You're unclean. There's none so base as a filthy whore. Gather round children. Look at her. Look at the whore in your midst.'

The neighbourhood kids had frozen when Gert first started up, but now they cast nervous glances at each other and started to giggle. There was something a little nerve-wracking about audience participation, but at the end of the day, they knew that this was all just like a rollercoaster ride—they would get all the thrills of real danger without anyone really getting hurt.

Gert seemed to be just warming up. As the dazed Sylvia pulled herself up onto her elbow, the old woman stomped on her crotch. 'Filthy whore. We all heard what you said. It won't be long before the whole world knows it too. Any day now they're all going to see the signs. They're all going to know!'

Sylvia yelped in pain. 'What?!'

'Everyone is going to know you're a prostitute when your belly starts to swell up. When your gut grows and your skin stretches. When that poison he squirted inside you makes you sick every morning. Everyone is going to know you're a whore just by looking at you, you filthy, filthy thing. Didn't you even know? Are you stupid as well as a whore?'

'I've never. I'd never...' Sylvia squealed as Gert ground her heel down.

'Everybody knows. There's no point lying about it anymore. You let a boy touch you down there. Let him put his dirty parts inside you and now you're spoiled. You're ruined. Won't be long now until everyone can see that you're pregnant, then your misery will really start. That will be your life over and done. The minute you squirt your filthy little bastard out onto my floor it'll latch onto you and never let go.' Gert's eyes were bulging out of her head. Her teeth were gnashing between each word. She'd never looked less human. 'Whoever you were going to be—whatever your dreams were —you've ruined them all just for some boy. Some man you can't even remember the name of. You've ruined everything for some man who paid you to lie down with him.'

The old woman's eyes flicked from side to side as she concocted the new reality, then she stamped her foot down again, setting Sylvia screaming. "You're nothing but a prostitute and you'll never be anything more. You took money from a man so you could buy more sweets to stuff your face. Then he stuffed you. Oh, you wanted to fatten up. Eat me out of house and home. Ruin your figure by gobbling up all the treats your whoring money could buy. Well, you've not even started yet. You've not even begun to see how vile and bloated that putrid little pink worm in your guts is going to grow. They'll see you coming from the other end of town.'

The neighbourhood kids were cracking up. Gert's own children looked a little put out by the ranting about how having children ruined your life, but it didn't take long for them to get back on board when Gert stopped talking and started kicking. She hammered her heel into Sylvia's crotch and when the girl tried to pull her knees together the old hag hissed. 'Too late for that now. Should have kept your legs together before it was too late. You filthy whore.' She growled at the nearest boys. 'Spread her legs for her. Don't worry about hurting her. You know she likes it like that. You know she likes spreading her legs for any boy that asks her.'

The boys stepped up readily. Their amusement turning into something darker as they grabbed Sylvia by the ankles and dragged her legs open as she screamed. Even her shrieks weren't enough to drown out Gert's roaring sermon. Every sentence punctuated with another stamp of her foot on the girl's groin. 'Women are unclean creatures. God doesn't love them the way he loves men. He's right not to love them. They're filthy. They're worms grovelling at the feet of men for affection and scraps. So desperate for their attention and their money that they'll do all manner of unholy things to get it. There's none more unholy than a prostitute. A woman who'd sell her most precious innocence to a man for a few measly dollars.'

Gert was beginning to tire. One of her kicks went awry and scraped over the knuckles of one of the boys holding Sylvia's legs up. He dropped her leg and for one awful moment the girl dangled, kicking, in the other boy's grasp, then he dropped her too and stepped back. Sylvia curled up around the burning ache between her legs and groaned. Gert staggered back and heaved in a few breaths before starting her ranting again.

'The Lord detests whores. And I'm a godly woman so I hate them, too. As all you children of God should. This miserable worm before us has taken money from a man. She has let him touch her down there in her special place. Now she is pregnant. She has ruined her whole life with her lustful, greedy, wicked, filthy ways. She is beneath you all. You should all hate her like I do. Every one of you. If you're good children, godly children, then you'll hate this whore.'

The laughter died away and the room fell into silence. The record had reached its end but nobody moved to change it. The regular thumping sound of the black disk completing another rotation was the only noise in the room apart from the soft sounds of Sylvia's sobbing.

With agonising slowness, Sylvia rolled onto her knees and started to get back onto her feet. Her arms were shaking with the pain, her fingers were leaving indentations in the unfinished plaster. She barely had the strength to stand. It felt like all the blood in her body was rushing down to where Gert had been kicking her and leaving the rest of her numb and useless. She went on groaning when she had the breath, not intentionally, not even consciously. The pain needed to find some way out, and her mouth seemed to be the only option. She wobbled on her feet for a long moment while the other children stared at her, then she lurched in painful half-steps towards the nearest empty chair. Gert got there faster. As Sylvia tried to lower herself gently, Gert jerked the seat away and the girl fell to the floor. She didn't scream at the surprise. After this long living with the Baniszewski children, discovering that her seat had been torn away from under her was practically the normal state of affairs. But when her aching crotch bounced off the bare floorboards it was like someone had shoved a red-hot poker up into her insides. She wailed.

Gert leaned over so far that she nearly toppled, staggering forward to loom so close to Sylvia's face that her ashtray breath ruffled her fringe. 'Whores are unfit for chairs.'

Petty Vengeance

Sylvia was no longer allowed to sit anywhere in the house. Even the pile of dirty laundry that she used as a bed was dispersed by Gert's kicking feet before she was allowed to lie down at night. The few times that Sylvia had tried to sit down without thinking had resulted in another screeching sermon from Gert on her filthiness, the filthiness of women in general, and then moved on to more general musings about the kinds of liquids that might come oozing out of a whore when she sat down. It had made Sylvia nauseated enough to never try sitting in the house again.

When she went to school the day after she had been kicked. She struggled to sit at her desk comfortably. Letting out a little whimper when she sat down and drawing a snigger from her classmate Stephanie Baniszewski. A snigger that she then accompanied with a lewd hand gesture to the girl sitting beside her by way of explanation. Sylvia didn't cry. She'd learned well enough by now that crying did no good. Instead of getting upset, she got angry, and while it wasn't in her power to hurt Gert directly, she could certainly lash out at her lesser tormentors.

During her school days, Gert had never been able to handle the rumours about her, riding on the wave of the ones that she could use, but never really understanding how they spread. Even as an adult she struggled to keep her secrets to herself, misunderstanding human nature so much that she believed the little favours she did in letting the neighbourhood children linger around her house would keep them from talking about the disgusting state it was in, or speculating about her children. In fact, her very deliberate attempts to suppress any information coming out of her home had created a kind of vacuum of information where people would believe almost anything about them, especially if it came from a source close to the family. Like a lodger.

Despite the humiliations that she had endured up until this point, Sylvia was fairly innocent, and even if she had intended on spreading a nasty rumour about someone she probably wouldn't have known where to start—if someone hadn't spent the previous night repeatedly screaming about an apparently evil act. The fact that Sylvia was so innocent just added more credence to the things that she was saying about the Baniszewski girls. After all, how would sweet, innocent Sylvia Likens even know what prostitution was if she hadn't seen it with her own two eyes? Jenny picked up the story from her at lunchtime, and by the end of the day, the whole school was buzzing with the rumours. Paula and Stephanie Baniszewski had been having sex with boys for money.

The Baniszewski girls never heard a word about it themselves, but they weren't stupid, they knew that something was going on when conversations suddenly dried up the moment that they came into earshot. They might not have had Sylvia's credibility or general likeability, but they did have a well-entrenched support network at the school. Friends soon began to hunt down the source of the rumours, without ever telling Paula or Stephanie what was happening, to spare them the embarrassment. Given that the stories included first-hand descriptions of the interior of the Baniszewski house, including areas that had been off-limits to visitors since Paula fell pregnant, it wasn't difficult to work out where they were coming from. Sibling rivalry wasn't non-existent in the Baniszewski household, but there were limits to how far any one of them might have gone to spite the others, limits that were largely enforced by how much Gert would be willing to tolerate before she'd consider these little betrayals to be giving her a bad name around town. It was obvious to anyone who knew the family that none of them would be spreading this kind of rumour, which left only the Likens girls.

Still, nobody wanted to be the one to tell them. The whole situation was gruesomely awkward to begin with, but when these new rumours intersected with both the events of the previous night and the persistent suspicion that Paula was pregnant, it created the kind of social hornet's nest that nobody wanted to go poking at.

As luck would have it, there was one teenage boy who knew about the situation and who suffered from a complete lack of social awareness and had no sense of self-preservation. Coy Hubbard was fifteen years old and he was in love. Stephanie Baniszewski was the first girl he had ever 'gone steady' with, so he supplemented his lack of real-life experience with movies and a great deal of fantasy. When he heard the rumours about his beloved, he was ready to start punching whoever was spreading them, and it was only the timely intervention of some of Steph's other friends that had prevented him from brawling his way around the entire school that day, redirecting his fury where they thought it belonged.

After classes were over, he headed straight to the Baniszewski house, where Gert greeted him with suspicion. This was a boy of her younger daughter's age, obviously fixated upon her and now lurking around near her bedroom. He wasn't a regular attendee of their open house and he seemed extremely pent up about something. It hadn't been so long ago that Gert could remember being that age, and her first assumption was that he was there for sex, so she tried to drive him off. It was only when he started rambling about 'teaching that bitch a lesson' that Gert actually started listening to him. She fell entirely silent as he explained the rumours that Sylvia and her sister had been spreading, and Gert's expression became more and more blank with every word. Eventually, she brought him into the living room and sat him down with a soda to wait. The two of them lingered in silence until the rest of the family returned home in a noisy rush with the Likens girls trailing along at their heels.

The moment that Sylvia stepped into the room, Coy rushed at her with grim determination. Gert sat back and watched the show. 'Why did you say those things about my girl?'

Sylvia was frozen in indecision. This was a boy from school, where it was safe, but she was in the house, where it wasn't safe. She didn't know whether she should fall silent like she did when she was receiving her abuse from Gert, or if she could talk back. She let out a little strangled noise.

'Why were you saying Stephanie was a slut? Stephanie isn't like that.'

Stephanie barged over. 'What were you saying about me?'

Sylvia's eyes flicked back and forth between them, then locked onto Gert where she was sitting, smiling, across the room from her. 'I didn't... I didn't say...'

'You told people that Steph was screwing guys for money. You told them she was a whore.'

Stephanie shrieked. 'You're the whore. Everyone knows that.'

'Whore,' Coy barked in her face.

'I didn't do anything... I didn't...'

'You know you shouldn't talk about my girl that way. I know judo. I'll mess you up. You say something like that again. There's going to be consequences. You understand me?'

Sylvia was pressed back against the wall. Tears were already pooling in her eyes. She had never expected anything like this. This wasn't how people were supposed to behave.

Gert's smile was slowly forced off her face. 'There'll be no stopping it now. It'll spread all around town. Everyone will hear these lies about my beautiful daughter. Everyone will think that your girlfriend is a whore. You're just going to let her off with a warning? What kind of man are you?"

Coy was already shaking with rage, but at that, his face flushed red and he lashed out. His fist caught Sylvia on the cheek and she let out a yelp, falling to the ground. She was weak from her long bout of malnourishment and even if she weren't, she had never taken a beating before and she didn't know how. Coy grabbed her by the front of her blouse and dragged her back to her feet. Gert called out in a stage whisper to her children. 'This is judo, is it?'

On her feet again, Sylvia swayed for a moment, then her whole world flipped upside down. Coy had grabbed her by the arm and the next thing she knew, she was lying on her back in the middle of the room, gasping for the air he had driven out of her. A fiery stab of pain shot up from her black and blue crotch and the air she was struggling to drag in escaped her in a whine.

The Baniszewski kids all shuffled back in silence. They weren't going to intervene on Sylvia's behalf, not when it was so obvious that Gert wanted this to happen, but they still felt uncomfortable with this stranger in their house doing violence. If it had been one of them it would have been fine, normal even, but for someone who wasn't part of the family to come and beat on Sylvia was like a stranger coming in and washing the dishes. They couldn't object, because they wanted it done, but it was still awkward. Gert met Coy's eyes across the room when he looked at her for approval and she gave a tiny nod before he leapt forward to drag Sylvia onto her feet again. He flipped her again before she'd even pulled in a breath to scream, and this time the floorboards bowed beneath them as he slammed her down and a chair toppled over. Gert frowned. 'You're going to smash up everything messing around like that. Pick her up.'

There was another long pause as everyone waited to see what was going to happen next. Coy wasn't one of her kids or even one of the neighbourhood children who she'd laid claim to. He could refuse her and everything that was happening could stop. He reached down and grabbed the gasping girl by her ponytail, hauling her to her feet. Then he looked askance. Gert gave another curt nod. 'Door to the basement is in kitchen. Nothing to break down there.'

Sylvia whimpered as he dragged her through the house by her

hair, but she understood her place in all this now. She wasn't going to risk enraging Gert by talking or contradicting her. In the end, she still had control over this situation, because she could control herself. This wasn't going to be forever. The boy would throw her around a little bit. She'd get some bruises. It wasn't the end of the world. She'd survived worse than this already. She repeated the same lies to herself over and over and he dragged her down the stairs into the basement. The floor was dirt and there was a single bare lightbulb hanging just low enough that Sylvia had to flinch away so it didn't sear her face. She cast a quick nervous glance back to the stairs. It was all right. Gert hadn't seen that. She was just coming down now. Coy didn't wait for further approval. He flung Sylvia into the wall.

Gert settled herself comfortably on the stairs to watch. Her silent glower the only constant in a world that seemed to be constantly in motion. Sylvia was flipped over and flung around so many times that even when Coy stopped she was still too dizzy to stand on her own. He was red-faced and sweating by the time he stopped. Sylvia had been getting colder and colder with each impact and his hands left slimy trails of sweat over her now. She would have shuddered if she wasn't already constantly shaking. Somewhere in the middle of that tempest of violence, she'd lost track of how many times he'd thrown her. How many times she had bounced off the walls and the floor. She ached all over. She was numb to it but now that she was lying still the pain was starting to creep back in. If this was how it felt now, she dreaded the next few hours and days. The platitudes she'd used upstairs didn't do her much good down here. At least it was over. The boy had his petty revenge. Gert probably felt like she'd been suitably punished. She didn't have to worry about anything but getting through this pain.

Coy staggered, half exhausted, towards the stairs, and he was almost past Gert when her hand wrapped around his thigh and he froze. The old woman looked flushed, he could hear her panting echoing back across the cellar as if she'd been the one throwing the girl around. 'You're good at that judo, but you could be better.'

'I'm the best in my class.'

She squeezed at the muscles of his thigh approvingly. 'Maybe you are, but wouldn't it help to be able to practice a little more? You know you can come back down here any time you want to work up a sweat.'

The perplexed expression on his face was starting to irritate Gert. 'If you want to practice your judo. You come back here and try it out on her some more. She deserves it. She deserves worse. Telling them lies about your girl. About my baby girl. It wasn't right.'

Coy lingered for another moment before grunting 'all right' and striding off up the stairs.

Gert stayed right where she was, sitting on the steps and watching Sylvia vibrating helplessly on the floor. She wet her lips. 'You just stay there tonight. None of my food is going to be passing those nasty lying lips of yours.'

She hauled herself upright and then flicked off the light. Leaving Sylvia alone in the cold darkness, waiting for the pain to come in like the tide.

Turning Inward

Sylvia tried to return to a normal life after her first night in the basement, but she was so bruised and battered that she was barely able to move when she woke up swollen and stiff in the morning. Her sister and the other children were already gone by the time she had crawled to the top of the stairs. Gert was waiting for her, perched on the one kitchen chair that was still intact. 'Everyone might have heard the lies you told about my daughter, but you can be damned sure that everyone knows you for a liar now. I don't need to punish you. You've brought enough misery down on yourself. Don't ever let me catch you with my daughter's names in your mouth again, whore.'

After the weekend, Sylvia returned to school, supposedly recovered from her bout of 'flu'. The bruises protruding beyond her deliberately prudish clothes had faded to yellow, and the Baniszewski girls were generous about sharing their makeup, at least until the yellowing had faded enough that it could just be passed off as bad skin. Sylvia completely withdrew from the Baniszewskis at school. She couldn't risk anything that she said or did trickling back to Gert, or for Coy to get mad at her again. It was clear that the protections any child enjoyed had been withdrawn from her, that anyone would be allowed to hurt her if she had angered Gert. It drove any possibility that Gert was just overzealous in her disciplinary habits out of the window. Despite the beating she had taken, and Gert's threats the next day, Sylvia still didn't feel like the axe had fallen on her yet. Doom followed the girl.

Still, life wasn't entirely terrible. When she was at school there were several friends she could rely on for distraction from her nightmarish home life. Anna Sisco was the closest friend she'd managed to make outside of her sister. She was thirteen years old, and if the Likens girls were sheltered compared to the more worldly Baniszewskis, they were nothing compared to Anna. She genuinely couldn't understand why she was never invited back to Sylvia's house, or why Sylvia wouldn't come back to hers and risk questioning about where she had been. There was a constant fear about bringing someone home to Gert. It was bad enough that Sylvia and Jenny were in the old woman's power. She didn't want to deliver someone else into the hag's clutches if she could avoid it. Worse yet, she had no idea how little Anna would respond to the treatment that she received in the Baniszewski house. If she tried to stand up for Sylvia or tried to report Gert, Sylvia had no idea what fresh hell would be unleashed.

Adding to the swirling chaos that Anna might have walked into in the Baniszewski house were the regular visits from Coy. He never abused Sylvia as much as he had the first night when he was in a rage, but Gert would still send him down into the basement with her, where Sylvia was expected to submit to his whims. Not that those whims ever seemed to extend beyond throwing her around. She didn't know how she could explain her ready acceptance to Anna in terms that would make sense to a sane person. She could barely rationalise it herself.

Eventually, Sylvia gave in to Anna's badgering and she brought her home on a weeknight when the swarms of teenagers that lingered around the house were likely to be thinner than usual. She thought that if she could show the younger girl the state of the house then she might be embarrassed enough on Sylvia's behalf that she wouldn't press the issue further. The record player was silent when they came in, which was a good sign. Gert was sitting in the living room, patiently waiting for some entertainment. Which was not a good sign. It was not a good sign at all. She caught Sylvia's eye and there was a glimmer of a wicked smile on her face for only a moment before she switched to her charming neighbourhood mother routine. 'What's this? A friend of our Sylvie? I'm so glad to finally meet you.'

Sylvia froze. She had only one moment to try and get control of this situation before Gert rolled right over her, the way that she always did, smothering her with her skewed version of reality until there was nothing that she could do except accept it. She opened her mouth, but it was already too late. Gert patted the seat beside her, all smiles and matronly approval. 'Won't you come take a seat. Sylvia hasn't told us a thing about you and we're all so curious. What's your name, girl? Come on now, don't be shy. Sit yourself down.' She turned to Sylvia with that same placid smile. 'Why don't you go and fetch your friend a soda?'

With feet that felt like lead, Sylvia trudged through to the kitchen and fetched the bottles. She had no idea what she was going to be walking back into. She didn't even have time to speak before Anna's fist caught her in the cheek. She staggered back into the hallway, completely aghast. Anna rushed at her again, swinging her fists wildly, barely connecting at the best of times and sobbing all the while. Eventually, Sylvia heard her shrill cries underneath the grunts of exertion. 'How dare you? How dare you tell people those things about my mother? You... you're a nasty liar. I'm going to tell everyone what a... I thought you were my friend!'

She pushed past Sylvia and rushed out into the street, tears streaming down her face. Sylvia was so shocked she didn't even try to follow her. Gert shook her head sadly. 'You really must stop telling lies, Sylvie. Otherwise, everyone is going to end up hating you. You wouldn't want that, would you? Wouldn't want the whole world to know that you are a vicious, lying little whore.'

Sylvia crossed the distance between them in a few strides and for one moment as she loomed over the haggard old woman, Gert's bottomless pit of confidence seemed to betray her. She almost flinched. It was enough to snap the girl out of it. She wasn't like the Baniszewskis. She wasn't a monster. She couldn't hurt people just for being cruel. She was better than that. She was better than Gert. She let some tiny part of that superiority show in her polite smile. 'Here is your soda. Mom.'

With the loss of Anna and the consequent rumours that began to spread about her untrustworthiness, Sylvia became completely isolated at school. Some small part of the rumours must have spread out into the adults of the community too, because before long teachers who would gladly cut her slack on account of her difficult circumstances turned cold to her. They started to treat the girl with suspicion in everything that she said and did. There were eyes on her constantly. It was like Gert had suddenly extended her reach, remaking the world in her image all over again. A world in which there was only one villain, Sylvia Likens.

Gert was unsatisfied with the way that her last torture had gone. She hadn't liked the spark of defiance that the whore had in her eyes, and that smug smile needed to be wiped off her face. She needed to know her place, looking down on Gert like she was any better than her. Gert had never spread her legs for money. She wasn't a whore. She'd been with her husbands, all legal and fair like the Lord wanted, and they might have bought her things and paid the bills, but that was how it was meant to be. Sylvia was the whore, and whores belonged on their knees. When Sylvia got home from the church social, where she had very carefully avoided eating much of anything despite the protests from her aching stomach, the house was packed with teenagers again. Stephanie hadn't bothered to come along, banking on the new clout that bringing Coy into the fold had bought her with Gert to excuse her from having to make nice with Reverend Julian for a little while. Instead, she had made the house into her own private party, inviting all of the kids from her year at school, the same teenagers who now looked at Sylvia with contempt and even outright hatred. Out of all the kids in the room, only one of them seemed furious enough to actually do something about it.

Judy Duke loomed over Sylvia, a head taller and almost double her weight after the recent bout of near starvation. She slapped Sylvia in the face then sneered as blood trickled out from between the smaller girl's lips. 'Why are you telling people my mom is a hooker?'

Sylvia glanced at Gert and sighed. How many times was this same script going to be played out? 'I don't even know your mom, Judy. I barely even know you. So why would I say something like that?'

Another slap. Softer but still stinging. 'I don't know why a lying freak like you says horrible things about other people. Maybe you're just horrible.'

'I didn't say anything about your mom, Judy. Somebody is telling you that so you'll fight with me.'

There was a long moment of silence before Gert's soft hiss cut through. 'Lies. Always more lies with this one.'

Judy kicked Sylvia in the shins with as much rage as she could muster, but there was doubt on her face, Sylvia could see it. They might have all been caught up in the maelstrom of chaos and wickedness that Gert sowed, but her pawns were still people. A couple of kicks later, it became clear that Sylvia wasn't going to fight back and Judy stormed out of the house, confusion still written all over her face. Gert was fuming. This wasn't what she had wanted at all. It wasn't good enough. She wasn't going to stand for it. She barked, 'Hit her.'

The music went on playing, a woman's voice crooning out, 'What the world needs now is love, sweet love,' obscene in the tense silence.

Stephanie squirmed. 'Who?'

Gert's eyes bulged. 'Hit the whore!'

Stephanie leaned away from her mother as the old woman vibrated with rage. 'No, mom. Who are you talking to? Who do you want to hit her?'

Gert cast her gaze around the room until they locked onto someone right beside Sylvia. With a dull sense of dread, Sylvia turned around to meet her sister's eyes. Jenny was already shaking her head frantically. Gert growled. 'Hit her. Hit the whore. Box her ears. I'll not have lying whores walking around unpunished. Hit her.'

Coy leaned over, 'I'll do it.'

'No. Her,' Gert snarled. 'She needs to be the one to do it. She needs to prove that she isn't on the whore's side in all this. That she'll stand by her family, not this degenerate.'

Jenny was shaking, tears already pricking the corners of her eyes. 'I... I won't.'

Sylvia shook her head. 'Do it.'

'I can't,' Jenny wailed. 'She's my sister. I can't.'

Gert lunged up out of her chair and crossed the room so fast that it was hard to believe. She slapped Jenny across the face. 'You do it or you get it instead. Hit her or I'll send you and Coy down to the basement for him to practice. Do it or you'll be eating nothing for the rest of the week. Do it. Hit the whore.'

Jenny was still shaking her head, even as Sylvia whimpered. 'For God's sake, just do it.'

Gert hit the girl. She slapped her so hard that Jenny's weak legs couldn't even support her. She cast around and snarled, 'Don't you take the Lord's name in vain. You filth. You aren't fit to speak his name.'

'Jenny, please. Just do it.'

Sobbing, the girl made a fist and lunged out. It caught Sylvia by surprise. She staggered back a step with a yelp of pain. This close, she could see Gert's eyes light up. She could hear her ragged breathing getting faster. The woman's face was a carefully tamed mask of misery, but there were little things like the flush spreading on her cheeks that told another story. She was enjoying this. Jenny hit her again with a sob. She beat Sylvia in the face until her knuckles were red and bruising before the hag dragged her off with a mock scolding. With her obligations as the evening's entertainment fulfilled, Sylvia stalked off to her room without another word. Gert's eyes bored into the back of her head every step of the way.

A Cure for Sticky Fingers

Sylvia showed up to school bruised and battered more and more frequently. Coy seemed to be enjoying having free range to toss her around, and his violence was beginning to escalate beyond practicing his judo into closed-fist beatings and a few brief bouts where he ground Sylvia against a wall with his body and wrapped his fingers around her neck. All of his dark fantasies could be fulfilled down in the dim lit basement, if he had the courage to go through with them. Until he got the guts to go further, he kept on escalating his beatings. After all, it wasn't like anyone cared what happened to Sylvia.

Despite all of this, life continued to move on around the Baniszewski house. Summer started to ease into autumn and fitness classes at the school remained outside. The shorts and shirt that her parents had provided were no longer enough protection against the elements, so Sylvia had to swallow the tattered remains of her pride and ask Gert to buy her a tracksuit. She thought that she'd caught the old woman in a good mood, but as it turned out, Gert didn't have good moods when it came to Sylvia. 'Wouldn't a whore do better if she didn't cover up?'

She bit back her denial. There was no point arguing. 'The school says it is the uniform. I've got to wear one.'

'Doesn't matter to me one way or the other.' Gert flicked ash onto the floor. 'There's no money for new clothes right now. Especially for the likes of you.'

'But I need it.' There was an edge of whining to Sylvia's voice that grated on Gert's nerves.

'And I don't give a damn what you need.'

At school before the next session of jogging around the field, Sylvia panicked. If she went out without a sweat suit, then the school would call Gert. They might even visit the house. If Sylvia brought that kind of attention down on the Baniszewski house, then she would be signing her own death warrant. Gert would blame her for everything and go berserk. She couldn't risk that. With a heavy heart, she slunk into the changing rooms before the bell rang and stole a tracksuit from one of the lockers. She didn't even know whose clothes she was taking but she hoped against hope that they could afford to replace them easily. Not that there was anyone at the school as bad off as her and her sister. She hid in the bathroom until everyone else was dressed then went out jogging onto the field with the rest of her class. Whoever she had stolen from must have had a spare kit because she didn't see anyone in their summer gear. She let out a little sigh of relief and tried to ignore the niggling guilt that raced after her when she broke into a run. She supposed that she should have been thrilled to get away with it with nobody being hurt, but she felt sick.

Gert spotted the new tracksuit when Sylvia tried to wash it. The old woman seemed completely obtuse most of the time. Barely literate as far as Sylvia could tell. Yet somehow when it came to things like this she was eerily astute. 'Where did you get that from?'

Sylvia froze on the spot. She couldn't help it. Every time Gert spoke to her it was like nails on a chalkboard in her head. There was no point in arguing or resisting. Whatever Gert decided to bellow would become the truth anyway. Gert snatched the clothes from her hands and stared at them long and hard. 'Stole it did you? I won't have thieves in my house. I won't stand for it.'

Sylvia kept her mouth clamped shut. The truth was that she had stolen it, but she hadn't really expected Gert to care. There was a steady supply of cigarettes and soda coming into the house each day, both in the hands of the Baniszewski kids and the visiting teenagers, and Sylvia knew for a fact that there was no money for them to buy them with. Every cigarette that Gert smoked had been stolen, but there she was puffing away on one and damning Sylvia for doing what she needed to survive. It wasn't fair. It just wasn't fair. Sylvia expected the slap. She was braced for it. She gave Gert nothing. No yelp. No flinch.

Gert hit her again, harder. There was surprising strength in the woman's wiry arms, a reminder that while she might have looked elderly and decrepit she wasn't that much older than Sylvia's real mother. When that still wasn't enough, Gert grabbed Sylvia by the hair and threw her down onto the filthy kitchen floor. There were still yellow stains here and there. A reminder of the last time they had been together in the kitchen like this that made Sylvia's stomach start to churn. Gert kicked her and took a long draw on her cigarette. A halo of blue smoke drifting around her as she hissed. 'Did you steal it, or did you buy it? Did you buy it with your whoring money?'

The next kick was to a familiar place. The bruises from the last time had finally faded but each time Gert's heel collided with Sylvia's crotch it set her whole pelvis alight with searing pain again. She cried out. She couldn't help it. Gert smirked. 'You like that whore? Can you even feel it after all the men that have used you? This is just another day for you, isn't it? Just another day lying on your back. Spreading your legs for whoever wants you. Is this how you got clothes money? When my babies have to wear hand-me-downs because you were too stupid to keep your legs shut when some man wanted you?'

Sylvia tried to crabwalk away, to get out of reach, but Gert pursued her. Eyes glazed. Heel grinding down into Sylvia's most tender parts at every opportunity. 'How many men did you fuck for those clothes? How many times did they squirt their poison inside you? You could have had a life. You could have been happy. But now you're nothing but a stupid, worthless whore. That's all you'll ever be now. Whore. Whore!'

Sylvia was screaming, still trying to crawl away. She didn't want to defy Gert but the pain, now that it was back, seemed even worse than the first time. It was like someone had shoved a red-hot poker inside her. Searing pain radiated up her body and her legs were limp and numb. Gert's cigarette tumbled out of her mouth as she bellowed, 'Whore! Whore!' over and over. It landed on Sylvia and she yelped in surprise. Suddenly, Gert was still and silent. When she spoke again, her voice was hoarse. 'You stole it. You... you're a thief. You need to be punished like a thief.'

She stumbled back across the room and lit another cigarette. Sylvia curled up in a ball around the boiling knot of pain inside her. Shaking and shivering. Trying to stay silent. Hoping against all evidence that Gert would just forget about her.

When she felt Gert's leathery hands taking hold of hers ever so gently and drawing them away from her body, she actually believed that it was over. That Gert felt like discipline had been dispensed. When her clenched fingers were uncurled with a firm but gentle grip, it was almost a comfort. The only time that anyone had touched her without the intent to cause pain in so long that she started sobbing. She could feel Gert's breath ghosting over the palm of her hand. 'Only one cure for thieves.'

There was no pain quite like a burn. It was instantly recognisable even though Sylvia had only ever touched the stove once as a little girl, so long ago that the actual event had long since fled her memory. She yelped and tried to pull her hand away, but Gert's grip on her was like steel. She entangled their fingers and held the weakened girl still without even a hint of strain. She moved the cigarette along to the next finger in line and then pressed down. The pain was immediate. Intense. It made her forget all about her battered crotch. She wailed and then sobbed as the cigarette was pulled away and then puffed a few times to get it hot again. Sylvia felt like she was going to go mad from the pain and that had only been two fingers. She still had eight left to go. When she tried to struggle away Gert sat on her, pinned her arm between clammy thighs and let out a high-pitched giggle. 'This is what thieves deserve. This is all you deserve.'

The Cola Bottle

If Sylvia had thought that her punishment was over just because every one of her fingers had been seared and she had passed out from the pain, she was sorely mistaken. Pain was only part of the lesson. There had to be humiliation, too. In the living room, in full view of all the neighbourhood boys, her skirts were lifted up and her panties were pulled down. Gert beat her with a belt until there were welts across her buttocks and thighs, then she dropped her onto the filthy ground. The children had all been informed of her indiscretion in one of Gert's sermons before the beating began, but now the time had arrived for them to participate in the punishment. Gert quietly encouraged them to burn the girl as a regular reminder that stealing was wrong. One by one, the children, some as young as twelve, stepped forward to put their cigarette out on Sylvia's bare flesh. She wailed each time, but that only served as encouragement for the more sadistic boys. Coy put his cigarette out on her thigh, as close as he could get to her vagina without accusations of infidelity from Stephanie.

From that day forward, Sylvia became a living ashtray for the Baniszewski house. Each burn was meant to serve as a reminder that she should not steal. Instead, they taught her an entirely different lesson. With no nutrition and almost no sleep due to her constant fear, Sylvia's body had stopped healing. The burns on her fingertips were still there, barely changed, a week after her punishment. Coy had come back for another session the day after he had burned her and while he was getting braver, he still didn't do much more than smack her around. The bruises, when they came up, were a dull dirty brown and they didn't fade. It was like her whole body was slowing down. She had been hungry for so long that she'd forgotten what it felt like to be any other way. It had become background noise to the more alarming pains that had started to develop across her body. Particularly in her pelvis. Her periods had stopped shortly after she arrived in the Baniszewski house, whether due to stress or starvation. Gert hadn't noticed yet, but when she did, it was certain to be used as more evidence that she was pregnant, despite never having been near enough to a boy who wasn't actively maiming her in the last few months. It became clear to Sylvia that she couldn't just keep on hoping and waiting for her situation to resolve itself. The burns on her fingers were a testament to that. Her body was shutting down. She was going to die if she didn't take action.

With the whole town convinced that she was a liar, she didn't have anyone to reach out to for help, so she returned to her original plan to deal with her starvation. She collected as many soda bottles as she could find around the house, then roamed the streets gathering more from the trash to trade in for pocket money. She knew that there were risks. Not just the very real risks of being a teenage girl roaming the street of Indianapolis at night, but the far more terrifying prospect that Gert would realise she was missing, but she had run out of other options. She needed to eat.

Her first night out of the house was a roaring success. She managed to scrape together enough money to buy almost a meal's worth of food, which she sat on a bench and ate before she headed home. She would have liked to have shared with her sister, but there was no guarantee that anything she brought with her wouldn't be confiscated. It would certainly have been used as evidence against her in the latest of Gert's witch hunts. With her stomach full for the first time in months, Sylvia made her way home and tried to sneak through to her room unnoticed in all of the usual evening hubbub. Gert didn't seem to be in the midst of the laughter and jeering tonight. For a moment Sylvia thought that she had gotten lucky for once, that the old woman had gone to bed early. The moment she stepped into her room she realised that luck was never on her side. Gert was there. Waiting for her.

She didn't even try to fight as Gert dragged her through to the living room. She tried to go away inside her head. None of this mattered. She had eaten. She was going to get her strength back. She was going to walk away from all of this. All of this was temporary. The bruises would fade. The shame, the humiliation, it would all pass. She was stronger than this. Gert tossed her into the room and every eye was turned her way. Sylvia should have been past embarrassment by now, but she still flushed as all eyes turned her way. Old habits die hard. Her shame wasn't helped by Gert's bellowing. 'Look what the cat dragged in. Our very own lady of the night has finally finished walking the streets.'

Sylvia glanced around nervously. A few of the neighbourhood kids were smoking. This could get very painful, very quickly, if she wasn't careful. 'What's the matter, whore? You're suddenly shy now? You spent all night parading your body around for men. Stripping off your clothes. Spreading your legs for them. Now you're blushing?'

Gert was right behind her. She could feel the weight of the monster's presence against her back. She leaned in close enough for her tarry breath to tickle Sylvia's ear. 'Are you too good for these boys? Is that it? You'll go whoring around all your fancy men, but these good boys here, you think you're better than them?'

Sylvia's eyes were still darting around the room. There were hardly any girls here at all tonight, and while she didn't think Gert's nonsense was really going to make these boys angry, everything was so confusing right now that they could all attack her at a moment's notice. That was the most frightening thing about what Gert had done. She'd stripped all of the rules away so that she could put hers in their place, but there were all these huge grey areas where anything could happen. Places where Gert hadn't made a decision yet. The old woman had drifted away from her now to go lean against the doorway, trapping her in the room. 'Go on then, whore. Give the boys a show. I know you want to. They know you want to. Everyone knows you're a whore. So do it.'

Sylvia had already started shaking and her voice cracked as she asked, 'Do what?'

'Strip for them, whore.'

Her hands moved with a will of their own. Her body betraying her. A month ago, Sylvia would have died rather than take her clothes off in front of a room full of boys, but now her pride and her shame had been ground down by terror. She slipped her skirt down her legs. Then unbuttoned her blouse and dropped it on top of the pile. She slipped off her shoes and kicked them forward too. She was trying not to look at the boys. She didn't know what she might see there and, if her humiliation had provoked lust, she didn't know if she could stomach it. She wasn't sure if she could manage pity either. It was safer to keep her eyes locked on the dust-crusted floorboards. 'And the rest. Whores aren't fit for clothes.'

Sylvia closed her eyes. She undid her bra and dropped it to the floor. She hooked her thumbs in her underwear and jerked them down. She was crying. It wasn't intentional. If it had been up to her, she would have given Gert nothing—this was just another way that her body was betraying her. The shaking legs. Her nipples tightening in the cold air. The hysterical sobbing that she was only barely able to hold back by keeping her eyes scrunched shut as tightly as she could. Pretending that she was all alone.

Gert growled. 'There's a good whore. Now give them a show. Let them see what you do for your money, whore.'

Sylvia didn't know what she was being asked to do. She stood there frozen. Resisting the urge to cover herself or run from the room because she didn't want to feel the sting of Gert's belt again. Being beaten while she was naked would have been more than she could stand. She felt something nudge against her hand, and despite desperately wanting to keep her eyes shut and the tide of tears held back, she couldn't help but look down. Gert was trying to put an empty glass cola bottle in her hand. Sylvia just stared at it. Eventually, with a few more nudges she took it, but it still made no sense. Why was Gert giving her a bottle? Was she admitting that she knew what Sylvia had really been doing all night? Was her punishment finally over? 'Put on a show. Like you do when you're whoring. Shove it inside.'

Nothing she was saying made any sense. Sylvia just stared at her blankly until Gert growled and seized her by the wrist, guiding the bottle down until it nudged against her bruised vagina. No. She couldn't possibly want that. Gert growled. 'Do it, you whore. Do it.'

The chant got picked up. The boy's usual pubescent voices seemed deeper than usual. Some animal part of them was growling out. 'Do it. Do it. Do it.'

Sylvia looked up and there was a dreadful hunger on their faces. Even though some of the boys were flushed red and looking ashamed of themselves, they still weren't looking away. Every eye in the room was on Sylvia, on that most secret and well-hidden part of Sylvia that was now on display for the world to see. She swallowed back the bile that was rushing up her throat and pressed the open neck of the bottle inside. It was cold, even compared to the chill of the room and her hands were shaking so badly that she almost dropped it. She wondered what would happen if she did drop it. Would Gert go and fetch another? Would she make her use the broken glass in the same way? She tightened her grip on the textured glass and shoved it a little further in. It was starting to hurt now as the neck got wider and the end went deeper. Sylvia was doing everything that she could to keep her hard-earned meal down, but it was a losing battle. She needed to hurry. If she could just get it done then she could sneak away. She could lie down in her room and go to sleep and pretend that none of this had ever happened. A little whimper escaped her as she shoved the bottle deeper inside and the boys, they leaned forward, practically salivating. Gert was losing patience. 'You keep all the men waiting this long? Hurry up.'

Sylvia tried to push on past the pain, but it was like the bottle had hit some sort of barrier inside her and couldn't go any further. Gert growled. 'I said hurry up.'

The old woman's hand darted out and she slapped the flat bottom of the bottle as hard as she could. Half the length of it vanished inside of Sylvia. Then the pain came. She fell to the floor, screaming so loud that it startled even Gert. Blood trickled down the glass to pool on the floor between Sylvia's knees.

Gert stood over her and scoffed. 'I'm sure you've taken bigger than that, whore. Now fuck yourself with it.'

Sylvia whimpered and tried to pull the bottle out, but even that slight motion had her screaming again. Something was wrong. Something was really wrong. It felt like something inside of her had torn. She shook and she wept. Her shaking hands pawed uselessly at the slippery, bloody glass. Trying desperately to pull it out. Tears were pouring down her face now, any attempt at stoicism lost in the agony of the moment. 'Please. Help me. Oh God. Help.'

Gert rolled her eyes in disgust. 'None of us want to catch your whore diseases. Touching your filthy slit. Pull it out.'

'I... I c-can't.' Sylvia sobbed.

Gert grabbed the bottle, drawing another shriek out of Sylvia. 'Ridiculous girl.'

She tore it out of Sylvia and another shrill wail came with it. There was a half inch of blood and other murky fluids pooled inside the bottle when Gert held it up to the light. That made her stop for a moment. When she turned back to Sylvia, the girl had passed out. With exaggerated disgust, Stephanie and Paula dragged her off to bed. The cola bottle was tossed out with the rest of the trash and forgotten about promptly.

The Basement

The next morning, Sylvia woke up in a puddle of her own blood-tinged urine. It had chilled through the night without waking her. The pain from her injuries was bad enough that she couldn't even stand, but she tried to bundle up the dirty clothes that she had wet and crawl through to wash them before Gert could realise. Of course, the old woman caught her in the act again. She looked down at the filthy, naked and bloodstained girl and sighed. 'You just aren't fit to live with humans anymore. Can't even keep yourself from pissing all over. You're like a dog. You're worse than a dog. At least a dog can be trained. I wish we'd got a dog rather than you and your half-wit sister.'

Sylvia lay on the floor of the kitchen and wept until Gert started to kick her. 'Down you go. Down into your kennel. You're not fit for chairs, you're not fit for clothes and now you're not fit for beds.'

Sylvia sobbed, 'Please. Please help me. I need a doctor. I need help.'

Gert's eyes narrowed. 'Do you have doctor money? Because I don't.'

She took a hold of Sylvia's hair and dragged her, wailing, across the floor to the basement door, then she kicked her inside. Every time that Sylvia managed to halt her tumble into the darkness, Gert would give her another boot in the ribs. She ended up down on the dirt floor of the basement again, weeping and aching like the first time that Coy had his way with her. Without clothes, it didn't take long for the cold to start seeping up from the ground into her body, but she welcomed it. If she was numb then maybe the terrible pain inside her might ease.

That night, Gert came down to study her. She had wet herself again during her fruitless attempts to find sleep. Her injuries had rendered her incontinent. Gert tutted at her. 'Filthy. Absolutely filthy. You'll have to stay down here, dirty girl. We'll have to scrub you down, too. You foul thing.'

Sylvia croaked. 'Please. I need help.'

Gert huffed. 'I'll need help. You've been stuffing your face for so long it'll be a wonder if me or the girls can lift you.'

She gathered up the most useful boys she could find upstairs. Coy, her son John, and another boy from the neighbourhood, Ricky Hobbs, who she had been keeping an eye on for quite some time. Between the three of them, the boys managed to carry the limp Sylvia upstairs and into the bathroom where Gert and Paula were waiting. There was one bath in the house, a claw-footed thing that had to be filled up with hot water boiled on top of the stove. Steam was rising up off the water despite the relative warmth of the room. Without thinking, Ricky dipped his finger in to check the temperature, then let out a yelp. It was scalding hot. Gert nodded to them. 'Dunk her in then.'

Ricky was holding onto Sylvia's legs, the smelliest job handed off to the youngest one. While the other boys made to throw her in, he pulled her back. 'Hang on now, that water will burn her. That's hot as a kettle.'

Paula, Coy and John all glanced nervously at each other, but Gert just laughed. 'Let me just talk with my new assistant here. You boys give her a wash. Paula, you scrub her with that salt when they're done.'

Ricky shook his head. 'This ain't right.'

'No it most certainly is not. Come on now. Let me explain some things to you.' Gert reached out and took his hand, leading him out of the room. He flinched when he heard Sylvia screaming, and he looked like he might run back for a moment, but Gert tightened her grip on his hand and led him through to the boy's bedroom. The only one in the house that still had a door.

She looked him up and down and pushed him onto the bed. 'How old are you now, Ricky?'

He glanced nervously from Gert to the door. He could still hear the sloshing water, but the screams seemed to have stopped. 'I – I'm fourteen, Mrs Wright. Fifteen in a few months.'

She smiled at him. Her teeth seemed longer than normal. Like her gums had crept back from them, or like they were growing out longer so she could take a bite out of him. He shivered. 'Fourteen years old. I never would have guessed. You look so mature.'

He wasn't immune to flattery. A little smile played over his lips. 'Thank you, Mrs Wright.'

'Please. Call me Gertie.'

'G – Gertie. That water. It was much too...'

'You have a girlfriend yet, Ricky? Handsome boy like you, must be beating them off with a stick.'

'No, Mrs ... um... Gertie. No, I don't.'

'Girls your age, hardly worth the time are they? No titties to speak of. Too scared to even touch a boy down there. You're probably just waiting for the right girl to come along, aren't you? The kind of girl that will treat you the way you deserve to be treated.'

She came closer and closer with every word. So close that he could smell the nicotine clinging to her clothes. He leaned back so that she couldn't plant a kiss on him, because that was what it looked like she was going to do, but she had another destination in mind for her lips. She slipped down onto her knees in front of him and unbuttoned his cords with deft fingers. She licked her lips as she looked up at him. 'I need an assistant, Ricky. Somebody to help me deal with that monster in the basement. Someone to help out with the lifting and carrying. I don't have any money to pay you with, but... I can pay you in other ways.'

He shuddered as her hands tightened on his thighs and she leaned closer. She'd done this plenty of times before to get her way, even when there was far less on the line than keeping a little squealer from going running and telling everyone her business. Men were easy to control if you knew where to apply the right pressure.

Three minutes later they came out of the bedroom. Gert clearing her throat and Ricky practically bouncing up and down with excitement. In the bathroom, Sylvia was letting out groans of pain as salt was scraped over her tender red flesh, but Ricky had mysteriously become oblivious to them. He hoisted the girl up into his arms all by himself and carried her down to the basement without faltering, except for a very brief pause to smirk when Gert commented on how strong he was. At the bottom of the stairs, he let Sylvia drop without a second thought. She let out a little cry of pain when she hit the ground, but it was so minor compared to all of her other suffering that it was more of an exhalation than a scream. Ricky didn't hear it anyway. He was already bounding back up the stairs to the daylight with a grin on his face.

The cleaning regimen continued over the following weeks. Once the initial pain of her internal injuries had passed, Gert had Coy and Ricky bind her hands and feet before carrying her up to the bath. Some days she wouldn't be cleaned at all. Just left alone down in the basement with only the smell of her own excrement for company. Other times, Gert would drag her up and scrub her two or three times over the course of the day. Food was even rarer for Sylvia now that she had been sent to the basement. Gert would bring her down a bowl of soup when she had made a pot, but she refused to give the girl cutlery. Sylvia was an animal, so she had to eat like an animal, trying to scoop the watery broth into her mouth with her bare hands. The only other time that she was allowed to eat was when Gert and the twelve-year-old John Junior came down to clean up the basement. They would scoop up her faeces with a gardening trowel, then Gert would pin Sylvia's jaw open while John poured her own excrement down her throat. When the smell of ammonia started to waft up into the kitchen, Gert threw a few buckets of water on the floor and gave Sylvia an old coffee tin to use as a toilet. Once a day, Gert and Ricky would come down into the basement and force her to drink its contents. The worst part was, those moments of agony in the bath, or humiliation and disgust in the basement, were the highlights of Sylvia's day. The only moments when she was allowed the simple luxury of light.

Missed Opportunities

The treatment of the Likens girls hadn't gone completely unnoticed by the people who had crossed their paths. Judy Duke, who had been goaded into fighting with Sylvia one night by Gert's lies, returned home confused and distraught. She had approached her mother and told her, 'They were beating and kicking Sylvia,' being careful to exclude herself from the guilty parties. Her mother seemed entirely unconcerned, having heard tales about the Likens girls. Their parents were carnies. It was hardly a surprise that they were nasty little liars, turning tricks. She took her daughter by the hand and explained to her that not every girl was as good and well behaved as her, and when a bad girl did a bad thing, sometimes the only punishment that she would understand was violence. Hearing that from her own mother was enough to calm Judy's confusion, but she remained withdrawn from the Baniszewskis' social circle from that point forward.

Not long after the Likens girls were "adopted" into the Baniszewski household, Gert got some new neighbours. The Vermillions purchased the house next to Gert's. The middle-aged professional couple of Raymond and Phyllis Vermillion saw how many children that Gert had under her roof and suspected she would make the ideal babysitter for their own children. Judging the state of her property, they also considered it an act of charity to pay her for that service. Still, they weren't even close to being as negligent as the Likens. Before even broaching the subject of babysitting, they invited the Baniszewski family over for a barbecue to get to know their new neighbours. Gert seemed to bring the whole neighbourhood's worth of teenagers and children with her and the whole event soon became rowdy. Even so, the Vermillions were delighted at the playful atmosphere. At least until they caught sight of one gaunt girl with two black eyes.

Phyllis caught Paula Baniszewski and asked her what had happened to the girl, only to be horrified when Paula proudly announced that she had been the one to give Sylvia the beating. She then vanished into the kitchen and returned with a mug full of boiling water, which she flung into Sylvia's face as Gert nodded approvingly. Needless to say, the Vermillions found a different babysitter.

Despite that, they made no attempt to contact the authorities about Sylvia's treatment. Everyone else in the neighbourhood treated the events that they'd witnessed as completely normal, and that normalised the violence for the Vermillions, too. Even when Phyllis stopped in at the Baniszewski house to borrow a tool for the garden and saw Paula beating Sylvia in the face with a belt until her lip split.

Shortly after Sylvia was condemned to the basement, another opportunity for rescue arose. Reverend Julian had an ongoing program that he had set up to visit his parishioners in their homes in an attempt to make himself seem more accessible. He sat with Gert in the kitchen, mere feet away from the door to the basement, drinking coffee and swallowing down her lies just as readily. 'That Likens girl. That Sylvie. She's been a terrible burden to me, Reverend. It pains me to admit it, but she has been such a blight on this family that it is a wonder I've held things together. If I'd known what she was on that first day when she forced her way inside my home I can tell you that I would have driven her right back out. She is a prostitute. The lowest of the low. The most unholy... not just that, she isn't just soiling herself, she is ruining good mens' lives, too. She services married men, Reverend. Then she comes back here gloating about it. She's pregnant you know. Got knocked up by one of the married men she lay down with.'

Paula wandered into the room in the middle of their conversation. Her stomach was already starting to swell with the baby she was carrying. She was several months along now, just starting to show but not enough that Gert had started dressing her up in baggy clothes. The reverend tried not to stare but Gert had a spark of fury in her eyes when he turned back to her. 'The nasty little liar has been going around trying to blame all her sins—all her crimes—on my sweet Paula. Saying that she is pregnant! It is ridiculous. My Paula is a virgin. As pure as they come. It is despicable the way that Sylvie has treated her. After she invited her into her own home, too.'

The reverend reached out to both of the women and took their hands. 'Let us pray for her.'

It only took a moment before their silent contemplation was interrupted by Paula blurting out. 'I've got hate in my heart for her.'

Gert silenced her with a pointed stare. 'You've got love in your heart for her is what you mean to say. Even though you should hate her for all the ways she's wronged you.'

Paula mumbled. 'Yeah. I don't hate her.'

The reverend scheduled another visit to discuss the troubles that the family had been having, walked out of the house and promptly forgot about it all.

Out of all the people in the world, there was only one that the Likens girls could reach out to. Their previous attempts to contact their parents had been thwarted by their constantly shifting address, information that only Gert was privy to. They had no aunts or uncles, and while they had a grandmother, she was ailing, impoverished and already taking care of Jenny's twin brother Benny. There was only one other family member who they had a hope of contacting. Their sister Diana.

When Sylvia was first condemned to the basement, Jenny sent a detailed letter explaining all of the torture that they had been experiencing at the hands of the Baniszewski family. A full accounting of it from start to finish. She begged her sister to send the police to the house to rescue them. Diana didn't believe a word of it. She was married with a family of her own, and it was far from the first time that her younger sisters had tried to move in with her and her husband. Diana didn't think that her marriage would survive their presence. She was already on the verge of a messy divorce when she got the letter and was faced with a prospect not dissimilar to the one that had faced Gertrude Baniszewski. Becoming a nineteen-year-old single mother was not a tempting prospect, and adding the burden of two more children was too terrifying to contemplate. With the Likens parents' tempestuous relationship, the begging and pleading phone calls from Sylvia and Jenny had become a fairly regular occurrence. Diana disregarded all of Jenny's fairly explicit descriptions of violence and degradation as regular corporal punishment that she was objecting to. She tossed the letter in the trash and went on about her day.

Something about the letter kept on niggling at Diana though. There were details in it, gruesome details, that she wouldn't have expected her little sister to have been capable of fabricating. So eventually she made a shopping trip into Indianapolis and swung by the suburbs on her way into town. One of the children answered the door when she knocked, squinting up at her in the late morning sunshine, but Gert appeared only a moment later. Diana greeted her with a smile. 'Hi there, I heard you're taking care of my sisters? I'm Diana.'

The response that she got just filled her with more apprehension. 'You aren't welcome here.'

'What?'

'Lester. He called me. Said you weren't to see the girls. Said you weren't even to come in the house.'

Diana boggled at her. 'Why on earth would he say something like that?'

'That's family business you've got to sort out between yourselves. But you aren't seeing the girls until I get his say so.' Gert closed the door on her.

All of this was just a little too strange for Diana's liking, so she walked a little further down the street, lit up a cigarette and waited. Almost two hours had passed by the time she got what she was waiting for. Jenny emerged from the house, dragging a sack of garbage almost as big as she was. Diana rushed up to her but instead of the warm welcome she was expecting she got a little yelp of fear. 'I'm not allowed to talk to you. Go away.'

It was all too bizarre. Diana called Indianapolis social services from a payphone and demanded that they investigate before heading home.

A few days later a social worker arrived at the Baniszewski house to find an exasperated Gert waiting for her with a story already prepared. Jenny was present and had been cleaned and dressed up to the best of the Baniszewski girl's abilities. Every word that Gert said, she nodded along with, every insinuation, no matter how vile she agreed with. Gert had cornered her before the social worker arrived and made one thing very clear. If she contradicted Gert in any way, then she was going to be stripped naked and cast down to live in the basement, too. It wasn't any harder to make two little whores disappear than one.

The story that Gert spun the social worker was partly a misdirection and partly the fevered imaginings that she had been inflicting on the Likens girls from the very beginning. Sylvia had been kicked out of the house several weeks ago after Gert discovered that she was physically unclean and a prostitute. Unwilling to expose her own children to Sylvia's lascivious lifestyle, she had decided it was better for them to part ways, but Jenny was silent proof that there was no problem in the house that had driven a teenage girl to turn to prostitution and run away from home. After all, if the good girl was still here, that put all the blame firmly on the bad one. Jenny nodded along. Eyes never once darting over to the door to the basement. She was twitchy and nervous but telling stories about a prostitute in the family was probably stressful enough to cover for her. After the social worker left, Gert gave Jenny a dollar to run to the store and buy herself a treat. After the social worker got back to her office, she closed the case. No more social work calls would be required at the Baniszewski household.

The Freakshow

Gert seemed to have secured her little kingdom for now, but while she had seen to its defences, her children had not been idle. While Gert may have been trapped in a web of her own fantasies, the children lived quite firmly in the real world, and in the real world, their family was on the poverty line. It didn't take long before neighbourhood boys came along who had missed the first 'striptease.' Boys who were eager to see a naked girl for the first time. John started charging boys a nickel to go down into the basement and take a peek. Soon demand began to outstrip supply, so he had to recruit his siblings into the venture. Rather than having their guests trail down into the basement to see her, the emaciated and scarred girl was forced up the stairs to be paraded around on display. She was pawed at, as much as the boys could get away with under the ever-watchful eye of Gert, who somehow still had the obliviousness to launch into searing sermons about the sinfulness of the flesh while having regular sex with a fourteen-year-old boy. Gert wouldn't tolerate Sylvia being used sexually, but violence wasn't just acceptable—it was actively encouraged. Every kid in the neighbourhood had probably taken a swat at the vacant-eyed girl by the end of the first week of displays. A few had stubbed out their cigarettes on her feet. One of the few acts of cruelty that could still draw some sort of response out of her. Sylvia was completely shut down, her motions sluggish and her voice slurring in the brief moments when she had the wherewithal to use it. Burning her drew out a low dull moan. It wasn't enough for the crowd, and the takings from an evening showing of their slave weren't as much as the Baniszewski children hoped to make. So, they started offering a special service. For a quarter, one lucky visitor could be the one to throw Sylvia back down the stairs into the basement.

The only one who was allowed down into the basement without Gert present was Coy Hubbard. She inexplicably trusted the boy, and his loyalty to Stephanie, despite the fact that their relationship had been gradually degenerating ever since the moment he first laid hands on Sylvia. Stephanie had no interest in furthering their physical relationship in defiance of her mother, while Coy got more aggressively sexual every time they were left alone together. Before long their 'relationship' was little more than some perfunctory kissing before he headed down into the basement for the main event. His judo practice with Sylvia lasted even longer now that she was constantly naked, and now that she had no clothes to grapple her with, he was finding new and unexpected hand-holds. He would emerge from the basement drenched in sweat and grinning, then putting Sylvia through her 'hygiene regimen' would be infinitely easier because she'd be too exhausted and sore to fight back.

Days stretched into weeks. Despite all of Gert's best efforts to break her, Sylvia still met the old woman's stares with defiance. It might have seemed to a normal mind that there was nothing more that could be done to the girl. That she had been brought to her lowest point and that the torture had failed. Worse yet, from Gert's perspective, there was no longer any excuse to punish the girl. After all, she wasn't capable of doing anything wrong when she was locked up alone down in the basement. Without sin, there was no reason to cast stones at her. Rationally, Gertrude must have realised that the longer she kept Sylvia down in the basement, the greater the odds that it was going to be discovered. She had total faith in her little army of accomplices, but she knew better than most that the world does not leave you alone just because you keep to yourself. On the 20th of October, they got a reminder of that when a stranger almost made it as far as the basement and the dark secret that they kept locked down there.

The Baniszewski children stole almost constantly with no repercussions from their mother, who could tolerate seeing no fault in her children. So, when a young man named Robert Hanlon showed up on her doorstep demanding the return of his property, she denied all knowledge. The kids had snuck into his basement through an open back door and helped themselves to several items, which were already gracing the shelves of a local pawnshop. Furious, Hanlon waited until nightfall and then broke into the house to try and retrieve his property. He made it as far as the kitchen before he was tackled by Ricky. Coy appeared only a moment later, and between the two of them, the boys were able to drag Hanlon outside and toss him into the street. Gert had called the police to report the intruder and a squad car had arrived shortly afterwards. It was far from the first time that the police had attended the Baniszewski house—Gert had been issued an arrest warrant herself just the year before for failure to pay the paperboy. But it was in all likelihood the first time that Gert had called the police herself, usually preferring to resolve disputes on her own. Hanlon was dragged off to the squad car but the Vermillions unexpectedly interceded on his behalf, explaining the whole situation to the police. It seemed like the police were going to search the house for the stolen goods. It seemed like there was finally some chance that Sylvia was going to be rescued. Then Gert casually asked the officers if any of them knew her husband John. Hanlon was taken down to the station.

After the police cars had all dispersed and quiet had fallen over the house once more, Gert came down to sit with Sylvia in the dark. Her matronly mask plastered back in place. 'I have been thinking about you, Sylvie. You've been in my prayers. I think that the Lord wants me to save you. I think he wants me to give you a second chance at life. Your time down here, that was you doing penance. Turning into something new. Something better than a whore. You want to be more than a toy for men, don't you Sylvie? You want to be free from your sins?'

Sylvia hadn't hoped in a very long time, and even with the ruckus upstairs earlier in the evening, she hadn't really considered the possibility that anything might change. She croaked. 'Yes. I want to be saved.'

'Then I'll help you. But you need to remember. This is your last chance. Your very last chance to do right. Otherwise, it will be back down here before you've even the time to open your filthy mouth. Do you understand?'

Sylvia struggled to wet her lips. 'Yes.'

She was bound hand and foot and carried up the stairs by Gert's boys. They tossed her onto one of the few real beds in the house and Gert crouched down beside her. 'If you can make it through the whole night without pissing yourself, you get to come and live upstairs again with the rest of the humans. Do you think you can do that?'

Sylvia wheezed. 'Yes, mom.'

She could not make it through the night without wetting the bed. While she might have held on to some hope that the very meagre provisions of water that she had drunk the day before would not be sufficient to cause a mess, the damage that had been done when the glass bottle was forced inside her had rendered Sylvia permanently incontinent. Gert came into the room sniffing in the early hours of the morning and then roared with rage, waking the whole house. She came at Sylvia with a knife. The girl looked up at her with helpless terror in her eyes. That one moment was everything that Gert had ever wanted from Sylvia. She used the knife to cut the ropes around Sylvia's wrists, then trailed the knife tip down the length of her body before doing the same with the ligatures around her ankles. She tossed a bundle of dirty clothes at

Sylvia and sneered. 'Get yourself dressed whore. I'll not have you parading around in shame all day.'

They made it as far as the living room before Gert's overexcitement had her changing her tune. The boys had migrated through to the living room for their morning smoke, and it didn't take long before Coy and Ricky showed up, like they did most days. The moment she realised there were no girls present, Gert ordered Sylvia to strip. 'Come on, whore. Give the boys one last show before you go back into the basement.'

Sylvia let out a little sob, but with numb fingers she began to undo the buttons of her borrowed dress, letting it drop to the floor with barely any shame at all. She wore nothing underneath because Gert hadn't given her anything. If the old woman had expected the sight of the naked girl to be exciting to the boys, then she was sorely mistaken. Any hint of sensuality had long since been beaten and starved out of Sylvia. She looked like skin hung over a wire frame. Her eyes locked on some distant horizon that none of the rest of them could see. Gert was furious with her. Even now she was defying her. The whore knew how to put on a show for men and she wasn't even trying. She was so superior. She thought she was better than Gert. She wasn't better than Gert. She wasn't. Snatching up a cola bottle, she slapped it into Sylvia's hand. 'You know what to do, whore. You've done it enough before.'

Sylvia's hand wasn't even shaking as she pushed the glass inside her. Even when she had to grit her teeth to push past the pain, she didn't stop until the bottle was in. She met Gert's stare. Implacable. Then she drew it out just as smoothly and handed it back to the woman. The whore had done exactly what Gert wanted, but it just made her angrier. She snapped. 'Get dressed. You're disgusting.'

Sylvia didn't even try to sit on one of the chairs, gravitating to one of the corners of the room, out of sight and hopefully out of mind. Gert slumped down on a seat in the middle of the room and waited for the rest of the household to filter in. Her plans were coming apart quicker than she could make them. She'd wanted Sylvia to move back upstairs so that she could start punishing her for her misbehaviour again, but instead, the stupid girl had wet herself and now she was going to have to go back into the basement. Then she was meant to be humiliated, putting on a show for the boys, and somehow she'd turned that against Gert, too. She was seething, staring at the girl as she looked off serenely. It was like she wasn't even here. Gert leapt to her feet and pointed a finger at her. 'I didn't forget what you did. You branded my daughters as whores! Now I... Now I shall brand you!'

She ordered the boys forward and they stripped Sylvia out of her clothes again, twisting a sleeve of her dress into a gag and shoving it into her mouth. The children were set to a task. They held one of Gert's sewing needles above a lit match until the metal was glowing orange, then the old woman snatched it out of their hands and advanced on Sylvia with a matching heat in her eyes. The boys pinned Sylvia down and Gert sat on top of her hips. Every one of her ribs was on display and her skin was so pale after a month in the darkness that it was almost translucent. As though she were fading away, unscathed. Gert growled and pressed the needle down into that perfect skin. Dragging a smoking line of pain down the girl's stomach as she thrashed and screamed. Now she was back in the room. Now she was back down here with Gert.

With the letter I completed, Gert reached out for the next needle. All the younger children were set to the task of heating them up, burning through box after box of matches. Gert got as far as 'IM' before she started to tire, and the stinging heat of the needle started to bother her. She handed the next one to Ricky Hobbs and he gleefully took over the punishment. Slowly the words of the brand came into sight. IM A. Ricky paused. 'How do you spell prostitute?'

With a tut, Gert scribbled it onto a piece of paper for him.

Sylvia didn't stop screaming through the whole process and the stench of her burning flesh overpowered even the usual miasma of filth that permeated the house. In the end the words 'IM A

PROSTITUTE AND PROUD OF IT' were left engraved into her flesh. Carved out and cauterised in one go. Gert licked her lips and stared gleefully down at the girl she had ruined. 'I'm a prostitute and proud of it. You certainly are, aren't you whore?'

With a contemptuous glance back, Gert left the room to go fetch herself another pack of cigarettes and a new book of matches.

Ricky was still holding on to the needle and without saying anything he passed it back to the ten-year-old Shirley Baniszewski to heat up again. He hissed. 'Slaves need a brand, so everyone knows that they're owned.'

He gleefully carved the lower half of the letter S into the middle of Sylvia's chest, but at the halfway point he stopped and looked down at what he was doing with growing horror. 'Jenny. Brand your sister.'

Jenny shook her head. He growled. 'Jenny. You do it or so help me...'

She squeaked. 'No. I won't.'

He cast a glance around desperately and then handed the needle to Shirley. 'You finish it. I.. I'm bored.'

Shirley took over the gruesome work with all of the sociopathic joy of a child, but when she was finished scraping the needle across Sylvia's breastbone the letter S had not appeared. Instead, the number 3 was there. Paula cackled at her little sister's stupidity. 'Isn't like you can rub that out and change it!'

Gert came back into the room, puffing away gleefully. She looked at the 3 on Sylvia's chest then chose to ignore it. She tugged the sleeve out of Sylvia's mouth with a cackle. 'What are you going to do now, Sylvie? You can't get married now. You can't undress in front of somebody. No man is going to want you. Nobody is ever going to want you again. What are you going to do now?'

Sylvia drew in a ragged breath but when she answered, it was in her usual voice. All of the fear had been burned away. 'I guess there's nothing I can do. It's on there.'

Even now she was winning. Gert couldn't stand it.

I'm Going to Die

Coy took Sylvia down to the basement and threw her around half-heartedly for a while, but without her terror, it had lost all of its pleasure. He slunk off home for the night, but the usual teenage party picked up in the living room before long. Sylvia lay there in the dark with a cold certainty running through her veins. A terrible, inescapable truth that she whispered when her sister crept down to sit on the stairs in the middle of the night. She whispered, 'I'm going to die. I can tell.'

Jenny tried to comfort her, but her platitudes were short lived. She had to scramble back up to her bed when Gert came around for a visit at about one in the morning.

Gert spent a long time just staring at Sylvia before eventually telling her, 'Come upstairs and go to your bed.'

When Sylvia was struggling, the woman hooked her hands into her armpits and lifted her up, supporting her as she climbed the stairs and then easing her down onto another unspoiled mattress. She gave the girl a pat on the head, then left her to drift off into nightmares that were little worse than her reality.

She slept right through the morning and was only woken gently at midday by Gert and Paula taking her through for a bath. She braced herself for the torture to resume, but the bath was pleasantly warm and full of soapy bubbles. The water stung at her wounds, both the brand and the open sores that had developed in many places over her body, but it was better than it could have been, so she found herself strangely thankful to her tormenters. Afterwards, they helped her get dressed and took her through to the kitchen, where they sat her down at the table with a pen and some paper.

It had been so long since she had dropped out of school in the midst of Gert's early torments that she barely even remembered how to hold the pen. It felt alien in her hand. Still, when the old woman smiled and began to dictate a letter, Sylvia moved to obey her, almost without thinking.

'Dear Mr and Mrs Likens,

I went with a gang of boys in the middle of the night. And they said that they would pay me if I would give them something, so I got in the car and they all got what they wanted... and when they got finished they beat me up and left sores on my face and all over my body. And they also put on my stomach, I am a prostitute and proud of it.

I have done just about everything that I could do just to make Gertie mad and cause Gertie more money than she's got. I've tore up a new mattress and peed on it. I have also cost Gertie doctor bills that she really can't pay and made Gertie a nervous wreck and all her kids.'

Sylvia moved to sign the letter, this obvious fabrication, but Gert snatched it away. 'No. You don't need to sign letters to your own kin. They'll know your writing.'

She turned away and Sylvia was forgotten again. She drifted in a daze for several minutes. Just enjoying the feeling of warmth again after so long in the cold and the dark. She was so disconnected from what was going on around her that she didn't even realise she was being discussed until it was almost over. Gert had her plan all laid out. With this letter as evidence that Sylvia was a runaway, all that remained to be done was to dump her somewhere. It was clear just from looking at her that there wasn't much life left in her. Gert told Paula her intentions. John Junior and Jenny would be told to carry Sylvia to the local garbage dump and leave her there. Exposure would kill her overnight. Once she was out of the house, Gert would go and call the police, and hand them the letter, explaining that Sylvia had gone off with some boys. It isn't clear whether it was due to Gert's mental breakdown or garden variety stupidity that she couldn't understand the flaw in her constructed timeline, but it is likely that the police might have gone along with it due to the renewed presence of John Baniszewski Senior in her life.

Regardless, Sylvia had heard enough. She got to her feet and ran for the front door, as fast as her withered and exhausted legs would carry her. She made it as far as the hallway before Gert scooped her up in her arms and dragged her back into the kitchen, pressing her back into the seat. 'How about some dinner, Sylvie?'

She made toast on the grill and laid it on the table in front of Sylvia with a flourish. Even the blackened, half-stale bread was better fare than she'd experienced in the last month, so Sylvia gobbled it up greedily. Or at least she tried to. Her throat was so swollen from her repeated chokings and the widespread infection that riddled her body that she couldn't force the bread down. She let out a dry sob. 'I can't swallow it.'

Gert's lips thinned. 'Let me help you with that, Sylvie.'

She walked over to the window and Sylvia assumed that she was fetching a glass of water until she heard the fabric tearing.

Gert rushed over with the greasy curtain rod in her hands. Grabbing Sylvia by the hair she tried to ram the end into Sylvia's mouth. Thrusting it in past the girl's cracked lips with a cackle. When Sylvia closed her mouth against the intrusion, Gert started smashing the pole against her teeth instead, eyes wild with some dark lust. 'Take it! Take it, you whore!'

Sylvia toppled onto the floor and Gert spat on her. John Junior arrived to see what all the noise was about and she snapped at him. 'Take the bitch back to her kennel.'

An hour later, Gert had regained her composure. She brought a plate of crackers down and tried to feed them to Sylvia, but the girl just turned her bloodied mouth away. 'Give it to a dog. They're hungrier than I am.'

Gert saw red again. She drove her fist into Sylvia's stomach, over and over until the scabs on her stomach cracked open and blood stained the pretty floral pattern stretched over her desecrated flesh. Gert stormed out of the basement, flicking off the light with a snarl and leaving Sylvia to one last night of total darkness.

On the next day, Gert and Coy came down into the basement together. Sylvia was still lying on the ground in the spot where she had been left. Gert had brought down a chair from the kitchen. She rushed over and swung it at the girl, but misjudged her distance and instead overbalanced and smashed it against the wall. Then she snatched up a paddle and tried to hit Sylvia in the head, but her swing went so wild that she hit herself in the face, blackening her eye. Coy watched, mesmerised by this feat of stupidity, before pushing her aside and hefting the curtain rail in his hands. He beat Sylvia all over her body with the stick, the rhythmic rise and fall of it punctuated only by the wet sounds of its impact. When they were certain she was unconscious, they abandoned her again.

Sylvia woke in agony in the middle of the night. She tried to scream for help but her throat was too badly damaged to make a sound. She managed to drag herself to the wall, where she found an old spade head, and for hours she beat it against the wall and the floor. Desperately trying to draw attention to her plight. She used every last bit of her strength, hammering away all night long. The noise woke several of the neighbours, but none of them thought to call the police. They were all used to strange noises from the Baniszewski house by now.

The next morning Gert sent Stephanie and Ricky down into the basement to fetch Sylvia for another bath before they disposed of her. They carried her up to the bathroom without even the slightest sign of a struggle and dumped her, fully clothed, into the water.

When her face slipped under the water and no bubbles came up, Stephanie realised that something was wrong. They pulled her out of the water and Stephanie tried to perform CPR but it was no use. The body was already cold.

Get Me Out

Jenny sat in the bathroom with her dead sister, staring at her intently and wondering, somewhat treacherously, how long it was going to be until she ended up in the basement now that it had been vacated. Panic swept through the Baniszewski house, but Gert was as solid in her delusions as always. Her plan was going to work just fine. The only thing that needed changed were a couple of minor details. She sent the boys to strip Sylvia and dump her back in the basement until nightfall when they would take her to the dump. Gert herself wandered across the street to call the police from a public phonebooth.

There was an unmistakable tension in the air when the two officers arrived, but Gert pressed on as if everything were fine. She handed them the note that she had forced Sylvia to write, then started waxing lyrical about how much of a burden the young runaway was, and about how inevitable it was that someone who prostituted themselves would end up coming to a gruesome end. The officers read the letter but seemed more perplexed by it than anything else. Even so, this was the wife of a fellow officer and they weren't about to start flinging any accusations around. They took a statement from Gert, and they were heading out of the door before one of them heard Jenny whispering. 'If you get me out of here, I'll tell you everything.'

That was enough to give him pause. He glanced at his partner, who didn't seem to have heard anything.

'I'm going to have to question everyone here. Standard procedure for missing persons.' The tension in the room suddenly mounted. He nodded to Jenny. 'You first, miss.'

The first words out of her mouth once they were out of Gert's line of sight were, 'Look in the basement. They killed her.'

He left Jenny in that strange bedroom with no door and went to his partner to ensure nobody left the building. Then he went down the staircase into hell.

Everyone in the house was arrested. Gert, Paula, Stephanie, John Junior, Coy, and Ricky were all arrested on murder charges. Everyone else was arrested for assault and injury to a person. Officers flitted out through the city, serving arrest warrants to everyone else involved in the horrific story and outside of Coy, Ricky and the Baniszewskis, every single one of them immediately told the police everything that they knew. From neighbourhood children to the local reverend. Everything came out, and all of it ended up in the court documents.

An autopsy was carried out on Sylvia's body to see which story was corroborated by the evidence. Gert's deranged tale of pregnant teenage prostitutes and roaming bands of torture hungry boys, or Jenny's even more disturbing story of matriarchal torment. Over one hundred cigarette burns were found on Sylvia's body. She had suffered second and third-degree burns. There was severe bruising, muscular and nerve damage. The cause of death seemed to have been multiple brain haemorrhages, but it was just as possible that the combined shock of all her injuries had just been too much for her weakened body to tolerate. In her death throes, Sylvia had bitten through her own lips, leaving them attached only by trailing threads of connective tissue. Her throat and vagina had swollen shut, although an examination of the canal revealed that her hymen was intact. Combined with the lack of rectal scar tissue, this made the obvious falsity of Gert's stories apparent to everyone involved.

The Trials of Gertrude Baniszewski

All of the lesser charges were ultimately dropped thanks to all the evidence that had been provided, with only the murder charge being upheld against Gert, her daughters, John Junior, Coy, and Ricky. When the case went to trial, the maelstrom of chaos that characterised their lives followed along with them. The charges against Stephanie were dropped before the case went to trial after she turned state's witness against her family—furnishing us with most of the story that we now know about the bizarre events within the Baniszewski home while downplaying her own culpability at every turn. Each of the plaintiffs had their own lawyer, with the exception of John and Coy, who were both underage and trying to pursue their youth as a defence. It had become apparent very early on that everyone involved was guilty to one degree or another, and only the degree of blame that would be individually assigned would determine which of them died and which of them escaped lethal injection.

Paula was rushed out of the courtroom during her first appearance to give birth to her daughter, whom she named Gertrude, after her mother, and from then the circus only grew more ludicrous. While the children all cottoned on to John and

Coy's tactic early on, claiming that they were merely coerced accomplices to Gert's madness, the woman herself seemed to be pursuing a completely different line of defence from her lawyer. The lawyer argued that Gert was old, infirm, and mentally impaired and that the children had done whatever they pleased in the absence of competent supervision in a sort of 'Lord of the Flies' scenario.

If anything, this argument was supported by Gert's own ridiculous behaviour throughout the trial, but after a certain point she began damning herself with her own testimony. She loudly announced to the court that Sylvia Likens had been the neighbourhood whore. Then she fabricated longwinded stories about the girl's trysts with married men, insisted vehemently on the girl's pregnancy and regaled the court with tales of all the times that she had started fights in her household, like some cuckoo hatchling snuck into the nest, intent on killing all the other chicks. She had no evidence to support her claims, and indeed it went completely against what much of the physical evidence gathered told the court, but she did have one witness willing to back up every single story that she told: her eleven-year-old daughter Marie. During her own testimony, Marie repeated everything that Gert had said, mostly verbatim, but during cross-examination she quickly broke down, screaming 'God help me!' before admitting that everything she and her mother had said up until that point was a lie. Her testimony, describing in blunt detail how her mother and siblings had tortured and ultimately murdered Sylvia Likens, was considered to be the turning point in the case. Gert was found guilty of murder in the first degree. To the dismay of the public, she was granted a sentence of life imprisonment without the possibility of parole instead of the death penalty.

Paula was convicted of second-degree murder. She appealed and was granted a second trial, but before she came to court she made a plea bargain, admitting to voluntary manslaughter. She served three years on that charge before she was paroled and then moved to a life of obscurity in Iowa at least until 2012 when she was exposed on Facebook and lost her job as a teacher's aide, in which she had been taking care of other people's children for years with nobody any the wiser.

John, Coy, and Ricky were all convicted of voluntary manslaughter and condemned to eighteen months in a juvenile detention facility.

John served his sentence, admitted full culpability to his crimes in interviews and seemed to be the only member of the family to experience true remorse. He went on to live a halfway-to-decent life, heavily involved with the church until complications from his diabetes resulted in his death in 2005.

Coy showed absolutely no remorse for his crimes and based on the evidence it is likely due to his being both a sexual sadist and a psychopath, just waiting for an opportunity to arise. He remained a criminal following his time in prison and was later charged with another double murder after a home invasion robbery went awry. While he tried to stay out of the limelight, attention to the Likens case has resulted in him being identified and losing several jobs over the years.

Ricky came out of the juvenile detention facility a changed man, but not for the better. He recognised his own culpability in Sylvia's murder and suffered a nervous breakdown shortly after his release. He lost a great deal of weight while imprisoned, and it was only after he had finally started to regain his faculties following his breakdown that he was finally diagnosed with late stage lung cancer. He died soon afterwards, riddled with tumours and regrets.

Gertrude Baniszewski appealed against her conviction on the basis of the extremely prejudicial atmosphere in Indianapolis, and the fact that the judge had been unwilling to let the case be relocated was considered to be solid enough proof of a mistrial, so her appeal for a retrial was granted. Without the damning testimony of her own preteen daughter, the jury was more lenient on Gert this time around. She was condemned to only eighteen years in prison.

She made herself into a model prisoner during her time inside, becoming a mother figure to many of the other inmates and working in the sewing shop. By the time that she came up for parole in 1985, she was widely referred to as 'Mom' by both the inmates and the guards.

Jenny Likens was adopted into the family of the prosecutor from the original case, Leroy New. He had several daughters of his own and she was well liked. She did her best to forget what had happened to her sister, but when news of Gert's parole hearing reached her, she felt obliged to take action. She made television appearances alongside many victims' rights advocates, condemning Indianapolis for even considering releasing the unrepentant monster. Even during her parole hearing, Gert still wouldn't admit to any wrongdoing. After a petition with forty thousand signatures was delivered to the parole board she was heard to exclaim, 'I'm not sure what role I had in it because I was on drugs. I never really knew her. I take full responsibility for whatever happened to Sylvia. I wish I could undo it but I can't and I'm sorry. I'm just asking for mercy and nothing else.'

After her parole was granted, Gert changed her name to Nadine Van Fossan and went to live with her daughter Paula. She was secretive during those years, with good reason. There was a whole, furious world out there that would have happily wrought revenge upon her for the death of Sylvia. She survived for only five years outside of captivity before succumbing to lung cancer in 1990.

It is quite possible that we will never know the truth about what happened to Sylvia Likens. Her story has now been shared in books and films, but every one of them has been based on testimony from the various members of the Baniszewski family, rooted entirely in their self-defensive lies. There have been many theories about what drove Gert to torture a young woman in the prime of her life to death, and indeed many of her Freudian slips throughout her ranting and raving seem to indicate that she saw herself in Sylvia. A version of herself that had not fallen so far from grace. One that could perhaps be kept right with strong enough discipline. Either that or Sylvia was simply serving as a punching bag for a woman so full of self-loathing that it overflowed and destroyed not only her own family but an innocent girl, too.

It is clear that Gert suffered from some sort of mental impairment which informed her actions, and it is entirely plausible that drugs or mental illness were clouding her judgement, but the death of Sylvia Likens was not a crime of passion. It did not happen in a moment of madness. The slow progressive torture that led to that girl's death went on for months. Even if we accept that Gert was somehow oblivious to the evil of her actions, that does not explain why the rest of the vast safety net of society completely failed the girl too.

There was an entire neighbourhood aware of the situation in the Baniszewski house, if not in full, then certainly in part. Yet not one of them contacted the police when they saw a girl shed half her body weight, wander the streets with open sores or black eyes. Not one person who crossed Sylvia Likens' path stopped and put in the bare minimum of effort that could have prevented her untimely demise.

There is no bottom to the pit of blame surrounding the death of Sylvia Likens. But you can be certain that at least some portion of it must be laid at the feet of the matriarch of the Baniszewski clan, whose delusions seemed to be so powerful that they could carry a dozen teenagers along for the ride and that could transform an unfortunate girl into the victim of what has been described as the single worst crime perpetrated against an individual in all of human history.

MAN-EATER

The Terrifying True Story of Cannibal Killer
Katherine Knight

Introduction

All that Kathy ever wanted was for somebody to love her as much as she loved them.

After a brief tussle, David was on top of her again, his sweat trickling down on her as he thrust inside her over and over. All of that weight—the mechanical inevitability of each thrust and groan—was like riding a mechanical bull, except she was trying to buck it off instead of the other way around.

Did David love her? She knew that she loved him. She wouldn't be lying here, legs all twisted up at odd angles, crotch aching and insides churning with cheap beer and agonising friction if she didn't. She tried to look into his eyes, to see her love reflected back at her from inside them, but he was staring into the pillow, eyes slack and unfocused, mouth hanging open and drool pooling at the corners, clinging to the stubble of the day. There were no answers to be found in that vacant face, not after a long night at the pub.

He didn't love her the way that her father had loved her mother, all sharp words and blunt fists. She knew that for certain. David was slow with his fists, even when some fool deserved it, and he was so soft on her that it made her feel uncomfortable sometimes. He was so soft that she could push her fingers right inside him like his skin was just the skin on a pudding.

He didn't love her in the way that the little animals that she'd rescued from the roadside and nursed back to health loved her, with the unconditional adoration and terror of someone meeting their god. He wasn't obedient and cowed like an animal would be. He certainly had some animal in him, but it only came out in places like this, when his rutting and grunting and growling were somehow acceptable.

She didn't even know if he could love through the haze of booze that had been hanging around him all day. When he'd picked her up on the back of his motorbike this morning, his breath was already strong enough to strip paint. He must have spent the whole night out drinking with his buddies. One last night of freedom, he'd said. Freedom. Like she was some prison he was being sent to. Like she would ever stop him from doing what he wanted instead of helping him on his way.

Who the hell did he think he was, talking about her like she was a punishment instead of being the only good thing in his shitty, little life? How dare he make a joke out of her? She started thrashing underneath him, raking at his back with her nails. Thrusting up against him as hard as she could, desperate to throw the rotten bastard off her. He probably couldn't even feel it through the booze. All he did was make appreciative little moans.

No matter how she twisted and pushed, he just seemed to love it more—maybe this was the only way he knew how to love her, with his big meaty hands clamped on to her hips and her hair spread across the pillows. Maybe that was enough, these moments of total adoration in exchange for spreading her legs? Her mother had always told her to just go along with what men wanted to make them happy. It had been about the only good advice the old hag ever gave anybody. Kathy was tough enough to take it. She was tough enough to take on anything.

She'd proven that every day in the charnel house. Men blanched when they saw guts and blood for the first time, but Kathy took to it like a fish to water. Her knives, her precious knives, moved through that dead meat like sharks through the water, smooth and perfect, never making a ripple out of place until she wanted them to. At work, they might have feared her smart mouth a little, but they feared those knives the most. She'd offered to settle any argument or score that folks had with her by the knife and not one of them had balls big enough to try. If it were up to her, she'd carry those knives with her everywhere she went, but her fist served just as well when one of the women or, more often, men, in the pub had a wrong word to say about her and her man.

Her man. It was worth it. To be loved, to be truly loved for the very first time in her life. It was definitely worth lying back and pretending that every drop of sweat didn't sting like acid. To pretend to be as soft as he needed her to be. As soft as he was under the tough mask that he put on to impress folks.

With just a little of his blood under her fingernails, Kathy stopped clawing at him. She could do this for him, she loved him and, at the end of the day, it wasn't really all that bad. She even found she could enjoy it when she wasn't trapped inside her own head. She envied David for having it that easy; for being able to close his eyes, inhabit his body and just feel things instead of spending all his time lost in the echo chamber of his memories, repeating some snide comment that one of his cousins made about their wedding ceremony being held in a registry office, and how it was no surprise that the bride wasn't wearing white.

Had Kathy had her knives with her, she would have painted that bitch's dress red at that moment. Instead, she'd let herself get dragged along by David, twirled out onto the makeshift dance floor in the bar for their first dance together as man and wife. He'd been so drunk that he trod on her toes and let out his stupid gruff laugh when she stamped on his in return. She reached up to cup his face in her hands. He was hot to the touch. She took him upstairs.

Eyes closed and grunting with the effort. Determined to hammer her right through the bed and into the floor. The headboard of the bed was clattering against the wall with every thrust and, on their hook above the bed, Kathy's knives jangled along like a musical accompaniment to their lovemaking.

She'd had more than a few beers right alongside David tonight. She was allowed to celebrate, too—it wasn't all about him. It wasn't all about him getting to haul her eighteen-year-old ass back to bed and grunt on top of her and then go off to hoot with triumph about it to all of his stupid friends. This was what she wanted. Kathy kept repeating that to herself every time he hammered into her, every time it felt like she was going to tear in half. This was what she wanted. She wanted the husband. She wanted to have kids and settle down and do everything right, the way that her own shitty parents had never managed to. She wanted it all. She wanted to be loved.

If that love burned a little, then she would let it burn her. There were far worse fates than to be warm at night, cradled in the shelter of a big, strong body. She wanted this. She had wanted this for as long as she'd been old enough to know what a man could be to a woman. It was true enough that she could never wear a white wedding dress without lying because she'd been chasing after this love since she was old enough to run. The boys back at school had been on the receiving end of her fists a lot more often than they'd gotten under her shirt, but she put that down to being raised by a pair of bad examples. Dad's example had led her to being free with her fists and mum's example had led her to being free with her tits.

Now, she was old enough to know right and wrong for herself. Old enough to recognise that the map her parents had laid out for her led to nowhere but loneliness and misery. Her reputation might have been tarnished by her school years, but she'd swung at anyone who tried to keep her dirty when she was trying to clean herself up. David wasn't the first man she'd ever been with, not by a long shot, but he was the first one that she felt like she could trust. The first one that she gave herself to fully, instead of trying to hide inside her head when the clothes came off, the way that she had when she was a little girl.

David was getting faster and faster, his eyes still squeezed shut, even though his face was held between her hands and Kathy was kissing him with a passion that surprised even her. The jangling of the knives above them was like sleigh-bells. His breathing had a hitch in it and, for a moment, sore as she was, Kathy felt the spark of lust light up inside her. She didn't just want this. She wanted him.

She'd wanted him after the two of them staggered home together that night. She'd wanted him when he picked her up, carried her over the threshold, kicked the door shut and dumped her into the bed. Right up until the moment that he'd stripped her out of her dress and climbed on top of her for the first time, she had been electric, desperate for him and arching up into every touch. But, the moment that he was actually inside her, she vanished back inside herself. Every grunt echoed in the dark cavity of her mind, coming back louder with a dozen bad memories coming along to keep it company.

The first time they'd ever made love, she bit his lip and he'd called her a bitch, but he hadn't stopped. Just like none of the others had stopped no matter how she squealed and hollered. She'd stopped biting him now. Her old defensive instincts had grown lax. She really was getting soft.

The first time that they consummated their marriage that night, she had given him nothing harsher than kisses and he'd given her nothing gentler than the same methodical, mechanical pounding that he always did. No matter what she did, it always turned out the same.

Ten minutes after that first attempt, she'd wrapped her lips around him and started off round two with a distended grin. She knew what was expected of her as a wife. She knew that she had to let him do everything to her and she had to act like she liked it. She'd learned that much at least. If this was how he showed his love then she wanted it all. Every sweaty, painful moment of it.

This third time, she'd climbed right on top of him the minute he finished and started slithering all over him. Smearing the two of them with sweat, dragging her smooth skin over his rough hairy chest and stirring his passion up all over again. This belonged to her. This night was all about the two of them and there was no way that she was going to let it end. He couldn't turn her down. He could never turn her down. All she wanted was his love. Rejection was an impossibility. A betrayal. It had taken only three slides up and down him before he was ready to go again.

Now, it was almost over. She could feel him clenching up above her. Felt those violent thrusts get harder, deeper and slower. He let out a noise like a deflating balloon when he finished, then he rolled off her, gasping, 'I swear, keep on like this and you're going to kill me, woman.'

She lay there for a long moment letting the cold seep into her. The ache was still there between her legs, but there was a sweetness to it now, a longing. This time, when she climbed back on top of him, it wasn't just going to be for him. It was going to be for the both of them. She was going to feel whatever it was that he felt when they were making love. She was going to be complete, like the other girls got to be with their sweethearts. She was going to feel the good as well as the bad.

David's cheek bristled her when she kissed it. His breath stung her eyes as it gusted out of him in shallow puffs. His eyes were shut, but they weren't clenched shut as they'd been in the heat of the moment—his whole face was slack, even looser than the beer usually made him. She climbed on top of him and fumbled around in the soggy mess where their bodies joined. She was trying to line everything up, but David was being awkward, flopping limply in her grip in a way that he never did. She let out a little growl and jerked at him, trying to get the motor running again.

With a dirty laugh, she leaned in close to kiss him on the lips, but she stopped when he made another of his little animal noises. Not quite a grunt, not quite a breath. Her eyebrows drew down. She knew that sound. A moment later, another snore joined the second. The bastard had fallen asleep. This was her night and he was sleeping through it. He wasn't here with her. He'd shut his eyes and left her behind. He'd abandoned her. It was their wedding night and he'd fucking left her.

She untangled her hands from his nethers and took a grip on his broad shoulders instead. 'Wake up, honey.'

It took all her considerable strength to lift him and drop him back onto the mattress, but he didn't even stir. She shook him. Slapped him. Hammered her fist into his shoulder. 'Wake up, you piece of shit!'

He was still ignoring her. Still leaving her behind. Her hands slipped up over his thick-corded shoulders, trailing up his collar, leaving tracks in the cooling sweat. 'David. Wake up. Wake up! This is my wedding night! Wake up, you miserable bastard!'

Her fingers were as calloused and strong as any man's from days on the tools and when they closed around his throat they were filled with terrible anger, born from pure, blind fury. When she crushed his windpipe in that grip, his eyes finally snapped open, but by then it was too late. His blushing, beautiful bride was gone and this other Kathy—one that he didn't even know—had slipped into her place. Her face locked into a rictus of rage and hands locked around his throat.

Even his Kathy's voice was gone. This one sounded more like a growling dog than anything human. 'I'll teach you a lesson you'll never forget, you bastard.'

The Sinners

In 1949, Ken and Barbara fled their homes in Aberdeen amidst a storm of scandal.

Barbara had been married since she was a teenager to a man named Jack Roughan and they had lived together in relative peace in the sleepy Hunter's Valley town of Aberdeen. The coupling had produced four boys, two of whom were in their teenage years by the time that Barbara's infidelity was discovered.

If you wanted to work in rural Aberdeen in the 50s, your options were extremely limited. Farm work was always an option if you happened to own a farm. Mining was the alternative that most of the men fell into, though it led to a short and painful life for most men who chose that route. Leaving was an option, too, one that appealed to many of the town's youth, particularly the better-educated ones who could expect to earn a decent wage living in one of Australia's bigger cities.

For everyone else, there was the slaughterhouse. All of the local farms produced animals, animals that had to be killed and hacked up into saleable portions before being shipped out across Australia. Even by employing almost every adult in the town of Aberdeen, the workload still outstripped the manpower and they had to look further afield to keep the gory machinery turning over.

Ken Knight was a boon for the slaughterhouse's operations. He was an itinerant worker who travelled from town to town looking for work in the meat processing facilities that dotted the Australian farmlands. Whilst he had a reputation as a hard man and an even harder drinker, he was still meticulous in his work, hammering through carcass after carcass in half the time that it took his local co-workers, no matter how dire his hangover might be. It probably would have earned him the ire of his co-workers if he weren't so gregarious. They all found it extremely difficult to stay angry at Ken.

Jack Roughan was one of Ken's local co-workers and, whilst he tried to keep some distance from the man who had become the star of the slaughterhouse, they shared friends and ended up going out drinking together quite regularly—although Jack soon found that he couldn't keep up with Ken in that arena, either.

It was during those marathon binge drinking sessions that Ken met Barbara. They'd crossed paths a few times when Jack's long-suffering wife came to collect him from the pub and drag him home, but it wasn't long before the next big night out for the abattoir workers had all of their wives in attendance. There was chemistry between the two of them and Ken flirted with her all night long, right in the presence of her beer-blinded husband.

Barbara had come to hate Jack by this point in her life. He'd been her sweetheart in school, but once her teenage hormones had cooled off, she found herself trapped in a marriage with a man who honestly didn't give a damn about her. There was no women's-lib in rural Australia in the 1940s—if a wife had needs beyond those that her husband was fulfilling, then she was expected to be quiet about them until she eventually died of old age. In Ken, she saw the opportunity to rekindle her passion for life. The idea of divorce never even entered her mind; with her conservative upbringing, she knew the kind of social death that a single mother would suffer, but an affair? They were practically commonplace. The dirty little secrets that everyone gossiped about but nobody ever confronted directly. The frayed edges on the bonds of the Aberdeen community. She didn't actually want Ken so much as she longed for change and he was the only change available at the time.

At the next night out, she flirted back. Not as outrageously as Ken did—his larger than life personality provided him with the perfect cover for that sort of behaviour—but with enough vigour that he was convinced of her interest. When Jack succumbed to the liquor and a few of his friends carried him off towards home, Barbara lingered. At closing time, only Ken and Barbara were still upright. Suddenly, shyness overtook her despite all of the liquid courage that she had consumed and she tried to go home to her husband.

Ken wrapped her wrist in his massive hand and led her away, through the dull grey of the pre-dawn streets until they reached his dingy one-bedroom apartment in spitting distance of the slaughterhouse. When she was bashful, he was forceful, when she was reluctant, he was persistent.

At the next night out, the two of them ignored each other entirely. Any burgeoning suspicions that might have been hanging around their co-workers evaporated and Ken went back to winking saucily at the poor bartenders, instead. Jack kept his arm around Barbara's shoulders anyway, a little statement of ownership that didn't go unnoticed by anyone. A statement that both Barbara and Ken were happy to acknowledge. It was better if everyone knew for certain that she was Jack's wife, that she was loyal to him and had eyes for no other. The more certain everyone was of those facts, the easier it was for the two of them to sneak around behind Jack's back without interruption.

Jack and Barbara's sex life had been on the decline from the moment that it started. She was repulsed by the sexual act and had endured it exclusively for the privileges that it brought to her in the marriage. With Ken, the situation was different—sex wasn't a penance to be endured in exchange for a roof over her head and babies in her belly. It was an act of righteous rebellion.

Once she had taken up with Ken, Jack was cut off entirely. With teenage children in the house, the arguments had to be conducted quietly, but they were intense all the same. Barbara found her grocery budget slashed, her free time filled with pointless, busy work—whatever petty miseries Jack could inflict to apply pressure on her to spread her legs, he did. He grew colder and angrier with her with each passing day and every little cruelty just reinforced Barbara's suspicion that all he had ever cared about was sex. He didn't love her. He didn't even pretend to help with taking care of their children anymore. Their marriage was a hollowed-out husk and she was bone-tired of pretending otherwise.

Things were at boiling point and all that it took to tip things over was a bruise on her thigh that looked like a handprint, if you squinted. Jack went mad. He beat Barbara until she was covered in bruises and threw her out of the house. Tossing her limited wardrobe out into the mud with her.

Whilst other cuckolded men in Aberdeen had the sense to keep things quiet, to prevent the shame and scrutiny that this sort of betrayal brought down on a family, Jack was too enraged to care. Within a day, all one thousand five hundred people living in the little town knew that his wife had been unfaithful.

The identity of the man that she had been having her affair with wasn't yet known, but it didn't take long before Barbara was found. Homeless and destitute, she had turned to the only person in Aberdeen who she was certain wouldn't turn her away or beat her even worse than Jack had. She moved into Ken's tiny apartment the same day she was thrown out of her family home.

The rumours about the two of them abounded and, before long, their shame was the talk of the whole town. Barbara's own children wouldn't even look her in the eye. The two younger boys had been shipped off to live with Jack's sister in Sydney, two hundred miles away, without Barbara even being informed. The two older boys sided with their father, going so far as to spit at their mother in the street when they saw her. The words 'whore' or, more politely, 'adulteress,' dogged her footsteps everywhere that she went.

With nothing left to tie her to Aberdeen, Barbara begged Ken to take her away. With only a pair of suitcases, the two headed off across New South Wales to find themselves a new place to call home. A place where nobody knew the shameful secret that had started their union.

They found that place in the town of Moree and he easily found work in the local slaughterhouse with the same jovial manner and practiced hands that had won him pride of place in Aberdeen society. Through letters and only a single court appearance, Barbara was able to secure her divorce from Jack Roughan, returning to her maiden name of Thorley for only a week before a hasty registry office ceremony branded her as Ken Knight's property, instead.

Whilst Barbara had lost all of her friends and contact with most of her family, the Knights were still a presence in Moree and they didn't care what circumstances had led their prodigal son back to them—they were just happy to have him nearby again. Their rapidly arranged wedding was conducted with Ken's locally famous brother, Oscar, as the best man and a few other family members as witnesses. Barbara was already beginning to show signs of her first pregnancy of the new marriage by the time that the ink was dry on the marriage licence.

Two boys were born in the years that followed, new sons to replace those that Barbara had lost when her first marriage disintegrated. Instead of chasing after the change she had so desperately craved, she instead found herself sinking further and further into an identical rut. The only difference was that this time, cold, angry looks were far from the only punishment she received for breaking away from her wifely duties.

Ken had always been an alcoholic, but amidst the hard-drinking culture of rural Australia, it wasn't immediately apparent that it was a problem rather than just another aspect of his gregarious personality. In isolation, with only Barbara and toddlers for company, it became immediately obvious that it was not merely a source of distraction but a crippling addiction. There was not a single day that passed without Ken getting so drunk he was slurring his speech. The good money that he made working in the local abattoir was whittled away in local bars before the family even got a chance to spend it on essentials. Whilst Barbara might have felt like a prisoner in a gilded cage with Jack, when she was with Ken, that cage began to tarnish and show its true colours.

Once again, she started to fantasise about how she might make her escape—eyeing the other men in Ken's life with an appraising eye and finding that none of them wanted anything to do with her. Ken's reputation preceded him in Moree and nobody wanted to cross the man, or his family, by getting involved in an affair. Painfully aware that a divorce could only end in her losing her precious children all over again, Barbara prepared to hunker down and endure the marriage with as little contact with Ken as was physically possible.

Ken did not respond well to the withdrawal of her affections. His sexual appetites had almost been a running joke back when they lived in Aberdeen and Barbara had adored the passion when they were still in their courtship phase. But, now that they were married, his ardour had not cooled even a little. He demanded sex constantly, sometimes as often as ten times a day. When Barbara refused him, he did not shy away as her first husband had. At first, he would beat her into compliance. Then, when even that began to fail, he simply forced himself on her.

Barbara was trapped in the house with two little boys, raped as often as ten times a day, beaten for every slight infraction against the rules that her new iron-fisted tyrant of a husband laid down. She might have escaped her nightmare life of boredom and mediocrity back in Aberdeen, but she had plunged headlong into a fresh hell of her own making; a poster-child for the puritanical beliefs about the sanctity of marriage that held sway at the time.

Her children were the only light in her life, but it didn't take long before both of her precious boys were learning the lessons that their father imparted through his actions as much as his words. By the time that they were walking, they were throwing punches at one another and at their mother. They treated their father with the respect that he considered his due, but their mother was little more than a slave to their whims. Alone and surrounded by vicious men and vicious men in training, Barbara longed for any sort of help against the tide of evil that surrounded her.

When she discovered that she was pregnant again, at the start of 1955, all of the usual delight that that discovery would have brought had been beaten out of her. The discovery that she was carrying twins just made things so much worse. There would be five of them. Five men, demanding and tormenting her, night and day. Stripping away whatever distant hope of escape that she might have harboured.

Imagine her delight when, on the 24th October 1955, she gave birth to a pair of non-identical twin girls in Tenterfield, New South Wales. Beautiful baby girls with her Irish red hair already curling on their foreheads. Allies.

Daddy's Girl

The younger of the two girls was named Katherine and the older twin, Joy.

Joy adapted quickly to life in a house full of masculine energy, becoming a tomboy and allying herself with the men against Barbara. Katherine quickly became her mother's only hope and only confidante.

She was a pretty little girl and she spent a great deal of her time playing with dolls and dresses. Despite his less than conservative actions, Ken was a conservative at heart. He deeply approved of his daughter behaving in what he considered to be 'feminine' ways and, whilst he treated his wife with utter contempt, considering her to be little more than a tool for his pleasure, in little Katherine he found—if not a kindred spirit—at least a balm to the hypermasculinity of his work environment, persona and lifestyle. Katherine was a quiet place that he could visit, where there was no judgement, no competition, no frustration and no backbiting, just the unconditional love of a girl who viewed her father as something akin to God.

But, if Ken was God, then he was the vengeful Old Testament version. He demanded obedience and compliance, not only from his battered sex doll but also from the children. The boys were raucous and rebellious, with nobody around who could control them all day long. Their only authority figure had literally and figuratively been stripped of all dignity in front of them far too often for them to listen to a word Barbara said, and the end result of Ken's brand of discipline tended to be bruises rather than life lessons.

Joy fell in with the boys, joining in their vicious games, but Katherine always held herself apart. She wasn't the most obedient child, but when she was stubborn, Ken looked on it as a virtue rather than a sign of defiance. He beat her with a dog leash when she was disobedient, switching to an extension cord when he was feeling generous or when he couldn't remember where he'd left the leash after his last drunken fury.

Whilst the other children received the same beating over and over, Katherine was a little quicker to adapt her behaviour. She was still the recipient of a great many unwarranted beatings throughout her young life, but they were rarely for the same reason twice. She was soft and pliant when he needed her to be and tough and rough when he wanted her to stand up for herself. She modelled herself on him and the ally that Barbara had been so desperately hoping for was co-opted by the enemy.

Barbara didn't take the loss well. She'd brought two daughters into the world after two awful marriages and both of them had turned against her in their own ways. She sunk into an even deeper depression, withdrawing entirely from the world, going through the motions of motherhood without seeking out any emotional connections or joy and enduring Ken's ever more violent violations with a cold stoicism born of total disassociation.

Her only small recompense was company. Katherine may have looked on her mother as too weak to defend herself, but she didn't overlook the woman's value as a teacher. It didn't take long before Katherine graduated from playing house with her dolls to trying to take over the running of the real household. She learned everything that she could about housekeeping, cooking and sewing from her mother. By the time she was old enough to turn the knobs on the stove, Katherine was already supplanting her mother in the kitchen, just as she'd supplanted her in Ken's affections.

As the girls got older, Barbara began talking to Katherine as though she were her confidante, even though Katherine had given her no reason to place her trust in her. Ultimately, she had nobody to tell. She was just as isolated as Barbara by their living situation and, with no basis for comparison, she assumed that every mother spoke to her daughters in the same way. Sharing explicit sexual details, ranting and complaining about all of the misery that had befallen her and sharing all of the sordid family secrets that Katherine would soon become the keeper of.

Rural Australia was not the most progressive place in the late 50s and the racism that the aboriginal people suffered on a daily basis made even America's civil rights history look positively heartwarming. Even the suspicion of aboriginal ancestry was enough to get a family marked as social pariahs. Whilst Barbara's Irish great-grandfather granted both her and her children their distinctive red hair—and a good deal of the European features that helped to disguise their true ancestry—her great-grandmother had been an indigenous Australian. Two generational infusions of white heredity had helped to mask the family's appearance, but as Barbara's sanity continued to decline, she began obsessing more and more over that ancestry, taking pride in being different from the men who abused her.

She taught her daughters about their aboriginal ancestry, making sure to instil the requisite fear of exposure in them. She had meant for it to bring them together as a family, but all it did was layer more pressure onto an already tense situation. Now, the girls believed that society outside of their immediate family was against them, that no assistance would be forthcoming even if they did eventually reach out for help. Their ancestry became another lock on the cage that kept them trapped inside the nightmarish Knight family.

As if the pressure in the Knight household wasn't already high enough, things worsened yet again in 1959, when Katherine was only four-years-old. Jack Roughan died and the two older boys who had been living with him were passed into the care of their mother. Already in their teenage years and suffering from a nasty shock after the death of their father, the boys submerged themselves entirely in the culture of their new family. If Barbara had hoped that the presence of the older boys might calm her new brood of hellions, she was wrong. The older boys had lost all respect for their 'whore' of a mother when she abandoned them back in Aberdeen and they were almost gratified to see how badly she was being treated. Some of this was idolisation of their lost father, but no small part was simply adaptation to their surroundings. Nobody else cared about Barbara, why should they?

If their contempt had extended only as far as their mother, then their contribution to the darkness that was gathering in the Knight household would have been negligible. Unfortunately, they swiftly learned from the example of their adoptive father and began to look at all women as disposable sex toys with no agency of their own: an example that was constantly reinforced by their peers and the other men in the community in more subtle ways than Ken's barbaric displays of dominance. Girls their own age had protections in place—the cultural expectation that they would wait until marriage, accompanied by the overbearing threat of violence from the girls' fathers and a whole whisper network to keep them from being left alone with boys like the 'new Knight kids.' All it took was a few fumbling attempts at molestation before the Roughan boys were blacklisted from every social event in town and every girl was given fair warning that they were after their virtue.

With no outlets for their burgeoning sexuality and no privacy within the family home due to the sheer volume of boys crammed into each room, they soon started looking a little closer to home for release. Joy was spared their attention thanks to her being 'one of the guys,' but the more feminine Katherine soon became the focal point for both of the older boys' sexual awakenings.

Between the ages of four and fourteen, Katherine was the target of a gradually worsening series of sexual assaults in her own home. A campaign of molestation that started with friendly touching, cuddles and gentle innocent kisses, gradually transformed into games where Katherine was stripped of her clothes and her dignity. As they grew old enough, the younger duo also started to join in with their new brothers' favourite hobby. Before she had even reached her teenage years, all four boys were using her for their sexual pleasure. If it hadn't been for her mother's example, Katherine would have been mystified by the strange actions of the boys, but Barbara was always more than happy to regale her girls with tales of her sexual exploitation, giving them all the explicit details of the 'disgusting' things that men would want them to do.

Katherine finally had the courage to ask, 'What do you say if you don't want to do those things?'

Her mother gave her the worst advice she would ever receive in her life. 'Just let them do what they want with you. It's easier that way.'

With that in mind, Katherine never reported her brothers' escalating sexual behaviour, even as they moved on to frottage and exploring her body outside the confines of the games that they'd played when she was young enough to believe they were only games. Just as Barbara became the receptacle of all Ken's sexual frustrations, so too did Katherine suffer that same fate—never speaking out and never truly knowing whether her life was normal or hellish.

As she grew older, Katherine began to seek out safe avenues of escape from her home life. Whilst she had no way of knowing that other families were not enveloped in the same maelstrom of chaos, she had found a few safe shelters outside of it. In particular, she discovered that she loved spending time with her Uncle Oscar.

In his youth, Oscar had been a champion horseman, famous in New South Wales for his skills and, whilst he had been forced to abandon that career as age wore away his competitive edge, he still maintained a horse farm where he tended to both his old champions and rescue horses that had been abandoned or abused. Katherine fit right in. She spent as much time as possible with Oscar, helping to care for the horses and any other animal that she found at the farm. Whilst her father's interactions with nature mainly involved butchering it, Oscar taught Katherine to love animals as more than just a resource.

Before long, she was rescuing injured animals and nursing them back to health in her room at home. She was fiercely defiant when Ken tried to take them away from her, to the point that she was able to make the brutal patriarch back down and let her tend to her wounded birds in peace. When she found larger animals in need of help, she called on Oscar and he took as many as possible into his stables or passed them along to a veterinarian who could provide the creatures with the care they required or the tender mercy of an overdose.

Oscar was a landmark in her life, a point that she could have used to navigate a new course. One where she didn't follow in her father's footsteps. One where the brutality of her home life was a distant memory instead of her daily reality. But, sadly, Oscar had his own struggles in life. Despite the brave face that he put on for Katherine, he was riddled with depression and in 1969, when she was only fourteen years old, he took his own life, turning the gun that he had used to put down so many injured horses on himself and putting an end to his own misery for once.

This was the breaking point for Katherine. The moment when all of the rage and misery that she had dammed up inside herself throughout her life finally cracked the veneer of good behaviour that her father had demanded. The next time one of her brothers tried to feel her up, she punched him so hard she nearly broke his jaw and threatened to castrate him the next time that he laid a hand on her. It was like a switch had been flipped, like a different person had just started to inhabit her body.

After the boy had fled to his brothers with this tale, the older boys approached Katherine and discovered that she was in just as good a temper as always, cheerful and charming despite her current state of upset. They discounted the younger boy's story as a misunderstanding. Over the next months, both of the older boys would suffer minor, yet painful, stab-wounds that they would blame on accidents in the kitchen. One of them walked around sporting a black eye that he claimed to have acquired rough-housing with his younger siblings in an accident.

None of them dared to talk about what Katherine had become capable of because that would lead to a conversation about what had pushed her so far over the edge. Even if the younger boys and girls had no knowledge of the world outside their walls, the older boys knew perfectly well what happened to rapists in rural communities like Moree and Aberdeen. There were plenty of farms around with plenty of the rubber tubes and scissors used for quick-and-dirty castrations on troublesome beasts. It is safe to say that, in those days, in those communities, there were very few repeat offenders.

After the death of Oscar, life in Moree began to sour for the Knight family. He had been their closest tie to the community and his minor celebrity status had helped to shield his brother from any criticism that his abnormal lifestyle and 'sinful' choices might have brought him. The people that knew Ken, outside of his family, all considered him to be a lovable rogue, but the community at large didn't have to contend with his personality when trying to disapprove— they only had to deal with the concept of him. After more than a decade in their new home, the old rumours about Barbara and her previous husband had finally caught up to them and it was as if the scandal had happened only yesterday.

Meanwhile, Barbara's family back in Aberdeen had started to soften in their stance towards her without the daily visual reminder of her sins in the form of the Roughan boys running through town. She had begun communicating with them through rather stilted letters, knowing them well enough to realise that they would never help her escape the fresh hell she had gotten herself into, but hoping that one positive relationship in her life, untainted by Ken's lust, might be a tether to hold her sanity together.

When the situation in Moree became untenable, it took very little prompting on her part to have the whole family relocate yet again, this time fleeing not further from the site of their original sin, but back to the scene of the crime. By the time Katherine was fifteen, they were settled back in Aberdeen, the town she'd consider home for the rest of her adult life.

Life on the Borderline

For the first year after their return to Aberdeen in 1969, Katherine had to catch the bus to Muswellbrook High School every day to complete her state-mandated education. She was an unknown element to the children of Aberdeen and so they began to test her, to find out what this new arrival was made of.

As it turned out, she was made out of harder stuff than the farm boys that took it into their heads to torment her. After only a week, the usual 'new kid' bullying on the school bus ground to a halt out of safety concerns. Katherine was polite and charming so long as nothing riled up her temper, but once someone had crossed her, it was like a switch flipped. She would defend herself readily against any insult using her fists, boots or cutting remarks, going well beyond the level of retribution that her would-be bullies might have expected, and into the territory of vendettas. Days after a girl tried to trip her as she walked up the bus aisle, Katherine came up behind her and snipped off her braided ponytail with a pair of scissors. When a boy made a lewd comment about her early-developing breasts, she responded by smashing his teeth against the back of the seat in front of him.

For as long as Katherine was enraged, the bus became a war zone, but when her teachers confronted her later, they were unable to align the stories that they were told about her behaviour with the polite, friendly and cheerful girl that sat before them. For the first six months, the burden of proof fell on her victims and even they had to admit that she had been provoked into her behaviour, even if that behaviour was completely out of proportion when compared to the minor slights it was in response to.

Having established herself as someone who was not to be messed with, Katherine settled into the educational routine. Even at fifteen, she still had only the most basic reading and writing skills, but in this, she wasn't drastically different from many of the children around her and what she lacked in polish, she made up for in ingenuity.

She was frequently at the top of her class, despite her academic shortcomings. Even the children who expected to go on to higher education and careers outside of farming, children who studied and worked hard, would struggle to surpass her. To the vast majority of her teachers, she was a model student. But, it didn't take long before her savage temper took its toll on her reputation and the lives of others there, too.

Bullying was common enough at the school—an extreme form of peer pressure that helped to instil conservative values in those children who were straying too far from the straight and narrow path of normalcy and stoicism that their community demanded of them. But, even in a school where insults and violence were the norm, Katherine was considered to take it too far, terrorising the younger children who had crossed her, to the point of tears on a daily basis. To her peers, she was to be respected, but to those in the lower classes, she was the bogeyman. All that a child had to do was get on her bad side and then their life would become hell. At least, until her dark mood had passed.

Even her ridiculous bullying behaviour was overlooked as a part of the normal school experience until the day that she stabbed one of her victims for the terrible crime of talking back to her. The knife that she used was small enough to hide in the folded-over top of her skirt, ready at hand whenever her foul temper demanded it, but close enough to her private parts that none of the almost entirely male staff would dare to go searching for it if word ever got back to them about it. Even when they were confronted with a bleeding young boy screaming on the hallway floor with Katherine standing over him, her excellent reputation among the staff protected her from consequences beyond a letter home about her behaviour. The teachers never found the knife that she had used. They barely even looked for it.

When Ken read that letter, slowly, using a finger to track his position in the text, he asked Katherine if her victim had deserved it and her answer of 'yes' was enough to satisfy him that justice had been done. If anything, he was proud of his favourite daughter for standing up for herself. Ken was trapped in the usual position of the overbearing patriarch. To him, all women were nothing more than property, but in the case of his daughter, she was his property. Property that he wasn't around to defend at all times. He wanted her to be subservient to both him and men in general, but also to defend herself against the dangers that other men, like him, would present to her.

She probably would have made it through her whole school career with her standing in the community unscathed if it hadn't been for the one fateful day that her favourite teacher gave her a bad grade.

Katherine had been quiet all the way through the class, staring sullenly down at the papers in front of her as if she were back to struggling through them like she had when she first arrived. Her teacher kept glancing over at her; the cheerful girl who usually bounced to her feet every time that he asked the class a question, had fallen silent and still. He wondered if perhaps she'd taken ill or was suffering from what the other teachers called 'woman's troubles.' He didn't want to pry if it was the latter—he knew more about that subject than he cared to already—but if she was actually ill, he wanted to see that she was taken care of.

'Kathy? You all right, love?'

She didn't even look up at him. Her hands were in her lap and she was fidgeting around. Maybe it was woman's troubles. He groaned internally. That was the last thing he needed today. Blood all over his classroom. The girls from town were all right, but some of this country lot, they'd make the whole place look like a slaughterhouse before they thought to put a stopper in it. Kathy had never let on about this sort of trouble before, but he'd heard enough from girlfriends through the years to know that things could change on you.

'Kathy, you weren't saying much today. Is something the matter?'

Her head snapped up. 'Is something the matter?' she snapped back, 'What do you think?'

She threw the loose papers at his face and they fluttered uselessly to the floor. 'Is something the matter? You're meant to be on my side. You're meant to help me. Why'd you fail me? Eh? You've just been leading me along all this time. Making me think you're on my side when really you just want to spit on me like those other pigs.'

She flung herself out of her seat and instinct kicked in. He backpedalled rapidly. Hands flung up in supplication. 'Calm down, Kathy. It is just one test. You'll have plenty of chances to make up for ... '

'Don't you tell me to calm down,' she snarled. 'You're just like the others. You never cared about me.'

He was still backing away. She was still advancing with the inevitability of the tides. 'Kathy, it was just one test! It doesn't matter.'

She roared. 'You don't matter, you cunt-faced son of a whore.'

His eyes widened. He'd heard rumours about Katherine's foul temper and foul mouth, but he'd never expected that he or any other teacher would be on the receiving end.

'Now, steady on. You can't talk to me like that!'

'Fuck you!' Her arm drew back and, for the first time, he saw the shimmer of steel in her hand.

'Kathy, no!'

He sidestepped the first stab, otherwise, it would have gone right into his gut. He danced back across the whole classroom with her in pursuit; his legs banged into his desk. He had nowhere left to run.

She slashed at him, tearing a ragged line through his leisure suit and his shirt but narrowly missing flesh.

'Kathy, stop!'

He tried to grab at her wrist and nearly lost his fingertips for his trouble. Her eyes were glazed over. Drool was flecking on her lips and her pretty little face locked in a rictus of fury. She couldn't hear a word he was saying through the roaring of blood in her ears.

Katherine drew the knife back and he then realised the truth. She wasn't going to stop. She was going to keep going until she killed him.

Instinct saved him again. Fight or flight. Before, his body had moved without thought to get him out of the way of the danger. Now, the other half of that survival instinct prevailed.

His fist lashed out and caught Katherine under the chin. She was strong for a fifteen-year-old girl, stronger than any of her peers, thanks to the manual labour she had done at home and at her uncle's farm, but, for all of that, she was a teenage girl and he was a grown man. When he hit her, it lifted her right off her feet.

She landed on her back, the wind knocked out of her and the vacant stare more likely caused by shock than frenzy. As soon as she managed to gulp air into her lungs, she started sobbing. Wailing. Loud enough for everyone in the building to hear and come running.

'Oh god, Kathy, I'm so sorry. Are you alright?'

He dropped down beside her. He just couldn't help himself. Even now he only wanted to help her. It was just luck that he knelt on top of the knife, and her hands found only corduroy instead of another opportunity to make herself a murderer. The student body pressed in at the door and it felt like an eternity before another teacher managed to wade through them and take in the scene.

'My god. What did you do?'

The teacher was suspended from the school following the incident, as was Katherine, but whilst he was wreathed in suspicion and contempt, she was allowed to play the victim, suspended from school to recover from the traumatic event. An investigation was carried out by the school board—people who had no direct interaction with Katherine—and suddenly the picture of her abusive behaviour came into stark relief.

The teacher was reinstated with back pay and an apology and Katherine was allowed back only under probation. She served out the last month of school in a silent cloud of rage, never once interacting with the man she had tried to kill and barely keeping her foul temper in check with the other members of staff. Without a constant stream of praise to sustain her, she left school at fifteen years old with no qualifications.

This became an established pattern throughout Katherine's life, a pattern that psychologists and criminologist clung to as an explanation for her erratic behaviour. She would eventually be diagnosed with borderline personality disorder (BPD), which explained many of these strange habits away.

Those afflicted with BPD suffer from emotional instability—in Katherine's case, almost always caused by feelings of rejection or abandonment. They suffer from cognitive distortions, where they see the world in black and white, with anyone who isn't actively 'with them' being considered an enemy. They are also prone to catastrophising, where they make logical leaps from minor impediments in their plans to assumptions of absolute ruin.

BPD is often characterised by extremely intense but unstable relationships, as the sufferer gives everything that they can to a relationship in their attempts to ensure their partner never leaves but instead end up burning themselves out and blaming that same partner for the emotional toll that it takes on them.

The final trait of BPD is impulsive behaviour, often characterised as self-destructive behaviour. In Katherine's case, this almost always manifested itself in her hair-trigger temper. When she was enraged, it was like she lost all rational control over her actions, seeing everyone else as her enemies. This manifested itself in the ridiculous bullying she conducted at school, in her lashing out when she failed her test and in the vengeance that she took on her sexual abusers. It is likely that she inherited this disorder from her mother, who showed many of the same symptoms, and that they were exacerbated by her chaotic home life and the lack of healthy relationships in the adults around her that she might have modelled herself after.

With Katherine, it was like a Jekyll and Hyde switch took place when her temper was raised. The charming, eager-to-please girl who usually occupied her body was replaced with a furious, foul-mouthed hellion bent on exacting her revenge no matter what the cost. In itself, this could have been an excellent excuse for almost everything that she did wrong in her life, up to and including the crimes that she would later be accused of. Unfortunately, this sort of 'flipped switch' argument doesn't hold up when you consider that her choice to arm herself with a lethal weapon was premeditated. Part of this may certainly have been the cognitive distortion that Katherine experienced, telling her that everyone else was out to get her and that she had to defend herself, but ultimately, she was choosing to give a weapon to a person who would use it to end lives, if she had the opportunity. Assuming that this division of personalities actually existed, then 'good' Katherine was an accomplice to 'bad' Katherine, giving her the material support and planning that she needed to commit her vicious attacks.

Of course, all of this is predicated on the idea that Katherine actually suffered from BPD. It is entirely possible that there was no imbalance in her brain chemistry that made her behave in the way that she did. That, if anything, her outlook on life was based entirely on the example relationships that she had experienced during her childhood, providing a roadmap for her entire future. The Knight household was home to the sort of dog-eat-dog anarchy that would prompt rational people to violently defend themselves, perhaps even making pre-emptive moves against potential abusers.

After her diagnosis of BPD in later life, the medication that was provided to Katherine never seemed to have its intended effect. No matter how high the dosage she received, psychopharmacology failed to inhibit her violent outbursts and twisted worldview. Casting the accuracy of this diagnosis even further into doubt was the fact that many of the psychiatrists who studied Katherine in later life did not agree with the diagnosis, whilst she herself clung to it as a defence against having to take responsibility for her actions.

Whenever Katherine was accused of wrongdoing throughout her life, she would go through the same patterns to defend herself. First, she would deny that her crime had ever been committed. Then, she would deny that she was responsible. When both of those failed, her final fall-back position was always that the person whom she had victimised had deserved the punishment. BPD offered her one final out; even if her victim didn't deserve whatever the latest cruelty was that Katherine had conjured up, it still wasn't her fault. It was her sickness.

Katherine's first port of call following the ignominious end to her educational career was the Aberdeen slaughterhouse. She went in with her father, first thing in the morning before the sun had even risen, so that she could beg for a job—any job. Her lifelong dream had been to follow in her father's footsteps and work the meat line. She had been studying the swift actions of his hands since she was old enough to remember, mesmerised by the way that the blades of his boning knives danced in his strangely delicate grasp. In her limited world, her father was a god and, in the community that surrounded them, that God was worshipped for his mastery of the knife.

The shift manager at the abattoir took one look at the waifish redhead and told her no, that it wasn't work suited to a woman and that she'd be better suited looking for work elsewhere. Thanks to the presence of Ken in the building, Katherine was able to keep her temper in check, otherwise, the polite conversation might have turned foul, very quickly.

Still, her dreams of living by the blade never left her. She found another factory job in one of the only other places in town, a clothing manufacturer, where it was her job to cut the fabric to size. She had considerable experience with clothes-making by this point in her life. Almost all of her own clothes were handmade; she'd been handling repairs on her brothers' forever torn trousers for as long as she'd been able to hold a needle and Barbara had gradually been ceding territory to her in regard to Ken's clothing, too. By keeping to herself and focusing on the work, she soon found that she excelled in her new role, earning considerable praise from her employers. With the fair wage she was earning there, she was able to move out of her parents' home and into a small apartment in town, near to the factory. It was the first time in her life that she was free to come and go as she pleased and it didn't take long before she realised that this pleased her very much.

The other women in the factory weren't exactly subdued, but they were a far cry from the sort of company that Katherine wanted, so, before long, she got into the habit of heading across town to drink with the slaughterhouse workers after her shift ended.

She became well-known among them for her foul mouth and ready fists. It took barely any time at all before the man who would have been her supervisor revised his opinion of whether she was too ladylike to work among the blood and guts. In terms of violence and grotesque language, she could hold her own with the men. Stories about her incredible work ethic, prowess with the knives and manual dexterity spread out of the factory and through the gossip network to reach the ears of the married men at the slaughterhouse. The only group at the slaughterhouse who wouldn't have been singing her praises were the single men and, as it turned out, Katherine's other hedonistic behaviour soon tackled that. It wasn't that she was loose with her affections. Quite the opposite, she went after each individual man with a hunger akin to desperation. A longing that they often found off-putting, rather than flattering.

Regardless of that one questionable habit, when she turned sixteen, Katherine went back to the slaughterhouse and asked for a second time about a job and, with the credentials that she had established in her year living alone, it was impossible for them to refuse her. So, in 1971, she turned in her notice at the factory and started work at her 'dream job' in the Aberdeen slaughterhouse, cutting up offal for dog food.

For Whom the Wedding Bells Toll

Katherine had always known that she would excel in the abattoir, but even she couldn't have predicted her meteoric rise. It soon became apparent to everyone just how skilled she was with her tools and, within a few weeks, they began testing her on more complex jobs around the slaughterhouse. She bounced from one production line to the next, proving her mastery of each job before being upgraded to an even more complex task the following week. This grand tour of the slaughterhouse gave her a chance to make the acquaintance of nearly every man who worked there and she most assuredly left an impression.

Those men who hadn't crossed her path before were in for a nasty shock when they tried to treat her like a girl. The first time someone on the line raised his voice to her, she quietly and politely offered to settle their disagreement with their 'fucking knives.' A suggestion that would arise regularly throughout her time in the slaughterhouse. Nobody was ever foolish enough to take her up on the offer. They'd all seen her work.

It wasn't long before she started to relax and come out of her shell, joining in with the foul-mouthed banter and establishing herself as a force to be reckoned with socially, as well as physically.

Still, she continued to bounce around the abattoir until 1972 when she finally arrived at what was widely considered to be the most complex and demanding task on the line: deboning. It was the job that had made her father's reputation and she ended up working alongside him when their shifts aligned. Ken hadn't become lax as the years went by, but he had achieved a certain level of excellence and then plateaued. Now, there was suddenly a new competitor for the throne and he was forced to push himself harder and work faster to stay ahead of the girl nipping at his heels.

For Katherine's part, she didn't even seem to be aware that she was competing. All of her life she had been waiting to get this job and now she was simply doing everything in her power to keep it. If one of the other men had surpassed Ken in his work, he probably would have accepted it as an inevitable part of his advancing years, but to see a teenage girl coming for his crown was disheartening— even if it was his own daughter who had trained at his elbow for years. They never argued about it, never even spoke about it. Ken worked harder than he ever had in his life and his example was an inspiration to Katherine, who worked all the harder to try to keep up with him.

The owners of the business weren't blind to the incredible work being done under their roof, or the way that Katherine's presence was driving all of her co-workers on to greatness. Efficiency in the slaughterhouse went up wherever Katherine went and it wasn't just her direct contribution. None of the other men wanted to be shown up by her and, once they had been, they strove even harder to try to wash that shame away.

With these deliberate and accidental contributions in mind, the owners of the slaughterhouse felt like they needed to reward Katherine, not with anything as dangerously disruptive as a pay rise, but with some little reminder that she was appreciated. Exactly one year on from her first day in the slaughterhouse, she was gifted with her very own set of personalised knives and a leather bag to carry them around in. She carried them with her to work every day from then on, honing their edge to razor sharpness and proudly displaying them on a hook above her bed when she was at home. They were her prized possession. A trophy and testament to her skill in the only area of her life where she'd ever felt truly valued.

The owners of the slaughterhouse would never have asked Katherine to serve as any sort of example, but her natural inclinations were sufficient to have her parading around the slaughterhouse, even on her days off. She liked to visit all of the different parts of the process, chat with the men about their work and watch them at their tasks.

Her absolute favourite place in the entire production line was the pig room. She would spend every lunch hour lingering there and chatting away with the old man who had the unenviable duty of killing the pigs in full view of the others in the pen. Whilst the cattle were typically slaughtered with a stunning blow to the head before the knife-work began, the smaller creatures were not afforded the same kindness. Their wailing squeals could be heard throughout the entire building over the course of the day. High-pitched, shrill and almost human-sounding screams. Katherine was fascinated. There were a lot of foul rumours circulating about the old man who slaughtered the pigs, mainly revolving around the fact that he enjoyed his work more than was appropriate and because of this he lived a fairly lonely life, with the exception of his new best friend Katherine, in whom he found something of a kindred spirit.

In his desperation to keep her engaged, it wasn't long before he began breaking the rules, killing the pigs in front of her in increasingly cruel and elaborate ways. Once, even skinning a whole pig in front of her whilst it was still alive and screaming. Even that wasn't enough for Katherine. She didn't just want to watch, she wanted to participate.

At first, he would let her step in and deliver the lethal killing cut to the throat—spraying arterial blood all over her waterproofed apron as she cackled with glee. But soon even that wasn't sufficient to keep her entertained. She would chase a pig around the enclosure, seeing how many cuts she could inflict before it fell down dead, snipping a ligament here and a muscle there to see how far she could twist the pig's movements whilst still keeping it fleeing from her in terror. She had transformed from the little girl who tried to save roadkill and nurse it back to health into a gleeful torturer of animals.

The full extent of Katherine's lunch-break activities obviously weren't known to the owners, who wouldn't have approved of the risk of meat getting spoiled by her antics, but the other workers seemed to be thoroughly aware of her sadistic capacity for cruelty and the stories about what she did to the pigs were sufficient to keep even those who doubted the threat that she posed, in line.

Despite all of the positive attention that Katherine was getting for her 'one of the boys' attitude and workplace achievements, she was on the receiving end of just as many romantic overtures from the majority male workforce that she spent every waking hour with. She headed straight from work to the pub with the rest of the men— following after her father's example in that respect, too— although she differed greatly in the fact that she didn't actually drink alcohol, faking her way through every single night with the assistance of the bar staff and a substantial amount of lemonade. Outside of work, she allowed her more feminine side to show, behaving more like the country-girl that the abattoir workers were accustomed to courting and beginning to garner attention now that she wasn't so desperately pursuing them.

She had an ongoing flirtation with an older man named John Chillingworth, but he was perturbed by the age difference between them. Despite being an alcoholic in the truest sense, he was never quite inebriated enough to take up the seventeen-year-old girl's offers to take him home with her. Some part of that may have been the looming presence of her intimidating father in the background of every conversation that they had, or perhaps it was simply an instinct for self-preservation. After all, Chillingworth had been one of the few men to press a workplace argument with Katherine beyond the shouting stage until she drew her knives on him. He had caught a glimpse of the madness behind her mask of civility and, whilst the wildness of Katherine might have intrigued him, he wasn't willing to risk his reputation as a decent man in the community by chasing some teenager, no matter how pretty or exciting she might be.

Still, for every cautious man like John Chillingworth, there were plenty of fools like David Kellett, who couldn't see underneath the paper-thin veneer of a pretty, young girl to the darkness inside.

Aberdeen was verging on being a company town for the abattoir employees, with terraced houses constructed by the owners of the 'meat-works' to provide low-cost barracks for all of their employees around the slaughterhouse itself. It was a good few streets away before you came upon property that wasn't under the Australian Meat Cutting and Freezing Company's jurisdiction, and a few streets more before you hit upon the commercial property that usually surrounded the hubs of industry like the abattoir. The town of Aberdeen had only two licensed establishments where alcohol could be purchased and consumed—a bar and a hotel—and both of them were sensibly situated in easy walking distance of the slaughterhouse, just beyond that line of demarcation between company property and the town proper.

The bar was usually the preference for the line workers and the hotel was preferred by management, though there was a lot of crossover as almost every man served the odd shift as supervisor when the need arose and there was little animosity towards the owners. Katherine's preference was definitely for the bar. She felt more at home there. She didn't like people who had pretentions and the hotel, for all that it was a little run down, still aimed a little higher than the lowest common denominator in the products it was selling. Still, sometimes it became necessary for her to go to the hotel instead of the bar. Mainly when she was banned after an act of brutal violence.

The latest of her many fist-fights happened in 1972 when she was seventeen. One of the new miners who had arrived in town took an immediate dislike to David Kellett, despite his general popularity among the workers in the abattoir. Whilst the two pillars of industry within Aberdeen rarely brushed against one another, this bar was one of the few places where both sets of workers would meet. The miners typically drank in their own union-house, where the prices were better and membership was a requirement, but when they were feeling amorous, heading out into the general population was the only way they could hope to meet women. It is possible that the gentleman in question had taken a shine to Katherine, who was currently quite fixated on David, but the exact nature of their disagreement still isn't known. All that is certain is that when he insulted David Kellett to his face, the slaughterhouse worker backed down instead of escalating the situation. David wasn't a line worker like the rest of them—he drove one of the delivery trucks that served the abattoir—still, despite that degree of estrangement, he was well aware that his comrades from the meat-works would back him if it came to a fight. Ultimately, he just didn't want that sort of trouble in his life. David was a relatively calm man of twenty-two years. If questioned, he would simply say that he had nothing to prove to anyone—that he was out for a quiet drink, not a brawl. The truth was, David was not a particularly physically imposing man and, in a small community of miners and heavy manual labourers, he just couldn't stack up in terms of bulk or raw strength.

Katherine did not share his compunctions or his limitations. Since she had started her new career in the meat-works, her father's genetics had won out. Any hint of waifishness had vanished as her muscles filled out and a final growth spurt had left her towering over David at six foot tall.

When the insult had been flung, her face turned beetroot red: a visual warning that would follow her through her life each time that her rage consumed her. She swung for the miner and she didn't stop until her knuckles were bloody and his teeth were scattered over the bare floorboards. David had to drag her off before she could kill the man—with the assistance of a good number of her stronger co-workers.

It was passed off by the other men in the bar as high spirits, as a drunken brawl, something that could happen to anyone. But what only Katherine and the bartender knew for certain was that her glass held only lemonade. She drank with the rest of them, held her own drink by drink because she never touched alcohol. She had seen how it robbed men of their power and she had no intention of ever feeling powerless again. The bartender had never shared that secret, assuming that the woman was just trying to protect herself against the lustful, leering men all around her, but he still knew and it still informed his decision to ban her. There was no liquor to excuse her actions; they were all just Katherine being Katherine.

With no bar to attend, both Katherine and David were forced to relocate to the hotel for the next night and it was there that they finally got together. He had been amazed that she would stand up for him like that, that any woman would throw a punch to avenge an insult against a man. In all of his life, he'd never felt so wanted.

It soon became clear that devotion wasn't all that Katherine brought to the relationship. Instead of subsisting on whatever could be scrounged up at the meat-works mess hall, David was soon dining on elaborate home-cooked meals. His clothes were being mended and their sex life quickly became a thing of legend. Everyone suspected that there was a little bit of animal in Katherine, but her appetite astounded David. And, when he was in his cups and talking about her, they astounded everyone else in town, too. Just as her father had ravaged Barbara up to ten times a day, so was his daughter equally insatiable in her pursuit of sex—not so much for her own enjoyment, but to prove her absolute devotion, body and soul, to David.

For a man like him, this was overwhelming. He was used to living a hard life and all of this kindness turned his head. More than that, the change in Katherine stunned him. He had only known her as the quick-to-anger co-worker; he had never experienced the soft side of Katherine that used to be her primary personality. Whatever reservations he had harboured about a potential relationship faded away rapidly and before long, the two of them had moved in together.

Twenty years on from when Ken and Barbara had been run out of town for living in sin, attitudes had shifted a little. The fact that Katherine didn't give a damn about the opinion of anyone who might be muttering helped, as did the expectation that even though the two of them were dallying at the moment, they were definitely on course towards marriage. They had a brief period of equilibrium when they were living together 'in sin' and working together in perfect harmony, but then, external forces began intruding. Katherine's flirtatious way of speaking to co-workers who were in her favour riled up David's usually subdued temper and he was soon being needled by their wives—by proxy—to tie the knot and keep everything respectable. Like Katherine, he was something of an outsider to Aberdeen society, so the pressure didn't trouble him too much.

Unfortunately, Katherine soon had the idea planted in her head that, without the guarantee of marriage, David was likely to leave her, and that the reason he was refusing to commit to marriage was because that had been his intention all along: to have sex with her for as long as it suited him and then to abandon her and move on to the next town when she became too much of a burden. In the echo chamber of Katherine's mind, these ideas bounced back and forth until they were almost deafening. Eventually, she went from dropping hints to outright demanding that David marry her. That, if he loved her, he would marry her. If he was faithful, he had to.

David had only been neglecting to marry Katherine because he thought that she had no interest. Now that her opinions had changed, he was happy to go along with her. He didn't think he'd ever meet a match like her again, so why on earth wouldn't he want to tie the knot?

There were certain formalities that had to be addressed before the wedding could move forward. Ones that both Katherine and David had been more than happy to avoid up until now. She took him out to meet her parents.

With decent savings filed away and his daughter still nipping at his heels, Ken had finally begun the slow slide into retirement. What was left of the Knight family had withdrawn from the meatworks' barracks—where their reputation had been in steady decline ever since their arrival—and relocated to a run-down farmhouse a little way out of Aberdeen town proper. Ken had cut back to only part-time shifts at the abattoir and was spending the rest of his time trying to get the house into some semblance of order. The vast majority of the land attached to the farm had been parcelled out to neighbours once the bank foreclosed on the previous tenants, transforming it from a source of income for the family into nothing more than an isolated dwelling in an advanced state of disrepair.

With his advancing age, Ken was finally starting to treat Barbara a little more gently, if only because he no longer had the energy to chase her around the house, batter her senseless and rape her ten times a day anymore. There was a stale quality to the air, where once tension had filled every living space. Ken and David had met before whilst working together, so whilst there was a little awkwardness regarding the fact that he was now dating Ken's daughter, they soon fell back into the usual comfortable companionable rhythm. Barbara was another story entirely. Much like Katherine, a decade without proper socialisation had left her a little rough around the edges. She'd always been prone to foul language—she was the font of knowledge from which most of Katherine's obscenities had been learned—but now it seemed to be almost all the vocabulary she had at her disposal. A brutally hard life had worn her down until she was little more than animal.

Eventually, Barbara cornered David in the heart of her domain, when he'd ducked into the kitchen to fetch Ken and himself another can of beer.

'You want to marry her, do you?'

He nodded, all the nervousness he'd carried into the house coming back to him in a rush now that it was being spoken about so bluntly.

'You sure about that? You know she's got a screw loose?'

David let out a startled laugh. He couldn't believe that Katherine's own mother was talking about her like that.

'I know she's got a little temper, yeah.'

Barbara tutted. 'Nah. You don't. Don't understand at all, do you?'

He shrugged and started backing away towards the kitchen door. Barbara was flushed, a few beers in herself and getting twitchy. 'You'd better watch that one or she'll fucking kill you. Stir her up the wrong way or do the wrong thing and you're fucked. Don't ever think of playing up on her, she'll fucking kill you.'

David chuckled. He'd been expecting this sort of warning from Ken, the old 'treat my girl right' threats that most fathers inflicted, but he'd never expected his future mother-in-law to be warning him about bad behaviour this way.

He smiled at Barbara. 'Don't you worry, I'll treat her well.'

'I'm not worried.' The woman was aged before her time, wrinkled and exhausted already. She stared out of the window and added, 'Ain't me she'll kill if it goes tits up.'

David didn't believe a word of it. He'd seen no hint of danger in Katherine, even when she drew knives on the men in the abattoir or beat a miner unconscious with her bare hands. To him, she was the perfect, charming wife that he had always hoped to secure for his future. He wasn't going to let anyone's wild suspicions ruin the best hope he had for his future.

With that settled and the arrangements made, the wedding day swiftly approached, pencilled into the calendar for just a few days after Katherine turned eighteen. There was no registry office in Aberdeen; the town was just too small to justify one. When the time for the subdued ceremony arrived, David had already been drinking heavily with his friends in the bar, both to provide him with some 'Dutch courage' and as a part of the celebrations. The indignant Katherine had to wait outside the bar in her handmade wedding dress until he came out, loaded her on the back of his motorbike and drove them, in a serpentine fashion, to the next town over.

The ceremony was the cheapest that money could buy, with the intention being to head back to the bar and spend the difference that they'd saved on a raucous party. Despite David's inebriation, he made it through the ceremony without incident and Katherine was so happy it seemed like she was going to let these minor slights slide. After they'd signed the license, they hopped back onto the bike and headed off down the dusty road back to Aberdeen.

The rest of the day was devoted to drinking, David's favourite hobby. In addition to all the usual suspects from the abattoir, his extended family was in attendance, along with as many of Katherine's relatives as could be convinced to make an appearance. The two groups did not mix. The Knights' reputation preceded them and whilst David's family were mostly visiting from Queensland, they had been forewarned by friends in the area about what they were likely walking into.

Over the course of the day, Katherine was insulted over and over by the Kellett family. They thought that she was too stupid to understand their little jibes, but whilst she lacked the communication skills required to make her intelligence apparent, there was a lethal cunning lurking just behind her eyes, and she had lived as the school bully for long enough to know when insults were being flung around. She blocked them all out. This was the happiest day of her life and if some piece of shit out-of-towners couldn't be happy for her then what the hell did she care. It was her day. Her's and David's.

In a state of advanced inebriation, the two of them made their way back to David's company-issued apartment to consummate their new union. Katherine was always enthusiastic, but on their wedding night, she was practically ecstatic, tearing David's clothes off and rushing him through to the bedroom so fast that they forgot to lock the door behind them.

They had sex three times in quick succession, with Katherine coaxing David on past the limits of his usual endurance. After that third time, he passed out immediately and Katherine was suddenly left alone in the tempest of her own thoughts and passions. When he started snoring, her fury bubbled over. All of the frustration of the day—all of the tension that she had been bundling up inside her that she was so used to unleashing immediately by lashing out at the earliest provocation—it all came boiling over. She beat at David with her bare hands to wake him up, slapping him and punching him until it became apparent that he was too numbed by alcohol to recognise any of her abuse. Then, her incoherent rage turned lethal. She climbed on top of his unconscious body, wrapped her hands around his throat and started to squeeze the life out of him.

Some spark of self-preservation was still inside of his drunken husk. Before brain-damage could kick in, David awoke. He was confused more than he was angry. The alcohol, lack of blood to the brain and his sudden awakening all combined to create a kaleidoscope of chaos that he couldn't comprehend, much less deal with. He didn't try to defend himself once he'd wrestled himself free of her strangling grasp. Instead, he staggered out of the room, gasping for air.

Pain finally started to penetrate the haze. The scratches. The slaps. The bruises forming all over his skin. He couldn't explain it. He couldn't understand what had happened to him when the only memory that he had of the moments before were of blissful, carnal joy.

'Kathy, what the hell?'

He could barely see her in the dark shadows of their unlit apartment. Her bare skin would give him pale glimpses in the moonlight, warning him where she was and how swiftly she was approaching, but he couldn't see her face. He had no way of knowing which of the two Katherines he was trapped here with.

Whether her face would be flushed red with her berserk fury, or if she'd faded back to her usual lovely self, the woman to whom he'd just sworn the rest of his life.

She lurched forward out of the darkness and pressed her lips to his, clumsily. 'Thought you'd fallen asleep on me there. Ready to go again?'

He wheezed out a pained breath that he hadn't realised he was holding. She was back to her normal self. Or as normal as Kathy got. David backed away from her and Kathy's hands flexed convulsively, like she wanted to grab onto him.

He groaned. 'You choked me?'

'What? Just a little.' She looked sheepish for a moment, like a little kid that had been caught doing something naughty, then in a snap, the fire was back in her voice. 'Don't be a pansy. You weren't waking up.'

She reached for him again and this time her fingers tangled in his chest hair before he could get out of reach. He growled, 'So you thought you'd just choke me, you mad bitch?'

'Don't you talk to your wife like that you ugly little bastard. You married me. That means you're mine.' She dragged him closer. 'So you get your lazy drunken arse back in that bedroom and fuck. You hear me?'

He took a hold of her wrists and managed to pry her free. 'You're nuts. You've got a screw loose. The old bag tried to warn me but I didn't listen.'

Katherine was lost in her own thoughts, too wound up to even understand what he was saying to her. 'Daddy did it five times. We've got to do it more.'

'What? What the hell are you talking about?'

Katherine's eyes were glazed over, lost in memory. 'On their wedding night, my Daddy did it with Barb five times. You love me, don't you? You love me more than that, right? We've got to fuck again. Two more times. At least two more. We've got to.'

He backed away from her, horrified. If the violence hadn't been enough to put him off any further amorous overtures—and there were plenty of men that it wouldn't have—then this talk about her parent's sex life, the explicit details that Barbara had poured out into her daughters, would have been enough to kill his passion. She blinked away her own confusion and gave him a coy smile, 'David. Don't worry about all that. It is just a little fight. Everybody has a little fight once they're married. Come on now. Come back to bed. I'll kiss it all better.'

He took a deep breath. He could still feel where her fingers had been biting into his throat. A deep, dull ache that didn't want to fade. A warning. Even the rush of adrenaline hadn't been able to drive all the day's drunkenness away, but some rational part of his mind was working now. Some basic survival instinct was picking up the slack.

'All right, love. You head to bed. I'll just ... nip to the loo and meet you there, yeah?'

She licked her lips. 'Don't be too long or I'll start without you.'

He managed to muster a smile before she skulked off. The bathroom was the only door in the house that had a lock and whilst he wouldn't be able to explain it in the cold light of day, he went into the bathroom, turned that lock and climbed into the bath to fall asleep. Katherine came hammering at the door not ten minutes later, but the booze-riddled sleep that had gotten him into so much trouble before turned into his salvation. Too drunk to waken, he couldn't get up to let the raging Katherine into the room.

Marital Bliss

After that initial hiccup, the marriage swiftly became bliss all over again. The two of them returned to their respective jobs, but whilst David slumped in from work, tired, all of the carnage that surrounded Katherine all day had her leaving the meat-works so full of energy she was practically bouncing. She washed all of David's clothes, cooked all of his meals, kept their communal living space absolutely pristine, and, when they were ready to move into a bigger place together, she handled all of the heavy lifting involved—both figurative and literal.

She was the perfect wife in every regard and within a week David had written off her marital night shenanigans as a misunderstanding that he had probably perpetuated in his drunken state. Like her teachers when she pulled a knife on another student, David was incapable of reconciling the two images that he had of Katherine, so he chose to believe in the one that benefited him the most. The beautiful young wife who willingly pandered to his every whim and who completely adored him.

This honeymoon period stretched out for weeks, then months. Katherine began to buckle under the strain of perfection, though. She was still able to let out her violent impulses in the odd workplace argument and the gruesome work that she did each day still gave her the same old satisfaction, but she was pushing herself every moment that she was with David to be the perfect wife and, eventually, something was going to have to give.

It did not escalate straight to another act of violence, but Katherine's temper began to manifest itself in other ways. She still performed every one of her many wifely duties without fail or complaint, but now she began to pick at any perceived faults in David. If he was home a minute later than he'd said he would be, she started to make wild accusations of infidelity. The pattern of a marriage was well established in her own mind and she saw none of the raw animal lust in David that had kept her parents together. Without that, she had to assume that their relationship would go exactly the same way as the first marriage that her mother had described to her in intimate detail. First, love, then marriage, then betrayal. To Katherine, the idea of David leaving her was so intensely painful, that just the thought of it began to poison their relationship.

The accusations persisted throughout the first year of their relationship when David was still working as a truck driver, out of her sight all day long. In a concession to her delusions, David took a job on the abattoir line at a fairly significant wage cut so that she could keep an eye on him all day long. He had assumed that if there were no possibility that he was being unfaithful, then her irrational behaviour would come to a halt and their happy relationship could resume. This was not the case.

By 1975, the constant accusations and foul treatment at the hands of Katherine were beginning to wear on David. It didn't matter anymore that her insane behaviour changed faster than the weather and that his beloved wife returned and did everything in her power to make things up to him; he was exhausted from living in a constant state of tension, just waiting for the next attack to come. On top of that, he was completely unsuited to his new job in the meat-works. Whilst his slight build had been a perfect fit in the cab of a lorry, on the abattoir floor he was dwarfed by the other men and he had to push himself to the limits of his strength just to keep up with the rest of the line. He began to go out drinking with his co-workers more and more often. Katherine's accusations came less frequently when they were in public and her other foul treatment at least had the benefit of earning him some sympathy from the other married men. Before long, the constant outings to the bar started to cut into the time that Katherine used for housekeeping and standards began to slip in their home. She was forced with the choice to either continue dogging David's steps to ensure that he was faithful to her or returning to the old routine in which she felt like she was being a good wife, one that was worthy of affection and devotion.

That particular internal struggle stretched on for many months, with Katherine flip-flopping back and forth between the two options, running herself ragged trying to do both, spending one night at home playing catch up and the next out with David, pretending that everything was fine. Desperately pretending that everything in their marriage was fine when she could feel him pulling away from her more and more every day.

One night, when the two of them were visiting Ken and Barbara for an awkward attempt at family bonding, Katherine came to an epiphany. Her father had his flaws, but he had never cheated on her mother and that had to be for a reason. Katherine still held that infidelity was a fundamental part of a man's makeup, but even the most broken and twisted relationship that she had ever encountered in her life had managed to resist it. She had to assume that it was because Barbara did everything that she was meant to do.

From that day forward, Katherine let David run free. She stayed home after work, put a beautiful home-cooked meal on the table every night and tended to his every whim when he finally elected to come home. She still fell into her rages, still made her wild accusations, but those were things that she considered to be outside of her control. Taking care of him properly was something that she could do.

A new equilibrium was established, one that probably could have been maintained forever if nothing else changed. David was willing to put up with her insane rambling, even managing to convince himself that it was just her way of showing that she loved him, because of the royal treatment that he received the rest of the time.

In August, she fell pregnant and her jealousy and obsession with David jumped into overdrive. The idea of being abandoned had terrified her before, but the idea of being abandoned whilst pregnant pushed the catastrophic scenarios that she was imagining to a whole new level. She was hyper-aware of absolutely everything that David said and did. Just a word out of place could set her off screaming and cursing him. One day, after a long shift at the meat-works, David came home to change into a clean shirt before heading to the bar. This was not his usual routine and Katherine latched onto it immediately.

Who was he getting dressed up for? Who was he sneaking off to meet in his fancy new shirt? The shirt she had sewn for him. The unbelievable bastard. All these months he had been lying to her, claiming that he loved her. Pretending that he cared about her. Now he'd knocked her up and he was off chasing after some other girl. Well, they would just see about that. Let's see how handsome she thinks he is when he doesn't have any new clothes to go dancing around in. Let's see how much of a hit he is with the ladies with just the shirt on his back.

She gathered up all of his other clothes in the bathtub, doused them in lighter fluid and tossed in a match. The ensuing blaze brought the haphazardly-assembled Aberdeen fire department to their door and, since half of those men were dragged out of the bar to come and throw a few buckets of water into the Kellett family bathroom, David came along for the ride, too.

The bathroom roof had turned black with soot, smoke had flooded out through the rest of the house, choking Katherine until she'd run outside. It was painfully apparent what had happened inside the house—the evidence was melted into the bathtub, after all. The whole world was now witness to Katherine and David's dysfunctional relationship and, whilst he burned with shame, she just turned her flushed face towards the whole town of Aberdeen and stared them down. Daring them to say a word.

Following the fire, David was too embarrassed to show his face in the bar for weeks. The two of them quietly relocated to a small house near to the abattoir when the cleaning required to make his apartment liveable again proved too extensive. He might have expected Katherine to be blissful now that she had him entirely to herself, but nothing could be further from the truth. She still accused him of infidelity on an almost hourly basis, like the slow machinery of her mind had developed a fault and kept clicking back into the same groove after it had been running unattended for too long. Their married life remained a constant alternating mixture of heaven and hell for David and, before long, he took to the bar again just to escape the onslaught.

One night, he returned home at about the same time that he usually staggered home for his dinner and Katherine ambushed him in their living room, screaming about him abandoning her, that he was off chasing after some other woman all over again. Burning his clothes hadn't been enough to fend all the loose women of Aberdeen off from him, so she decided something else needed burning. When he came home, she had been ironing what little wardrobe David had been able to piece together. With a roar, she swung the scalding hot iron at his face. It burned a thick gash across his cheek, searing through almost to his cheekbone. If he hadn't flinched away at exactly the right moment, the blow would have cost him his eye. He retreated, screaming in pain, to the bathroom—his old sanctuary from her violent outbursts—and locked the door before she could get to him. She hammered at the door with the iron, leaving burn marks and dents in equal measure until the rage left her just as suddenly as it had come on and she started weeping and begging forgiveness, whispering under the door that she was sorry, that she would never do it again, that she just missed him so much that it made her crazy. Despite the pain and disfigurement he had just suffered, David believed her. He unlocked the bathroom door and the two of them embraced. She wrapped his face in gauze and lavished kisses on his unmarked cheek. Before long, they moved into the bedroom, where she did her best to distract him from the pain.

David didn't sleep all night. Not because of Katherine's amorous attentions, although they were plentiful, but because of the awful pain in his face. He knew that if he called an ambulance then the paramedics would be obliged to report his injuries to the police and he didn't want to see Kathy get in trouble over something that had happened in a moment of passion. He lay there in the dark, with his wife snoring beside him and held back his screams.

The next day at work, David's supervisor took one look at the injury and drove him to the hospital to have it seen to. Without the emergency call, the police were not informed about what had happened. David got the help that he needed and Katherine got to avoid repercussions. It was the best of both worlds and all that it had cost was David lying in agony for eight hours instead of seeking medical attention for the grizzly burn scar that would remain his most prominent feature for the rest of his life.

In the aftermath of that assault, David began to make some new concessions to Katherine to help keep the peace. When she felt like he was running late, she would become upset with him, so he formalised his evening arrangements to prevent any more 'misunderstandings.'

Before they went their separate ways after work, he would list off his plans for the evening and she would either approve them or demand alterations. In her continuing quest to appear the perfect wife, she tried to let David feel like he was making the decisions, but she lacked the communication skills necessary to manipulate him with any sort of subtlety, so, more often than not, she would end up barking, 'No!' at him over and over until he accommodated her poorly-expressed demands.

He learned the hard way that this method of managing Katherine had its setbacks. One night, he lingered slightly too long at the bar before heading back towards the slaughterhouse and their company-provided home on 'Honeymoon Lane.' He was so close to being on time that it didn't even occur to him that Katherine might have a problem with it.

When he was one minute late, Katherine began to get anxious. She started to imagine that he had run off with someone else, that his long-awaited betrayal was finally here. She was now six months pregnant. The slaughterhouse kept dropping less and less subtle hints that she needed to stop working the line. She was going to be alone and unemployed with a baby. A baby that she didn't even know that she wanted.

When he was two minutes late, her catastrophic vision of the future faltered in the face of her blinding rage. He'd better not come home after making her wait this long. If he came home, she was going to slice him to pieces. She was going to make him pay for betraying her, running off with his women and abandoning his wife to suffer in silence, all alone.

When he was three minutes late, the capacity for rational thought had entirely escaped Katherine. Her mind was still rattling through elaborate plans for bloody revenge, but it was more like a series of flashing images shuddering past her mind's eye than any sort of coherent pattern.

He arrived back at the house four minutes after he was due to return. The lights had been turned out and it was completely silent. David let out a little huff of relief. Even if he didn't think Kathy was going to mind him coming in so close to her crazy curfew, he still didn't really want to deal with her right now. If she'd made him dinner and sulked off to bed early, like she did every now and again, then he was in for a nice, relaxing evening, followed by some of the vigorous lovemaking that Kathy always went in for when she was well-rested and feeling guilty about neglecting him. The night was looking up already.

Keeping it nice and quiet, he pulled open the door to the kitchen and stepped inside with a smile on his face.

He blinked once or twice. He was looking up at the stars. Why was he looking up at the stars? His stomach lurched. Where was he? The last thing that he remembered, he had been walking home. He had been at the bar. Maybe he was drunk? Maybe he'd fallen somewhere and hit his head. It felt kind of sore, but that pain was far away in the distance like it was on its way but hadn't quite arrived yet. He fluttered his eyes open and shut a few more times. Home. He had to get home. If he was late, Kathy would be furious.

He tried to sit up. That was when the pain caught up to him.

The bones in his head felt like they were grinding together. Like his whole skull was grinding and shrieking. The pain was intense, immediate and all-consuming. A blinding light in the darkness of the night. The only reason that he didn't scream was that his throat was clogged up with the wave of vomit that trying to move had conjured up out of him. It was splattered all over him now; his face was slick with it down one side. His mouth was sour with stale beer and bile. The pain wasn't distant now. Without movement, the grating had stopped but it still felt like molten metal was trapped inside his head.

Something had happened.

What had happened? It was almost impossible to work it out with the pain dragging him back every time he tried to think, every time he tried to remember. When he tried to move, the pain got worse, he wanted to die every time he moved. He let out a little whimper, but even that slight vibration set his skull thrumming all over again. There was an echo of that sound that dragged his memory back into the light. A noise like a gong being sounded.

The cast-iron frying pan swung at the back of his head with all of the brutal force that the powerful arms of Katherine could muster.

David let out a whimper and raised a nervous hand up to touch the wetness on the back of his head. He half expected to find it caved in and it was almost a relief when his fingertips touched blood-soaked hair. Almost a relief, because the moment that he applied any pressure, he could feel his skull shifting beneath his skin. The pain rose like the sun, blinding him to everything else.

It took him an hour to drag himself inch by painful inch to the back door of the neighbouring house. Twenty minutes more to muster the strength to scrape and bang loud enough to draw some attention. By then, he was completely incoherent. His neighbours, the Macbeths, couldn't do anything but call an ambulance as he sunk back down into nightmare-haunted unconsciousness.

David awoke the next day, just ten miles from where he'd fallen, in Muswellbrook Hospital, with his wife simpering by his bedside, holding his hand, with tears in her eyes.

A number of scenarios could explain what he chose to do next.

It is possible that he was taken in by Katherine's 'perfect wife' act the way that he had been so many times in the past. Despite everything that had happened, David was deeply in love with Katherine, or at least his idealised version of her. He may have thought that this would be a turning point in their relationship, a pivot back on to the right course. Guilt over one irrational act had been sufficient to reshape many people into better versions of themselves—it wasn't entirely wishful thinking that the harmless-looking, sobbing pregnant woman at his bedside would be one of them.

It is equally possible that he was frightened to think what Katherine would do to him if he spoke out against her. They were in a hospital, he was weak and helpless and she still had every bit of the terrible strength that she had unleashed against him the previous night.

One final factor was the testosterone-drenched culture of rural Australia in the 70s. A place where men were meant to be tough and women subservient. It would have been a dreadful blow to David's ego and his reputation in the community if it became known that he was being beaten by his wife. The shame of everyone knowing how Katherine had burnt his clothes had been enough to drive him into hermitage before, and that was widely-excused as a common act of hysterical womanhood that could be mocked and made light of. This was something much more serious, something that could strip him of his manhood entirely if he let it.

When the police arrived to take the couple's report of what had happened the night before, David explained it away. Katherine had been left home alone when he went out drinking and when she heard someone trying to get into the house she acted in self-defence. An accident, rather than an act of malevolent brutality. It was an easy-to-swallow story for the New South Wales Police, who preferred not to get involved in domestic violence cases when the man was the perpetrator in those days, let alone this strange, flipped version. Katherine was happy to reiterate his story to them from her perspective, being sure to look at him pointedly every time she repeated how late her husband had been in returning home.

With the concussion and subsequent damage to his brain, it is possible that David genuinely couldn't recall the events of the previous night properly and he was forced to accept that Katherine's version of events was genuine due to having no alternative explanation to hand. After all, it wasn't like she had explained why she was assaulting him before swinging at him with the skillet. She had been too lost in her fury to even formulate words, let alone sentences. Her limited vocabulary was a hindrance at the best of times, but in moments of duress, she became almost entirely mute, letting out little more than snarls and growls like some sort of wild animal trapped in a human body.

A few days later, when the swelling around his brain had eased and the doctors were convinced that the fragmented sections of his skull were beginning to knit back together, David was released into Katherine's custody and she took him home. He was guided to their bed with her arms hooked under his, laid out carefully on a heap of pillows and kissed gently on the cheek. If he had been hoping for a change in Katherine, then this was surely it. The perfect wife had returned. She pampered him for the rest of the week, tending to his every need and desire with the same brazen admiration she had shown him when they were courting. David truly came to believe that his nightmare was finally over.

When David returned to work, Katherine finally gave in to the boss' prodding and stayed home, after getting assurances that her job would still be waiting for her when she returned from her unofficial maternity leave. Alone in the house all day, it didn't take long for Katherine's imagination to start running away from her all over again. Worse yet, David seemed to have lost all fear of crossing her. Now that she was showing him nothing but sweetness, he had forgotten who he was dealing with.

It didn't take long before she reminded him.

One night, less than a month after the first near-lethal assault, her veneer of benevolence started to chip away. She had been taking long drives in the countryside during her empty days, swerving to hit cats and dogs when she saw them. It was the only amusement that she could come up with for herself that didn't involve any strenuous physical activity or company. David had dinner with her after he'd finished work, then immediately got up to leave for a darts tournament at the bar. He checked that Katherine was all right with this plan and took her smiling agreement at face value, but before he left, she made sure to confirm what time the tournament would be over. Once she knew it was 11 pm, she settled in for another night of quiet crafting, working on new clothes for David and the baby.

When 11 pm arrived and David hadn't, she didn't immediately fly into a rage. She had been working on her temper as a part of her plans to keep David sweet, so instead of letting herself descend into the usual downward spiral of imagined slights, she phoned the bar and asked to speak with him.

'I thought you were coming home?'

He actually had the courage to sound annoyed with her. 'I am,

I am. The tourney is just running a bit long, is all. Shouldn't be more than an hour.'

'But you said you'd be back at eleven.'

David was in front of all of his friends from the meat-works—if he went skulking off at Katherine's beck and call, he would never live it down. 'Well, now I'm saying I won't.'

She was waiting for him when he got home. Frying pan in hand. This time he was ready for her. He ducked out of the way of her first swing, caught the second one on his arm instead of his face. Katherine had turned completely red. She was huffing instead of breathing. She looked like some sort of mythical monster more than she looked like a woman. The next swing missed him entirely and knocked a light switch off the wall instead.

In the darkness and screaming chaos that ensued, David managed to get out of the house, running back down the road towards the bar and catching up to his drinking buddies before they could all disperse. He spent the night on one of their sofas, delaying the inevitable retribution until the next day.

He went to work as usual and fully expected Katherine to show up there to claim him, but instead, he just had a whole day of back-breaking labour with the constant threat of violence hanging over him. People in prison were living better than him.

For all that he was in love with Katherine and overflowing with forgiveness, David Kellet finally came to a conclusion whilst he was scraping marrow out of bones that day. If he didn't get away from her, she was going to kill him.

The idea had been percolating in his head for quite some time, but the attack the night before had just cemented his certainty, in no small part because Katherine's suspicions about him were actually correct.

Ever since Katherine had first started wildly accusing him of infidelity, David had been alienated and isolated in his marriage, so he had done the only thing that made sense to him. He'd gone looking for affection elsewhere. It hadn't been an active search, but it had been a fruitful one and, shortly before Katherine seared her mark into his face, he had formed an ongoing relationship with a girl whom he knew in Queensland. After his concussion, he had stepped up his plans to be with her and just a week before she had informed him that she, too, was pregnant with his child. She wanted him to leave Katherine and for them to be a family. The whistle of the frying pan being swung at his head the night before was like the sounding of a starter pistol. He needed to escape; he had somewhere to escape to. Now all that he needed was the opportunity to get out alive.

He returned home that night to find that Katherine had transformed back into her loving and devoted personality. He apologised profusely for being late the night before, explained that he completely understood why she was angry and did everything in his power to make it up to her, even bringing her flowers and some freshly-cut pork chops for dinner. She was so smitten with the gesture that all of his sins were forgotten.

He spent the next month and a half walking on eggshells, just waiting for the opportunity to grab his things and get the hell out of town, but the chance wouldn't arrive until May of 1976 when Katherine went into labour.

Katherine's parents were called and they rushed over to drive her to Muswellbrook Hospital, leaving David behind to pack a bag for her and follow after. He packed all of his surviving belongings into that bag, walked down to the slaughterhouse and handed in his notice. With a spring in his step, he got into his car and drove out of Aberdeen as fast as he could, before anyone could report back to the Knight family. He was free, at last.

Alone in the Dark

Katherine went through a long and painful labour to bring her first daughter, Melissa Ann, into the world, and she spent almost every moment of it asking for her husband. Sobbing. Screaming his name with each contraction all through the long night. Her sister was sent off from the hospital to scour Aberdeen for any sign of him. He had left the vast majority of his belongings behind—whether out of guilt or simply a desire to travel light and get away fast—which obscured the fact that he was truly missing. His car was gone, as was the case that he was meant to have packed for Katherine, so the abiding assumption was that something had happened to him on the road to the hospital. Joy swiftly recruited some of his friends from the meat-works' barracks to search for him and it wasn't long before a half dozen cars were flying about the back-roads around Aberdeen in search of a crashed car.

Joy was a little more suspicious than David's friends, however. She had grown up in the same household as Katherine, hearing the same gruesome and lewd stories about the qualities of men from their mother. She knew the evil that lurked in their hearts and, whilst Katherine had found a way to master it, Joy still lived in fear of it. None of the men in his usual haunts had seen David. None of the neighbours wanted to get involved in another of Katherine's screaming rages, which were gradually becoming legendary about town, so they were all struck blind to his movements, too. It was only when dawn rolled around that it occurred to Joy that there might have been some sort of work emergency that dragged him away from the birth of his first child. She went to the abattoir to ask after him and discovered that he'd quit.

By the time that Katherine had given birth and was capable of independent thought and movement again, she had sunk into a deep rage. Despite her blood loss during labour, that familiar red flush filled her face. Those that were unfortunate enough to know her recognised these signs and retreated with as much tact as they could muster, but the hospital staff didn't get much more than grunts and growls from her when they delivered the baby into her arms for feeding, or when they plucked Melissa off her breast when the tiny baby had drunk her fill.

Whatever love she might have felt for her daughter at that moment, whatever bond a normal mother would make with the tiny life that she had just brought into the world, was washed away by Katherine's black mood. Her eyes darted to the door of the ward every time there was movement, but David still had not arrived. At the moment when she was most vulnerable—when she needed her husband by her side the most—he had abandoned her. Her vengeance was going to be a gruesome thing, a bloody nightmare, the likes of which Aberdeen had never seen. She was going to do things to David that would have made the old man who tortured pigs for laughs sick to his stomach. She had her knives hanging above her bed at home and by god was she going to use them. That worthless scumbag would never walk again. Let's see how far away from her he got when he couldn't even walk, when she snipped every tendon in his legs and left him limp as the worthless, wailing little lump in her arms. He would never leave her again—she'd keep him like one of the broken-winged birds she used to hoard in her bedroom, powerless and desperate for every bit of attention she gave him—just as soon as she got her hands on him.

Joy had always been in her sister's blind spot, never a victim of her cruelty, nor an authority figure who needed to be appeased or navigated. She may very well have been the only person in the world whom Katherine actually considered to be a friend. Out of all the people in her life, only Joy could deliver the news of David's escape safely, without fear of violent repercussions.

She expected Katherine to rage and scream—to lose her mind to the fury that still clearly consumed her—but instead, she had to sit and watch her sister break. The red flush faded from her face, the knotted muscles of her jaw went slack and her eyes went dead. She was too devastated to even cry. She whispered a soft, 'Thank you,' then rolled away onto her side.

Normally, a mother was released from the hospital a few days after the baby was born, but both Katherine and Melissa Ann seemed to be sick. They lay lifeless and limp in a bed together. The only sounds being the occasional shriek of the baby as it demanded something. Katherine did not speak to her daughter. She barely even looked at her. Psychiatry was still in relative infancy at this point in history, isolated in specialist hospitals away from all of the 'normal' patients. So, there was an assumption that Katherine's illness was due to some complication of the birth, that her lifelessness and muteness were due to a lack of blood, or some damage to a nerve.

Eventually, the doctors were forced to give up and release her. Her father drove her home to the abandoned house. Neither father nor daughter had a word to say to the other the whole trip. Ken delivered the pram, which the Knights had bought the baby as a gift, to the doorstep right alongside his daughter, then turned and left without another word. What was there to say?

That first night, Katherine went through all the motions of being a good mother, just like she had always wanted when she was growing up. But, just like her own mother, it wasn't long before she started to pour her misery out onto the baby, too. Regaling the child with endless stories about David's imagined infidelities, shortcomings as a man both in and out of the bedroom and, more generally, about how wicked he was to abandon the two of them. Whatever answer she was hoping to get from the baby did not seem to be forthcoming.

It took only a few weeks of being trapped alone in the house with Melissa before the darkest parts of Katherine's psyche took the helm. She'd always had limited patience with being stuck indoors and the addition of the constant shrill screaming of a baby pushed her past that limit in moments. Each morning, Katherine would rise with the sun, the same way that she always had, then she would load the baby into her pram and start walking up and down the streets of Aberdeen, desperate for some distraction from the misery of her life. People could not look her in the eye. At the best of times, an abandoned mother would have been a shameful sight, someone to be pitied as well as treated with contempt; but, in the case of Katherine Knight—the hellion of Honeymoon Lane—that pity never managed to come to fruition. There was too much fear of Katherine for anyone to reach out to her. Everyone knew that it was just a matter of time before she violently exploded in exactly the same way that she always had before and nobody wanted to be in the blast radius when it finally happened.

Her isolation was complete. Whether she was trapped in the house or roaming the streets, Katherine moved in a bubble of silence, pierced only rarely by the screams of Melissa. It did not take long for Katherine, sunken into a deep and dark depression, to loathe that sound. To long for the silence and isolation that had until now haunted her. She would never be able to pinpoint the exact moment that she started to hate her baby, but it is possible that Melissa served as a reminder of David's betrayal each time that Katherine looked at her. The thing that should have been her greatest joy, her greatest triumph in her pursuit of traditional conservative womanhood, had instead become a lead weight around her neck. A symbol of all the ways that her life had gone wrong.

By the end of May, Katherine was past her breaking point and diving headlong into cartoonish villainy. People twitched back their curtains to watch her as she went by, screaming and raving at the three-week-old baby in her pram. She took off, running down the streets, paying no heed to the way that the baby was flung around as she went over the potholes and bumps. When even that wasn't enough to calm Melissa, she started flinging the pram from side to side as she ran, battering the helpless baby off the hard sides of the pram as she mock-screamed right back into the tiny girl's face.

The Aberdeen police had learned to fear the wrath of Katherine Knight, even if they hadn't been on the receiving end of it themselves and had only seen the mess that she left of the people she raised her fists to. When they received a call about her that morning, they were far from surprised—it had always just been a matter of time before they were forced to face off with her. In such a small town, rumours ran rampant and a decent police force knew exactly how to turn that to its advantage. Community policing may be a buzzword of modern law enforcement, but in a town like Aberdeen, it was unavoidable and essential. The police lived in the same communities that they were policing and they heard the same whispers as anyone else—whether directly or through their wives—and that informed the way that they pursued their cases. The Katherine Knight that they knew was only one unlucky day away from a murder charge. They'd heard all about her treatment of David Kellet and, whilst they shared the same assumptions as everyone else at the time about her acts of domestic violence being retaliatory rather than predatory, they were also aware of just how easily self-defence could turn bloody—particularly out here, so far from the centres of civilisation.

Three officers were sent out to confront Katherine after her reckless endangerment of the baby had been called in, but the sight that confronted them was not what they had prepared for. Instead of the raging monster of bar-room legend, they were confronted by a helpless woman in tears. She started to sob as soon as they approached her, her face completely flushed and her voice quavering with every word she tried to bark out. Once again, when confronted with authority challenging her for her crimes, she managed to make them all someone else's fault.

Whilst they believed her fragmented story of abandonment and betrayal, the police still couldn't let her go roaming free, not when there was a child at risk. They offered her a ride home, offered to take the baby to her parents for the night and then drove her to the nearest hospital equipped to deal with mental health patients before she could realise what was happening around her.

St Elmo's Hospital in Tamworth was quiet about its area of specialisation, so as not to spook the local population. Everyone agreed that there should be hospitals for the insane, but nobody wanted one in their own back yard. The odd rumour might occasionally spread about the place, but if it did, it had never reached as far as Katherine's ears all the way out in Aberdeen. She had no idea why she was being taken to the hospital, loudly insisting at every turn that she wasn't sick, until eventually one of the nurses sat her down and explained exactly why she had been taken into their care. It was during this first stay in the hospital that the groundwork for much of the psychiatric casework about Katherine Knight was built.

There were strong suspicions, created from their gathered reports about her behaviour and her own strange admissions, that she suffered from BPD, but in the short term, all that they could prove conclusively was that she was suffering from a bout of post-natal depression, a mental condition that often presents in a failure to bond with the baby and, in extreme cases, results in attempts on the baby's life. Additional testing after that first day showed that Katherine had lost the ability to read and write since falling out of practice following her grand exit from the education system, and this, in turn, prompted the doctors to administer an IQ test, on which Katherine scored in the low 80s.

Even at this early stage in her diagnosis, the doctors began to suspect that the results that they were getting were not accurate. Whilst she lacked the education required to pass an IQ test, she did not lack in raw animal cunning. Coupled with the violent outbursts that she exhibited whenever she felt wronged, this drove one of the psychologists to describe her as being possessed of a 'primeval intelligence.' She operated on a very base level, akin to what you might expect from a caveman, rather than a woman in contemporary society. He was one of a few medical professionals who felt Katherine's mental health problems could more easily be explained away with a different diagnosis— psychopathy compounded with narcissism.

This tiny cabal within the hospital believed that Katherine was deliberately manipulating the other staff members so that she would be absolved of responsibility for her actions.

Throughout Katherine's life, she had a set pattern that she worked through if she was ever confronted by someone in a position of authority about her atrocities. At first, she would deny that her actions ever took place, as she had often done with her schoolyard bullying, violent threats towards her molesting brothers and vicious words towards others in the workplace. When that failed, due to evidence or testimony, she would instantly switch to admitting that the event had taken place, but it was at the behest of some other party for whom she was now taking the blame. This happened frequently during her week in St Elmo's, when she would fling accusations at other patients. Finally, when all else failed or there was no patsy to pin her crimes on, Katherine would admit to having committed them but insist that it was out of retribution for some slight against her—that her actions were a reasonable response to provocation from the party she had maimed or abused. With a formal diagnosis of BPD, Katherine would have had the ultimate freedom from responsibility for her actions. Her crimes would no longer be hers at all, even when there was nobody else to blame— they would be because of the BPD.

For this reason, among others, this minority of Katherine's

carers intervened to ensure that her insanity defence was only temporary. Post-natal depression is an appalling, crippling mental illness, but it generally has a short run—even when it goes untreated. Katherine would be free to go after a short week in the institution, having undergone talk therapy—that she mainly responded to with grunts—and the beginnings of drug therapy that would go on for the rest of her life. With a paper bag full of pills and a clean bill of health, Katherine was released from St Elmo's less than seven days after her first attempt on Melissa's life.

She collected the baby from her parents in sullen silence, then went back home to the empty house that she had planned to share with her devoted husband for the rest of her days.

There was no sound from Katherine's house throughout the next day. The constant tirades of screaming that had accompanied every noise that the baby had made previously had given away to a more eerie silence. It was like the calm before the storm. Every time there was a sound, the neighbours would cast a fearful eye out of their windows, just waiting to see what new madness Katherine Knight might achieve, but nothing manifested, and by sunset many of them were starting to suspect that perhaps Katherine's stay in a mental hospital might actually have cured her, that the chaos and viciousness that they'd all been living with for years might finally have been brought low leaving nothing more than a lonely woman. Their hopes were misplaced.

'Old Ted' had worked in the mines for many years before an injury drove him out and now he lived a vagrant life, panhandling, foraging and receiving donations from the businesses around town to keep him fed and clothed. Despite his eccentricity and rather lax hygiene standards, he was fairly well-liked in Aberdeen, considered by many locals to be something of a local landmark. He had never run afoul of Katherine in his years of roaming about town. Not because he was beneath her notice—Katherine was strangely egalitarian with her viciousness, lashing out at all layers of society equally—but rather because he seemed to possess that same animal cunning that she did. Whatever else you could say about Old Ted, he was a survivor. And, he had lived as long as he had by recognising danger before it turned its attention on to him.

Whilst it would have been very easy for Ted to stay in the loop about all of the town's gossip, he wasn't inclined to seek it out and, more pressingly, he had spent most of the day since Katherine's release out of town, searching for game to hunt or crops that nobody would notice had gone missing. He knew nothing about the drama surrounding her, or the silence following her release.

So, as he trailed along the side of the train tracks in the cool evening, searching for the little brown mushrooms that sometimes grew between the wooden sleepers, oblivious to anything that might have been awry in town, he didn't think much of it when he heard a baby crying from up ahead. People about town left him alone, so he did his best to return the favour. If someone wanted to hold a crying baby by the train tracks, he wasn't going to stop them. Live and let live, that was his philosophy. But even his happy-go-lucky attitude began to get a little dented as the baby's wailing went on and on. He didn't have kids of his own, so he didn't have the experience to know the difference between a baby's cries, but this one was grating on him. It wasn't like it wanted something. It sounded pained or scared. He wished that its mother would just settle it down, just so he didn't have to hear it anymore. Not that he'd ever be so crude as to voice that opinion. He wasn't an animal.

The baby went on wailing and he went on tramping along the side of the tracks, doing his best to ignore it. There were a few mushrooms growing about here, so Ted crept a little closer to the tracks to pick them. That was when he felt the vibration running along the metal. A train was on its way and if he had any sense, he'd stand well clear. Most of them didn't stop in Aberdeen—they blew right through and, at that speed, they could lift a man right off his feet with the turbulence of their passing. Still, that baby went on crying up ahead. Ted finally felt like he should say something. The folks dithering by the line might not have known that a train was coming. He left the last of the mushrooms and jogged along the line, looking around but seeing no sign of anyone standing. He was almost standing on the baby before he realised what he was looking at.

Little Melissa was laid down on the tracks. Her head rattling on the rail as the train approached. With a yelp, Old Ted scooped her up, fumbling her as he tried to settle the wriggling lump safely in his arms. There was no time—he held Melissa out in front of him like a struggling cat and ran. The train ripped by a moment later, close enough on his heels that he felt it tugging on his coat-tails.

If he'd taken just a moment longer, the train would have run right over the baby, with nobody on board any the wiser.

Katherine had not been idle since abandoning her baby on the train tracks. She had walked back down into town in a fury, the likes of which Aberdeen had never even seen. Her face was flushed completely red, her brows drawn down so low that her eyes were lost in dark shadows. She seemed to have lost all ability to speak, huffing breaths in and out with a growl in her throat. She made a beeline for the general goods store in the middle of town, snatching up a wood-axe from the display and storming out into the street with a guttural roar.

The police were already on the scene by that point, having received a slew of informal warnings that Knight was on the move. She walked for a short distance down the road, swinging the axe back and forth in a figure of eight, but it didn't elicit the response she was looking for from the cowering onlookers. They might have feared her, but she could still see that disgusting pity in their eyes. They felt sorry for her. Mad little Katherine, abandoned by her cheating husband with a baby in tow. They wouldn't dare look at her like that again, not after what she had done tonight. That mewling little bitch Melissa was gone and Katherine was going to wipe Aberdeen off the map. Every one of these people was going to die until there was nobody left that could remember what had happened to her. She'd kill all of them, then she'd kill David, then she'd just go away somewhere and start over. It would be easy. She would be free again.

The police didn't dare come close to her. She was taller than any one of the officers sent out to fetch her and, with that axe in hand, she had enough of a reach to take a lump out of any one of them if they tried to come at her with billy-clubs. They trailed along, just out of reach, keeping everyone else out of her way as she stalked back and forth, swinging the axe around and around, growling and spitting and snarling, working herself up enough to make her charge.

She was almost ready to do it. She had almost built herself up enough that she really thought that she could kill them all. That was when the piercing wail cut through the tense silence of the standoff. Old Ted had come staggering down into town with a baby in his hands. The axe tumbled from Katherine's grip and the police rushed in to seize her. She let out an awful matching wail as she saw Melissa alive in the old man's arms, then she was buried under a pile of police trying to subdue her.

Her return to St Elmo's was brief. She was well-rehearsed in the correct things to say to be given a clean bill of health now and the staff were ready to admit that the dosage of her medication clearly hadn't been enough, calculated for the average woman rather than a lady of Katherine's bulk. Once she had been forcefully medicated, all traces of the raging berserker that had stalked the streets of Aberdeen were washed away once more. She was back to the charming, dim-witted girl whom they'd released only a day before. She signed herself out after spending a night in the hospital, then called her parents to come and collect her.

Ken and Barbara may not have been geniuses, but they recognised the pattern that was emerging and, for all of the personal evils that dominated their actions, they still couldn't bear the thought of their granddaughter being hurt, or worse. Ken drove Katherine home, but Melissa was not returned to her this time. He promised that the baby would be taken care of until Katherine was well again and no amount of threats or pleading were enough to change his mind.

Katherine was left completely and utterly alone.

The same dreadful silence descended over her house, but this time not even the cries of the baby punctured it. The neighbours kept watch on Katherine, both out of concern for a fellow human being and as an early warning system in case her murderous wrath was next directed towards them, but, yet again, there was nothing to see from dawn till dusk. This went on for three days. Three days of watching and waiting.

The Macbeths had always been relatively sympathetic to Katherine despite living right alongside her and hearing the worst of her screaming. They had been the family to help David receive medical treatment after his head injury and perhaps it was with that in mind that Katherine went to them on the night of the third day after her release.

Hearing a banging on the back door, 16-year-old Margaret Macbeth rushed to answer it, thinking that there was an emergency. Katherine was out there in tears. 'My baby is sick and I don't have my car. I need to get to her. Will you take me? Please?'

All of the foreboding stories that Maggie's parents had been sharing about Katherine went out the window the moment she saw those tears and heard those words. 'Of course. Let me grab the keys and my brother.'

'Your brother?' Katherine paused, lurking in the doorway.

'I'm babysitting him tonight. Don't worry. He'll come along with no trouble. Just head out to the car, I'll be with you in a second.'

Katherine was already in the passenger's seat by the time Maggie got shoes on her brother and shoved him out the door. They climbed into the car and were already in motion before Maggie asked, 'Where is your baby? At your parents'?'

'Queensland. We're going to Queensland.'

'What? That's a thousand miles away. What's your baby doing there?'

'Who gives a fuck about the baby? We're going to get David. His mum lives in Queensland. He'll be back on her apron strings. Him and his whore. They'll both be there with her. I'll see to them all.'

Maggie shivered and darted a glance over at Katherine. There was a butcher's knife resting in her lap. The dull yellow streetlights glinting off it as they passed under them. 'Kathy, I'm not sure I can drive you to Queensland. Is there somebody else who could ... '

Katherine growled, 'Shut up and drive.'

'I've got my little brother in the back. He's got school in the morning. I can't ... '

The knife was like an extension of Katherine's hand. For all that she stomped about town and clattered around in her house, there was a fluid grace to her movements now that she had a blade. It flicked out, almost of its own accord. Katherine didn't even have to look. It tore a line across Maggie's cheek. Deep enough that she could taste blood on the other side. Despite herself, Maggie screamed. The car swerved dangerously into the other lane before she got control again.

'Just shut up and drive, or I'll open you up. You hear me?'

It hurt to talk. Every time she opened her mouth, it pulled on the fresh wound and set a new rush of blood down her face. Her little brother was screaming. Katherine was screaming back, 'Shut up! Shut up!'

Maggie yelled over the chaos, 'All right! All right! I'll take you to Queensland, but we need to stop and get petrol, okay? We won't make it on an empty tank.'

Katherine growled and glowered, but she couldn't argue with the logic. They weren't going to get far without fuel.

On the edge of town, there was a petrol station, one of the last places that David had been sighted during his flight from Aberdeen. Maggie pulled into the station and silently fuelled up the car whilst Katherine sat immobile inside it. Her little brother was still in there. If she made any mistakes, if she gave any indication of what was going on, then Katherine could turn that butcher's knife on him. With the tank filled to the brim and as much of a delay as Maggie could muster to think, she headed inside to pay. The moment she was out of Katherine's sight, she ran for the till. 'Please, you've got to help me. Me and my brother. We've been kidnapped. It's Katherine Knight, she's got a knife. She wants me to drive her to Queensland. She did this to my face. Please. Call the police. Please.'

The police hadn't exactly been waiting for this call—they didn't even know that Katherine had been released from the hospital, or that it was possible for her to just sign herself out after she had been more or less incarcerated. Two officers rushed out to the petrol station, where things had already begun to deteriorate.

Maggie hadn't gone back to the car. She couldn't bring herself to get back in, even if it meant her little brother was in danger. Her cheek was throbbing with pain and her hands wouldn't stop shaking. Katherine's patience ran dry only a moment after Maggie went into the petrol station, but with no clear course of action to follow, she sat there growling and ranting to herself until the girl came back into sight.

The girl and the woman stared at each other for a long time, neither one of them willing to make the first move, but neither one of them willing to meet in the middle. That was when the boy in the back seat decided to take his chance. He unstrapped his belt and was halfway out the door before Katherine caught him by the back of his collar. When straining with all his strength proved insufficient to free him from her grasp, he wriggled out of his shirt and dropped to the tarmac with a yelp. Katherine was out of the car and on him before he could move more than a few feet towards his sister. The huge woman rode the boy down to the ground before placing the blade of the knife against his throat and dragging him to his feet by the hair. She nicked him once or twice in the scramble to their feet and little trails of red ran down his bare, dusty chest. Maggie covered her mouth to hold back a scream.

'Get over here and drive this car.'

Maggie shook her head. She didn't trust her own voice to work.

'You get over here or I'm going to gut him like a hog. You want to wear his guts? You want him dead? You're the one killing him, not me. Get over here, you little slut.'

This time, Maggie managed a little wail from between her fingers.

'You get in that car right this fucking minute or he's going to be squealing like a stuck pig, you hear me? I ain't going to kill him quick. It's going to hurt. You want to watch that? You want to hear that?'

She let out a little whimper, 'No.'

Maggie took a step forward, but the gruff old man from behind the counter had caught her by the arm. 'Don't do it.'

'I've got to,' she whimpered. 'You don't understand. He's my brother. I'm ... I'm meant to be taking care of him.'

He croaked back. 'If you give her what she wants, she doesn't need him anymore. She'll kill him. You stay away, or she'll kill him.'

The police car tore up the dirt road, throwing up a cloud of dust that blocked out the stars. Katherine spun on the spot, her sunken eyes tracking any movement, every bit the primeval predator that her doctors accused her of being. Her grip on the boy's hair never loosened, but the blade didn't bite any deeper, either. She was keeping her options open.

When the police came out of their car, it was with their hands held up. Both of them had been present for her arrest earlier in the week. They knew how dangerous this woman was and they didn't want to risk another innocent life being flung onto the train-tracks of her impending insanity. 'Let's just put that knife down now, eh? We're all friends here, aren't we Kath?'

She hissed, 'Fuck you and the mother you rode in on.'

'No need for that now, Kath.' They were more than used to the kind of venom that Katherine liked to spit. 'It's all over now, just you put that knife down and we can talk this through. No reason anyone needs to get in any trouble.'

'I'll slit his fucking throat. You take a step towards me and you're killing him.'

'Nobody is going nowhere, Kath. We're just standing here on a fine summer's evening, having ourselves a conversation.'

Katherine was not equipped to talk her way out of the situation and she couldn't fight with the boy in her arms. She made a snap decision, releasing him and kicking him towards the police in one fluid motion. 'Lucky little bitch.'

The situation shifted, one officer darting forward to drag the boy clear of Katherine, the other trying to circle around and place himself between her and the other civilians. Katherine went for him.

He got his arms up in time, and what could have been lethal or disfiguring blows just left nicks on his knuckles. The bellow that he let out was enough to startle her—similar enough to a bull being slaughtered— that for one moment she forgot where she was, the knife in her hand slipping into the next position of her deboning technique.

The policeman took his opportunity and tried to rush her, but she was too quick and too canny, even when her mind was completely elsewhere. She was the veteran of more bar-fights than could be counted, her body moved on its own, slamming a fist into his jaw and opening up his arm from elbow to wrist with the flashing tip of her knife. This time, the scream was definitely human. Katherine grinned.

With the boy safely stowed away in the car, the other Aberdeen policeman tried to creep up behind her, but he nearly caught her knife in the ribs for his trouble. They couldn't get close enough to subdue her, not when she had the knife. She spun from one of them to the other, her wild grin never faltering. Her eyes were dead, but she was laughing away the whole time that they were trying to arrest her. All of her life, she'd hidden this away inside of her. The vicious edge of Katherine that nobody ever wanted to see that only broke the surface when her mask of humanity was worn too thin.

The police were not equipped to deal with a problem like this.

They were used to pulling apart the odd bar brawl—a maniac who'd spent her whole life training with a knife was a bit outside of their experience. Beyond that, their physical equipment wasn't up to the task, they had no reach on the huge woman, and that knife of hers could flick out and back so fast that they'd be more likely to lose a finger than make contact if they did try to hit her.

Once again, the petrol station attendant came to the rescue. He threw a pair of brooms that he'd been using to sweep up the forecourt to the police. Working together, they closed in on Katherine and managed to bat the knife out of her hands. Even with her disarmed, it still took both of them to wrestle her to the ground. She screamed, clawed and bit at them until she was handcuffed and even then she almost broke one officer's nose by flinging herself at him as they tried to wrestle her into the car.

This time, Katherine bypassed her old friends at St Elmo's and was sent directly to the high-security Morisset Psychiatric Hospital, where the correct paperwork was finally filed to restrain her movements until treatment could be proven to be effective. She remained in their care for almost a month.

Afterwards, she did not speak about her experience, but other residents of Morisset have shared plenty of horror stories about the quality of care that they received there. None of her usual manipulations were effective when she was taken outside the context of civilised society. The successes that she had achieved so far in her life were predicated almost entirely on everyone around her believing that she was normal, that her violent tendencies were just the run-of-the-mill outbursts of an ill-tempered woman. In Morisset, all of those deceptions fell away. When she was violent, they sedated her. When she was rude, they punished her. To begin with, she railed against it—spitting her medication in the faces of the staff, tearing her wafer-thin mattress to shreds and causing as much chaos as possible out of pure spite—but, before long, she fell back into the rhythm of institutionalisation, a pattern of behaviour that was all too familiar thanks to her upbringing under Ken's ironclad laws.

Her parents had no interest in fighting to see her freed. She had no friends. It would have been entirely possible for this to have been the final residence of Katherine Knight, if it hadn't been for the one man in all of the world who loved her.

Following her institutionalisation, it became clear to the staff of the hospital that David Kellet was in danger from Katherine. In her weekly therapy sessions, she had talked at great length about her desire for revenge against the man who had ruined her life, even detailing the fantasy that she had hoped to fulfil on the night when she had abducted and permanently scarred Maggie Macbeth.

She was going to drive to Queensland and torture David's mother until she gave Katherine his new address. Then, she was going to kill the old woman and hunt him down. She planned to kill him and the new girlfriend that she was certain he was with, along with any witnesses or bystanders who got in her way. Then, she was going to come back to Aberdeen and kill anyone who might have helped him in his escape, starting with the local mechanic who had recently fixed his car, allowing him to get away in the first place.

Patient and doctor confidentiality becomes moot when a patient is threatening to act on their violent impulses. The police were informed of her plans and took no time in tracking David down in Queensland and informing him of his still-wife's current mental state.

David was horrified by what he had done. He took all the blame for Katherine's actions on himself and drowned in self-loathing. Before the month was out, he had abandoned a second pregnant woman on the cusp of giving birth to one of his children. Along with his mother, another of Katherine's potential victims, David relocated back to Aberdeen, rejecting the new life that he had been building for himself in favour of returning to the waiting arms of a woman who desperately wanted him dead.

Once he had established himself back in Aberdeen and picked up his old job, he filed with the courts to have his wife released into his care, with both he and his mother offering to act as caretakers for the woman, ensuring that she would take her medication and do no harm to herself or others.

However dubious anyone who had followed the case of Katherine Knight up until this point may have been about the odds of their success, the decision was in the hands of the courts and the courts wanted as few able-bodied citizens of Australia confined in mental hospitals as possible.

On the 9th August 1976, Katherine was released into her husband's care, contingent on him ensuring that she continued to take the frankly ridiculous doses of antipsychotics and sedatives that had been prescribed to treat her condition. They drove straight from the hospital to Ken and Barbara's house to collect their daughter.

On arrival, David left Katherine and his mother in the car and went to get the baby himself. Katherine was still feeling fragile after everything that had happened to her in the last month and that was manifesting in a dark mood that filled both of her caretakers with fear. They quietly conferred before arriving at the elder Knight's farmhouse and decided that it would be for the best if Katherine didn't come face to face with the parents who had abandoned her in her hour of need. Katherine did not handle abandonment well, and they wanted to keep her as calm as possible. Any violent outbursts could have led to a more permanent return to Morisset, and all three of them knew it.

When David knocked on the door, it wasn't Ken who answered. He'd been afraid it would be Ken, afraid that this would turn into a physical altercation that he was certain he wouldn't win, but instead, he was confronted with silly, old Barbara. She lunged at him and caught him by the hair. 'What did you do to my daughter you cheating piece of sheep shit?'

David was so surprised that she barrelled him right off his feet. He tumbled backwards, with her fingernails scraping over his scalp as she tried to keep her grip. 'You destroyed my Katy. You drove her crazy. You just couldn't keep your dick in your trousers, could you? You had to ruin everything!'

She started stamping on him as he lay there on the gravel path and, whilst she lacked her daughter's size, she had the same tenacity and cruel aim when it came to kicking a man when he was down.

Katherine came storming up the path so fast that David's mother didn't even have a chance to shout out a warning, let alone try to stop her. Her fist caught Barbara under the chin, sending the old woman flying back to her own doorstep. 'Don't you ever lay a hand on David again! He saved me. You left me to rot and he came back for me.' A predatory growl crept into her voice. 'He's mine! Mine! You never even look at him again!'

Katherine stepped right over her bleeding mother and strolled into the house. She moved from room to room like she was in a dream, picking up everything that belonged to the baby as she went until finally, she found Melissa, fast asleep in her father's arms. He handed the baby over without a word of admonishment, without even a hint that he was surprised to see her, either.

Then, as fast as they'd descended on the house, they were gone. Zooming off down the dirt roads back to the little flat David had been renting by the meat-works. A home that would only last them a few days more, before change swept through their lives again.

Katherine could not stand the stares of the people around town and whatever benefits to her mental stability the familiarity of Aberdeen might have brought, were grossly outweighed by the terrible memories that she had of the town. David had no attachment to the place. His mother had only lived there a couple of weeks and already loathed it. All of the spite that Katherine used to fling at David seemed to have been burned away by the fires of the tribulations that she had been through in the last month. Either that or harshly curbed by the medication which had her moving through a hazy world devoid of sharp edges. She was every bit the loving, pliant wife that David had always hoped she would be, so when she begged him in tears to take her away from this horrible place, where their worst moments had been, he didn't have to be asked twice.

The couple relocated to Woodridge, a quiet suburb of Brisbane, where neither one of them had any family ties, nor where there was any way that whispers could follow them. His mother continued to live with them and, with that addition to the household, Katherine realised that her presence within the house was almost entirely unnecessary. All of the cooking and cleaning naturally passed along to the older woman and, after the first few months, even the care of Melissa became just another of her mother-in-law's chores.

With all the hours of the day to fill, Katherine started a job hunt and it wasn't long before she picked up a new job on the line at the Dinmore meat-works in nearby Ipswich. She took to the work like a fish to water and, before long, she had fallen back into her old rhythm, surprising her new employers and co-workers with her skill with the custom knives that she had brought along from her old job. Knives that she would spend a solid ten minutes sharpening before every shift.

She remained on her medication, which slowed her down a little, but that also meant that the number of 'incidents' in the workplace remained relatively low. She would still inflict complicated schemes of revenge upon anyone who crossed her, but they were more often practical jokes rather than violent outbursts. In her home life, all of the pressure to be perfect around the home had been removed thanks to the assistance of her mother-in-law, and the extra money she was bringing in gave them a more comfortable buffer between their regular life and bankruptcy. She was living the kind of life that she had always dreamed of living, with a loyal husband, a happy baby and all of the support she could ever have wanted. She was miserable.

The only moments in her life when she was happy were when she was cutting into the meat of some slaughtered animal or when she was on the long, silent drive back to Woodridge after a day at work. Even that was only a treat because sometimes an animal would stray onto the road and she could swerve to hit it. She had gone from being the little girl who saved injured animals and nursed them back to health to being the killer of animals of all shapes and sizes. Every time she heard bones splintering against the grill of her car, that old, wicked smile crept back over her face. The old Katherine was still there, just under the surface, lost but not forgotten.

The Dark Knight Returns

Katherine sank into the dull monotony of her new life, doing her best to forget everything that had happened to her and that she had done. To her neighbours in suburbia, she barely even drew attention. In Aberdeen, she had been a legend, the subject of fear and ridicule but known to everyone. Out here, she felt like she was invisible, like she was fading away. For years she went through the same repetitive motions, rising with the dawn, driving to work, slicing her way through another day before turning back and mechanically delivering all of the things that David Kellet needed to convince himself that his wife actually loved him. One of those mechanical deliveries of affection came to fruition on the 6th March 1980, in the form of Natasha Maree Kellet, the second of Katherine's children.

David stayed by Katherine's side throughout the whole of her labour, driving her to the hospital and holding her hand through every grunt and strain. Neither one of them spoke about the birth of their last daughter or the darkness that had followed. Neither one of them was so foolish as to dig up the past when it already haunted their every waking moment.

Katherine took time off work to be with her baby and soon found that her mother-in-law was an intrusion rather than a help.

This time, she felt that she had the opportunity to get things right. This time, she could bond with her baby, have the kind of relationship that she had always wanted to have with her own mother, but Old Mrs Kellet always seemed to be in her way. Eventually, given the options of a violent outburst or going back to work, Katherine elected to go back to doing the one thing she had ever been praised for. She sank back into that routine like she hoped it would drown her, but the distractions of work, roadkill and family life were never enough.

She was constantly bored out of her mind. All of the things that used to bring her joy had become numbed and even the satisfaction of her work never seemed to reach her. The treacherous voice that exists inside of all of us, demanding that we destroy our lives and go back to the freedom we knew before, wasn't a whisper in Katherine's mind, it was a primal scream. Her thoughts were dominated by fantasies of escape from this mediocre life and, before long, that resentment began to turn outwards. She grew colder and colder towards David, completely ignored his mother—who still lived in the house with them—and even her precious children began to receive the same treatment.

On Natasha Maree's fourth birthday, Katherine's misery came to a head. Four years after the birth of her first daughter, she'd had Natasha to look forward to, but now there was nothing. She packed up her things the next day, collected the children and drove back to Aberdeen.

David's abandonment of her had been one of the most catastrophic and defining events in her entire life. An event that loomed so large in her mental landscape that it had threatened to kill her and a half-dozen others. Yet, her abandonment of David was almost casual, like she was discarding some tawdry thing that she just didn't need anymore. David was upset, of course, but at the same time, he was relieved. He could see the clues that the old Katherine was clawing her way back to the surface and, as much as he may have loved his idea of Katherine Knight, the reality that had seared a line into his face and smashed his skull was too frightening to forget.

For the first month back home in Aberdeen, Katherine and the children stayed with her parents, out of sight of the town gossips in the countryside. She filed for a divorce, which David didn't even try to contest in a startling display of self-preservation that seemed entirely out of character.

Shortly after the divorce was granted, Katherine rented a small house in nearby Muswellbrook and picked up her old job in the Aberdeen meat-works again, as if she had never left. Eight years had passed since she laid down her knives and spiralled into madness, but for her, it was like yesterday.

Tragedy struck only two years after her return to work in Aberdeen. Whilst she was hefting the carcass of a particularly heavy hog, Katherine injured her back. She was rushed to the hospital by her supervisor, but the damage was already done. The wear and tear of her job and the rough life she had lived had put an end to her career working in the abattoir. The heavy lifting that the job required might have been possible for her once or twice a day, despite her injury, but each repetition would have just made her condition worsen. The job that had been the only constant in her life, the only truly good thing, was over.

She was put on to a disability pension and filed for workplace compensation through her union representative, and the government provided her with a Housing Commission apartment on the outskirts of Aberdeen, as she no longer needed to be in close proximity to the abattoir.

In 1986, Katherine turned 31 and realised that she still had another thirty years or more stretched out ahead of her. Her kids were pretty poor company, although she had done her best to patch up the relationships that she had left to rot for so long when they lived with their father. Melissa was old enough to truly understand her mother by this point and became the friend and confidant that her mother had always hoped for. Katherine shared all of the gruesome details of her life with her daughter but made sure not to repeat her own mother's mistake of reinforcing them as the natural order of things. She warned Melissa about men in no uncertain terms, but she also acknowledged her own loneliness, even if she didn't quite have the vocabulary to really explain it to her daughter.

In the evenings, Katherine began leaving Melissa in charge of her little sister and going out to bars again. She didn't return to the height of her youthful exploits, spending as much time just listening to the bustle around her as wading into every argument, but that was likely because she no longer felt like she had a group to belong to. The abattoir had always had a high rate of employee attrition and the men who came drinking from there each night were almost all strangers to Katherine.

But then again, strangers were really what she needed—people who had never heard the stories about her. All the older folk of Aberdeen had kept her reputation alive in her absence and whatever notions of dating she might have been entertaining soon vanished in the face of the town's long memory. Anyone who knew who she was by reputation alone fled from her, leaving only the company of a few outcasts and stragglers who remembered her from before Melissa was born, a decade before.

Luckily for Katherine, not everyone who drank in Aberdeen was from Aberdeen. Thirty-eight-year-old David Saunders worked in the nearby mines and liked to come into town for a drink after a long shift down in the darkness. He mostly kept to himself—he was more than a little socially awkward after a lifetime of isolation and back-breaking labour—so he wasn't privy to all of the stories about Katherine. When she approached him in the bar one night, it was like a dream come true for him. She had started wearing thick glasses and, over the years, the sun had done its wearing work on the skin of her face, but her red hair made every freckle seem like an addition rather than an imperfection. More pressingly for a man like David, she had lost her waifish figure after years of work and replaced it with a toned body that she wasn't shy about showing off.

Combined with the way that she was predatorily sexual, he thought that he had hit the jackpot.

She took him home with her that first night and, within a month, he had more or less abandoned his own apartment in nearby Scone in favour of living with her full-time. Home-cooked meals and a family that he could slot into like a missing puzzle piece—David had never been happier in all his life. When the other men in the mine realised who he was dating and started trying to warn him off, he didn't believe a word of it. He convinced himself that they were speaking out of jealousy or spite. Even when they recounted the whole story of her abduction of the Macbeth children, he claimed it was just a misunderstanding. He hadn't seen any sign that Katherine, his beloved Katherine, could have done anything like the horrible things that they were describing. At least, not at first.

They would fight relatively frequently. Katherine was suspicious of his movements when he wasn't with her. After work, he still went for the odd drink and sometimes the shifts in the mine were irregular, depending on how rich the veins they uncovered happened to be. She would accuse him of philandering at the slightest provocation, but he took it all in good humour. He could tell that Katherine had a fiery temper, but even when the screaming was at a fever pitch, he never really felt any danger; after all, she was just a woman.

Sometimes she would throw him out and he'd go sleep in his flat in Scone for a night or two before she showed up, begging his forgiveness and lavishing him with so much affection he barely knew how to respond. He kept a few bare essentials in his old apartment, but the majority of his clothes and belongings came with him to Katherine's government-supplied house.

On the anniversary of their first meeting, he returned home from work with a little bunch of flowers purchased in town, expecting a feast laid out and a night of exertions on par with every other. Instead, he found Katherine in a dark mood. She tossed the flowers aside without even looking at them and continued her pacing around the tiny kitchen.

A few weeks before, David had bought a dog for his new family. The girls had been delighted, with Natasha, in particular, being completely smitten with what she called 'the dingo pup.' Katherine didn't seem to care too much for the animal one way or the other, but she tolerated its presence in her back garden as a small price to pay for Natasha's delight. Still, she always made sure to call it 'David's dog' rather than accepting it as a part of the family.

He tried talking to her, tried to tease the reason for her foul mood out, but she just kept pacing around the kitchen, slamming cupboards and chopping vegetables in sporadic bursts of fury. He had almost given up when she suddenly darted out of the back door. David followed after her, profoundly confused about what was going on until he heard the pitiful squealing outside. Katherine had the puppy by the scruff of its neck, dangling it by a fistful of fur and skin, level to her eyes. It was letting out a piteous wail that kept distracting David, but she did nothing else until he looked at her. Then, the chopping knife in her hand flashed out and the bleeding started. She slit the dog's throat, so deeply that he could see its spine glinting white in the mess of gore. Its wails turned to gurgles, then to dreadful silence as she dropped it to the ground.

'If I ever catch you running around on me, that is what I'll do to you.'

David backed away from her, horrified. She dropped the knife into the dog's corpse to stand on end, then stalked after him. He backed into the kitchen, babbling, 'I'd never be unfaithful to you, Kath! You have to believe me. I've never even looked at another woman since you came along. Never.'

Her eyes narrowed, but she couldn't really see him, not now that the red rage had descended over her vision. He was just a shape now, a looming shadow that she poured all of her rage into. She snatched up a frying pan and swung for him. He managed to get an arm up in time, but the heavy iron hit even that with so much force that his bones cracked. She brought it down on him again and again as he curled up in a ball, his piteous screams not much different from the sounds his dog had made. Eventually, she tired, dropped the pan and dropped to her knees beside him. 'Why did you do it, David? Why would you do that to me and our family? Why?'

He could not answer, he had been knocked unconscious.

Once he had regained consciousness, he spent a week in his own apartment in Scone, ignoring the phone, refusing to answer the door and only scurrying outside for long enough to resupply with medicinal whiskey for the pain, or to work a short shift down in the mines once the worst of the bruising had subsided. He had never been a fearful man before, willing to wade into dangerous stretches of tunnel where other miners feared to tread, but now he flinched at every bump and bang of equipment. The other men began to make a joke of his twitchiness, but some of the older natives of Aberdeen did their best to curb that mockery. They knew what Katherine was capable of doing to a man—many of their number had been on the receiving end of her fists through the years.

She ambushed him on his way home from work one night, camped out in front of his apartment door. He was paralysed with fear the moment that she came into sight. She wept. She sobbed. She threw herself on the ground at his feet, begging him to forgive her and, fool that he was, he did. Everyone deserved a second chance in David Saunders' mind and, as far as he could see, from the broken woman in front of him, Katherine had a moment of madness that she didn't deserve to lose the love of her life over.

He'd made a few mistakes in his life and been grateful for the forgiveness and as she dragged him into his flat and stripped off their clothes, he realised just how grateful Katherine was going to be.

The honeymoon period lasted for a couple of months before Katherine started to draw back from David all over again, vanishing back into her own mind and slipping into the self-destructive patterns that were ingrained there. It would have been just a matter of time before her internal turmoil exploded outwards in the form of violence again, if it hadn't been for a lucky coincidence.

Katherine was pregnant again and, for David, that changed everything. He got rid of his flat in Scone and put down the deposit on a house. It was a tiny two-bedroom weatherboard house on MacQueen Street in Aberdeen, not much to look at from the outside and dark and dismal on the inside. Its flaws aside, it was the first home that Katherine had ever truly owned any part of and she adored it. She had spent her entire life in other people's houses, in rented apartments and homes that belonged to authority figures. For the first, time she felt like she was free to make someplace her own, like she wasn't just passing through. She set to work immediately, decorating every surface of the walls and even the ceilings with her own special brand of interior design. Animal pelts, taxidermy, skulls, rusty animal traps, leather jackets, machetes, rakes, boots, pitchforks and, of course, her beloved knives, covered every inch of the tiny house. Just brushing against a wall was liable to give you tetanus.

Sarah was born in June of 1988 and David had absolutely no warning of how the arrival of the baby was going to affect Katherine. She fell almost immediately into another downward spiral of depression, trapped in her memories surrounding the birth of Melissa and the chaos that had followed. He went on with his life, oblivious to the doom that was swiftly approaching, unaware of how little it would take to push Katherine over the edge into violence once more.

In early 1989, when their relationship had deteriorated, to the point that Katherine was barely even speaking to him, her worker's compensation finally came through in a lump sum. It was more money than she had ever seen in her life and she knew exactly what she wanted to do with it. She paid off the house on MacQueen Street, essentially buying the house out from under David. The house had been the only thing that Katherine stood to lose if she lashed out at him, and now, with that last tenuous restraint severed, his time was up.

As Katherine had grown colder, David's temper had begun to flare up. Where before he would have accepted any treatment from a woman, his brief taste of domestic bliss at the beginning of their relationship had now spoiled him. When housework was left untouched, he shouted at her. When the baby was left filthy and untended, he shouted at her. One day, in 1989, he returned home to find that all of his clothes were dirty. Katherine hadn't bothered to do the washing all week. It was the proverbial straw that broke the camel's back. He bellowed for Katherine and when she finally sulked into the room, he pointed at the heap of dirty clothes. 'Will you do something about this? It's been sitting there all week whilst you've done nothing.'

She turned on her heel and stalked out of the room, returning just a moment later with scissors in her hand. She held up one of his shirts and started cutting. Through the first shirt, he just stood there in shock. Through the second, he flushed with rage and, when she hefted the only pair of trousers he had without holes in the knees, he darted forward to snatch them.

He stopped abruptly with his hands still reaching out for the denim. At first, he couldn't understand what had happened. He couldn't understand where the pain was coming from. Then, he looked down and saw the scissors jammed into his stomach. The blood spreading out in a perfect circle across his gut. He looked up into Katherine's eyes, expecting to see surprise or horror at the accident that had just happened, but her eyes were merciless and dark, like she was staring right through him to a future that he didn't feature in.

She twisted the scissors as she yanked them out, and it set David howling. Shock kicked in, numbing the pain and giving him the precious moments that he needed to ensure his survival. Katherine had dropped the bloody scissors and was fumbling for her trusty iron to finish the job. David didn't hang around long enough to give her the chance. He ran for his life, leaping into his car and tearing right out of Aberdeen without pause.

The stab wound in his gut proved to be superficial, missing any vital organs by sheer luck, but David knew that he wouldn't be so lucky a third time. He rented a room in Scone for a few nights, returning to Aberdeen for only as long as it took to file for a leave of absence from his job in the mine. His foreman had been brought up on tales of Katherine Knight. He didn't have to be asked twice before he gave David the leave he needed to escape her.

It was almost three months later when he returned to Aberdeen to try and rescue his daughter from Katherine's clutches. He even entertained the idea of trying to rescue her other daughters, too. Surely they had spent enough time with their mother that they recognised the danger they were in? He never even made it into town before the police pulled him over. There was an outstanding Apprehended Violence Order against him, something like a restraining order with more immediate legal consequences, filed by Katherine on the day that he left and outlining a long history of domestic abuse on his part. David was given two options, leave town immediately or go to jail. He chose to leave and, thanks to the AVO outstanding against him, he didn't have a hope of securing custody of Sarah or access to the house that he had paid the deposit for. Katherine had won again.

The Last Survivor

John Chillingworth came back into Katherine's life towards the end of 1989. He had lived an entire life in the time since he had last seen her working the line in the Aberdeen meat-works. Shortly after rejecting the teenaged Knight, he'd met a more stable, if less exciting, woman and married her in short order, moving away to the city for almost a decade before his ever-worsening drinking problem led him to make one stupid decision too many. He arrived back in Aberdeen freshly divorced and more than halfway to being pickled in alcohol. A bit of luck at the abattoir meant that the new supervisor had once been his co-worker and, instead of the miserable remnants of a man slumped in the chair in front of the interviewer, his younger self was recalled—The John Chillingworth who would always pick up an extra shift and help his co-workers with the tricky jobs. His next stop after securing the job was to pop into the housing office, where he was offered an apartment in spitting distance of the slaughterhouse. His third and final stop was the bar in town, where he fully intended to drain the last dregs of his savings before he had to report for work on Monday.

Katherine was there. Waiting for him like a memory brought to life. He was still ten years her senior, but now that she was no longer a teenager, it seemed to be less of an impediment than it once had.

John was appallingly bad at taking care of himself, having leaned heavily on his wife to handle even the most basic functions of his life so that he could focus on the two pillars that he hung his personality on: working and drinking.

As a teenager, Katherine's raunchy flirting had been uncomfortable, almost comical, but as a full-grown woman, it had become intensely appealing to John Chillingworth. The two of them remembered each other well and, over a night of heavy drinking, he eventually confided in her just how tempted he had been by her offers all those years ago. Offers that she was more than happy to present to him again in short order.

He didn't even sleep for one night in the barracks housing that had been provided to him. Katherine took him home with her to MacQueen Street and whatever horror he might have felt when he looked at the horrific decorations that coated the inside of that dwelling were soon forgotten at the first glimpse of her naked flesh. In a strange way, he was the perfect fit for Katherine Knight. His drinking brought all of his animal instincts to the fore and stripped away any need for the kind of complex conversation that she was so uncomfortable with. They fucked, he went to work, he drank, and they fucked again. Sometimes she'd provide him with a meal in between and sometimes he'd hand over whatever change was left from his paycheque after he'd settled his bar tab. It wasn't the formal arrangements that Katherine had become accustomed to, but it suited her well, appealing to that savage part of her psyche that just wanted with immediacy.

None of the men that Katherine had pursued through the years could have been called soft—her tastes had been shaped to the mould of tough guys like her father—and, whilst she liked to physically dominate her lovers, that didn't mean that she could abide any sign of weakness in them. Despite all of that, the men she had dated all seemed to be relatively soft in the grand scale of things. They had lived as sheltered a life as the time and place of their births would have allowed and their instincts were those of civilised men. Chillingworth was different. The exact details of the traumas that had driven him to drink have been lost to history, but they had left him with a very different set of responses when confronted with conflict to the startled 'deer in headlights' approach of the Davids that Katherine had been dating before. He had a survivor's instincts. When he was pushed, he would push back. He had experienced enough pain in his life to know that it doesn't end without somebody ending it.

When Katherine first threw a tantrum at him for an imagined affair with another woman, he had sat through the foul language and flying spittle without flinching, a bemused expression on his face that just enraged her even more.

When Katherine took a swing at his face, he ducked under it and countered it with a quick slap that left her ears ringing. She had thrown him out of the house for that, startled and unsure what to do when confronted with a victim who wouldn't just sit there and take the abuse that she felt compelled to dole out.

John spent his first night in his assigned barracks apartment after that argument, but by morning, Katherine was there begging him to return to their cosy little arrangement and lavishing him with the sort of attention that he had spent his whole life starved of.

The house on MacQueen Street was always loud, always busy. Katherine didn't much care that her children heard her screaming arguments, or her equally deafening lovemaking, and it didn't take long for John to adapt to the racket. He spent all day surrounded by the squealing of animals being slaughtered; a houseful of kids crammed into a spare room was hardly worse than that, even if they were a little more persistent.

By this point, Melissa was fifteen years old and had already left school to begin dating men up to five years her senior, much to Katherine's delight. She spent only a small fraction of her nights sleeping in the house and when she did, she was forced to share a bed with her younger sisters. Circumstances had forced her to mature much faster than her peers and, by 1990, she was treated as more or less an equal by her mother. A friend. Which was why, when she heard about his one tiny act of violence against her mother, she was enraged. She confronted John, screaming in his face, her own countenance turning the same bright red that characterised her mother's rages. John was halfway past drunk and having none of it. He slapped Melissa just as he had done her mother.

It was Melissa's first brush with first-hand violence, beyond her mother's attempts on her life, which she was too young to remember. It shut her up promptly and ended the argument permanently.

Katherine fell pregnant again, at about the same time that all of this was coming to a head. John made some noises about making their arrangement a little more official at the time, but when he realised that Katherine wasn't going to push him for a marriage proposal, he didn't press further. He was already living with her and doing as much as he would have done for her as a husband—he didn't see the point of doing any more.

He was not prepared for the emotional tempest that surrounded pregnancy in the mind of Katherine Knight. Her occasional accusations of infidelity went from a monthly occurrence to an hourly one. After her screaming rages, he would often just leave the house rather than have to deal with a pregnant woman getting physical with him, spending his evenings drinking and then sleeping it off in his apartment.

It wasn't long before this pattern became apparent to the women of Aberdeen. Despite his age and his drinking, John was still considered to be an attractive man. He had become accustomed to having certain needs fulfilled by Katherine that she was no longer in any sort of mood to entertain, so before long he began to do the thing that she accused him of. He didn't go on a campaign of conquests or anything so vulgar, but once his judgement was sufficiently impaired by alcohol and attractive women started falling all over him, a certain inevitability set in.

Towards the end of 1990, Katherine gave birth to her first and only son, Eric. His father was present at the birth and offered all of the support that he could muster. Almost instantly, all of the imagined sins that Katherine had heaped at his door were forgiven and he was welcomed back into the family home with open arms. This new, maternal Katherine was one that John had never seen before, but he liked it. She was the domestic goddess that had lured in her previous partners and the gentle, loving wife that had kept them ensnared even when her violent tendencies began to show. John was completely taken in.

He was so taken in by the illusion of softness and kindness that his conscience began to nip at him. He had been unfaithful to Katherine at a time when she was feeling her most vulnerable and if he didn't make it right then he knew that guilt was going to drive him right back down to the bottom of a bottle and make his whole life fall apart. So, he confessed.

Katherine's rages had always been incandescent, but this one burned with a cold fire that should have served as a warning in itself. She walked calmly through to the bathroom and punched the glass containing John's false teeth into fragments, with the enamel teeth scattering over the yellowed tile in a chatter.

Even then, John didn't grasp the depth of the trouble that he was in. 'Oh look what you've done, now. I've only got the one pair I'm wearing to last me 'til I get those fixed.'

Katherine eyed him up, then swung her fist again. Breaking the set of false teeth in the jar had been an inconvenience to him. Breaking the set that was still in his mouth was a lesson. He spat out the fragments along with a mouthful of blood. There was no fear on his face. If that was what she'd been hoping for, she had grossly misjudged the man. Instead, there was a careful, assessing expression. He was a survivor, and he was calculating his odds.

That night, he slept in his own apartment, but the next day, he came back to the house to collect his things. That was when he found her lying nearly-dead from an overdose of sleeping pills on the bed. Just like that, he was ensnared again. He panicked, snatched her up and drove her to the hospital. Her stomach was pumped and she was saved, but she ended up back in a mental institution for observation for a week, to ensure that the threat of suicide had passed. During that time, Chillingworth watched her children and drove out to see her through every visiting hour. He was horrified by what he had driven her to and all of his safety concerns faded away in the face of the reality of losing her over his own foolish choices. When she was released, his apology was accepted and life returned to the same strange equilibrium it had before. John thought that life was getting back to normal, but he did not realise that the proverbial Sword of Damocles was hanging over his head.

The broad strokes of the legend of Katherine Knight had been preserved in Chillingworth's absence, easy enough for him to pick up from anyone he wanted to talk to in town. The specific details of the horrors that she had wrought on Aberdeen were less readily available. Everyone thought to warn John about the murder attempts on her previous partners, the near-death of her baby and her commitment to a mental hospital, but nobody thought to warn him about her long memory, or the months or years she would wait to spring an ice-cold revenge on those who'd wronged her.

She memorised his schedule every single day. She knew exactly where he was going to be at any given time and, on those nights when he went to the bar, which was most of them, she knew exactly when her old friend the bartender would gently nudge the man towards the door. When he came home from the bar after a long night at work and found her spread-eagled on the bed with another man thrusting away between her legs, he knew that it was deliberate. She had chosen to make him see that, to see her affair right in front of his eyes. To know that it could have been going on for months or years without him ever knowing until this moment when she wanted him to know. He was done. He left the house and never came back. It took him less than a week to put his affairs in order, during which time he was lucky enough to avoid Katherine, who considered him to be sulking and nothing more.

After his brush with Katherine Knight, John Chillingworth got his life back in order. He moved to the big city, joined a program, quit drinking and eventually got a full-time job as a counsellor, helping addicts who were trying to break free from the cycle of brutality and addiction. Out of all the partners that Katherine Knight chose for herself, he was the only one to escape without permanent injury and it seems that he wanted to pay that good karma forwards to the other men in the world who might have been in similarly dire straits.

Unfortunately, there was nothing that he could do to help a man who was already in the clutches of a dangerous and self-destructive addiction but completely unwilling to try to get out on his own. There was no saving a man like John Price.

The High Price of Living

John Price, known as 'Pricey' to his friends, was the man that John Chillingworth had caught Katherine in bed with. Their affair had been going on for almost a year before Katherine decided to use him as a blunt instrument of vengeance against her partner, but as uncomfortable as he was with the whole situation, it wasn't enough to keep him away from Katherine. He was a grown man with a less than amicable divorce in his past. In 1988, he had split from his wife, leaving her to raise their two-year-old daughter but taking his two older children with him to Aberdeen.

He was well-respected in the community of Aberdeen and well-liked by everyone that he met—a real rarity in such a small town. Pricey even had a good reputation in the mine, where he was known for his skill as a first-aider, one of the first responders whenever there was an accident down in the dark beneath the hills. There was something in Pricey that brought out the best in Katherine. Even when it seemed that their sexually-charged affair was transforming into something more stable, he was able to guide her gently into that next phase without any outbursts. She met with his two children, Becky and Little John, and was surprised to find that they liked her. Her own children were very taken with the new, gentler man that their mother had taken up with. In normal circumstances, it would have been an ideal situation, but there was nothing normal about Katherine and John's relationship.

Just as she always had in the past, she soon began accusing John of infidelity. Just as she always had in the past, her screaming and cursing turned to violence—although it was more restrained now than it had been with the men in her past. She did not jump straight to acts of outright brutality for fear of losing Price, just as she had Chillingworth. It is possible that she was not restraining herself but that she was merely mellowing as middle age swept in; just one look at her proved that this was not the case, though. The red flush that had once marked her berserk tantrums had now permanently discoloured her face, like she was trapped in that state permanently. A visible warning to anyone who met her of the personality hidden behind those bottle-thick glasses.

John took all of her aggression in his stride, for the most part. He'd already been through a cold and loveless marriage and he generally interpreted her assaults as signs that she was passionate about him. It was also difficult for him to take her concerns about infidelity as anything more than slightly flattering jealousy, since it was clear to everyone that he was completely devoted to her and smitten, to boot.

Warnings about Katherine Knight had not fallen on deaf ears when it came to John, but with rose-tinted glasses on, he tended to interpret events differently from those who'd lived through them. He adopted Katherine's version of events wherein she was a victim, struggling back against an unfair and oppressive system and any parts of her story that weren't protected under that dubious interpretation he fed into his own delusions of machismo. The men who had come before him were weak and that was why they considered Katherine's passions to be something worthy of fear. He was strong, so he could weather the storm and receive his just rewards on the other side of each frenzy.

By 1993, even her ranting and raging on that subject of infidelity had begun to fade in favour of a new argument. She wanted to know, if he was so devoted to her, why he wouldn't propose marriage.

In John's mind, marriage was the end of happiness. He'd had a healthy and happy relationship with his first wife before they got married and from what he could gather about Katherine's first husband, he got the very same impression about their relationship. If they could live a happy life together, then why did they need to go and put the stamp of doom on their relationship by announcing it as formal in front of friends, family and the government?

After two years of the same question, answered a dozen times with varying degrees of bellowing, John decided to take their relationship to the next level and get her off his back. In 1995, he invited Katherine and her children to come and live with him and his. He was a supervisor up at the mine, running shifts on his own most of the time and, as a result, he was making good money doing a job that he genuinely enjoyed. That, in turn, had led to a good house, one with enough rooms that all of Katherine's kids wouldn't have to be piled up in a single bed at night. With his three-bedroom bungalow on St Andrews Street, it would have been madness for her to refuse the offer of such a comfortable life, but she still wasn't willing to give up her own little nightmare home on MacQueen Street. In the end, John didn't force the issue. His prosperity was so assured that he didn't need Katherine to sell her house to make sharing his home economically viable. The strange collection of skins and bones were left hanging in her empty house, whilst everything that lived came to stay with John in his.

For almost a year, they were in a honeymoon period. Her pointless, petty arguments all seemed to have been crushed by his invitation to live with him. They lived as if they were married and, indeed, under common-law, they were considered to be a married couple. The children all got on well with each other and Katherine became increasingly maternal towards John's kids, too. It seemed like a fairy-tale relationship where nothing could go wrong. Then, she started asking him to marry her again.

The arguments went on and on without a moment's respite for either one of them, but whilst they exhausted John, fighting just seemed to give Katherine more energy. It was like she took some twisted delight in badgering and harassing him, day in and day out. It went on and on for a year, ever-worsening until eventually, in 1998, she went too far.

The mine had recently replaced all of their first aid kits, tossing the rest into a dumpster to be destroyed, but the thrifty John Price had lifted them out of the trash and brought them home. Their contents may have been past their 'best by' date, but the majority of them were still perfectly functional and he wasn't in the habit of getting rid of something that could still save a life.

One day, whilst he was at work, Katherine took the video camera that he'd bought her for Christmas and filmed all of the kits, providing a running commentary about all of the things that John stole from his workplace. With the same deranged grin on her red face that she always displayed during her most self-destructive acts of cruelty, she mailed the tape to his bosses at the mine.

By the end of the week, John's entire life had fallen apart. The job that he had spent his whole adult life working had fired him for stealing company property. Even after the situation was fully explained, they didn't care. It seemed to be a punishment for associating with characters like Katherine Knight as much as it was retribution for any theft.

He drove home from the mine, gathered up all of Katherine's things and threw them out into the street. When she arrived home, she found that the locks were changed. They stood on the doorstep and had a screaming argument for upwards of two hours before, finally, on threat of police involvement, she snatched up her belongings and stormed off back to her little house on MacQueen Street.

It was like a weight was lifted from John. No longer would he have to endure the insane demands and ramblings of that woman. Even if it had taken the loss of everything else in his life, at least now he was free of her.

Work was never easy to come by in Aberdeen and men found that, unless one mining company hired you out from under the nose of another, there was little chance of employment underground. There was no official blacklist, but people talked and none of them wanted a thing to do with Katherine Knight or any of her men. Nobody wanted to invite that chaos into their lives or their businesses. The whole town knew what Katherine had done to him and, whilst there was some sympathy and pity, there was just as much contempt. They'd warned him about Katherine Knight and he'd still gone along with her like a fool.

He didn't even care that they looked down on him; he was just glad to be free of her. The pay was terrible but he found work at the abattoir before the month was out. His savings were depleted and the big house was now a massive strain on his finances, but even if he had to tighten his belt, he was going to survive.

Of course, it wasn't long before Katherine crossed his path again. She still lingered on the periphery of the meat-works crowd more often than not and whilst, she'd avoided the alcoholism that plagued Aberdeen up until this point, she had now turned to the bottle, just as her father had before her.

Every night she was in the bar, just out of sight, like a memory lingering on the edges of John's life. Every time that he saw her, he remembered the good times that they'd shared. He remembered the kindness and the love. After a few weeks without attention from another woman, he started to recall the carnal aspects of their relationship with some affection, too. With the kind of animal cunning normally only reserved for ambush predators, Katherine waited until he approached her before she sprung her trap.

By the time the clock struck midnight, she was back in his bed and their relationship had resumed the intensity that had tricked him into forgetting all of the stories about her the first time around. But, even that proved insufficient when the cold light of dawn shone over them.

Katherine had expected to move back into the house immediately, to pick up right where she had left off. John wasn't as foolish as that. He might have let her back into his life and into his bed, but he wasn't inviting her to live with him any time soon.

Despite that little bit of distance, the story of their reconciliation swept through Aberdeen before midday and it wasn't even the end of his working day before John was confronted by a group of his friends with an ultimatum. They had no intention of watching him destroy himself. They refused to just stand by and watch as he ruined the life he had struggled so hard to put back on track once he had rid himself of that 'devil woman.' For as long as he took up with Katherine Knight, they were going to have nothing to do with him. His calls would go unanswered and his friendships would go untended until they went their separate ways.

Even with that ultimatum delivered, his friends still didn't truly abandon him. It pained them to see him putting himself through the same torments over and over, so they reached out to the only person that they thought he might listen to. David Kellet.

Katherine's first husband had been in hiding ever since the relationship broke down and age was starting to wear heavily on him after the hard life he'd led. The scar on his face was still angry and red, hot to the touch. He approached John in the bar one night when he was sat alone drinking. He'd been called back into town by his old friends to add his experience to their warnings.

He told John every single story that he could remember, illustrating each one with a new scar. He warned the man that Katherine Knight was not to be trifled with, sharing the warning that he'd received on his own wedding day. 'If you cross her, she'll kill you. Do you understand? This isn't a joke. She will kill you.'

It was obvious from the bemused smile on John's face that he wasn't getting through to him, so David bade his sad farewells to his old friends and took to the road before Katherine had a chance to hear that he was in town. He still lived in fear of her, even decades after their relationship had ended. He still woke up gasping for air and scrabbling at his throat. She haunted his nightmares.

Life fell into a new routine, with Katherine in a state of limbo, allowed to come into John's house to cook for him, or for what they termed 'date nights,' but never allowed to overstay her welcome or feel settled. Her old arguments about marriage fell by the wayside as she demanded more and more frequently that he let her and her children move back in. The kids had been welcomed back into John's home with open arms—he had never held them responsible for their mother's actions, even when she tried to use them as the justification for them. Even spending every other night in his bed, Katherine was still uncertain of her place. She wanted his house to be hers again. It isn't clear whether she entertained ideas of taking it from him when their relationship finally degenerated or if she was not thinking that far ahead. Once again, that animal desire for comfort was winning out over whatever more complex motives she might have possessed. And that desire was being thwarted at every turn.

This went on and on, escalating from harassing questions to screaming arguments that would end with her tossed out into the street and, finally, almost inevitably, to violence. By the year 2000, every day had become a battlefield.

'Why can't I just live here? It'd be easier for us. Easier for the kids.'

He had just come in the door from work and he was already regretting letting her keep a key to the house. 'You know why. You know what you did.'

'Haven't you forgiven me yet?' Her attempts at emotional manipulation fell flat. She could say the words, but her expressions never matched what she was aiming for. 'That was years ago. That was a mistake. I wouldn't do nothing like that again.'

'I know you won't because you ain't moving back into this house.'

Tears would have worked, a quaver in the voice, but Katherine didn't understand sadness or sympathy, she only had rage. Her face went from rosy to scarlet. 'Don't you trust me? After everything I do for you?'

She'd go on and on like this for the rest of the night unless he nipped it in the bud. Once she'd had a good scream to let her frustration out she usually wound down again quick enough. Then it came time to kiss and make up and if there was one thing Kathy was good at, it was kissing and making up. John sometimes thought that those moments were the only reason he had to put up with her at all.

'I ain't a fool, Kathy.' He shook his head. 'I'm never letting you hold nothing over me again. Not ever. When you lose your temper, it doesn't matter what you've promised.'

'Temper?' She growled. 'Temper?! You've never seen me mad, John Price. You think you know fucking everything, don't you? But you know fuck all. You've never seen me angry.'

She sprang up from her seat and tore across the room in a wild charge. John got his hands up in front of his face before she could start slapping. This was all business as usual. She'd wear herself out and have a little cry and show him just how sorry she was. Katherine at her best.

The blows never fell, but something warm and wet was spreading across his chest. Had she thrown a cup of water on him? He nervously moved his arms away and looked down. There was a knife sticking out of his chest, sunk in deep enough to stand proud, but not deep enough to kill him. The tip was scraping on his rib.

He let out a roar and grabbed Katherine by the scruff of her neck. He dragged her to the front door, cast her out into the street, slammed it shut behind her and then sank to the floor, gasping for air. His hands were shaking as he reached up to pluck the knife from his chest. It tumbled from his numb fingers to clatter across the floor beside him. She nearly killed him. If she'd been a half inch down, that knife would have sunk right into his heart. The back door.

He scrambled to his feet, still chill with shock and half-drunk with panic. The back door was sitting slightly ajar to let a breeze through the house, the way it usually was. He could hear the dog bounding about happily in the sunshine just beyond it. It felt like he'd run a mile by the time he reached it and locked it tight.

Not a moment later, he heard a fist thump against it. He'd been right. She was still trying to get in. He did a mental inventory of the house. Dashed around, making sure all the ground floor windows were locked up tight. Then, finally, he staggered, breathless, to slump in his chair in front of the nook in the living room. That had nearly been the end of him. This couldn't go on any longer. It didn't matter what sweet nothings she whispered in his ear, or any of the other things that she could do with that body of hers. If he kept this up, she was going to kill him. He could see that now.

After a fretful night spent worrying that Katherine was out there with a key to his house, a new day dawned. February the 29th. John took himself to the Scone Magistrate's Court a little after dawn and took out a restraining order against Katherine. All that he had to do was show the court the knife-wound in his chest and they were quick to capitulate.

With that done, he went to work just the same as always, although all of his friends noticed that he had a hunted look about him. By his lunch break, the wound on his chest had oozed through his shirt and he had to seek out a first aid kit to patch it. News of his injury spread through the town like wildfire and all of the people who had turned their back on him because of his relationship with Katherine seemed to come out of the woodwork to offer him solace and advice. To each and every one of them, he said the same thing. 'If I don't show up for work tomorrow, it'll be because she killed me.'

He couldn't bring himself to head home when his shift ended, instead being buoyed along with the rest of the crew to the pub, where he was surrounded by well-wishers and more than one of the town's insufferable gossips, desperate for any fresh details to add to the local legend of Katherine Knight. Every one of his friends offered him a safe bed to sleep in at night, no strings attached, no commentary on his love life, just safety. He turned every one of them down. At first, they thought it was just bravado, that he thought he was tougher than the monster that had sunk a knife into his chest less than a day ago, but eventually, he broke down and told the truth.

'If I'm not there and she shows up ... If she can't get me, she might kill the kids. I can't ... I can't risk that.'

He went home late to discover that the kids were already gone. Katherine had sent them to sleep over at a friend's house and they'd left him a note so he didn't worry. He let out a breath that it felt like he'd been holding all day. His babies were safe.

Less than a minute after that relief, the door rattled in its frame as somebody hammered on it. John froze on the spot. Was it Katherine? There was no way to look out without her seeing him and he hadn't locked the door on his way in. Old habits die hard. Swallowing the cold knot of fear, he strode over to the door and flung it open. He almost collapsed with relief when he saw his neighbour on the doorstep. 'All right, mate?'

The neighbourhood knew all about Katherine Knight and nobody was willing to let her have a good man like John Price without a fight. There wasn't much that they could do to save the man from himself but they could try their best to watch him whilst they could. He spent the rest of the evening lounging around in their garden, sharing bottles of beer and stories of happier times, before he eventually wandered home at eleven to slump into his bed in a drunken stupor.

That was the last time that anyone saw John Price alive.

The Last Supper

Katherine's day had gone in a very different direction to John's. Whilst her shadow stalked his every step, her mind was completely focused on the task at hand. She knew nothing about restraining orders, his mounting desperation to escape her, or anything else that he had done. All that she knew, deep down in the instinctual primordial chaos of her mind, was that he had crossed her and she was going to make him pay, however, she could.

Once she was fairly certain John was gone, she headed over to his house to see the kids. She took her video camera along to make a home movie. She spent the morning filming the children at play, providing a soft, deep-voiced commentary over the whole proceeding, talking about which of the children was to receive which of her belongings when she was gone, talking about who should be given care of her children, if she and John Price should suddenly disappear off the face of the earth. Already, she was trying to construct a narrative. She had no experience with the forensic sciences, she had no knowledge of how cases were composed, but she knew just how to spin a story so that she was the victim, not the perpetrator. She'd been doing it her whole life and doing it so well that, despite everything she had done, she still walked about as a free woman.

With all of the children filmed and accounted for in this video-will, she packed up their things into overnight bags and sent them off to stay with their respective friends for sleepovers. She drove around, dropping them off at their destinations and simmering over the fact that not one parent would come out to greet her. Nobody treated the kids badly—they wouldn't punish them for the sins of their mother—but nobody wanted anything to do with Katherine Knight if they could avoid it.

After the last child was handed off, she drove into town with her very meagre savings in her pocket and bought the fanciest black lingerie that she could find in what she probably thought was the fanciest department store in town. She had never spent so much money on clothing in her life and certainly not on clothing that nobody was ever meant to see outside the bedroom. She wanted to make tonight special.

The rest of the day she spent alone in her little house on MacQueen Street, lost in her thoughts, surrounded by her things, just sitting in silence until the sun went down.

She drove over to St Andrews Street at about eleven o'clock when she was quite certain that John would already have gone to bed. Then, she quietly let herself in. She settled herself in front of the television at first, basking in the normality of it all. This was her home and John was her husband. He had gone to bed early, but now he would be waiting for her. She went through to the bathroom and took a shower, scrubbing herself thoroughly until her skin was as red as her face, then she patted herself dry and dressed up in her new lingerie, admiring herself in the mirror. That John Price, he was a lucky man, to have a wife like her, to do all those things that wives do for their husbands. Sex and cooking, just like her mother used to do for her father. Sex and cooking and cutting. Those were the only things Katherine was good for, but she was so good at them it made up for everything else.

John was lying on his back in bed with the covers flung off in the midsummer heat. His breathing came out in gentle wheezes. He wasn't a snorer like some of the men she'd had. John had been caught young enough by another woman and trained to behave himself. He was used to another person in the bed, so he didn't flinch when the mattress dipped. He didn't stir as she ran her fingers through the hair on his chest. Even when she reached down and stripped off his underwear, he barely responded except to make a little mumble and shift his hips to make it easier for her. John Price, her man, was a creature of habit and she knew just how to use that to her advantage. She worked him with her hand and mouth until he was ready, then climbed on top of him and started to rock her hips. Softly at first, as if she was scared to wake him, then harder and harder, until the fierceness and the intensity of their lovemaking started to shift the bed. Still, she didn't stop, she didn't slow. John's eyes opened slowly, lust-drunk and night-blind. 'Kathy?'

She leaned down and silenced his murmurs with a kiss. Moaning into his mouth. It was like she'd breathed life back into his body. His hands came up and seized her hips, the silk of her lingerie making everything strangely cool and slippery as he fought for a better grip. For more traction.

A little delighted sound slipped out of her as he started to move, not for the pleasure that it brought her—she could bring herself enough pleasure without his involvement—but because it meant he was giving in to her, that he was succumbing without a fight. After the sex, he'd be soft and pliable. She could make him do whatever she wanted, the same as she always had. She just needed to get here and take him in order to win, and now she had.

The bed hammered into the wall over and over, setting her bag of knives jingling above it. They were hanging above his head, right where she'd hung them when she first moved in all those years ago. Of course this house was hers, otherwise, her knives wouldn't be there. Of course this man was hers, or he'd object to her riding him. With a surprised grunt, John finished inside her. She tried to keep moving, to keep this moment going forever, but those strong hands on her hips plucked her right off him and pushed her aside.

John's eyes were open now. Open, awake and aware of what had just happened. There was fear in his eyes. He was scared of her. She'd done that for him, trussed herself up like a Sunday roast, degraded herself for his pleasure, and now he was going to reject her? He was going to toss her off him like she was nothing. Like she was just another one of his whores to be discarded the moment he was done with them. No. She wasn't going to tolerate that. She wasn't going to be thrown out in the street. She wasn't going to be his victim anymore.

Neither of them knew how she got the knife in her hand—that was how quick and instinctive her movements were. One moment she was kneeling there with her face turning scarlet and the next she was lunging forward, the shimmer of fine-edged steel in her hand. It slipped into him so easily that he barely even felt it, so sharp that only the tell-tale wetness that came chasing it out of the wound gave away that he was injured at all. John was still dazed, barely aware of what had happened a moment before and not even slightly conscious that his lung was now collapsing. Her hand snapped forward again, and another little red mouth yawned open on his stomach. The next thrust went in the other side, the blade flipping and twisting in her hand as she shifted its momentum. That one sliced into his liver.

Pain finally cut through his confusion. Pain chased right on its heels by terror. He leapt up off of the bed, too scared to even realise he was dying. He turned heel and ran for the bedroom door. The broad expanse of his back was an easy target for Katherine. She stuck him twice more, cobra-swift. Two more tiny fountains of blood started spraying out his life onto the carpet.

She had been excited before. The dull beginnings of a greater pleasure had built up at the base of her stomach before John had let her down again. But this was better than that; this was better than anything she'd ever felt. Her cheeks ached with smiling, her senses soared. She could smell him, sweat-slick and terrified. She could hear his feeble one-lunged whimpers for help. Wetness clung to her, his sweat, his seed, his blood, she had taken it all from him and now it ran over her skin as she lunged out of the bed after him.

Again and again the knife lashed out, but still, John was too stupid to know he was dead. He ran for the front door, the wash of blood making him too slippery for Katherine to get a good grip. What the mind didn't perceive, the body still couldn't ignore. His limbs were losing strength and his numbed feet were turning under him with each step.

In the hallway, by the front door, he went down. Katherine mounted him the moment he fell. Hammering the blade into his chest and guts as she ground herself against him.

Rage had always been the easiest thing for her, ever since she first let it out. Everything that she saw made her angrier and angrier, every person more loathsome. There wasn't a single waking moment when Katherine wasn't simmering with hatred and resentment for every living creature around her. To let it out like this, to finally be completely honest—it was a revelation.

She knew rage; she could trust rage. Love, which had always been out of reach. Even when she thought that she'd found it, it always seemed to slip through her fingers. She could never tell what a man was thinking or feeling, not really. Her first husband's abandonment had proven that for certain. She never knew what was in any man's heart before this moment, but now she could feel it. Her hand was pressed flat against John's chest to support her weight whilst she stabbed him over and over and she could feel his heart thumping against her, the last desperate throes of a dying animal.

Tapping some reserve of strength found only in the shadow of the valley of death, John bucked her off and grabbed at the door handle. The two of them were more alike than they'd like to admit. Katherine was a creature of habit, too: she'd forgotten to lock the door behind her.

John lunged out into the warm night air, the stars above him shining like pinpricks through the ever-darkening veil that was enveloping him. He opened his mouth to scream for help, but there was no air in his lungs. He tried to crawl out into the street, but her hand was locked like a bear-trap around his ankle. He got one last glimpse of the sky, then she dragged him back inside.

He didn't struggle once he was back in the house. He didn't have the strength any more. The pain was getting more and more distant with every thrust of the knife until he could barely feel them at all. Somewhere between the twentieth and thirtieth stab wound, he died.

Katherine had never been more at peace in her entire life than in the moment that she realised he was dead by her hand. He would never leave her. He would never cross her again. She had her revenge.

Then the reality of it all came crashing down on her: John was dead, she was a murderer, people were going to find out. She was going to get in trouble. She needed to get away. She needed to find someone to blame. She needed to make an excuse. She needed to make it his fault, somehow. With a grimace, she looked down at herself. She needed to have a shower before she did anything else. She looked like she'd spent all day working the line at the meatworks, coated from top to bottom in gore.

After a brief sojourn in the shower to clean off the worst of the mess, Katherine let herself out the back door and drove into town. In the moment, everything had made sense. In the moment, all of the fear and confusion of the modern world had faded away. She had let her primal instincts guide her and she had been elated. Now she was being crushed by the enormity of what she had done. She found an ATM and used John's card, pilfered from his bedside table, to withdraw all of his savings—around a thousand dollars that he'd managed to rebuild after the last time she destroyed his life. It was enough for her to make a run for it, get set up for a month somewhere to lay low and let the madness that was going to erupt on discovery of John's body pass her by. She already had a bag full of her most prized possessions in the car. She could go now and never look back if she wanted. She could give in to that most primal instinct to flee from danger and see just how far from this nowhere town she could get.

But if she did run, then people would know that she had done it. They would blame her for what she had done. There wouldn't be consequences until they caught up to her, but the whole town—already hissing and whispering about her behind her back—would know that she had killed him for no good reason at all. That she was the bad guy. She couldn't tolerate that. Not when a brief stop at John's house to plant some incriminating evidence would be enough to cover it all up. She'd spent her whole life subject to this town's gossip—she knew just what to say to turn public opinion around.

She pulled up to the house in the early hours of the morning with a dull ache in her bones. All of the excitement had drained out of her body, leaving her feeling hollowed out. The adrenaline rush was over and now she faced the arduous process of cleaning up her own mess.

When she tried to push the door open, it hit against something. With a growl of frustration, she slammed the door into the obstruction over and over, until it was pushed out of the way and she could force her way in. It was only when her footsteps produced a squelch from the carpet that she remembered what she had left lying behind the front door of the house.

She looked down at the heap of meat on the floor. He had done this to her. He had ruined everything. John Price should have loved her like she loved him, but he hadn't. None of them ever had. They weren't men at all. They were swine. Pigs in human skin. Beneath contempt.

Her fingers tangled in his blood-matted hair and she hauled the carcass up to eye level. She spat in his face. 'You. You did this. You did this to me.'

Her knives were still hanging in the bedroom and it only

seemed natural to reach for them. All of the confusion that had wracked her only moments before was washed away in the familiar warm rush of anger. He had done this to her and now he had to pay. She'd made the same cuts a million times before on other swine, blade-tip grazing across the spine as she severed the soft tissues and cartilage, easing into the groove between the vertebrae when it came time to separate the head entirely. He was a pig and he deserved to be served up like one.

With a grunt, she lifted his severed head and tossed it into the empty aluminium pot on the stovetop, the one she'd left out to cook him his dinner before he'd thrown her out into the streets over nothing. A splash of water from the tap and some furiously hacked up vegetables joined his head, then she turned on the heat and stalked off. That was how her mother had always prepared pigs-head and that is how she was going to serve it up to his children.

She let out a snort, not unlike a pig's, at that fantasy. Setting John down on the table for his kids to eat, watching those treacherous little cuckoo bastards gobble him down then watch the colour drain out of them when she told them what they'd just consumed.

It still wasn't enough. Not enough for a meal and not enough to sate her other hungers. He had to suffer the way that she'd suffered. She had to strip him of everything that made him John Price. She returned to the rest of his body and continued her work.

If she'd cut a head off a pig a million times, then she'd skinned one a million more. It was tricky, delicate work if you didn't want to score the precious layer of fat underneath. The kind of job that required a more skilful touch than most of the meat-works employees could muster. She made one long, graceful cut along the length of the pelt, then set to separating it from the subcutaneous layers with small, gentle cuts, like she was scraping away the body from inside it more than cutting the hide from the beast. The pot began to bubble and, before long, it smelled just like her mother's kitchen back home. That smell intermingled with the offal and iron of the slaughterhouse, all of Katherine's happy memories, all in one place at last.

She didn't know what to do with his skin once she was finished cutting it from his body, so she hung it from the architrave of the door in the living room and turned back to the meat. A pig's head might make a fine soup and gravy, but there wasn't much eating on it. She really needed more if she was going to provide John's kids with a filling meal. There were a few choice cuts on this particular pig, but the rump had always been her favourite. She sliced each of John's buttocks off with one clean cut a piece, then portioned one in two because she'd taken a little extra meat on that one and didn't want them to cook unevenly. It would be terrible if the kids got food poisoning whilst eating their worthless swine of a father's ass.

She put the meat in to roast, along with a few more handfuls of vegetables. Then, she laid out plates and set the table, scribbling names on a piece of kitchen towel tucked under each plate. 'Beaky' for his daughter Rebecca, and 'Jonathon' for little John.

Finally, she strolled back through to what was left of the corpse and hefted it up into John's favourite seat. It didn't look right. She crossed, then uncrossed the limp cadaver's legs, but it still didn't look like John. Eventually, she got it posed and tucked a bottle of lemonade into the crook of its arm. She started trying to plan out a disguise to cover his corpse with, pawing through his clothes in his room to find a hat or hood so the kids wouldn't notice that their daddy had no head, but it proved useless.

Whilst she waited for the meal to cook, she took a long, slow stroll around the house, smashing every picture that she could find with her bare knuckles. It was only as she ground her hand into the last one, of John and his kids on some sunny afternoon, that she remembered why she had come back to the house to start with. She picked up a pen and a scrap of paper and wrote:

'Time got you back Johathon for rapping my douter. You to Beck for Ross — for Little John. Now play with little Johns Dick, John Price.'

It fell apart a little due to her inability to write in clear English, but the message was essentially conveyed. John Price had been a paedophile, an incestuous child molester who had raped both of his own children and Katherine's, too. It was a baseless accusation, but it was also a lie so hideous that everyone would believe it. Katherine had seen men run out of town on far less evidence than a note from a wife. Her memory, her legend in Aberdeen, would end with her as an avenging angel for the helpless. She would be a folk hero, instead of the bogeyman that the parents of Aberdeen used to threaten their children to sleep.

When the meal was ready, she served two portions of meat out onto the kids' plates, heaped them with vegetables and drizzled them with gravy. It smelled delicious, even though she knew what it was made from.

The third cut of meat lay there in the roasting tin, tempting her with the glisten of rendered fat. One bite would be all that it would take to know for certain if it was as good as it looked. One bite and every part of John Price would belong to her forever. She took that bite, but she couldn't stomach it, spitting it into the sink half chewed and then washing it away. She threw the rest of her portion out into the garden so that the dog could have it when it came home from wherever John had left it.

There was no way that the kids would eat this meal. There was no way that she could trick anyone, let alone the confused and suspicious children of the man she had just murdered. Even this last little attempt at a plan fell apart in the face of reality and, suddenly, it was all too much for Katherine. Her pills were in the kitchen cabinet—the only thing that John had allowed her to keep in his precious house. She fetched every packet of them out and began gulping them down as she dithered around the scenes of her greatest brutality, soaking it all in. The rage was gone and the edges of the world began to darken as she swallowed down packet after packet of sleeping pills, scattering the blister packs across every surface of the house.

In the end, she went back to where the evening had begun, sinking down into the blood-soaked bed and pulling the bedsheet over herself in a makeshift shroud. She had done what she set out to do, and now she could rest.

No Remorse

When John didn't show up for work the next morning, a coworker was immediately dispatched to check on him. They found the smeared, bloody handprint by his front door. The signs of a body being hauled back inside. The co-worker wasted no time in calling the police and soon the scene was swarming with them.

Katherine was discovered almost immediately, still alive but comatose from her overdose. That was the least disturbing thing that the officers on the scene discovered. It was like a scene from a horror movie. It took the first responders a solid five minutes to work out what the object hanging from the doorway was. It took the lead detective to point out the nose and pubic hair before they could grasp what they were looking at. These were small-town police, unaccustomed to violence of this sort and it took a dreadful toll on every one of them just to observe it. Most left the force soon afterwards, some committed suicide and even the hardiest of them were changed, with those few resilient men suddenly developing an aversion to meat that lasted for years.

They painstakingly pieced together the events of the previous night, measuring the temperature of the boiled head to determine the exact time of John's death.

John's body was taken to the coroner's office, where it was

discovered that he had suffered thirty-seven separate stab wounds prior to his death. It was abundantly clear that whoever had killed him was an expert skinner, because the incisions that had been made were so perfect that, when the autopsy was over, the coroner was able to stitch John back into his skin, leaving him looking almost as he did when he was alive.

It was two days later that Katherine woke up. The police were on hand to question her, but they quickly discovered that the hardened killer, whom they thought was in their clutches, had severe mental health problems. From the very beginning of her questioning, she claimed to remember nothing about the events of the night, but she was careful to cast doubt on any claim that she was responsible for John's death, talking at great length about how much she loved him. Were there no other witnesses to the rest of Katherine's life, it is possible that she would have convinced the police of either her innocence or insanity to a degree that she would avoid conviction, but that was not the case. When the police began canvassing the area for any witnesses, they were approached by a delegation of the townsfolk of Aberdeen who begged them to ensure that Katherine never got out. Every person in Aberdeen lived in fear of her and they dreaded what new heights of horror she could achieve if she were set loose again.

Her trial began surprisingly quickly following her arrest, with the courts desperate to get through it before news of the horrific details had spread too far and compromised too many jurors. Even as it was, it was almost impossible to get jurors to sit for her trial. The few who hadn't already heard rumours about the atrocity had the scene of the crime described to them before they took up their position on the jury, and the threat of having to see pictures of her victim was sufficient that many of them begged off. It was with some relief that the judge was able to dismiss the jury after her lawyers had entered a guilty plea.

Sadly, this plea came with some strings attached. Katherine would admit to the lesser crime of manslaughter in exchange for a reduced sentence. The judge, Justice O'Keefe, refused the plea outright. This was one of the most horrific crimes he had ever heard of and there was no way that he was ever letting the perpetrator walk free again.

The plea was switched to 'not guilty' and the jury trial began again in earnest, but before it could progress too far, O'Keefe dragged it to a halt once more, sending Katherine off for a psychological evaluation to prove that she was competent to enter a not-guilty plea, rather than an insanity defence.

It was during these assessments that the formal diagnosis of BPD was finally attached to Katherine, even though some of her old carers came out of the woodwork to deny it. With the BPD diagnosis, Katherine was able to claim that she had been suffering a period of disassociation during the gruesome acts of March the first, explaining her missing memories. Her lawyers ran with the diagnosis, committing to several bouts of theatrics to convince the jury that Katherine was not culpable—or at least, not fully culpable—for her own actions. The largest of these theatrical events was when Katherine begged to be excused during the descriptions of her crimes, and when that was refused, launching herself into a hysterical fit that ended with her being sedated.

Despite all of these tricks, the jury saw through her and she was found guilty of premeditated murder, along with lesser crimes associated with her treatment of John's body. The judge sentenced her to life in prison, with a special addendum added to her file: 'never to be released.' This essentially denied her any hope of parole, making her the first woman in Australia to ever receive such a harsh sentence.

Mulawa High-Security Prison has been Katherine Knight's home since the day of her sentencing, but it is difficult to punish a person who lives like an animal at the best of times. A typical day for Katherine begins at seven when she is woken by the four guards who will serve as her escort for the day. She eats breakfast at a table away from the other inmates and is then walked to her job in the prison's earphone factory. She is manacled to her workstation, out of reach of any other inmates, and sets to work assembling the tiny pieces by hand for up to six hours, depending on her shift. Her work ethic and skill is widely praised by the prison staff and she commands the highest wage in the entire factory, but those aren't the only traits that the guards comment on.

The other inmates call her, 'The Nanna,' and she is widely-considered to run the female side of the institution. When there is a dispute between inmates, she is called in to resolve it, and whatever her judgement is pronounced to be, is taken as law. Even when there is a dispute between the guards and the inmates, she is usually referred to. Everyone is terrified of her and she basks in the kind of respect that she had always dreamed of.

A prolific artist, her single person cell is filled to bursting with craft projects, knitting, crochet, drawings, paintings and pottery. It is her private space that nobody is allowed to enter, whether they be inmate or guard. Indeed, the only comfort that Katherine is truly denied is a cell-mate. It has been decided that there is too great a risk to the life of anyone put into a domestic situation with her to justify the savings that might be made.

Her artwork decorates the visitors' and guards' sections of the prison, with many pieces being sold off with her approval to help fund some of the education and entertainment programmes on offer. Katherine is very careful never to sign any of her original artwork, despite basking in the attention that they bring her. She does not want any true crime fans out in the world buying her art simply because she was the one who made it.

Any friends or family have long since abandoned Katherine to her fate, with only a single exception. Whilst her children, co-workers, parents, and brothers have turned their backs on the murderess, her twin, Joy, still comes to visit whenever she is able, riding the bus for hours to get to the prison.

In 2006, she launched an appeal against her sentence, claiming that it was too harsh for the single murder that she had committed.

A panel of three of New South Wales' most prominent judges gathered to review the case and promptly ratified her original sentence. Katherine had never shown any sign of remorse for her actions and, without remorse, there can be no basis for parole under the Australian system. It is for this reason that a guilty plea is often preferable to a prisoner than a not-guilty one, even when a reduction in time to be served is not offered.

In the time since her arrest, more accounts had been gathered about her personal dealings that had helped to seal her fate. In particular, a series of conversations with her brother, Kenneth and niece, Tracy, when she said, 'I am going to kill Pricey and I am going to get away with it. I'll get away with it because I'll make out I'm mad.'

Justice McClellan responded to her appeal with one additional statement, which seems to reflect the views of everyone in Australia. 'This was an appalling crime, almost beyond contemplation in a civilized society.'

The 'primitive intelligence' that drove Katherine Knight to commit her heinous crimes against her fellow man exists inside each and every one of us. Buried under layers of guilt, conditioning, education and intelligence, there is a primal part to every psyche driven exclusively by raw emotion and need. In a narcissistic psychopath like Katherine Knight, civilisation is a mask to be worn over this primal reality. The truth that others are different from them, that people have depth and understanding beyond what the psychopath thinks and feels, is impossible to comprehend. It is as though the psychopath is completely alone in the world, with no friend or ally, and reversion to savagery is the only way that they can ensure their own survival. For a woman like that, remorse would be a display of weakness that others might exploit. The full depth of her emotional state is always going to be beyond the psychologists and criminologists who pore over her crimes and profile because even if she possesses complexity beyond that which she displays, she lacks the tools required to communicate with others. Something that decades in relative isolation within a prison certainly has not improved.

It is possible that Katherine Knight felt bad about what she did to John Price, just as it is possible that the lioness feels bad as she tears out the throat from a gazelle. The unpleasant truth is that the predator's feelings do not matter in the face of the material reality of their actions. And, in the case of Katherine Knight, those actions are now considered to be one of the worst crimes to have ever been committed in Australian history.

TRUST ME

The True Story of Confession Killer Henry Lee Lucas

Hear My Confession

The car lay unmoving by the side of the highway; not with the cold stillness of a dead thing, but the waiting stillness of a coiled rattlesnake, just waiting for its time to strike. Out here in the middle of nowhere the desolation of the American South was abundantly present. There were deserts and icebergs with more life spread across them than this little slice of nothing. Nothing to see, and nothing to do, except each other.

There was no urgency to the sex—the car wasn't even rocking on its suspension. There was no love and not even much desire if truth be told. Ottis's face was pressed into the fabric of the backseat, his snaggletooth snagging on the tattered stitching when he turned his head for air. They were both slick with sweat, their clothes plastered onto the hard planes of their bodies. The windows were fogged up and the air was muggy with the air conditioning turned off. Henry loomed over Ottis's back, his mouth hanging open in a perpetual silent moan. In the dim light of the car, with his brows drawn down and furrowed, it looked like he had no eyes at all—two dark caves instead of the one empty socket that was usually on display. There was no love, no urgency, no desire, just the mechanical rocking motion that helped them to pass the time until the phone rang.

That was the one feature of this stretch of nowhere that nobody had mentioned before: the payphone standing proud out of the sand at the roadside, just waiting to be used when some poor unfortunate broke down out here with no help in a hundred miles. You wouldn't think that a phone like that would even have a number to receive calls, but you'd be wrong. It was the reason that Henry and Ottis were waiting here. The sharp song of that phone ringing was what they both strained to hear over the sound of their own harsh breathing and grunting. It was due any moment now.

The sun dipped low towards the horizon, cherry red and wavering behind the rising heat of the day. Sunset was the appointed time for their call, but the fall of darkness here and the fall of darkness down in Florida could be at different times. Neither Henry nor Ottis had the education required to decipher it themselves, so they waited patiently by the phone, doing what came naturally while the hours rolled on by.

There was no end to this for either one of them. In the heat and the dark, they were too exhausted to exert the efforts required to push over the edge into a moment of real pleasure, but their lusts would not settle until they'd been sated, so they rocked on and on.

The phone began to ring.

Henry slipped out of Ottis and out of the side door of the car before the other man had the time to even groan in protest. By all rights, Ottis should be the one answering the call. He was the one who had been chosen. He was the one who had been marked by his grandmother and the devil. Henry made him weak, made him hand over control of the things that should have been his, and his alone. That was just how powerful Henry was, how majestic.

Henry picked up the phone with his jeans still halfway up his legs. Wasn't like there was anybody out here to see him anyway.

'Tell me, child, do you accept Satan as your lord and master?'

Henry chuckled into the mouthpiece. All confident swagger even in the face of a question like that. 'You know that I do.'

The voice on the phone was guttural and monstrous, enough to turn the hair of lesser men white. 'And will you serve the dark majesty with all of the strength in your body?'

'Most definitely.' Henry was still smirking like this was all a game to him. Ottis had tumbled out onto the tarmac, knees near searing at the touch of it. He flinched every time Henry was coy with their masters. Every little joke or jibe that he made filled Ottis with terror.

'Are you ready to fulfil your purpose in the grand design of our Lord and master, Satan, the Dark Angel!?'

Henry gave Ottis a wink. 'Just tell me where to go and what to do.'

'There is a town, four hundred miles to the west of where you now stand, and outside of that town, you shall find a girl. Her hair is long and dark. Her skin is pale and freckled. She will be carrying a backpack with a purple lotus flower embroidered upon it. You shall know her by these signs, and you shall take her. Kill the girl and bring our master's plan of chaos closer to fruition. Do what you will with the body afterwards. Take whatever pleasure in it that Satan will allow you. But first, be sure to send her soul down into the pits of hell for him to feast upon.'

'As you command.' The words came clumsily to Henry's cocky mouth. He didn't take kindly to orders, even when they came from the Prince of Darkness himself. 'You are our hands, and through you, we shall work His infernal will. You are the Hands of Death, and with each killing, we shall spread more terror and dissension across this great nation until it falls to its knees.' The next words seemed to be drawn out of Henry involuntarily, like a howl. He threw back his head and bellowed, 'Hail Satan!'

'Hail Satan!' echoed both the phone and Ottis, Ottis from his place in the dirt at the roadside.

Then silence fell back over the desert again. Henry dropped the phone handset back into place and turned to Ottis with a grin and a hunger.

He took the other man there in the dirt by the roadside, roaring out the devil's secret names with every thrust, making Ottis into an offering just as surely he would this poor, simple girl that the Hands of Death cult had chosen as their latest victim.

Before the moon had fully risen fat above them, they were tearing off down the highway to the west, eager to fulfil the will of their master, bound to his demands, revelling in evil at his behest. No man could resist the will of Satan, so they could hardly be blamed for the things that they would do next or the sinful things they had done before.

'Stop.'

The sun had barely risen when they spotted the hitchhiker by the side of the road. She was the one. The one that their dark lord had chosen to be their next victim. She was the one that...

'Stop. Stop with all this devil worship nonsense. It doesn't make any sense.'

Henry's well-practiced recitation of his crime ground to a halt. 'What's that now?'

The detective on the other side of the table leaned forward to offer him another cigarette. They needed to keep the room good and smoky to cover up the unique reek that seemed to seep out of every one of Henry's pores. He'd been poisoned as a kid. That is what the prison doctors said. That was why he oozed that eye-stinging smell. It was the collective opinion of everyone on the force that a good wash would probably deal with most of the smell, but the medical eggheads insisted.

'The Satanism stuff.' The detective sighed. 'Nobody is buying it, Henry.'

Henry cocked his head to one side and scratched at his empty eye-socket. It wasn't easy with his wrist chains fed through the hoop in the middle of the table. 'What that you're talking about, now?'

'Nobody believes that you were sent on a mission by Satan to murder all these girls. I don't know who put this idea in your head that you'll get a lighter sentence if you bring the devil into it, but you won't. Just tell us the truth, and nothing but the truth. Okay?'

Henry looked genuinely perplexed. 'But the Hands of Death? What about them, huh?'

'Florida PD have been through the Everglades. They've gone to all the places that you said these cults had their meetings. There was nothing there. No sign of anybody. No human sacrifices. Nothing, Henry. It's just a fantasy, and I'm tired of hearing it.'

Henry wet his lips. 'All right, all right, all right.'

He took a moment to compose himself then launched back into his story as if he hadn't just been called a liar.

They pulled up alongside the hitchhiking girl, with twin alligator grins plastered across their faces. 'Hey now, what's a pretty little thing like you doing out here all by your lonesome?'

It was dark inside the car. She could see the shine of their grins but not the hunger in their eyes. She was upset, she needed somewhere to vent her frustration, and two friendly strangers seemed to be just the ticket. 'I just broke up with my boyfriend. I'm all done with men. They're the worst.'

'I would take offence, but I am inclined to agree with you there, Miss. I ain't never met a man, outside of my good buddy right here at my side, that I could stand for more than any length of time at all. Why I'd bet that boyfriend of yours isn't even worth spitting on if he's on fire.'

There was a strange charm to Henry, the same charm that had ensnared Ottis so easily and so deeply. He was like some old black and white movie star that had come out of the screen and roamed around. He was larger than life. People got caught up in his wake, and the whole world seemed to reshape itself around him. Nobody could charm a girl into a car like Henry. He was the gift that just kept giving, as far as Ottis could see.

The girl fell under his spell readily, bursting into giggles. 'Well, he isn't all that bad.'

Henry didn't even have to switch gears. As smooth as a Vegas hustler, he replied, 'I'm glad to hear you say that. As a matter of fact, because that boy of yours, I have to tell you, he is feeling mighty sorry for how he's crossed you. He stopped me and my buddy here and begged us, down on his knees begged us, to come out here after you and take you back to him. He knows he's done wrong, and he wants to make it right.'

'Wait'—a scowl crossed her face—'Kenny sent you?'

Henry chuckled, 'Well, I hope you didn't think I was in the habit of just stopping to chat up every pretty girl I came across at the side of the road. Of course Kenny sent us. He wants us to take you back to him so that he can make his apologies to you proper.'

It was hard to be suspicious in the face of Henry's overwhelming charm, but she still made the attempt. 'Why didn't he drive out here himself if he's so sorry?'

'Wouldn't you know it? That is a part of this sorrowful story, too. Your young man was all set to come a roaring out of town after you when he burst his dang tire. Nail right through it. That's how we met Kenny to start with, you see. We saw that poor boy pulled up on the side of the road trying to wrestle a jack under his car and, being the good Samaritans that we is, we hopped right out to help him. But would that boy hear of it?'

Ottis shook his head on cue. 'Nope.'

'No, he most assuredly would not. He said to us, "Don't you tarry here. I've got a girl out there in this merciless sun, and she needs rescuing. You good boys want to help me out? Then you get yourself back into that car of yours and you go find that girl of mine before she gets too far, because I've done wrong by her and I need to make it right."'

'That's what he said.' Ottis nodded along.

The girl dithered on the roadside. Henry was certain that she wasn't doubting his word, so the only alternative had to be that she was doubting her boyfriend. He leaned back in his seat. 'Listen here, Miss. I ain't got no attachment to your boy Kenny. If you tell me you never want to see him again, I'll give you a ride to wherever you've got to go to get away from him. I ain't even heard his side of things, only him hollering that he's sorry, so I don't know what sort of situation me and my buddy here just got wedged into the middle of.'

That seemed to cinch it. 'No. No, I'll go listen to what he's got to say. If nothing else, he owes me that apology.'

She opened the back door of the car and climbed in, wreathed in the smell of cigarette smoke and sweat.

'And this was on the twenty-eighth?' The detective interrupted Henry again, pen tapping on his clipboard.

'What's that now?'

'You picked this girl up on the twenty-eighth of August. Is that what you are saying?'

'Yeah, that's right. Of course. The twenty-eighth. Ottis strangulated her that afternoon. I fucked her. Then we buried her out by the rickety barn, right where I said you'd find her. You've dug her up, right?'

'Oh yes, we found the body exactly where you said it would be.' The detective nodded along. 'But here is the thing. You didn't kill her.'

Henry was getting angry. His empty eye-socket began to weep. 'I done already told you Ottis did the killing and I did the fucking.'

'I've got a pay-sheet from a job you were working on in Richmond, Virginia. Says that on the twenty-eighth you were roofing some old girl's house. How could you have been in two places at the same darn time?'

He took a long draw on his cigarette. 'What is this? You don't want my confessions no more?'

The detective sat back with a sigh. 'We want the truth, Henry. That's all we ever wanted. The truth.'

'Well, maybe that one was just Ottis then. Can't remember every little thing. You do enough of them and they all mix up. You remember every shit you ever took?'

The detective reached across the table and drew the packet of cigarettes out of the murderer's reach. 'Well, let's see if we can't jog that memory.'

The Son of a Whore

On August 23, 1936, Henry Lee Lucas was born onto the raw dirt floor of his family's log cabin in the backwoods of Blacksburg, Virginia. What would have been the cause for celebration in any normal family was an irritation and a serious imposition in the Lucas household.

His mother, Viola, was in her fifties but still working hard as the town prostitute, and every day that her genitalia were out of commission due to yet another unwanted baby was a day that the family was losing the pittance of money that she got paid for sex—typically, about ten cents per customer. It wasn't like his father, Anderson, was bringing much in to support his wife and the thirty-odd bastard children that she had spawned. While he used to make an acceptable living working on the railroads, his alcoholism soon cut that, and him, short. One night while blind drunk, he passed out on the tracks and a freight train rolled right over him, severing both of his legs. He survived the experience but spent the rest of his days in a little wooden wagon that he pushed around with a broom handle.

It was the last time that he tasted liquor. The moment that Viola became the breadwinner she asserted herself as the matriarch and master of the whole family, holding the purse strings of their extremely meagre fortune and using them as just another of her many tools to dominate and belittle everyone around her.

Even when Henry was a baby, his mother would pinch at him each time that he cried or fed. There was no kindness for Henry that didn't come with pain in equal measure. As soon as he was old enough to survive solid food, Viola put him down and never picked him up again. Affection was something to be purchased, not something freely given. But suffering—she had plenty of that to spare for her last-born son.

There was no plumbing in the cabin, no electricity either, just a wood-burning stove that Viola used to prepare meals for herself, her pimp, and very occasionally, her husband. Hot food was a luxury that little Henry would never experience. When she caught him trying to steal scraps from his father's plate one night, he was banished from the house to live in the chicken coop.

Henry was often seen gnawing on the woodwork of the coop as his teeth began to come in. He chewed off substantial amounts of the lead paint that coated it and, combined with the absence of any sort of cleaning routine, it wasn't long before he was suffering from several different types of poisoning—lead poisoning from the paint and cadmium poisoning from the chicken droppings and insecticide that was sometimes stowed away in there. By the time that he was old enough to walk, these poisons had already impregnated his body to such a degree that the smell of cadmium seeped constantly from his pores. By the time that he was old enough for school, the reek of it was enough to make his fellow students' eyes water. In the schoolroom he was seated beside an open window, no matter the weather, but even that wasn't enough to alleviate the stench—or the hatred that it instilled in the other students. Henry was loathed by teachers and students alike. He was completely isolated from the community in Blacksburg, with only the dubious company of his family elevating him from being a total pariah.

His parents—such as they were—remained more or less unreachable by the school or authorities, with any message that

Henry carried back to them being discarded without a second thought. But eventually, one of the many demands that the boy be washed to deal with his ungodly smell finally made it through to Viola, and it sent her into a rage. She dragged the terrified boy out to the small pond bordering their property, stripped him naked and then held him under the water while she scrubbed and molested him in more or less equal measures.

'They wants him to be a pretty smelling little girl, then that's what we'll give them.'

She still had clothing from all of her older children stowed away for use as hand-me-downs, but one item held a particular pride of place amongst the belongings of all Henry's many half-siblings—a beautiful floral dress that had been intended for his older sister to wear to church. Viola forced Henry into it, then paraded him through town, bellowing, 'Look how beautiful my daughter is. I thought I had a son, but I guess that I was wrong.'

She marched him all the way through the school gates and into the building before scuttling back into the woods. Henry had to sit in the dress throughout the whole school day before he was finally allowed to run home, sobbing all the way.

It was far from the last time that he would wear that dress. It became one of Viola's favourite punishments for the boy to force him into girl's clothing. She had spent enough of her life at the mercy of men that having the opportunity to get some revenge on that gender was all too welcome. She loathed and feared all men, so being able to take the power away from them in any way was a massive thrill for her. She had long been using emasculation as a tool to control her husband. Every time she had a client come calling, she would prop her husband up in the corner of the room and make him watch. Soon, that disabled man was joined by what appeared to be a remarkably ugly girl. Henry was pinned in place by fear of his mother, repulsed and appalled by the things that she did for money. Whatever last embers of humanity might still have been burning inside of the boy despite all of the abuse that he had suffered died in that dimly lit cabin, watching man after man mount his mother and leave a few pennies behind in payment.

Henry was in desperate need of a friend. His older brothers had sensed their mother's particular antagonism to Henry, and they feared to suffer the consequences of seeming to be in cahoots with him. His father was wracked with constant pain, denied the alcohol that he had always used to numb himself before, and forced to watch man after man lying with his wife. He was completely lost in his own misery. If Henry ever came close, he lashed out at the boy with the broomstick he used to punt himself around.

There was nobody who could help to shoulder the unbearable burdens of his horrific childhood. No human being would have anything to do with him for fear of being dragged into the maelstrom that surrounded him, but he did find one creature in all of Blacksburg who seemed to care for him—a mule that he stopped to visit each day after school.

The nameless animal was the property of one of Anderson's old work friends, and it was serving no purpose lingering around his property. So when he discovered the delight that young Henry was taking in playing with the animal, he was more than happy to gift it to the boy.

Viola eyed the animal warily when Henry led it into their yard on a ragged rope. She didn't understand why the boy had brought it, and it took several rounds of vicious accusations before she calmed herself enough to listen to his fumbling explanation. She looked from the boy to the beast and back again, saw the affection in her son's eyes, the admiration of an animal that most would have overlooked entirely. The moment that she recognised it as love, she was consumed by jealousy. Viola loathed Henry, she wanted nothing to do with him even at the best of times, but she could not stand the idea of him finding comfort or love in anyone else, either.

Living on the fringes of civilization with domesticated animals of their own, the Lucas family needed a gun. It was very rarely used, and barely even thought of most days, but Viola could find it among the dark rafters by touch alone. The shotgun was kept loaded in case of emergencies, and the look in Henry's eyes, the softness and kindness there, that constituted an emergency in Viola's view.

She shot the mule, right in the face. Henry was sprayed with blood. It blinded him. With both hands, he wiped his eyes clean. He could feel a scream rising up his throat, but Viola's firm backhand cut it off before it could escape. 'What did you have to go and do that for? Now I've got to go and pay somebody to haul that useless carcass away, you worthless, stupid little rat-shit.'

She hit him again, an open-handed slap that dropped him to his knees with a gasp. There was blood on his hands. She kicked him in the ribs, hard enough to make them creak.

It was his fault. He shouldn't have loved that mule. This was what his love brought with it. Viola stamped on his hand as he held it up to her in desperate supplication. He'd been taught young that love came with pain, that joy came with a price. Why hadn't he listened? Why hadn't he learned?

Viola continued to punch and kick him until he was unconscious, then she dragged him back to the chicken coop to sleep it off. It wasn't the first time she'd beaten him like this, and it certainly wouldn't be the last.

The campaign of abuse that she inflicted on both Henry and his father to 'keep them in their place' was relentless. She insisted that both of them watch as she serviced her clients, sometimes dressing up Henry as a girl and threatening to rent him out alongside herself, sometimes just pushing them into one corner of the room so that they wouldn't disturb her 'gentleman callers' too much.

Henry never seemed to be numbed to that particular pain, no matter how many times he was exposed to the same routine. He would still flinch at the sound of flesh hammering into flesh, still struggle to keep the bile from climbing his throat. The first time he'd tried to run, Viola had been on him like a shot, like something out of a nightmare. Naked, bloated, and pale in the firelight, she'd dragged him back into the room by the ankles, and the man who'd paid to fuck her lay laughing on the bed as she kicked her son in the head.

After that, she'd gotten more creative in her punishments. She'd let him run, but every moment that he was out of her sight, his terror grew. He knew that she'd come for him when she was finished. He knew that the torments she'd inflict would be all the worse for him denying her immediate satisfaction. After she'd finished up her business, Henry would walk right back into the house for his beating, feeling every inch the helpless, terrified coward that she accused him of being as he wept and bled, begging her for mercy.

This violence reached its peak when he was just nine years old. Viola had set him the task of repairing the fence around the edge of their property, alone, and acquired some scrap wood in trade for her services. He laboured at this task all through the day, gladly missing school where he was treated like dirt, and finding some small measure of satisfaction in doing good work with his hands. His fixation on the task was so intense that when Viola called him, he didn't come running. She had a client waiting for her, already halfway to undressed in her bedroom, and Henry wasn't coming when called. The same old fury bubbled up in her. She rushed over to the wood stack, grabbed a two-by-four and swung for the back of Henry's head. The crack was so loud that they probably heard it in town, and he tumbled onto his face in the yellowed grass. Viola spat on him, then went back to her whoring without a second thought. That would teach the boy some respect; he'd wake up sore in the morning and regret even thinking of crossing her.

Night came and went, Viola's busiest working hours and drinking time all rolled into one. A few hours after sunrise, she climbed out of bed and went to the chicken coop to give the boy a piece of her mind now that he was conscious enough to hear it. There was no sign of him. With a snort, Viola turned on her heel and headed back to the cabin. 'Fool boy thought he could run away to school and be safe from her. Didn't he know that he just got it worse every time he ran? Little coward. Little idiot. Did he want to get beaten bloody?'

She was almost back to the house when she spotted the dew-covered lump out in the grass. Right in the same spot where she'd dropped Henry yesterday. Lazy little swine didn't even crawl back to his coop. She took a little run and then kicked him as hard as she could muster in the backside. Her ankle started to ache. 'Get up, you lazy little pig shit. You got a fence to finish.'

Henry didn't move a muscle. She kicked him again. Then again, hard enough that his limp body rolled right over and his slack-jawed expression was exposed to the morning sky. It was enough to make even Viola pause. With a tremor in her hands, she touched his face. He was cold. She moved her hands down to his lips and held them steady. His breath tickled over her fingertips, and the breath that she'd been holding herself came out in a whoosh. 'Get up, you lazy little bastard. Go on. Wake up.'

When it became apparent that Henry wasn't going to move under his own power, Viola set a couple of his older brothers to drag him inside and prop him up in the corner where he wouldn't get in the way. Anderson was parked in the opposite corner, utterly ignored by the swarms of children as they went about their day. Both of them forgotten.

Henry lay there for a day, forgotten. Then another. Viola had put him out of her mind. Anderson would have been powerless to help him, even if he hadn't been so lost in his own misery that he'd barely noticed the boy's state. Henry would have died there and then, on the dirt floor of that cabin, if it weren't for the most unlikely of benefactors coming to his rescue.

Viola's pimp, 'Uncle Bernie', had been coming and going as usual over the past few days, bringing her trade and returning for his cut of the takings, and he had noticed the injured boy. Eventually, his basic humanity won out over his desire to stay detached from this horrid little family drama. He picked Henry up, tossed him in the back of his pickup truck, and drove him to the hospital.

Even a few minutes of concussion-induced unconsciousness is cause for medical concern, and Henry had been lying in an unmonitored coma for three days. The medical staff couldn't believe that the boy was still alive at all, and they certainly didn't expect him to ever regain consciousness after suffering what they assumed was extensive brain damage. It took a week before he regained consciousness, and when he did, it was alone in a strange, white place, completely unlike anything he'd ever experienced before. The people there spoke to him softly and kindly. Slowly enough that he never had to question them or doubt his own recollections. For the longest time, he thought he'd died and gone to heaven, but then the tests started in earnest. The needles and the endless questions.

What had happened to him? How much could he remember? When had he been exposed to cadmium? When had he been exposed to lead? What school did he go to? Who was the man who had brought him in? He couldn't even begin to understand some of those questions, let alone answer them. They took his dumbness in the face of questioning as a sign of amnesia or oxygen-deprived retardation. They accepted that accidents just happened sometimes.

When Uncle Bernie came back in to check on the boy, they could think of no good reason why he couldn't go home.

The seizures didn't come until later. Brutal, crushing things that Henry couldn't even remember afterwards. Every muscle in his body would contract, shaking and straining against every other one. His eyes would roll up into his head. He would froth at the mouth, let out little yips or screams. Back then, the doctors called them 'grand mal' seizures—violent convulsions that would wrack his whole body and leave him aching for days in their aftermath, even though he didn't even realise they'd happened. One moment he would be fine, the next he would be flopping around on the ground, helpless and lost in the black static of his own brain.

After that harrowing experience, Henry shied away from his

mother. Viola would have punished him for that before, beaten him bloody and tormented him even more, but at the urging of Uncle Bernie, who didn't want to see his meal-ticket going to jail for child abuse, she eased off on Henry.

With the obvious danger of calling down Viola's wrath finally gone, his half-siblings were delighted to welcome him into the family. The girls took pity on Henry, taught him how to wash properly, how to clean his clothes so that he wasn't so obvious a target for the school bullies. The boys, they were just glad to have a new playmate after so many years of stagnation. They would run, whooping and screaming through the woods around their house. They would rough-house, wrestle, swim in the creek, and hunt for squirrels until long after the sun had set and they had to trudge back to the never-ending misery of their parents.

By the time that he had reached the age of ten, in 1946, Henry was beginning to become as normal as it was possible for someone of his upbringing to be. He was starting to find some minor success at school, and the bullies who had plagued his early days eased off after they discovered—the hard way—that he carried a knife in his belt at all times, just like his brothers did.

Those knives were a daily part of the Lucas kids' lives. They used them to whittle crude toys for themselves out in the woods. They used them to skin the squirrels that they caught. There are a hundred small uses for a knife in rural life. Most importantly, though, they used them to fight. Not just with outsiders, but to settle arguments within the family, too. There wasn't a single Lucas child without a knife scar somewhere on their body, and as weak and starved as Henry was after his early years of neglect, he carried more of them than most.

Since his coma, Henry's movements were sometimes erratic and clumsy, like he had forgotten how his mind was meant to fit into his body. In the semi-playful knife fights of the family, this made him as much a danger to others as to himself, lurching around unexpectedly into harm's way.

It was during one of these playful little stabbings, on a sunny day in the forest, that Henry lunged forward unexpectedly, impaling his own eye on his half-brother's knife. The eyeball burst immediately, sticky vitreous sliding down his cheek and drawing a scream out of his brother's throat. Henry didn't scream. He didn't even shout. He seemed to be too surprised to even respond to the stimulus. He fell down to the ground as if he was going through the motions, then a seizure wracked him while his half-brother ran around looking for somebody to help drag him back to the cabin.

Viola took one look at her son, with blood and leaves caked to his face, and she shrugged. 'Ain't nothing to be done about it now. Just, don't be stupid again.'

His siblings did their best to wash out the now empty socket as Henry cussed at them all with surprisingly colourful language. As per usual, Viola had no intention of seeking out medical attention for her injured child, and with no frame of reference, the kids just went along with her. Somehow, despite a dirty knife inflicting the injury, soil and decomposing leaves getting rubbed into it, water from a stream being used to wash it out, and no hygiene being practiced by anyone involved, the injury did not get infected. Three weeks on from losing the eye, it was healing so well that the teachers at Henry's school assumed that it had actually been treated.

Henry had started to develop a little bit of a personality now that he was out from Viola's shadow. He had a wry sense of humour that passed most of the children his own age by but occasionally drew a chuckle from his teachers. He was far from being a favourite, and his presence was still more often than not a disruption in the classroom. But he was quiet and attentive, even if he couldn't get to grips with any of the more complex subjects. He left the teachers alone and they left him alone.

The same could not be said for all of his classmates. They were the usual mix of clowns and bored children that comprise most schoolhouse populations, and they received their fair share of punishment from their teachers as a result.

Henry was sitting one day, minding his own business and doing his best to be attentive to what his teacher was saying when the boy beside him started cracking jokes to a buddy. Henry paid them no attention either, but before long the constant guffawing had enraged their teacher. She turned and flung a ruler at the boy. She missed. The little slip of wood hammered into Henry's empty eye-socket and stuck there. All the noise that he'd never made when he lost the eye came pouring out of him now. He sounded like a pig being skinned alive. His teacher rushed over in a panic and tried to pull the ruler out, but it was stuck solidly in the soft tissue. She had to twist it to get it loose.

After that little incident, infection set in. Nothing life-threatening, nothing that would even impact his life too severely, but a persistent little culture of bacteria that would last for the rest of Henry's life, making his empty eye-socket weep milky tears at inopportune moments whenever he didn't have a glass eye in place.

Growing Pains

By the winter of 1949, the strain of living with Viola had become too much for Anderson. He had done his best to raise his children with some decency and dignity despite everything, but he had been marginalised so thoroughly by Viola that his lessons never took root. By the end, he simply whacked at his children with his broom handle whenever they came around to torment him. He had been reduced to less than a man—less than an animal—by their treatment, and he could have lived on for another twenty years in that same daily living horror if he hadn't had one brief moment of self-reflection. In the middle of the night, he dragged himself out of the cabin and into the snow. He kept on dragging himself forward for as long as he could, his atrophied muscles given new strength by the knowledge that there was an end in sight—that his suffering would soon be over.

That last desperate dash for freedom was a complete success. By the time the kids found him in the morning, he was already half dead from exposure. Even after he was taken to the hospital and pneumonia truly set in, he never regained consciousness.

By the spring of 1950, Anderson Lucas was dead and gone, and every attempt that he had made to instil values or restraint in his children were forgotten with him.

Puberty hit Henry Lee Lucas like the freight train that took his dead father's legs. He went from having no interest in the girls outside his family to having entirely too much interest in the course of a few weeks. He spent the summer of 1950 relentlessly pursuing every girl in his class and being quite brutally rejected by every single one of them in turn. He didn't have the social skills to navigate around his reputation around town, nor around his pungent aroma. The charm that he eventually developed wouldn't surface until a good few years down the line.

As a fourteen-year-old, the outlets for his sexual impulses were extremely limited, but once again, his brothers came to the rescue. They had spent many years hunting squirrels and rabbits in the woods around their cabin, but it was only now that Henry's sex-drive began to ramp up that he discovered why his older brothers still pursued such childish games. They were having sex with them. The same fate would probably have befallen his beloved mule if Viola hadn't intervened so early.

Henry took to his brothers' lessons so well that before long he was the one leading the hunt and expanding both the repertoire of animals that they would molest and the specific techniques that they used to maximize their pleasure in each case. It was Henry who discovered that slitting the throat of an animal just as he was approaching his orgasm led to it bucking around in a particularly thrilling way, and it was Henry who proved time and again that he was quite happy to go on fucking an animal after it was dead.

About this time, Henry's academic career came to its end. The woods were full of animals that were calling to him, his hormones were soaring, and he had no interest in any sort of work; not when his extended family had already turned his head to a far more lucrative way to spend his time. Cousins—kin of Viola for the most part—were forever passing through the Lucas house, with all of Anderson's family wisely distancing themselves from him after he made the fatal error of marrying her. And while not every one of them was a criminal or a drifter, enough of them were to leave a permanent impression on young Henry.

A series of burglaries started up across Virginia, mostly centred on Richmond, but extending well out in every direction. From scattered reports and sightings, it seemed like there was some roaming gang of teenagers and young adults hitting targets almost at random, taking very little care to avoid detection and trusting almost exclusively in luck to see them through. Still, no matter how far he roamed or how much money he managed to fence his goods for, Henry returned every time to Blacksburg and his mother's ever-waiting malice.

With money came better prospects for the boy. He was fifteen years old in 1951, as wealthy as he would ever be in his life, and learning some confidence for the first time thanks to the long periods of time that he was spending outside his mother's influence. Absence seemed to make the heart grow fonder, and many of the girls who wouldn't give him the time of day when they went to school together suddenly had an interest in the only boy their age who drove a car instead of a tractor. His interest in women was never romantic so much as it was an expression of his endless carnal desires, but he learned to play the game, at least a little. And the more that he acted like he was just interested in dating the girls that he pursued, the more success that he had with them—up to a point.

Henry devoted an inordinate amount of time and attention to wooing the girls that he pursued, obsessively attempting to purchase what he considered to be the natural conclusion to their arrangement. The girls, meanwhile, had been well-warned about the dangers of premarital sex, and the depths of depravity and destitution that it could lead to—often with the Lucas family being used as examples in the conversation.

After a month-long attempt at courting, interrupted only by his trips away to do a little breaking and entering, and the intricacies of keeping their relationship a secret from everyone in town, Henry came back to find the object of his affections just as reluctant to progress beyond heavy petting as she had been when he departed.

Off in his car, deep in the woods, far beyond the usual spots around Blacksburg where necking teenagers usually haunted, he laid out an ultimatum. 'You either give it up to me like you're supposed to, or we ain't going to see each other no more. No more flowers, no more drives whenever you feels like it. No more nothing.'

Despite that persuasive argument, her knees did not part. 'I'm not like that, Henry.'

A tremor ran through him—not a convulsion but rage. After all he'd done for her. After all the money he'd spent. She wasn't like that? He'd make her like that. He'd make her so she was however he liked, whenever he liked.

He scrambled on top of her, his hands grasping, not for her chest, as she'd assumed, but for her throat. His hands shook as the corded muscles in his arms stood out. The girl didn't even have time to think, didn't have time to change her mind or to fight back. By the time she realised what was happening the world had already started to go dark. The last thing that she saw was Henry Lee Lucas looming over her, teeth gritted, eye-socket weeping with frustration and effort.

Once she was dead, he made swift work of her underwear, slicing it off and tossing it aside. He was intimately familiar with the mechanics of sex, having spent so much of his life with a front-row seat in a whorehouse, and it didn't take him long before he was happily humping away at the still-warm corpse.

With his urges sated, Henry looked down at the girl with disgust and regret; not that he'd killed her—he didn't care whether she was alive or dead—just that now he was going to have to deal with the body. He dug a shallow grave out by the fire road and tossed her in, still partially dressed. As he filled it in with dirt, Henry pontificated on the situation. Sex with dead girls was always going to be better because they couldn't say no to anything that you asked them. If he'd skipped straight to killing that bitch then he'd have saved himself a lot of work and money, and he'd still have got exactly the same thing in the end. It was just like fucking critters with his brothers. The thrill of the hunt adding a little edge to his arousal.

The killing did nothing for him, as it turned out. He knew some of his kin revelled in it—they had a real blood lust—but for him, it was as empty as any other act. A necessary step to get what he wanted, perhaps, but not something to be remembered or cherished. He cared so little about this girl, that when the time came to confess for his crimes, he couldn't even recall her name. Her body still lies somewhere out in the woods of Virginia, undiscovered in an unmarked grave or dug up and torn apart by scavengers. If her family missed her, there is no sign of it in the official records.

Later, Henry's account of this crime shifted. He described an entirely different set of circumstances, a completely different girl whom he had picked up at random from a bus stop, beaten unconscious and taken off into the woods to rape. He claimed that she awoke during the act of penetration, and tried to fight back, prompting him to choke her unconscious. Later still, he recanted both of these confessions claiming that he had never killed anyone at all.

The truth was always a moving target for Henry Lee Lucas, and with no body and no forensic evidence to examine, it is impossible to know which of the three versions of reality actually happened and which were spawned by deception and confusion. More recently, this confession has been linked to the disappearance of seventeen-year-old Laura Burnley, but no additional evidence has ever been produced to confirm that link.

Eventually, Henry's crimes caught up to him. Not the murder, nor the numerous sexual assaults that he had committed over the years before finally coming to his murderous revelation, but the petty theft that had been his only income. In 1954, he was convicted of several counts of burglary and sentenced to six years imprisonment. Rather than sending him to an adult jail and exposing him to the privations he'd be likely to face there, Henry was committed to Beaumont Training School for Boys.

It was not a successful placement. He was intensely disruptive and rebellious, and he seemed entirely incapable of absorbing any of the lessons that the school tried to instil in him. One of the staff later described him as 'a boy gone feral'.

Within a month, he made a successful escape from the institution, running all the way back to Blacksburg and the searing contempt of Viola. He had nowhere to vent his frustrations for the month inside that institution; nobody to be the recipient of his vile carnal interests.

One of his nieces, from an older half-sister, had been left in Viola's care. She was twelve years old and more than a little terrified of her wild-looking teenage uncle. That fear was well founded—he raped her out behind the chicken coop that had served as his home throughout his childhood, and threatened to slit her throat like a squirrel's if she said so much as a word about it to anyone.

Despite all the signs that he was a sociopath, Henry still clung to family as something sacrosanct. Despite all of the evil that he inflicted on them and that his mother had inflicted on him back in her day, he still wouldn't willingly kill his niece, even though their only connection was a tenuous one through genetics rather than any sort of bonding.

His well-thought-out plan of running away from the low-security prison may have gotten him home, but it was only a day later that he was picked up by the local sheriff and handed back over to the state. Once he had been committed to an adult prison, court proceedings went ahead and more years were slapped onto his sentence. But by that point, Henry didn't give a damn. Prison was heaven.

For the first time in his life, he had a bed of his very own. He got to eat hot meals for the first time, and he was guaranteed them, too, no matter whether he worked hard or not. There was no Earthly paradise for Henry that was sweeter than his time in that jail.

Where before he had only his family to educate him in the ways of crime, now he had hundreds of men, all arrested for a wide variety of crimes, with their expertise at his disposal. Even so, he didn't actively seek out any new criminal enterprises to indulge in, preferring instead to enjoy the good life while he could.

Even his appearance improved while he was imprisoned, with the doctors taking one look at his empty eye socket and immediately fitting him with a glass prosthetic to prevent the constant infections that had plagued him. In an instant he went from hideous back to merely unpleasant; some might even say rugged.

There are many men who indulge in opportunistic bisexuality when their environment demands it. Prisons, military forces, anywhere that there is segregation by gender, there are men or women finding love amongst their fellow captives. This was the case for Henry. While he'd shown a preference for women outside of prison, this was primarily due to a lack of education. He was not aware that men could have sex together, but once he had made that discovery, his little slice of heaven got that little bit more heavenly. Needless to say, he became extremely popular among his fellow inmates.

That popularity rippled out through the prison, and with his new friends and support network, Henry began to flourish, becoming a whole person for the first time in his life, developing a personality and a little bit of the charm that would serve him so well as time went on. He began to write to women through the prison pen-pal service, and while he lacked the artistry of some of his fellow prisoners when it came to pretty words, his honesty and almost child-like excitement to receive news from the outside world made him fairly popular in that regard, too.

By the time that he was offered early parole for good behaviour, Henry was actually well on his way towards being an at least partially reformed character. For the first time in his life, he believed that he could be somebody, that he could make something out of his life. As long as he was held out of the reach of his family, and more specifically the poisonous influence of Viola, Henry had a chance at living a real life.

The Dying Light

In 1959, at the age of twenty-three, Henry was granted early release and headed out into the world. Now that he'd experienced positive relationships, he had enough perspective to shy away from Viola on his own. Instead of trailing back to Virginia and the hovel that had been his home throughout his childhood, he went to stay with his half-sister, Opal, in Tecumseh, Michigan.

Henry had a great many relatives across the states, and despite everything that had happened in his life to date, almost all of them would have been quite willing to play host to him until he got back on his feet. Opal had never been much closer to Henry than any of his other relatives. Apart from being the girl for whom the dress he'd spent so much time in as a child had been bought for, they didn't have any special connection. Even so, she welcomed her little brother into her home with open arms and no questions about his plans and prospects for the future. He was hardly the first in their family to have spent a little time in prison, and he surely wouldn't be the last, so there was no judgement in that regard either. The fact that Opal worked long shifts at all hours certainly helped to make their cohabitation go smoothly, as did the disciplined cleaning habits that prison had instilled in him.

Even so, he had little intention of overstaying his welcome.

There was already another home calling to Henry. The home of a woman who had already announced her willingness to be his bride in many letters before his release.

Stella was not a prize catch in the eyes of most of the population of Michigan. There was a reason that she had turned to the prisons of the world in her search for love. She was not considered to be a particular beauty, her personal habits sometimes verged on the odious, and she fully expected to rely on Henry to fuel her drinking habit once they were wed. None of that mattered to Henry. For the first time since he was a little boy, he had found someone to love; someone who seemed to love him back.

For the love of this woman, Henry was ready to turn his back on his criminal past, to set aside the horrors of his childhood, and to at least attempt to become a decent person. Prison had given him the freedom to become a better man, but in Stella, he found a reason to want to. He set about finding work in the city—real paying work rather than just another opportunity for crime. While he wasn't going to be winning anyone over with his employment history or skills, there were plenty of manufacturing jobs where intelligence and skills were pretty low on the list of priorities, which consisted of 'turns up to work at least fifty per cent of the time' and 'has arms to pull the levers.' Even the fact that he was a felon didn't count against him, as he had just enough sense to lie about where he'd been over the course of the past decade.

With his life on track, he made his play for the kind of normal life that had always eluded him, getting down on one knee in the Michigan snow and proposing to Stella after he'd picked her up for their regular date. With delight, she said yes, and they headed out to get thoroughly drunk to celebrate.

On his return home for the night, he shared all of his good news with Opal, who was delighted to hear that her little brother was finally getting his life on track. The very next morning, while he was still sleeping off the festivities, she started making rounds in the family to spread the joy.

When the news reached Viola, she was less than pleased that it had come to her via a third party, and even less pleased that Henry had been out of jail for weeks without even stopping by to inform her.

In the intervening years since Henry's arrest, life had taken a downward turn for Viola. After she shot a client in the leg with her shotgun for talking back to her, the trade from town finally began to slow. Her ever-advancing age did nothing to tempt Johns in, and even her longstanding arrangement with Uncle Bernie soon fell apart in the face of the economics of her declining appeal. In short, she was broke, unloved, and alone—not for the first time in her life, but certainly for the rest of her life. All of her children had gotten the hell out as soon as they were old enough to run from her, and they had scattered across the United States, some making it as far as the opposite coast in their desperation to escape her reach.

As she went into decline, Viola settled upon a course of action. She would need one of her children to come back and live with her, to pay for her and care for her in her advancing years. Preferably someone weak-willed with no real ties outside of the family. Someone she could browbeat and bully into subservience with the barest amount of effort so that she could get back to relaxing and enjoying the produce of Anderson's old moonshine still until death finally took her.

Naturally, her favourite choice for this joyless task was her youngest, and most broken, son. Henry getting his life together, neglecting what she saw as his duties and hiding from her all interfered with her plans. So, for the first time in many years, Viola left the old log cabin, went down into town, and boarded a bus for Michigan.

She arrived in Tecumseh just after nightfall on January 12, 1960, and it didn't take her long to track her daughter down. Opal was delighted to inform her mother that she had to go to work the night shift, and therefore wouldn't be around to entertain her, but old Viola made it excessively clear that she wasn't here to see her daughter anyway. Her sights were set on Henry. So, with only a little twinge of guilt, Opal sent Viola his way. Only a few minutes in her mother's company had been more than enough for Opal. But the way that she saw it, he was the one who had brought the old woman down on them, so he should be the one to suffer through her visit the most.

Henry and Stella were out at a bar when Viola arrived, having a proper, formal celebration of their engagement with her friends and his co-workers. The new Henry, the outgoing, happy Henry who was going places and making a life for himself, shrank back into the shell of the old Henry at her approach. He was struck almost mute as Viola stormed in, and it was only when Stella prompted him that he explained. 'Momma.'

Stella tried to greet Viola warmly, but she received nothing but a sneer in return. 'I ain't got no time for you. I'm here to see my boy.'

She pushed past Stella and took a hold of Henry's shirt. 'What're you thinking boy? What filthy little thoughts are sliming around in that head of yours?'

He couldn't even meet her eye. 'I'm getting married, Momma.'

'Ain't no woman ever going to marry you. You're scum. Girls would toss out their boots if they got you smeared on 'em. Nobody could ever love a dirty little bastard like you, Henry Lee. Not nobody.' She leaned in close enough that he could smell her foul breath. 'Not once I tell 'em all about what you did. Once they know what you are, ain't nobody is ever going to love you.'

For the first time in months, his missing eye began to weep. 'Momma, please.'

'Please? I don't remember you never saying please to me before. Don't remember you saying please to none of them animals or them children you put your dirty little pecker into, neither. Did you think I didn't know Henry? Did you think nobody knew what you were up to, you filthy little bastard? You monster!'

He wasn't sobbing, but water was streaming down both of his cheeks. 'Here is what you're going to do, Henry. You're going to say goodbye to your little whore here. You're going to pack up your shit. Then, you're going to get on the bus with me and we'll be going back home to where we belong. Wouldn't you like that, Henry? To come home like you was meant to when you got out of jail?'

Somewhere deep inside the crumbling husk of Henry Lee Lucas, that last dying spark of hope flared up. It drove him to stand up to his mother for the first time. 'No, momma. No. Stella loves me. We're getting married.'

From this close, Viola's shriek was almost deafening. 'No? You don't say no to me, boy!'

She started slapping him at first, then switched to closed fists when it became clear he was just going to cower and take it. 'You don't say no to me. You don't never say no to your momma.'

Her fists were a blur, blending the present moment with all the hundreds of beatings just like this that Henry had taken before. But then, suddenly, it stopped. Like an avenging angel, Stella had risen up between Viola and her prey. The two women were screaming at each other, shouting over the other. Neither woman getting an opportunity to get a word in edgewise. Still, Stella stood her ground, keeping her body between Henry and his mother like a shield. 'You can't treat him that way!'

Viola shrieked right back. 'Don't need no trash like you telling me how I can treat my boy!'

Then her fists were up all over again. If Stella had thought sanity or general decency were going to protect her from the wrath of Viola, then she was sadly mistaken. While there had been a grim fury on the old woman's face as she beat her son to the ground, it was now replaced with dark delight. This was what she had wanted from the very beginning. All that she had wanted was to come find the little bitch that would dare to take her baby boy away from her and knock her teeth out. It was like a dream come true.

She had knocked Stella to the ground and started kicking her before the bar's bouncer finally intervened, dragging the raving old woman out of the bar and ejecting her into the snow-covered street.

Henry rushed to his beloved's side and tried to sweep Stella up in his arms, but she pushed him away. She scrambled out of reach as his grasping hands came after her again. She was horrified to see this side of Henry. She had known some small part of his sordid history from their time as pen-pals, but she had no idea of the monster that had raised him, nor how powerless he was against her. With her hands still shaking, she stripped the engagement ring from her finger and threw it at Henry. She sobbed. 'I can't deal with this. That thing was your mother? That is what you came from? I can't marry you. This is just too much.'

Her friends swooped down on her, helped her back to her feet and formed a protective bubble of bodies around their fallen friend to keep Henry's grasping, begging, and pleading away from her. Somewhere in the press of bodies and the hubbub, Stella managed to escape him unseen.

To her friends, she said that she just needed some time to think things over. And after the initial shock had passed, it seems likely that she would have welcomed Henry back into her life. She would never get that opportunity, though. That train had already come off the rails, the passengers just didn't realise it yet.

He sat in the bar until they turned the lights out, drinking to numb the pain of his face and his heart, toying with his penknife the way that he always did when he was distressed. Flicking it open and shut with his thumb. He was blind drunk by the time they forced him into the streets, drunk and maudlin in a way that he wasn't accustomed to. He knew that he was sad about Stella leaving him, he knew he was sad about the way his mother treated him, but he didn't make the mental connection to the better life that he had planned for himself. He didn't understand that Stella being scared off by his mother was just the beginning of the death throes of his dream of a normal life.

He let himself into Opal's apartment without knocking. He knew that she was working all night, and it wasn't like any of the Lucas boys had ever had any trouble getting around a lock. He felt unnaturally heavy as he trudged to bed, like there was something huge and heavy hanging over him that he just couldn't see.

It was about a half-hour later that he woke to the steady drumming of a broom handle on his skull. Viola loomed over him like a nightmare that had followed him up from sleep. She was roaring and swinging for all that she was worth with the broom, and each blow set off fireworks in his half-drunk skull.

'Disrespecting me! Running around with some whore! Talking back to his momma!' Every bark punctuated with another strike.

He rolled out of bed trying to shield his head and scrambled past Viola into the living room as she went on raining blows all over his bare back. 'Momma, stop! Momma, stop!'

Begging had never worked before and it didn't start working now. Viola was relentless. She hit him with the broom until it snapped, then she switched to wild slaps. All of Henry's hopes and dreams were crushed under that flurry of wild swipes. She spat on him. Cursed him. Did everything that she could to remind him that he belonged in the dirt at her feet grovelling for attention. She could not see the man that he had become—in her eyes he would always be the snivelling little nothing, begging for her scraps. With each blow, she drove him back, drove him further and further inside himself until he began to believe it, too. Until there was nothing left of Henry except fear, pain, and despair. Until he finally reached the limits of his humanity and stepped over the precipice into raw animal instinct.

He didn't even notice his fist moving until it had already happened. It was a clumsy, wild swing that caught his mother in the neck rather than the jaw. Whatever he'd done was enough, though. Viola tumbled to the floor of the dark apartment, unconscious, or at least stunned long enough for Henry to make his escape. He bolted out of the front door without ever looking back or looking down. If he had, he might have noticed that his penknife was still in his hand, sticky with blood, and that he'd fallen asleep before folding it shut again.

He ran out into the street, hotwired the nearest car, and fled Michigan, still half-dressed and wild with terror.

Regressed as he was to his childhood state by Viola's last round of abuse, it should come as no surprise that he reverted to the behaviours of childhood, too. He knew he'd done something wrong, even if he couldn't fully grasp the magnitude of his own actions. He knew that his mother was going to be furious and that delaying would only ensure that his punishment was so much worse than it had to be.

Henry drove through the night, all the way back to Blacksburg, Virginia. He fled all the way back to the cabin and squatted down on that dirt floor, sobbing and waiting for his mother to come home and punish him. Cowering in dread, but certain that this was the right thing to do. That his being here would please his mother. That she might go gentle with him because he'd done this to placate her fury.

He was there for a full day before he realised that something was wrong. But even so, he crept out of the cabin cautiously, fully expecting her wrath to descend on him the moment he stepped out into the sunlight. She must be waiting for him to come back to Opal's apartment. He felt so stupid for thinking she'd come here instead of staying put. Stupid, stupid, stupid. Just like she'd always said he was. He climbed back into his borrowed car and started the long drive back to Tecumseh, but he only made it as far as Toledo, Ohio, before the local sheriff pulled him over on an outstanding warrant. It was only once they'd secured him properly that they told him what he was even being arrested for. The murder of Viola Lucas.

Their version of the story was repeated to him in excruciating detail to force his confession. After his mother awoke him in the middle of the night to continue the argument he had started back in the bar, he had taken his knife—the knife that he still had in his possession when they arrested him—and stabbed her in the throat with it. She had not died quickly. In fact, the tiny cut that he had inflicted had barely even nicked the artery. The blood had not drained from her body in a great rush. It had trickled out drop by drop while his mother lay abandoned and alone on the floor of a strange apartment in a strange city. It took all night for her to bleed to death. But by the time Opal had returned home from her long night shift, it was over.

At first, Henry tried to explain that he hadn't known the knife was open, that he'd forgotten it was in his hand but that story was too dubious to even justify a response beyond contempt. Next, he tried to argue that it was self-defence, and the forensic evidence certainly supported that interpretation to a degree. Henry was covered in bruises, the broken broom handle was found lying just out of Viola's reach, and her history of violence could certainly be taken into account. But nobody could believe that a young, healthy ex-convict in his physical prime could not prevent a woman in her seventies from attacking him without resorting to murder.

In Michigan, he stood trial for his crime, and the jury was even less inclined to believe his pleas of innocence than the police had been. They did not believe the prosecution's claim that the murder was premeditated, but they absolutely believed that Henry intended to kill Viola when he hit her. Some guilty part of Henry had to admit the truth in that sentiment, too. In that moment, as much as he loved his mother, he had wanted her dead. She had taken everything from him, and now, in one final act of spite, she took his freedom. He was sentenced to forty years imprisonment, eligible for parole in twenty. They had to carry him out of the courtroom, a broken husk of a man headed for Southern Michigan State Prison.

A Boy Named Sue

On March 5, 1947, another boy was born in barely more fortuitous circumstances. Jacksonville, Florida, was not the sterile sprawl that it would one day become in 1947. Beyond the reach of the central city hub, where all the traffic ran through, there were still communities living uncivilised lives within easy reach of the urban amenities. The Toole family lived in what would now be considered suburbia but was then just another development thrown up hastily and haphazardly to contain the latest influx of rural settlers hoping to escape their lives of poverty, and finding instead a whole new life of poverty waiting for them. Money was tight and liquor was plentiful—in short, it was a powder keg.

Ottis was not the healthiest child, suffering from severe epilepsy that sent him into grand mal seizures at the drop of a hat. After years of these seizures, a doctor eventually got involved, diagnosing the epilepsy but offering nothing in the way of treatment or preventative measures. An IQ test was administered to the boy at the time of examination, and he was discovered to have a mild mental disability, likely a result of brain damage following his seizures.

With the poor understanding of epileptic fits at the time, there were murmurs among the more religious fringes of the community that the boy was possessed. But pursuing an exorcism or any other kind of religious intervention would have required either one of his parents to give a damn about him.

From a very young age, Ottis's mother made it clear that she had wanted another daughter and had no use for a son. She dressed him almost exclusively in hand-me-down dresses from his older sisters, referred to him in public as a girl, and called him Susan at every opportunity.

Susan was by far not the prettiest girl in the Toole household, but she was the most defenceless. When Ottis's father entertained the other neighbourhood alcoholics, it was that five-year-old boy who was forced to tend them while his older sisters stayed well out of the way, fearful of the filthy old men and their groping hands. If he hadn't been wearing a dress the whole time, it is possible that they wouldn't have troubled him. If his father hadn't seen dollar signs the first time that a hand went up the boy's skirt to fondle him, the whole course of Ottis's life might have changed. But he did, and it wasn't. Ottis's father rented him out to his friends for a few cents a turn. It didn't matter how Ottis screamed or slapped at them. They were deep in their drink and the screams just added to their excitement.

After that first night, Ottis's father tried to prostitute the child again, but in the cold light of day, all of the drunken rapists saw their actions in a new light. Every once in a while, he would find someone new in town with the right proclivities, but Jacksonville was just a stop on the highway for most people—there wasn't a lot of return custom.

Despite the infrequency of his prostitution, the knowledge that 'Little Susie' had been a whore completely changed the already abusive familial relationships that he had. He was treated like filth by his devout mother like it was his fault that men had held him down and raped him while his father laughed. News travelled fast around the neighbourhood, and the girls who had once looked on him as an oddity and a cause for pity now considered his enforced cross-dressing to be a sign of depravity. Sexual assault and molestation became an everyday occurrence, not just by a couple of the neighbourhood men who had that inclination but also by the girls, including his sisters and mother who would grab at him under his skirt while making disparaging comments about his manhood.

One day, while fleeing from this horrific treatment, Ottis ran out onto the porch of the family home, even though it had been disused for many years due to rot. His weight was just enough to punch through the sodden wood and he fell right onto his face. In itself, this would not have been a memorable moment of misery in Ottis's life—pain was not unusual to him. What was unusual was the exposed nail that the fall had driven right through his skull, two inches into his brain. His mother pulled it out without thinking twice, and suddenly his usual seizures became much more frequent.

Ottis's father left one day without a word to anyone, one spring evening in 1957. He had been an alcoholic for years and a travelling salesman for longer, so it wasn't all that much of a surprise to anyone involved. He'd always drunk more than he made, so there wasn't a financial strain involved in the abandonment. But without his calming influence, Ottis's mother became more and more zealous in her persecution of the boy on a religious basis. It is likely that this would have reached a lethal conclusion if it weren't for the intervention of a more powerful figure in the family cosmology than God himself: Ottis's grandmother.

Where others saw his fits and sexual history as signs of demonic influence, Ottis's grandmother saw… exactly the same. But while to the Christian community of Jacksonville this was considered to be a terrible thing, his grandmother and her fellow Satanists took it to be a blessing.

She took Ottis under her wing, calling him her 'Devil-Child' and curbing the worst of his mother's excesses with the application of some good old-fashioned fear of the devil. She dressed him in boy's clothing, embraced his oddities as signs of infernal intervention, and cared for the boy in her way. With that care came a new set of obligations for the child. No longer did he have to serve as a house servant in his mother's paltry home. He had a higher calling now, and a far grander master to perform for.

There is a great deal of debate about how much of Ottis's reported childhood of satanic rites actually occurred, and how much was conjured from his fevered imagination. The self-mutilation that he later described was certainly corroborated by the patterns of scars on his body, and there were many reports of grave-robbing that line up neatly with his described activities. But the stories of human sacrifice that he claimed to have witnessed and the cannibalistic feasts—an inversion of the Catholic sacrament—have no evidence to support them. There were certainly missing people around Jacksonville at the time, and it is possible that some of them fell under the blade of some cultist, but it is just as likely that these stories were mere inventions of Ottis during one of the phases when he was trying to concoct a greater meaning to his actions; much greater than simple hedonistic pleasure.

Puberty hit Ottis hard and it hit him early. By the age of twelve, in 1959, he began showing hints of stubble, and he was forced to admit that he was indeed different from the other boys, who were now no longer a source of fear and confusion for Ottis and had instead become the cause for unexpected arousal.

Never one for lying, Ottis was honest with his family about his burgeoning homosexuality, even talking a little with his sisters about a boy whom he had been maintaining a relationship within the neighbourhood. The news was not well received. The fervour with which his mother had tormented him in his early years returned threefold. He was beaten at every opportunity on the most spurious of evidence, and before long he began to sleep in abandoned buildings rather than take the risks that came with returning home.

There were no shortage of abandoned houses in Jacksonville, with the rural families trying to start over discovering rapidly that opportunity did not await them there, so Ottis had little trouble finding places to stay in night after night. The only thing that troubled him in the beginning was the cold. It took him longer than he would have liked to admit to work out how to build a fire in the houses where he slept, but even once he had worked out the basic mechanics of it, he was still sloppy. Less than a month after setting his first fire, he lost control of one and it burned down the house where he had intended to spend the night.

Something in his brain clicked at the sight of that fire. It was like the flames were the catalytic agent that his burgeoning sexual awakening required to complete its formation. He began to set fires more frequently, more deliberately. He became aroused when he set those fires, and before long, every house that he slept in went up in smoke the next morning. The fires became the reason, more than his safety, that he slunk around abandoned houses at night.

By 1961, at the age of fourteen, Ottis had abandoned any hope of living a normal life. All of his days he had been called a freak, a deviant, a monster, and he had never seen any evidence to the contrary. He dropped out of school, where his contributions were barely missed, and began a career of extremely petty crime: selling along salvaged goods from abandoned houses before he torched them, panhandling, and eventually offering his services as a prostitute.

There were few gay bars in Jacksonville, but the fourteen-year-old Ottis became a regular at every single one of them. Initially, it wasn't out of a desire for trade, it was out of a desire for companionship. He desperately wanted someone like him, someone who could understand what he was going through. Instead, the men took one look at him and judged him. He was poor, a little bit dirty, in a way that wasn't entirely unappealing, and there was only one thing that a boy like that could have been after. They might not have been able to offer him the understanding he so desperately craved, but sex and cash were readily available. Ottis took what he could get.

There was a small gay community in Jacksonville, but a

disproportionate percentage of that population was comprised of male prostitutes, thanks to all of the travellers passing through. While they didn't appreciate the extra competition that Ottis presented, they weren't made of stone. When the confused boy found his way into their care, they did what they could to keep him right. The local gay scene didn't like to see its members preying on the community, so it wasn't long before Ottis learned to pick up his clients from truck-stops and the like rather than lingering in bars. He made a clear division between his working life, where he had sex with travellers out by the roadside, and his extremely tenuous social life spent drinking and flirting in the gay bars in town.

One night, Ottis was picked up by a travelling salesman. That was enough to make him uncomfortable in itself, tangling up with his memories of his father's abuse, before the situation had even begun to develop. Not all of Ottis's clients were particularly kind to him, or even complimentary, but he was very rarely frightened for his life. This client was different. The moment that he got Ottis into the car, he tore off down the freeway without a moment's pause, laughing all the way. In the middle of nowhere, ten minutes out of town, he swerved off the road and slammed on the brakes, flinging the unsecured Ottis into the dashboard and knocking the air out of his lungs. He dragged the dazed boy out of the car and forced him down onto all fours in the glare of the headlights. There was no pause for preparation, no hint of humanity at all. He raped Ottis, taking delight in the boy's screams and sobs. 'Go on, yell. Nobody is going to hear you out here.'

When he was finished, the salesmen tossed a handful of change onto Ottis's prone form and staggered back towards his car, fumbling with his trousers and laughing all the way. He stopped in front of the car to light a cigarette and looked back at the night's prey with another little giggle. He stopped laughing abruptly when he realised that the boy was gone. He turned and made a dash for the driver's side, but Ottis got there first. Blood, and worse, trickled down his bare legs to stain the upholstery as he slammed the door shut, but he didn't give a damn.

Ottis slammed the car into reverse, then hammered it forward into the salesman with as much acceleration as he could muster. The thump of the impact would have been loud enough to alert people for a mile around, but the salesman had made sure that they were somewhere that nobody could hear them. Ottis reversed back over the man and got the car back up to the side of the road. He got out to retrieve his trousers and to check that the salesman was dead. He was. His skull had been crushed to a pulp. Another man might have spat on his rapist, but a darker passion than vengeance had enveloped Ottis. He reached down and masturbated over the corpse of his first victim until he had, what he would later describe as, the best orgasm of his life.

With that done, he took whatever cash he could find, got himself dressed, and drove back to the edge of town before abandoning the car in one of the hundreds of disused lots—his first murder complete, and the connection between killing and sex firmly cemented in his mind. The last puzzle piece of sex, pain, and fire finally slotting into place: death.

For almost a full three years, Ottis lived the life of a vagrant teenage prostitute, sleeping in a different abandoned house each night, staying well clear of his family, in particular his grandmother, who still held an almost unnatural sway over him. It is entirely possible that he could have gone on living like that on the fringes of Jacksonville forever if it hadn't been for a state governor who had decided that being hard on crime and immorality was going to secure him the votes he needed for an upcoming election.

The seventeen-year-old was arrested by plainclothes police during a sting at one of his regular pickup spots in August of 1964. They couldn't prove that he was engaged in prostitution, primarily because the evidence that they often used to convict prostitutes was possession of prophylactic devices such as condoms, and Ottis lacking any sex education beyond the mechanical had never even heard of them. He received six months in jail for 'loitering with intent,' even if they couldn't prove what that intent might have been.

Much like Henry Lee Lucas, Ottis found that his time in prison was far from the punishment that he had imagined it might be. He didn't have to work for his supper, and the only sex that he was having was fully consensual, which was more than he could ever have said before. Most importantly, his imprisonment severed any ties that he still had to the community in Jacksonville and filled him with new confidence that he could survive outside of his family's shadow.

When he was released, Ottis had the whole world at his feet, nothing to tie him down, and the whole of America as his backyard. He stole himself a car from just a couple of streets away from where the prison bus had dropped him off and set out to explore this brave new world. Drifting, panhandling, and prostituting his way across the southern states, under the radar of law enforcement, and slipping between all official records for years.

Making the Perfect Killer

Henry Lee Lucas was in a pit of despair when he returned to prison for the second time. Jackson State Penitentiary in southern Michigan was everything that his first prison had not been: filthy, underfunded, and full of men driven past the edge of reasonable behaviour by their circumstances. Fights were frequent, overcrowding was prevalent, and Henry, lost in his own thoughts, did nothing to take the initiative and establish a place for himself in the ecosystem.

All of the progress that he had been making towards a normal life was in tatters; any hope that he ever had of humanity had been stripped away. Whether he had killed his mother by accident or with intention was irrelevant—he was still the man who had killed his own mother. The rest of his family had been surprisingly quick to forgive him—either because they believed his story of accidents and self-defence or because they were simply glad that the monstrous woman was finally out of their lives—but the one person who could never forgive the crime was Henry himself. Viola had taken very little time to instil values in Henry, but the one that had been hammered home time and again was the importance of respecting and obeying your parents. Henry had broken the one sacred rule that had ever been given to him and he could not live with the terrible shame.

His first suicide attempt was very nearly a success. He fashioned a noose for himself out of his bedclothes and hung himself in his cell for almost twenty minutes before a patrolling guard noticed. The makeshift rope had not been tight enough to properly cut off the blood supply to his brain, just interrupt it badly enough to render him unconscious, and possibly add a little to the extensive brain damage that he had already suffered. The injuries were minor enough that the doctor didn't even report the suicide attempt—too much paperwork and too much effort all around setting up a watch for some nobody.

Henry was returned to the general prison population, went through the motions obediently to keep the guards happy, and about two months later, when he had recovered his strength and he was certain that nobody was watching him, he tried it again. He got the rope right the second time around, the sheets twisted tight enough to bite right into his neck, to knock him out instantly instead of the agonising, lingering gasps for air that the first suicide attempt had brought. What he hadn't accounted for was a changed guard rotation. He was only dangling for two minutes before the guards found him and hauled him off to the medical block. This time, there was no question about reporting it. It had gone from one foolish mistake to a pattern of behaviour, and a pattern of behaviour meant that Henry Lee Lucas could be foisted off on some other overcrowded government-run facility instead of remaining their persistent problem.

The recipient of this burden would be Ionia State Mental Hospital. It was there that the complex web of misery that comprised the mental state of Henry Lee Lucas finally came under some scrutiny. When asked about his suicide attempts, he eventually admitted that he had heard his mother's voice telling him to do it. Day and night. Even in death, Viola would not leave her son in peace. There was no prescription for guilt or ghosts available in Ionia State. Nor was there any real way to help a patient who had been raised from birth to keep every detail of his life a secret for his own protection, someone with a history of criminality so brutal that divulging secrets in therapy would likely lead to the death sentence or life imprisonment. All that they could do was treat that sole symptom, the hallucinations, as though it were the sum of his problems.

He received an extensive regimen of sedatives to keep him calm and compliant during the rest of his therapy, and for what the doctors termed 'schizoid delusions' he received weekly electro-convulsive therapy. In essence, triggering the grand mal seizures that had plagued him since childhood in the grim hope that eventually he would wake up with his brain 'reset' to normal.

With his brain damage suitably aggravated by the electrocution, and the more aggressive elements of his personality more or less entirely suppressed by the medication that he was on, Henry became one of the favourite patients of the staff. They soon recognised the spark of intelligence still burning in Henry, carefully tempered by the haze of sedation, and set him to work in the filing room, organising the files of the other patients. The hospital was home to some of the worst criminals in the local states. Those who had committed crimes so grievous that they were considered to be beyond the actions of the sane. A full account of every one of their crimes was contained within the files that were handed over to Henry, along with a full explanation of all the holes in the criminal justice system that these criminals had been able to slip through, ensuring that their crime sprees could continue long beyond the point that logic would suggest that they could be stopped.

Sitting alone in the stuffy file room for days on end, Henry got an education in how to avoid detection and capture; a masterclass from some of the world's most despicable criminals and most competent law enforcement. He discovered that moving from one state to another could completely stymie an investigation as the different departments failed to communicate properly. He discovered the various means of countering forensic investigation, by destroying the body of a murder victim or moving them around to rob the police of corroborating evidence. Ultimately, he learned that patterns were the enemy of every mass murderer. Using the same methods to hunt victims. Using the same methods to dispatch them. These were the amateur mistakes of lesser killers who soon got caught. By moving around, by destroying evidence, by switching the mode of murder, Henry slowly realised he could go for years without the police ever drawing any connection between his crimes. So far, he had committed two murders, and only the one, where there was an obvious and direct familial connection, had ever caught up with him. Randomised victim selection was added to his list of methods to avoid capture.

At this point, all of this was entirely academic. He had no intention of committing any further crimes. Indeed, by the time that he was released from prison, he expected that he would be too old to pursue any of the pleasures that had once formed the backbone of his existence. His sentence to forty years imprisonment had not been lessened by his transfer to the hospital. If anything it had been lengthened. Now, he would not be free until he was judged by the medical staff to no longer be a danger to himself and others—something that Henry knew in his heart would never happen.

He was, at his core, a killer. Now that he had a few years to think about the death of his mother, he accepted that his part in it was no coincidence. He had always had the instinct to kill buried underneath the mesh of terrors that had been his childhood. The fact that it had only come to the fore a couple of times in his life was more thanks to a lack of opportunity and luck on the part of his potential victims than on any sort of restraint. He had broken the only rule that had ever been laid down for him and walked away from it without consequences. He was truly free to do whatever he wished. If it weren't for the constraints of imprisonment, he had absolutely no doubt that he would kill again, and again, and again; for his own amusement, for his own advancement, maybe even just for the sake of seeing someone die.

It was a small comfort to him that he was never going to be faced with making the decision of who lived and died. At least until ten years into his sentence, when he was suddenly informed that he was being released.

'There's got to be a mistake. I ain't even up for parole for another ten.'

The doctor looked up from his clipboard, calm and assessing. 'There is no mistake, Mister Lucas. This facility is suffering from severe overcrowding, and you have shown a remarkable recovery in your time with us. Provided that you continue with the regimen of medication that is prescribed to you, I can see no reason that...'

Henry interrupted. 'I'll kill again. If you let me out of here, I swear I'll do it.'

'Mister Lucas,' the doctor sighed, 'you have shown no indication of any schizoid behaviours since undergoing your therapy, and it seems quite clear that the circumstances of your crime were... unique, to say the least.'

'No, doc. They weren't. Ain't ever going to be a shortage of necks and knives. If you send me out there, why, I'll leave a body on your doorstep.'

The doctor finally looked uncomfortable under his thin veneer of professionalism. 'Regardless of your feelings on this matter, I'm afraid that the decision has already been made, at a higher pay grade than mine. Tomorrow morning you will walk out of here a free man, Mister Lucas. I suggest you use this time to say your goodbyes to any friends and to turn your mind to more positive avenues. Consider profitable ways that you could make use of your freedom. The ways that your newfound clarity might help others.'

His psychological profile listed off a wide variety of symptoms that could have been tied to just as many different disorders, but the majority of his issues were attributed to head trauma alone—indeed, one psychologist said that Henry was fundamentally healthy except for being 'exceptionally needy' as a result of his childhood neglect.

The very next morning, on August 22, 1970, with crushing inevitability, Henry was released. This is, once again, where the reality that he described in his confessions and the reality that could be proven, diverge. Within sight of Ionia State Mental Hospital, Henry would later claim to have met two girls, pretty teenagers of the sort that he had always preferred. He took them somewhere private, plied them with liquor and strangled them, one by one, while the other was distracted and insensible. He took his time, having sex with their dead bodies through the night, then stole himself a car and drove out of town the next morning. No evidence can be found of this double homicide, and Henry later recanted his confession, but once again, there were a great many missing persons cases in the area that went unsolved. It isn't outside the realm of possibility that he committed these crimes and hid the evidence with sufficient skill that the bodies were never discovered. After all, he had just spent ten years studying criminology.

It would have made sense at this point for Henry to vanish entirely, to drift, as Ottis Toole had chosen to do, and to use his new specialised skills to gratify all of his darkest urges, but there was still one tie binding him to humankind. His family tree stretched out like kudzu across America, massive and complexly tangled. In this time of uncertainty, it was them that he turned to. For the next few years, Henry attached himself to his various cousins, uncles, half-brothers, half-sisters, and in-laws like a lamprey, living off each one for as long as they would tolerate until they eventually drove him off. It became a running joke in the family, with a warning call being sent out to all nearby relatives every time Henry was excised from one household that he would soon be on his way to another. Henry wasn't exactly loathed by his family. He had a pretty good temperament compared to the majority of the Lucas clan, he was relatively charming and provided that he was never left alone with anyone's children, there was never a problem. There was always one sure-fire way to be rid of Henry when the time came. All that anyone had to do was mention the death of Viola to stun him into sullen silence. He'd move on shortly after being reminded of his mother, without fail.

In 1971, he tangled with law enforcement once more, firstly for attempting to pick up a fifteen-year-old girl in his car, using a spiel about her boyfriend being angry at her to try and trick her into the vehicle. When that failed, she told the police about the incident and they promptly picked him up, only to discover that he was in possession of an illegal pistol; a violation of his parole. This earned him a fresh four-year stint in a Michigan prison. For Henry, this was a return to form, a little jog of his memory about just how comfortable regular hot meals and an actual bed could be. It was enough to convince him that he might like to settle down for a time. He turned to the prison pen-pal system all over again, finding an inexplicably willing woman named Betty in Port Deposit, Maryland.

It took him quite some time to discover exactly what was wrong with Betty. Nobody looking for love behind bars was doing so because they had a buffet of options in the outside world. But unlike Stella, Betty did not seem to be one of the dregs of society like Henry. Eventually, she admitted to having two pre-teen daughters. But if she had expected that to put off her new beau, she was sadly mistaken. He enquired after the girls extensively, restraining himself enough that his interest seemed to be parental rather than prurient. Betty thought that she had finally found herself a keeper.

In 1975, Henry had finished his sentence, and within only a few hours of his release, he was on a bus to Maryland and the waiting sofa of his cousin Wade, who lived conveniently just a short drive from Port Deposit.

Betty was smitten with her new husband-to-be, and it took no time at all before Henry had secured himself a job at the local scrapyard, where it turned out all of his years breaking into cars had given him all of the vital skills required to break them down into their valuable component parts and even to rebuild them, ensuring enough stability that Betty was willing to commit when he asked her to marry him.

Without Viola's interference, planning rushed ahead and the ceremony—well attended by the Lucas clan's local branches—was conducted on December 5th of that very same year. The happy couple and Henry's two newly acquired step-daughters moved into a reclaimed mobile home in Lot C3 of Benjamin's Trailer Park in Port Deposit, Maryland.

Things started out quietly enough for Henry and Betty until he discovered that by driving around using his wrecker tags he could completely circumvent the DMV and police detection. That was when Betty found that he would go missing for days at a time, returning reeking of booze and the faint hints of perfume. She assumed that if he was philandering, some word would work its way back to her through the gossip network of the town. But whatever women Henry was going off with must have just vanished afterwards, because not a single rumour ever made it back to Betty.

Henry wasn't a perfect husband in any respect, but his drinking was usually reasonable. He paid for everything, he never lifted a hand to Betty, and he was fairly charming. The only thing that sat wrong with her was the way that the girls seemed to have chilled to him all of a sudden. In the beginning, the prospect of a new dad had been the cause of great excitement, and Henry had been almost overbearing in the kindness that he lavished on them. Gifts had been well received, but the attention had been what they were really craving. After so long with no father and a mother working long shifts to support them, Henry's open adoration of the girls had meant the world to them. Until suddenly it didn't.

She didn't know what she was looking at. She had no basis for comparison. Even when she realised that something was wrong, Betty couldn't put the pieces together, until one awful morning when she went to change the girl's sheets and saw the tell-tale silvery stains, rust-speckled by her daughters' blood.

Henry was late home that night, with the faint aroma of bourbon clinging to his lips when he tried to press them to Betty's cheek. She didn't raise a hand to him—she still didn't dare risk anything of the sort after the years of beatings from her first husband—but she pulled away and couldn't bite back the words that hissed out between her teeth. 'You bastard.'

Henry just smiled, the way that he always did, disarmingly and softly as a kiss. 'Now what am I meant to have done wrong this time?'

'I know what you done, Henry.' Betty was not charmed. Her voice was cold as ice. 'There's no question about what you done. I'm just trying to decide what to do about it.'

Her old husband had a look about him when he was about to start yelling. His eyes would narrow, his face would go red. Henry wasn't like that. He hardly raised his voice at all if truth be told, but in those moments when she'd seen him riled to anger it, was invisible. Whatever expression had been on his face before stayed plastered there like a mask while he acted out his fury. Even this close, Betty couldn't tell if he was insensible with drink, genuinely puzzled, or readying himself to knock out her teeth. The mystery of him had been appealing in the beginning, but now, nearly a year since he'd come out of that prison and into her life, it grated at her. He could have been thinking anything and she'd never even know.

His voice was almost unnaturally soft when he finally replied. 'I ain't got a clue what you're talking about, and I'll bet you ain't got a clue neither.'

It wasn't a threat exactly, just a statement of how Henry wanted the world to be. A broad accusation like Betty had just laid down would have had the mind of any normal person scrambling through all of the little secrets that they kept, trying to work out which one they had to protect. Henry was not so divided in his purpose. Every one of his secrets was enough to earn him a life sentence or worse. The only question on Henry's mind was the level of response that was going to be necessary.

'You've been touching my girls. You've been going in their rooms at night and...' She cut off in a strangled sob.

The tension in Henry loosened just a little. Was that all? That was hardly worth making a fuss over. 'I ain't never done nothing like that, Betty. I'd never lay a hand on either one of them girls. Swear on my mother.' If that was meant to be ironic, Betty would never know.

'I saw the...' She trailed off with a shudder. 'I spoke to the girls. They told me what you done. There's no point lying about it now. I know, and pretty soon everybody else is going to know, too. I'm going to tell the whole world that Henry Lucas touches little girls.'

There was another moment of his odd stillness. He then seemed to settle on a course of action. 'Now listen here. If you had enough with me, then that's fine. You just say the words and I'll pack up my bags. But don't go telling folks no lies about me just to drive me out. You want the trailer? It is all yours. But don't never go telling lies about how I touched them girls of yours. I took care of them like they was my own, and I don't know what sort of dirty stories you been planting in their heads, but I ain't going to sit here and listen to this.'

She was crying, gently, but maybe this was what was best for everyone. 'You better get out of here, Henry. I see you 'round here again, I'll tell everyone. I'll call the police. You hear?'

'I got my family reunion down Virginia way this weekend.' Henry was still speaking softly, still working the thought through. 'I'm going down there with Wade. We'll be gone a few days. Maybe that'll give you some time to think this over. Decide if you want to keep lying or if you want me around.'

She hissed. 'You're filth, Henry Lee Lucas. Worse than the dirt you walk on.'

'I'll bet you take that back too after you been missing me a couple days.' He gave her a glimpse of that old charming smile again. It didn't work, not even a little. 'Don't ever come back here. Not ever.'

The smile faded away to blankness. All emotion slipping out of his voice. 'Don't go ruining them girls' lives just to get one over on me.'

Betty shuddered. 'Get out, Henry! Get out!'

A road-trip with Henry was usually a fun time, and Wade had been looking forward to the run down to West Virginia. He was aghast to discover that his usually cheerful cousin had fallen into a dark mood.

It took a hundred miles before Wade's poking and prodding got Henry talking again, but once the flood gates were opened there was no shutting him up. 'Betty's trying to get rid of me. She's gone against me. She's telling all sort of nasty lies. Going to go spreading them lies around. Ruin my life. Evil bitch.'

No matter how Wade tried to change the subject, Henry just wouldn't stop. 'I can't go back there, cuz. I can't go back. Betty'll ruin everything if I do. Spread her filthy lies around. Make me look like a monster. I can't do it.'

This went on and on until they rolled to a halt in the traffic. A bridge was under repair up ahead, narrowing the road to just a single lane and causing the backup. Henry cranked down his window, still mumbling to himself about Betty.

'You talking to me, buddy?' There was a lorry parked alongside them, waiting for the chance to cross the bridge, a big freight hauler with the driver hanging half out the window.

'Just jawing to myself, mister.'

The trucker chuckled. 'Well, that's one way to make sure you don't get no surprises.'

Henry smiled up at him without even meaning to. He just looked at him for a while, then he finally asked. 'Where are you headed?'

There was a white-toothed grin under the trucker's moustache. 'I'm on my way to Shreveport, Louisiana. How about you?'

Henry glanced across at Wade, contemplated his options, and said, 'Well, I guess I'm heading to Shreveport, too, if you'll give me a ride?'

The trucker chuckled. 'Hell, I ain't got no company. Come on up here then.'

Just like that, Henry's brief attempt at normalcy fell to pieces all over again. He vanished from official records and began to drift. In Shreveport, his new friend gave him a stolen car to drive to Los Angeles, but it never quite made it there. Even in criminal circles, Henry became a ghost.

A Match Made in Hell

For a while, Henry Lee Lucas was nothing but a story. The one-eyed drifter of campfire tales. He travelled far and wide, with sightings of him now recorded in Wilmington, Delaware, and Hurst, Texas. He stopped for a while with Opal, who had forgiven him pretty readily for bringing murder to her doorstep when it came with the opportunity to be free of her mother forever, but stories gradually made their way through the family grapevine back to Opal.

He had been staying for a month with their other sister, Almeda, when she discovered that he was molesting her granddaughter, and sent him packing with the local sheriff on his heels. Opal had children of her own now, and as much as she might have cared for her goofy little brother, she wasn't blind nor stupid enough to let the same sort of situation develop there in Michigan.

All the doors that used to be open to him slammed shut as stories of his depravity managed to outpace him. His last real contact with his family was another visit to Almeda. She greeted him with a shotgun, but he insisted he wasn't there to see his grand-niece, nor even Almeda. He was there about scrapping work for her husband, who owned the local yard. While he was at the yard, he stole a partially refurbished truck and the wrecker's tags that would allow him to drive around in it without leaving an official record.

The next sign of Henry Lee Lucas's existence was towards the end of 1977 when he popped up very briefly in Beckley, West Virginia. Following some sort of injury, he found himself briefly hospitalised, and then unable to drift for a few months. So Henry did what he always had, found himself a simple woman to prey upon, and found the kind of job where a man of substantial strength could make some cash with no need for papers being filed. The woman in this case was a local legend named Rhonda Knuckles.

They say that men are attracted to women who remind them of their mother. And when presented with evidence like Rhonda Knuckles, it is hard to dispute that idea. She had more children than could be easily counted with more fathers than could be easily named—a veritable smorgasbord for a child predator like Henry Lee Lucas.

He found work in the local carpet warehouse, hauling product around and measuring it out for cutting and distribution, and he lingered for just a little while longer than he had intended to. Allegations of child molestation, not only from the Knuckles brood, but also from other children around town started up, and it was mentioned to Henry by his supervisor that the folks in these parts weren't overly attached to the letter of the law. There was an old lynching tree not far out of town that hadn't seen any use in some years, but it still looked sturdy enough to hold one body at least.

Henry left town the next morning in a borrowed pick-up truck, heading south and east to the one corner of the American South that hadn't yet served as his home.

By the spring of 1978, he had arrived in Florida. Flat broke and with no leads for work, he found himself standing in line at a soup kitchen in Jacksonville, Florida, which was where he bumped into the man who would become the centre of his world for the rest of his days.

The soft boy that Ottis had been was left long behind him. He bore the stubble and scars of a man now, looming over everyone around him at 6 feet, 8 inches. Henry fell into step with the lisping giant, fascinated by the juxtaposition of a clearly dangerous man and such effeminate mannerisms. Henry was no stranger to sex with men, but in prison and on the rough fringes of society where he'd dwelled, it had always been something secret, something shameful. Ottis had made homosexuality into a part of his personality, part of his identity. He had taken the thing that others would have used to shame him and worn it like armour. Henry could hardly take his eyes off the man.

To begin with, Ottis just took him for another closeted admirer, but after laying down a few hints that he would be amenable to spending some private time together, he was surprised to find that Henry genuinely seemed to want to be his friend. Neither man had ever had much luck or experience with friendship. Henry was too introverted and secretive to share much about himself, so those early days were spent trailing after Ottis as he went about his usual routine, rather than trying to seize control of the situation like he normally did.

There were two very specific moments in that first week that cemented the trust between the two men. The first was when Henry came with Ottis to visit his mother. She had died only two years previously, and every time that Ottis passed through Jacksonville he made sure to stop at her grave and pay his respects.

While Henry stood there, Ottis sank down onto the bare dirt and let out a sigh. 'It feels warm, you know? And if I just lay here for long enough, sometimes I can feel her moving underneath me. Like she's trying to give me a hug.'

The fact that both of them were haunted by their own mothers' ghosts was enough to convince Henry that the connection between them ran deeper. But he was still reticent to share any details of his own life, even though Ottis had now picked up on the underlying mystery of his new admirer and started prying at it. As evening rolled around, he asked Henry if he'd like to go for a drink, and ever his father's son, Henry most certainly did.

They made one brief stop at Ottis's car before they headed out for the night so that he could change. It was almost like a test, to see how far Henry could be pushed. A test that he passed with flying colours, both by openly admiring the other man's bare body as he stripped out of his dirty clothes and by voicing no objection when Ottis pulled on a sequinned dress.

In the first bar, they got a lot of dirty looks, and more than a few laughs, but nobody was deep enough in their drink to cause any trouble yet. Even in the second bar, Ottis was a source of amusement rather than anger. Henry found himself bobbing along in the other man's wake, enjoying his company and his sharp-tongued comments. It was only after the second bar, as they were heading towards the third, that the trouble started. Some local meathead hurled a mouthful of abuse at Ottis. The word 'abomination' came up. It only had time to come up once before Ottis was on the man, fists swinging wildly. The local had friends, and before Henry knew what he was doing, he was in a fist-fight in the streets, defending the honour of a man in a dress whom he'd met only a couple of days before. They held their own against that first crowd, but then a second wave of locals came pouring out of the bar and came after them. Henry had to grab Ottis by the arm and bodily drag him off the man whom he was beating to a bloody pulp. 'Come on, now. Ain't no trouble worth dying over.'

For one wild moment it seemed like Ottis was going to turn his unbridled rage on Henry, too, but then his eyes seemed to focus. He leaned in and gave him a kiss on the cheek, then the two of them ran for their life back to Ottis's car. There was only one man from the crowd of their attackers stupid enough to chase them down. Only one man consumed enough by hate that just the sight of a man in a dress made him think that he could take the two of them on. He caught up to them in an alleyway just a street from where they'd been heading, screaming slurs at the top of his lungs as he rounded the corner. The sight that awaited him was enough to steal the scream from his throat. Ottis had reached into his purse and pulled out a revolver. With a grunt of carnal delight, he pulled the trigger. Not just once, but six times. Stalking closer as the man fell to ensure every bullet hit its mark.

He turned back to Henry, eyes hazy with lust, blood splattered across his dress. 'You alright with that, sugar?'

Henry smiled right back at him. 'Most definitely.'

The Grand Tour

Their first meeting in Florida precipitated a rapid exit. Both Henry and Ottis were more than accustomed to skipping town ahead of trouble, and this time was no different. Except that it was. They weren't running off alone, scattering to the winds—they were together. For the first time in their lives, Henry and Ottis had both found someone who could know the entirety of them and not flinch away in fear. It was a terribly empowering experience for both of them, to know that they were not alone in the universe, to know for the very first time that they were not the sole recipients of minds completely different from those of everyone around them. In the sweaty confines of Ottis's car, the two of them traded stories of their lives, punctuated by their murders.

Ottis had managed to avoid detection as a murderer up until this point simply because his drifting habits happened to coincide perfectly with the 'best practices' that Henry had learned from his time reading sealed records and crime reports. He would commit a few crimes here and there, still relying almost entirely on prostitution and petty larceny to support his low-cost lifestyle. But by the time the local police caught wind of him, he had already moved on. Once or twice he had been arrested and jailed for lesser crimes, but because none of the justice departments around the country communicated with one another, each time he was caught, it was treated as his first offence rather than a pattern of criminal behaviour. On top of that, his incredibly effete mannerisms really helped to curb any fear that a jury might have of this lumbering giant of a man. The same thing that made people think of him as a freak outside of the courtroom also conferred on him a layer of unexpected protection inside it.

Both men had developed a taste for killing by this point in their lives. Henry as a means to an end and Ottis as a source of unique moments of pleasure in an otherwise dull and grey world. Neither man shared the same perspective on murder, but it didn't take them long before they realised that the diversity in their viewpoints was actually to their advantage. Ottis killed because he loved to kill. Because it aroused him. Henry killed out of practicality for the most part, and to procure a sexual outlet when willing warm bodies were in short supply. There was no reason that the two of them could not co-exist perfectly, fulfilling both of their needs with each victim.

It did not take long before they tested that theory. On their way out of Florida, the duo realised that they were short on funds, so they staged a quick liquor store robbery in Alabama. Just before they walked in the door, Ottis tossed the gun to Henry with a grin. Their relationship was intense so far, but it was also new, and Ottis had no real way of knowing if all of the things that Henry was telling him were the truth. This was his way of getting to the truth fast. Either Henry was a killer, or he wasn't. If he was, then they were going to have a real good time. If he wasn't, then there was no reason to be scared of putting a pistol in his hands. Either way, Ottis would get all the benefits of a robbery with none of the potential backlash for swinging a gun around. He was smarter than he looked.

Henry did not disappoint his new friend, storming into the store with the gun already pointed at the clerk without even a moment's hesitation. 'Listen up, you. Give us all the cash or I'll splat you all over them cigarettes. Hell, give us some of them cigarettes, too. And a bottle of whiskey. Move it or lose it.'

The clerk panicked, eyes wild and darting back and forth between the two men. To Henry, he looked like he might just be about to do something crazy.

'Don't you try shit, boy.'

Panic overrode whatever logic was operating the clerk's body. He tried to make a run for the door to the back room. Ottis's revolver was almost deafening in this enclosed space. Each of the three shots roared out of it and echoed back at them. All three bullets hit the running clerk in the back. Square in the middle. Tidy as any firing range cut-out.

When his hearing came back, Henry was almost deafened all over again by Ottis's whooping. He found himself wrapped in a gangly armed hug and had a stubbly kiss pressed to his forehead. 'Oh, you did it, sugar. You did it just right.'

Ottis didn't even bother with the cash register; he went straight for the dead body and started to unbuckle the dead clerk's belt. Henry just stood there staring, mesmerised as Ottis got the boy's trousers down far enough to serve his purposes. After the gunfire and yelling, the store was almost deafeningly quiet. Henry could hear every panting breath coming out of Ottis. He moved over to the counter silently to collect the cash, but his eyes never left the scene by the back wall. Ottis let out a little moan, then glanced back, suddenly aware of the eyes on him. 'You can go wait in the car if you like. Or you can watch if that's what takes your fancy.' Henry leaned back against the counter and stared at Ottis, almost defiantly. 'Oh, so you're the watching kind, are you, sugar?'

It was another little challenge. Another little push to see just how far Henry would go. As it turned out, all the way. They had sex for the first time in the garbage-strewn back seat of Ottis's car just a few miles down the road from that murder. Both of them all worked up by the night's work. Henry didn't want to talk about it afterwards, and Ottis had already pushed him so far for one night that he didn't dare go any further. After all, he still had the gun, and now Ottis knew for certain that he was ready and willing to use it.

The two of them roamed the southern states for months on end. Aimlessly killing, raping, and robbing as they saw fit. Their sex life was inconsistent. If they found themselves in the middle of nowhere and Henry had no other outlet then he would happily take Ottis in the back seat of the car, but if there were women about, his preference was pretty clear. The times that Ottis interfered with Henry's flirting were among the only times the two of them disagreed at all.

Henry Lee Lucas and Ottis Toole working in tandem, was a thing of nightmares. For a year, they were on the road sharing the lessons that they had learned, screwing and arguing, and getting blind drunk by the roadside until all those things blended into one long, loud blur. Henry taught Ottis the things that he needed to do to circumvent the methods that the police might employ to catch him; how to mangle a body before burying it so that it couldn't be identified, how to strip the plates off a car and run it around with wrecker's tags so that it was always overlooked. In return, Ottis taught Henry new depths of depravity. Their sexual relationship didn't show Henry anything that he hadn't seen a dozen times before in prison showers, but their criminal relationship was something else entirely. Necrophilia was part and parcel of Henry's usual behaviour, but Ottis kept pushing him to go further. To have sex with the decomposing bodies of their victims when they had to wait out a day before the cover of darkness could cloak an improvised burial. To eat the flesh of the dead, grilled by the roadside on a tiny barbecue that Ottis hauled from one stolen car's boot to the next. Henry tasted it only once before declaring that he didn't like Ottis's barbecue sauce and never indulging in cannibalism again. It seemed strange that he was the one with more scruples for the first time in his life, but it grew stranger still when it became apparent how much he dominated the relationship. After their first night together, Henry no longer felt any need to prove himself to Ottis, and with the arrival of that fresh influx of confidence, the other man suddenly discovered an overwhelming attraction to Henry. Ottis made the most foolish mistake in a lifetime full of them: he fell in love with Henry.

There is no telling how many people they killed in that first year of travelling together, in no small part due to the number of confessions that the two men made, recanted, and then made all over again when it suited their purposes. When you piece together the details of their confessions and see where they overlap, it was clear that the presence of another killer drove each of them to new heights. They spent a surprising amount of time trying to top the other's latest activities.

One story that both men told in vivid detail was about the time that they spotted a young couple hitchhiking through Texas. Henry was driving that night, trying to settle his backside into the pristine seat of the freshly stolen car they had picked up only a few towns back. They had to put some distance between them and the vehicle's owner before it was reported to the local sheriff. That was why they planned on driving through the night, intent on burning through the whole tank of gas and a whole strip of the highway before anyone knew anything was amiss. The kids by the roadside were in their late teens, or maybe early twenties. The girl hung back behind her boy as if he could protect her from all the things that went bump in the night. They were perfect, both of them the very image of white picket fence America.

Henry nudged Ottis awake and pulled over. The boy held up a hand in greeting as the passenger side's door swung open. Ottis held up a gun in answer. He blew off half the boy's fingers with the first shot, then turned his aim towards his torso, rattling out the other five bullets so fast that the girl didn't even have a chance to scream. Henry was not sitting idle as his friend and lover went to work; he had sprung out of the car and rounded it before the last shot was fired. The girl tried to run, but horror had turned her feet to lead. She stumbled and staggered as she turned towards the desert, and before she'd made it a step Henry was on her. His dirty hands tore at her clothes. His stale beer breath swept hot over her face as he pawed at her. She managed to clench a fist and swing at Henry's face, but it was like hitting a brick wall. His grin didn't falter. He didn't even seem to notice. He just wrapped his arms around her waist and lifted her clean off the packed sand. There was one awful dizzy moment when gravity let go of her, alongside all other logic and reason, but then she was orientated to the earth once more, slung over this monstrous man's shoulder with a clear view of everything he had trod on, and the empty stretch of nothing that was all she could see in any direction. She screamed anyway, not out of any hope of being heard, but as the only outlet for the absolute terror that filled her. All that did was make him laugh.

She could see everything that was happening behind her. She could see what the other man, the huge lumbering monster, was doing to her dead boyfriend. She could hear every grunt and every groan even when she pressed her eyes shut against it. Henry patted her on the backside as she went limp, and she had a terrible premonition of her future. She cracked the back of her head on the frame of the car door as he tossed her into the backseat, filling her head up with ringing darkness. As he climbed on top of her, she tried to chase that darkness down into the safety of unconsciousness, but her body betrayed her. It brought her back up to feel his callous fingers dragging over her bare skin, his browned teeth nipping at her stomach.

Ottis got back in the car while Henry was still raping the girl in the backseat, more than satisfied with his own evening's entertainment. He preferred his men hot to cooling, but he wasn't fussy, and killing a man came with its own special zing. It sounded like Henry was still going to take a while, though, and they had places to go, so he started up the car and they took off down the highway, screams trailing out behind them.

Neither man was a stranger to the road, but while Henry was just learning all the ways that belonging to nowhere made him free,

Ottis was different. He had a longing to live amongst other people, even if they hated him. He was hopelessly lovesick over Henry, but their constant isolation and proximity was making the sweetness of that love turn bitter. He wanted Henry to love him back, but the other man didn't seem capable. Whether that was because Ottis was a man, or whether it was because of the echoing void in Henry where other people would keep their emotions, didn't much matter. Ottis could already sense how easily his love could transform into resentment and hatred if things went on as they had, and he had no desire to turn Henry into an enemy. If they settled somewhere then other people could serve as a buffer, an inoculation of social interaction to make it seem like Henry wasn't the only other person in the world.

For Ottis, home meant Florida. He hadn't stopped by his mother's grave for a whole year, the longest he'd ever stayed away, and while he loathed his family, he still felt their absence keenly. Henry didn't want to go. He didn't want to settle anywhere. He dug his heels into the ground and railed against it. Then they drove down to Florida.

The intense relationship that he'd cultivated with Ottis was a double-edged sword. He knew every soft spot in the other man's psyche, but he had left himself just as exposed and open to manipulation. Ultimately, neither of them was ready for the ride to end just yet, and they were both willing to make some compromises to stay together.

The Child Bride

Ottis's family did not know how to respond to Henry. They didn't know if Ottis was bringing home a friend, a lover, or something in between. The way that the men behaved together gave very little away, and while Ottis was so flamboyant that his sexuality was often apparent to people several streets over, Henry was a closed book. They drifted around the periphery of the Toole family, never quite welcomed in, and never quite rejected fully. The duo stayed with several of Ottis's sisters during their first few months in Jacksonville, bouncing from one apartment to the next as their presence became a nuisance. Ottis's sisters had been a font of constant misery to him in his earlier life, but now, with their mother and her constant incitements to torment him gone, they had all fallen into more traditional familial relationships. Henry swiftly found himself occupying exactly the same role as Ottis in those households, an honorary uncle to all of Ottis's nephews and nieces, including Frank and Freida, the twin children of his eldest sister, Drucilla.

Drucilla was a single parent working well past the limits of her own endurance to try to support her family, and she was incredibly relieved to find a pair of ready-made babysitters snoozing on her living room furniture at all hours of the day. She might have found something suspicious about the way that this near-stranger Henry took an interest in her children. If he favoured one or the other, he made a point of lavishing attention on both of them equally, even taking them with him and Ottis when they went on short road trips around Florida.

Henry honestly didn't care for Frank much—he considered the boy to be a whimpering simpleton for the most part—but he endured his company in exchange for the access that it granted him to Frank's sister. At ten years old, Frieda was the apple of Henry's eye, and he took a more than paternal interest in her, just as he had in the children of his ex-wife.

Almost immediately after meeting her he started calling her 'Becky' in private. Neither of them cared for her given name, and she thrilled every time she heard him whispering the one that he had given her. Henry had read the records of many child abducting paedophiles in his time—he knew just how easily they got caught out when taking their pliant victims in public just because they slipped up and called them by their real name. He was training both himself and Frieda for that possibility. To this day, nobody is entirely clear on what it was about Frieda Powell that was so incredibly appealing to Henry Lee Lucas, whether it was her close connection to the uncle that Henry was unwilling to admit that he loved, or if there were something in her pubescent personality that meshed perfectly with his own networked web of psychoses. Whatever the attachment was, both of them called it love, and when the time came to be moving on, Henry dug in his heels all over again.

He wasn't ready to give up on the road entirely. Even through the months when they had been staying in Jacksonville, the duo often took extended trips out on the highways and byways, preying on any pedestrians they found outside of civilisation and committing armed robberies where they dared—but Henry wasn't ready to break off his tenuous relationship with Frieda, either. It wasn't clear if he had begun sexually abusing her by this point, although later arguments that the duo would have in earshot of witnesses would seem to indicate some degree of chastity on Henry's part for possibly the first time in his life.

Ottis took a wife in 1979, a train-wreck of a relationship that saw him publicly outed as gay to everyone in Jacksonville by her fierce rumour spreading after the whole relationship fell apart. She never named the lover that he had brought home and kicked her out of her own bedroom to have sex with, but to everyone who knew Ottis, it was abundantly clear that the lover was Henry. It created an extremely uncomfortable situation for Ottis, who would normally have skipped town after creating such a fuss, and he had many hissed arguments with Henry to that effect.

To stay close to Frieda, Henry, and by proxy Ottis, had to get jobs in town. Southeast Color Coat was a roofing company in Jacksonville that Henry somehow managed to impress with his technical skills, and by the end of his interview both men were on the company payroll, although their wages were often docked for failure to show up to work—the call of the highway and the life of crime that they both adored was just too loud to ignore some days.

According to their confessions, this was the most fruitful time in Henry and Ottis's careers as murderers, and while the thousands of murders that they confessed to could not possibly have all happened, there is one murder that definitely did.

In Georgetown, Texas, a hitchhiker from Oklahoma died. Her body was found dumped by the side of the road, stripped completely naked with the exception of a pair of orange socks. To this day, she has not been identified, although there was so much publicity around the case that her lack of identification is likely the most miraculous thing about her death at this point. She died by strangulation at the side of Interstate 35 and was tossed over a barrier to fall into the dirt, where she would later be discovered. These are the certain facts of the 'Orange Socks' murder. Beyond that, everything is shrouded in lies by either one serial killer or the other.

According to Henry, he picked up the girl when he was travelling alone, and they had consensual sex by the roadside. When she refused to have sex with him for a second time, saying 'not right now,' he had swerved the car to the side of the road and strangled her to death while raping her.

According to Ottis, she was a regular lover of Henry's whom he had murdered in a fit of jealousy at seeing his lover in the arms of another. Initially, Ottis claimed to have slit her throat while the two of them were having sex, but upon hearing about the forensic evidence, he altered his story to include garrotting with a pair of stockings. Regardless of which story was the truth, the duo were able to provide some very specific details, both about the location of the body and some material evidence found around the corpse that only someone who was present at the scene of the crime could have known—details that were not even included in the police reports because they were considered to be irrelevant, like a folded hand towel that 'Orange Socks' had been using in lieu of a sanitary napkin.

Despite their near-constant absences from work, Henry and Ottis managed to keep their heads down well enough to hold onto those jobs for two whole years. Years in which Henry had more time to ingratiate himself with the ever-flattered Frieda. Henry and Ottis maintained that holding pattern, working, robbing, killing, and raping as they needed to throughout all of that time, just waiting for the catalyst that would remake their lives all over again. It arrived in 1981, when Ottis's sister, and the twins' mother, hung herself in their apartment. The children were the ones to find her.

Henry and Ottis immediately swept in to lay claim to the children, now twelve years old, over the widespread protests of the extended Toole family. The other sisters were in no better position to care for the children than Ottis, and the kids barely knew most of them by this point, having spent almost two years in Henry's loving care.

From that moment on, both children rode in the back of the

pickup truck everywhere that Henry and Ottis went, sitting outside their roofing jobs in the sweltering heat and parked outside the petrol stations in the cool of the night while their ersatz parents went in to rob and murder. There are few secrets in so confined a space, and there are even fewer that can't be seen with just a glance through the bug-crusted windshield. Both children understood exactly what their new guardians were doing, but they responded to that information in completely different ways.

'Becky' had already fallen deeply for Henry, in the way that only extremely naive young girls can. His perfection had become a cornerstone of her worldview, and anything that might disrupt that idealisation would have hurt her, so her rejection of such, along with the law, was a guiding force in her life. If Henry broke the law, it was because the law was wrong. If he killed people, then they needed killing.

Frank went mad. Whether this was a symptom of the mental weakness that Henry had always ascribed to him or the inevitable result of so much disruption in his young life is unclear. His whole life fell apart with the death of his mother, and the people who were meant to take care of him turned out to be hardened criminals with very little interest in his mental state most of the time or even an interest in his survival. In a fictional retelling of these events, he would have witnessed one of Henry and Ottis's gruesome murders, and his mind would have broken. But in reality, it was just the slow grind of life in their care that drove him into the near catatonic state he was in by the time the slow gears of child protective services finally started turning.

Both children were taken from school to juvenile homes where they would remain in the care of the state until they turned eighteen. From there, Frank was soon transferred to a hospital for the mentally infirm, where he remained for the rest of his short life.

In the home, they called her Frieda, and it felt like a lie each and every time she answered to it. She wasn't Frieda anymore, she was Becky, his Becky. The other girls in the house picked on her for her name or for being dirty, or for whatever fresh excuse they had conjured up that day, but all of their little barbs passed her by.

She didn't belong here. She belonged out there on the road with the man she loved. Every night she would press her face to the window pane and stare out into the clammy darkness beyond the bars. From up in this room she could see the road beyond the high wall and its mask of trees. She had been staring out intently ever since she first arrived, certain in her gut that this wasn't the end for her, positive that her love would never abandon her. She stared out at that road as if she could will a shabby looking pickup truck into existence. She imagined it so intently that when she finally set eyes on the car idling out there she was almost certain that it was all just a dream. From here she couldn't be certain, she didn't know that it was Henry who got out of the passenger's side and slunk over to the wall, but she had been waiting for this too long to care.

Sneaking downstairs wasn't hard—there was a steady flow of movement throughout the house as they all went to the communal bathrooms at odd hours, but the front door was going to be hard to get around. They locked it at sundown. She needn't have worried. By the time she made it down, Henry was already there, crowbar in hand and a grin plastered over his face. If they were smart they would have run. But they were romantics, so he scooped her up in his arms and kissed her like a hero in a movie.

At the wall, he boosted her up, and for the first time all night, anxiety slithered through her. It was a high wall. How was she going to get down on the other side? 'Just drop, sugar, I'll catch you.'

Ottis was there, smiling just as wide as Henry had been. She fell into his arms with a little yip, and her uncle gave her one last squeeze for good measure, so that she knew that she was safe, so that she could know for certain that she was home again.

They went on lingering around Jacksonville for almost a full year after breaking Becky out of juvenile detention, but by January of 1982 the authorities were closing in on them. Their crimes had gone almost entirely undetected up until this point thanks to the invaluable education that Henry had received in Ionia State. But Becky could not avoid attention. There was an official record of her escape from care and there was an active effort to return her to state custody. Confronted with the choice of staying in Florida and being separated from Henry, or fleeing across the country with the two men, there wasn't any choice to be made at all.

This time, when Ottis and Henry set off drifting across the southern states, it was with a girl in the backseat of the car. She was the perfect addition to their little family unit; willing to overlook the two of them rutting in the dirt by the side of the car when they thought she was asleep, willing to turn her gaze away when they robbed and butchered with abandon, and serving all the time as the perfect camouflage. The two men alone were frightening, even with Ottis's flamboyance. But with the addition of a girl that the two of them looked on with obvious love and care, they were able to slip right under the radar of anyone on the lookout for danger. Victims came willingly into their reach. Suspicion passed them by entirely. Everything was easier when there were three of them. While they were together, it was the happiest time in their lives. But even for serial killers, all good things have to come to an end.

Abandonment Issues

Less than three months into their journey together, Ottis took ill. He had been a devoted alcoholic since he was old enough to open a bottle on his own, and with time the liquor had eaten away at his liver, causing all manner of minor medical problems. This time, he took on a jaundiced appearance, grew sluggish, and vomited each time he tried to ingest food. Neither Henry nor Becky had a clue what to do to help him. They turned around and headed back to Florida, delivering him to the first hospital that they found, then turned tail and fled before the authorities could notice Becky's presence. Ottis had never been so thoroughly abandoned before. His family had always been toxic, but they had been persistent. They may have hated him, but they would never ever have let him go.

It took almost a month more before he had recovered enough from his illness to get out of the hospital, and by then he had no way of tracking his lover and niece down. He was stranded, angry, and trained to kill without detection by one of the best minds in the serial killing hobby. It didn't take him long before he found an outlet for his frustrations.

At first, he fell back into old patterns, setting fires for the rush of arousal that accompanied each act of arson, but after experiencing the intensity of murder on a regular basis he found that arson had lost its thrill; at least until he started setting fire to buildings in Jacksonville that he knew had people sleeping inside. Two people died as a result of the fires that he had started, and while that aroused him greatly, it also drew unwanted attention. He stole himself a white Cadillac and went for a drive all the way down the east coast. It was there, in Hollywood, Florida, that Ottis would have his next brush with celebrity.

Adam Walsh didn't want to go to the shop. He was six years old and department stores had very little appeal to him, particularly on balmy days at the end of July when there was baseball to play. The mall was kind of cool, he supposed. The air conditioning was kind of nice after a long, sticky few months. The mall even had toy stores and stuff that he'd really rather go visit than Sears, but his mother had her heart set on some lamp that was on sale, so he went along quietly, the way he went along quietly with just about everything in life. He didn't like to be the centre of attention, and he didn't like it when there was trouble. If he could keep his head down and keep his mother smiling, then that was exactly what he would do, especially if it meant they might go by the toy store on the way out of the mall.

Sears was just as boring as ever. Adam could feel the boredom settling over him like a heavy blanket. Even his mother, lost in conversation with the first salesperson she could lay hands on, noticed him slump. That was when something caught her eye and a little smile lit up her face. She dragged his unwilling body over to a small crowd of other boys a little bit older than him, over by the boring microwaves and stuff. There was bleeping and music coming from in the middle of the press of jostling bodies, like at the arcade. The weight of boredom lessened slightly as she pressed him in close enough to see the display. An Atari! The other boys were taking turns playing the games. Adam wanted a shot so badly, but he could see that there was already a kind of queue, one that was already kind of shaky without him wedging himself in. Mother had already vanished out of sight by the time he thought to look back. That was fine. This was way more interesting than some stupid lamp.

The other boys were getting excited. They were shouting, and if Adam had a little more courage he might have been shouting with them, but instead, he just lurked at the back of the pack, ducking and bobbing to see the screen through them all. One game ended and another began, but there was some confusion over who had the next turn. One of the boys was still holding tight to his controller and another two were trying to snatch the other out of each other's grasp. It escalated to pushing and yet more shouting before the long shadow of a security guard loomed over them. 'All right, that is enough. Out you go.'

He held out his arms and herded them along, and Adam was herded along with them. The other boys were bigger, ten or twelve; they were probably here on their own. But Adam had to get back before Mother found him missing. He kept trying to say something, to find his voice through the shyness, but it just didn't come. Before he knew it, he was outside, not just back in the mall but out on the street, and the guard had lumbered back inside. He turned to talk to the other boys, but they were already striding off down the street together, laughing and jostling each other like nothing had even happened. Adam didn't know where to go. He didn't know what to do. He'd heard about 'getting lost' but he'd never once thought that it could happen to him. He was a good boy who always did what he was told, so no bad things could happen to him, right? There were adults passing by him in the street, but none of them even looked down. If he went back into the shop, would the security guard still be waiting for him? Would he get in even bigger trouble? His mother would not be happy with him. She would be mad, like the time he went out into the garden to play without telling her first. Complex decision making was not part of the six-year-old skill-set, so when he heard a soft voice cooing to him from the roadside, it was a relief more than anything else. Even if going over to the car was the wrong decision, at least someone else was making it for him. 'You all right there, sugar? Where's your momma?'

There was a big white Cadillac sitting there by the side of the road, like something out of a movie, and that voice, it sounded like something out of a movie, too. Like some Disney character had come to life. 'Are you lost, little boy? You want to come with me? I've got a ton of toys to play with in here. Got some candy, too, if you're hungry.'

It was a ploy right out of some after-school special, but Adam was too young to have even the beginnings of a fear of strangers instilled in him. He walked up to the car slowly, out of shyness rather than fear. Inside, Ottis was waiting for him. 'You ever get to ride up front when you're out with your folks?'

'N-no.'

'You want to give it a try? Have a roll round the block and look for your momma?'

Adam nodded and reached for the handle. It was a better plan than the nothing he'd been able to come up with. Inside the car, it smelt kind of funny, like his clothes after he'd been playing baseball all day in the sunshine, but he didn't say anything to the nice man. That would be rude. The nice man looked a little bit funny, too. He was really big, and his stringy hair was getting kind of thin on the top like he was smuggling a big egg underneath it. But he was smiling down at Adam really friendly, so he decided not to worry about it. They drove along the street and turned to the left, just like the man said they would. Adam pressed his nose to the glass and stared out at the crowds, but there was no sign of his mother anywhere. She was probably still arguing about her stupid lamp with some salesperson in Sears.

'You know, I've been thinking, I'd like a little boy like you for myself. My buddy, Henry. He got himself a little girl. My niece. And if he has that, why can't I?'

Adam turned slowly in the seat to look at the man, confused and still too shy to say much of anything. Ottis didn't falter. 'I mean, sure, you're kind of little compared to her. Folks ain't going to mistake you for my wife or nothing. But you and me, we could work out just fine. You could be my son. Not ever going to have none any other way. And I'd take good care of you, and you could love me like a boy is supposed to. How does that sound to you, son?'

Adam was more confused than afraid. What was the man talking about? They carried on straight ahead instead of turning left at the next junction, and that was enough to finally force words out of him. 'I need to go back.'

'Ain't no need for going back, sugar. You're with me now. You'll keep me company. You'll love me. You'll do anything I ask you to, just like folks that love you are meant to.'

Adam was scared now. Actually scared instead of the make-believe scared he was in his games. He wanted his mother. 'I want my mom.'

Ottis chuckled like the kid was just being silly. 'I'm your mom now, sugar. I'll feed you and clothe you and...'

'I want my mom!' Adam insisted, finally finding his voice.

Ottis's fist lashed out, nearly as big as Adam's whole face. Adam didn't feel the punch. One minute there was a sense of motion then the whole world just went white. The pain crept in a moment later and tears started streaming down his reddened face. 'Let me out! I want my mom!'

Ottis's face was frozen in a rictus of frustration. A quick smack was meant to quiet the kid down, not rile him up even more. 'No. No!'

Adam scrabbled at the lock on the car, trying to fling himself out on the side of the highway, but Ottis was having none of it. He hammered the little boy in the head with his meaty fist, over and over. Screaming to drown out the sounds of the little boy's sobbing. Then, it was finally quiet.

Ottis drove until the sun was slipping behind the mangrove trees, then he pulled off the dirt track he'd been following to deal with Adam more permanently. When he reached in to drag the boy out, he couldn't believe that the kid was still breathing. Still grumbling at being woken from his concussed slumber. All of the rage and bitter disappointment that Ottis was feeling after Henry abandoned him came bubbling up. He wrapped his fingers around little Adam's tiny throat and he squeezed as tightly as he could until he could feel the bones. Then he let the tiny corpse drop to the dirt, and his training from all those years with Henry kicked in.

He fetched a machete out of the trunk and with three brutal cuts took the boy's head clean off. The rest of the body he would take back to somewhere more familiar and burn away to bones and ash, but the head made it too easy to identify. Dental records were the thing Henry kept banging on about. Easiest just to dump the whole head somewhere it would never be found. Ottis tossed Adam's into a little canal near where he'd stopped and went back to clean up his mess. Whatever satisfaction he'd been hoping for was nowhere in sight.

The abduction of Adam Walsh became one of the most widely publicised crimes in American history, resulting in the passing of multiple laws for the protection of children, the creation of 'America's Most Wanted,' which was hosted by Adam's father for its duration, and a manhunt that would not end until 2008, when the police finally confirmed Ottis Toole's involvement. Prior to that confirmation, there was a great deal of speculation about who had killed young Adam, after his head was recovered from a drainage ditch early in the search for him, on the same day that a $10,000 reward was offered for his safe return. Interestingly enough, it would seem that Ottis Toole was not the only serial killer at the Hollywood Mall that day.

Jeffrey Dahmer lived in Florida at the time of Adam's abduction, and a man fitting his description was seen several times around the mall that day, including in the toy section of the Sears in question. Years later, the police confronted Dahmer with this evidence and demanded his confession, and he laughed in their faces. He was imprisoned on multiple life sentences with no possibility of parole, and he had quite happily confessed to every one of his crimes once he had been caught. He pointed out the flaw in the police's logic. If he had committed the crime, he had nothing to lose and everything to gain by admitting it, so when he denied it, they could believe him.

Ottis returned to Jacksonville the following day, found an abandoned refrigerator, and used it as a makeshift incinerator for the rest of Adam's remains—the same solution that Henry had been using to dispose of their victims for many years when circumstances allowed. He started a few more fires, started a few bar fights, and let the days and weeks pass him by in a grey haze of misery. He would never find love again, and he had no way to chase it. All that he could do was wait, and hope.

Without Ottis to drive them on, Henry decided to try and create some sort of settled life for him and Becky. She had grown enough now that the prospect of them being a couple wasn't so ridiculous to the outside observer, so they took on a rented apartment in Maryland under the pretence of being newlyweds. Henry found himself work at the local scrapyard, and they began to settle into the sort of routine that in anyone else's life might be considered normal, but that for both Henry and Becky was now a bizarre deviation from their usual behaviour. Play-acting, at normalcy.

Becky was completely isolated from everyone around her. She dare not get to know the neighbours in case details of her life came slipping out, and while Henry was free to come and go as he pleased, staying out until the middle of the night sometimes, she soon discovered that there was an invisible tether holding her in easy walking distance of their tiny flea-ridden apartment. With no other outlet, her feelings for Henry intensified. He became her whole world. She was nearing fifteen years old, and all of the idealised romance that had defined their relationship thus far was now confronted with the hormonal reality of a developing teenager. Henry was her husband, in every way except for the ones that mattered, and she wanted to change that. She knew that he was having sex with other women when he was out on those late nights. She knew that he had needs that weren't being fulfilled by their relationship, and it made her furious. She was his wife, and she wanted him to be her husband in every way. Including in the bedroom.

The first time that she tried to mount him while they were kissing, he nearly flung her across the room. The next time, he sat her down and gave his best rendition of a talk about the birds and the bees, along with several heavy-handed comments about her still being a little girl; comments that really did not go down well.

Sex became a major source of tension within their household, with Becky trying to pressure Henry into taking their relationship to the next level while he tried to resist the temptation—something that he had never been particularly successful at. The more that she pushed him, the more that he avoided her, and the more certain she was that he was out every night having sex with other women, driven wild with lust by her clumsy, fumbling attempts at seduction.

The unfortunate truth of the matter was that Henry was going out to satiate his sexual appetite in exactly the same way as he always had: through rape, murder, necrophilia, and sexual assault. His ability to intimidate and manipulate his victims had only improved over time, and all of the amateur mistakes that he had made in his early criminal career had served as useful lessons to him. He managed to last for months without a single whisper of his crimes making it to the police, despite being in a small town with a healthy gossip network. Then, one of the local girls, a teenager only slightly younger than Becky, came forward with her story about him forcing her hands down his trousers.

Henry was arrested for the sexual assault, and Becky was caught idling in their apartment. For a 'first offence,' he received a relatively short sentence of only three months in the local jail, but Becky's fate was considerably more permanent. She was easily matched to the missing persons records from Florida and shipped back there immediately, returned to the last relative that had official guardianship of her, with the intention that her family would put her on the path back to salvation. Ottis met her at the police station in Jacksonville with a grin on his face. Becky was back, and Henry would surely follow.

With his sentence served, Henry caught a ride on a freight train heading the right direction and made the whole journey without stopping for a rest. When he showed up on Ottis's doorstep, Becky and the lumbering giant swept him into a crushing hug. They were all right back where they belonged. The party that followed lasted almost a whole week, with all three of them drunk and dazed, but by the end of that week, every one of them was twitching to get out of Jacksonville again. They loaded into yet another 'borrowed' car and headed for California.

For Henry, this was the ideal situation. He got to have the relationship that he wanted with Becky, spend the time he enjoyed with Ottis, and had the other man there to serve as a buffer whenever she started to push for a sexual relationship. For the other two, it was less ideal. Becky wanted Henry all to herself, and her mounting jealousy started to drive a wedge between her and her uncle. For Ottis, it was like his worst nightmare come to life; seeing Henry every day, watching as his ever-developing relationship with Becky took him further and further out of his reach.

They stayed with friends and acquaintances, bouncing from one place to the next. In Hemet, California, they squatted in the home of Jack and O'Bere Smart, spending almost four months restoring furniture to earn their keep. The Smarts wanted rid of them after just one month, but the trio gave no real cause to put them out. They were loud and their love triangle was a little nauseating once the Smarts understood it. But beyond that, they did good work on the furniture and they kept mostly to themselves in the manner of people who have too much to hide. Eventually, O'Bere hit upon a solution. Her elderly mother had been haranguing her for years to come and care for her in Texas, and now they had a full set of handymen and housekeepers willing to work for room and board. Kate Rich was eighty years old, the proud matriarch of her family now fallen on hard times. Money wasn't a problem, but maintenance required people to be physically present, and with her kids dispersed across the states, that was something Kate was sorely lacking.

On the road to Texas, things finally reached a boiling point when Becky caught Henry and Ottis having sex while she was sleeping. She issued the first of her many ultimatums. Henry had to choose, there and then, which one of the Tooles he wanted to keep in his life. He could have Becky as his wife, body, and soul, or he could hold on to whatever sordid little relationship he had been sneaking about with Ottis to maintain. He was given until they reached Texas as a deadline to make his decision. Henry was not a man inclined towards introspection. Decisions in his life up until this point had served one of two purposes: survival and feeding his lusts. This was likely the most strenuous mental activity he had ever undertaken, and he hated every minute of it. All three of them travelled in sullen silence, their usual jokes and chatter muted by the impending dissolution that awaited them.

Ottis was miserable. There was no doubt in his mind whom Henry was going to choose, and he had spent the entire time that they were in each other's company avoiding this very conflict. He knew Henry preferred women. He knew that Henry was never going to love him the way that he wanted to be loved, but he had been able to hold out hope for as long as Henry kept him trailing along behind him. When they got to Texas, Ottis didn't even attempt to sway Henry in his favour; instead, he did his dearest friend one last kindness by taking the difficult decision out of his hands. Both Henry and Becky were dumped at the roadside, and Ottis drove off with tears in his eyes. It was the last time that the men would ever see each other.

Alone at Last

So it was, that Henry Lee Lucas and the girl known as Becky found themselves stranded on the side of the highway with a hundred miles of Texas between them and the closest shelter. Henry had been so lost in his first intellectual exercise that he had forgotten all about his own survival and comfort. He was not happy with Becky. She had taken his ideal life and ripped it to pieces in the name of her dream, and a more introspective duo might have realised that he was never going to be able to forgive that. As it was, they trudged together, weary and sun-beaten along the side of the road with their scant luggage and their thumbs held up hopefully towards every passing car. Time stretched out slow and lazy in the heat. Every minute could have been an hour. The midday sun beat down on them like they had done it some personal insult, and before long, Becky's litany of complaints started to tumble out of her. She was too hot. She was tired. Her feet hurt. Henry's hands clenched themselves into fists at the sound of her voice. He could have killed her there and then for what she had done to him, but then he would have been left with nothing at all. She was all that he had left in the world and letting go of that was too hard, even when the sound of her whining voice set his teeth on edge.

When a car finally stopped for them, Henry didn't even realise it at first. He was so beaten down. It was only when the driver stood up and loudly declared, 'Well, my children, you look like you have been through the wars,' that Henry finally snapped out of it.

'Hey, mister, any chance of a ride?' He didn't have the energy to muster a spiel.

Luckily, this was one stranger who didn't need reeling in. A stranger with his very own set of ulterior motives. 'Why of course! I didn't pull up here in the middle of nowhere for the good of my health. Whereabouts are you headed to?'

'We ain't fussy.' Becky groaned. 'Anywhere with some shade.'

The man grinned at her. 'Well, hop right in then, lovebirds! Let's get this show on the road!'

The car was cramped but clean, and with all the windows rolled down there was enough of a breeze to make it a vast improvement over standing out in the sun. The radio wasn't working, but the driver more than made up for that, filling every empty moment with more words. 'So, tell me, dear children. Would I be right in thinking that if you do not have a particular destination in mind, that might mean that you also have no place to hang your hat and call your own? That you are itinerants?'

Henry cocked his head. 'I don't know about that, mister, but we ain't got no place to be running back to if that's what you're asking?'

'Lost and in need of a shepherd, just as I suspected when I first set my eyes upon you. Allow me to introduce myself properly. I am the Reverend Ruben Moore, father, and preacher to the House of Prayer. We have ourselves a little place out here along this road. A little home for those without one. A place that you might call your own, were you so inclined.'

Henry chuckled. 'So you're just offering us a place to stay? No strings attached?'

It was like Moore already had the whole patter memorised. 'The only bondage I would set upon you would be the ties of friendship and community, my child. You would be free to come and go as you please, though I'd rather you didn't bring any sin or temptation down among the more vulnerable of our numbers. Newlyweds like you, you need the best start in life that the world can give you. I'm just doing as the Lord would want. Offering up what I've got and don't need to them that need but don't got.'

Henry was still dubious, but one glance back at Becky, all wide-eyed and excitable, told him exactly what she wanted. She loved to do the newlywed bit, and if they were living on some Jesus commune, she'd get to play that part to her heart's content.

'Alright, Rev, we're listening.' Henry settled back into his seat with a sigh. 'Tell us all about it.'

By the end of the day, Henry and Becky were settled into the 'honeymoon suite' of the House of Prayer's commune on the outskirts of Stoneburg, Texas. It was ideally situated for Henry and Becky, just a short drive to the south from Ringgold, where they were meant to be caring for Kate Rich. They had met a few of the other drifters and homeless people that Moore had reeled in with his patter and promises of a better life. Most of them now worked for the Reverend in his main enterprise, running a joinery and roofing company. The commune was as much a company town as it was a religious organisation, and it was as much a homeless shelter as either of the other two.

Henry barely got the door closed before Becky was on him, and this time he did nothing to fight her off. He had tried to keep their relationship pure. He had tried to keep from hurting her. But right now he was angry and confused with only one familiar thing to grab hold of, and he was going to hold onto it for all that he was worth. He hurt her, just like he'd been scared of doing. She wouldn't let him stop even as she bled. At long last, all of her dreams had come true. At long last, she was his wife in every way that mattered.

The next day, they borrowed one of the trucks from the commune and headed off to work. Kate Rich took an immediate liking to Becky and was willing to overlook her sullen husband in exchange for this new daughter. To Henry's eyes, the work that Becky was putting in seemed a lot like pottering around the house rather than actually doing anything, while he was doing hard manual labour every single day they were on the Rich property. But it was a small price to pay to keep the old bird sweet while he milked her bank account for everything that it was worth. The extensive repairs and refurbishments to the big old house came with a lot of material costs, costs that Kate had to sign so many cheques for that she eventually just started signing a few at a time and handing them off to Henry to finish with the details. This wasn't his usual kind of crime, but he'd done enough reading on the subject to know how people usually got caught out. When he started making out cheques for himself, he kept it small. Fifty dollars here. Fifty dollars there. Tiny amounts to someone with as much money as Rich. Amounts that could have been for any number of little things around the house. Going big would get him noticed, but skimming a little bit here and there he could keep this up forever, while still drawing a paycheque from the old lady to boot.

Kate Rich lived up to her name, with enough money in the bank to keep her well into her dotage without any trouble. She wouldn't have given any of those little cheques a second thought, and Henry's plan to defraud her would have gone perfectly if it weren't for the Smarts living up to their name, too. They had always suspected that something was awry with Henry and Ottis, even if they'd never quite been able to put their finger on it. They had kept a close eye on them while they were under the Smarts' own roof, and they had half expected them never to show up in Texas. They were half right. Ottis had vanished. Henry was a changed man without him, and suddenly that little girl Becky who they thought might have been his daughter was his wife? It was all too strange, so they took a close look at the situation, trying to find anything out of place.

In her finances, they found about a hundred and fifty dollars out of place, taken in small amounts over time. When Kate asked Henry to account for the missing money and set her fretting daughter's mind at ease, he responded by vanishing. Neither he nor Becky came back to work the next day, and nobody had any means of contacting him. Kate was prepared to forgive and forget, but O'Bere took personal offence at the man she had sheltered for all those months. The man now trying to rob her mother. So she filed a police report that would later prove instrumental in bringing Lucas's campaign of terror to an end.

Back at the House of Prayer, Henry was ready to pack his bags and get out of town before both Becky and Ruben himself intervened. They took turns extolling the virtues of their current living situation to Henry. Ruben was happy to put them up rent-free until Henry got a new job. Becky had found herself surrounded for the first time by a community that wasn't judging her as inferior, where she didn't have to hide anything to be accepted. This 'new normal' was giving her the self-confidence to speak out even when she wasn't desperate, and she had no intention of throwing it away for nothing. Between the two of them, they managed to convince Henry to stay put, and by the next morning, he had a new job on one of the Reverend's roofing crews.

A month rolled by, then another, with no excitement to speak of. Becky and Henry continued their sexual relationship, although it brought him very little joy—after so long, the hunt and the violence had become integral to his pleasure. He wasn't like Ottis, needing to kill every time he wanted sexual satisfaction, but he needed more than the timid fumblings of some love-sick teenager. He missed his old life. He missed Ottis. But even the things that used to be reliable reminders of that old life were being eroded in the House of Prayer.

Becky was becoming a believer. She thought that she could seek salvation from her former life in prayer and virtue, that she could become more than the white trash that everyone had always assumed that she was. She might well have succeeded if for a single moment she had let go of her tight grip on the weighty anchor of Henry. When Henry looked at her now, he could barely see Ottis in her face. He could barely remember why he had ever wanted her. He did his best to ignore her new Jesus talk, did his duty in the bedroom, and brought home enough money for them to eat.

There was no liquor in the House of Prayer collective, and that wore on him heavily. Just as Becky was revelling in no longer having to hide anything, Henry was feeling like he was under the most intense scrutiny of his life. He couldn't go out drinking. He couldn't go out looking for girls to prey on. He was trapped. Pinned in place on this blank spot on the map by obligation to a girl he could barely stand to talk to anymore. Things would come to a head soon. His temper would boil over and he'd take off into the great wide nowhere all over again. Maybe he'd find Ottis, maybe he'd go it alone. But he never got the opportunity. Becky's personal growth and ever-growing belief in the teachings of the Reverend Ruben Moore had finally reached the point where she felt ready to confront her old demons. She was old enough now that the system in Florida was unlikely to try to seize control of her again. And if it did, well then that was surely a small penance to pay in return for the forgiveness of her family. She came to Henry with a simple request. She wanted him to take her back to Florida. Away from all of this. He could not have been happier to oblige.

When they set off in the car, it brought a flood of good memories back to Henry. It reminded him of just how sweet their life had been and gave him hope that the two of them could get back to that. There were a lot of states between Texas and Florida. A whole lot of fun was waiting just beyond the horizon. The kind of fun that he'd been missing out on while he was shackled to a job and a home and a wife. Henry wanted to turn back the clock and start over with Becky, to get things back to the way they used to be when he was so happy just to see her. Sadly, the person who she used to be no longer existed.

It didn't take long into their journey before Becky started laying out the reasoning behind her pilgrimage home. She had done wrong in her life, she had sinned in more ways that she could readily count, and she knew in her heart that she would not be forgiven and granted a place in Heaven if she did not try to make apologies and amends to those she had left in her wake. Henry just nodded along to all the Jesus stuff the way that he always had. Soon she'd start badgering him to get on board with it, too, and he'd change the subject enough times that she'd eventually give up. 'Confession is the first step to forgiveness, you know?'

That pulled him out of his reverie. Confession was a very dangerous word. If Becky wanted to confess to all of her sins, she would most assuredly be tarring him with the same brush, and while she had seen some portion of the evil he'd done, she had no idea just how dark the path he'd tread had gotten. If she was out there running her mouth about all the bad things they'd done together, it was just a matter of time before it came back on him and people started looking into his history more closely than he would like. 'But ain't you just going to upset folk all over again? Rehashing all the bad stuff you did to them? Ain't it better to let it lie?'

It was the first time Henry had spoken since Becky had broached the subject, and even if he was arguing with her, at least he was talking. If he would talk and listen, then maybe all of this was fixable.

'It ain't about what is easy for them or for me, it is about what is right. There's wounds that can't never heal if you just keep covering them over. Reverend Ruben says you got to shine a light on the dark places. Uncover them secrets that are hurting y'all.'

Henry bit back his first reply. 'But some secrets is there to protect folk. You go telling everyone everything then their feelings are going to get hurt, or worse.'

'Reverend Ruben says...'

'I've heard about enough of what Ruben says. Now listen to what I say. You go running around making sad eyes and sorries to all your folks, and it is just going to bring a whole heap of trouble down on us. You want to go to jail? You thought juvie was bad, you ain't seen nothing until you get to a state prison. Think that you and me'll have a life together then?'

She turned her eyes back to the dark highway. Steeling herself.

'You got to make sacrifices to do the right thing. Sometimes that's how it is. 'Specially if you've done wrong.'

'So you just don't care that I'll be gone?' Henry's voice came out in a harsh whisper. 'You don't want me no more?'

She didn't have an answer for that. Henry was no longer the centre of her universe. She was still profoundly attached to him, but as she got older, the cracks in his façade were starting to show, and she was starting to think about her life as her own instead of as some part in a white trash fairytale romance. By the time she was old enough to drink, he'd be fifty. By the time she was his age, he'd likely be dead and gone. Even before she started to seriously consider the immorality of his life, she had that age difference to contend with, and while the attention of an older man had been flattering as a child, now she felt like she could see Henry clearly. They rode on in silence for a time, then almost without warning, Henry pulled off the road into a truck stop just outside of Bowie, Texas.

Inside the cafe, Henry made good use of the free coffee and facilities, and when the waitress came around they had as good a meal as a truck stop could provide. All of this was conducted in frosty silence. Henry didn't have a thing to say to Becky right then. His mind had turned back to the old subject of survival, and the least painful way to maintain his freedom.

They walked around the back of a trailer, heading for their car, and the neon of the truck stop blinked out, leaving them in nothing but moonlight. Becky turned to him, skin glowing in the darkness, and he could see that same old smile on her face, the one that said she was a little nervous but she trusted him to see her through. He closed his eyes as his fingers tightened around her throat. At least this was the end of it.

When he opened his eyes again, Becky was gone. The girl that he had fallen for all those years ago had emptied out of this body like water spilled from a glass. Now there was just another girl, another set of motions to go through to maintain his freedom. It was easier now that she wasn't watching. By the time he'd made it out into the middle of nowhere, he couldn't even recognise that the body used to be Becky. He drew out his machete and set to work, severing each of the limbs at the joints, taking off the head and burying it by the roadside before heading out into the big dark emptiness to scatter the other parts to the wind. It wasn't Becky. Not anymore.

Afterwards, Henry just sat in the car and tried to plan his next move. Even that simple a process was hard when he was feeling so numb, so he had to trust his instinct. He couldn't lie to Ottis. He couldn't go back to Florida and face the uncle of the girl he'd just butchered with any hope of seeing love on that man's face ever again. It was too soon, too raw. He needed some time to get that final image of her face out of his mind. He needed to move. He needed to run as far away as he could get. But to do that, he was going to need some money. Luckily enough, he knew somebody who had cash to spare.

The Downward Spiral

Kate Rich hadn't forgotten about Henry and Becky, despite the long months since the last time she had seen them. She had asked about town for them on occasion, even though she often struggled to get out and about on her own. She had felt some kinship with Becky when the girl was still around—seen some hint of her younger self in those big, sad eyes. Kate didn't know every detail of her situation, but she suspected plenty based on the interactions she'd witnessed between Henry and the girl. So when somebody came hammering at her door in the late evening, she half expected to walk down the stairs and find a runaway teenage girl waiting for her. Henry was an unwelcome surprise. 'What exactly do you want, Mister Lucas? Haven't you had enough from me already?'

His eyes were red like he'd been crying. 'I'm sorry, Mrs Rich, but I didn't know who else to turn to. You were always a good friend to us, and I feel just terrible about how things happened. It's Becky, you see. She's gone missing and we don't have any other people in these parts that I can ask for help. We're all alone out here.'

That stopped her dead in her tracks. 'Becky is missing, you say? You'd better come in then.'

Henry slunk in, eyes darting up and down the street like he was visiting his mistress. What a strange man. Kate shook the thought away, this was hardly the time. 'Now why don't you tell me exactly what happened, so I can help you.'

'We got in a fight, she was mad at me and she stormed off. We was at a truck stop, heading back south to see her folks, and she just ran off and now I don't know what to do to find her. Won't you help me?'

'Well, I'd say it sounds like she doesn't want you to find her.' Kate pursed her lips. 'Or that you're spinning me a yarn.'

Henry's sorrowful expression melted away into a grin. 'What is it about old bags like you that they can always see right through you?'

'Once burned, twice shy. That is what they say.' She straightened up to meet his smirk. 'So you're here with some deception to rob me once again? You must realise that I shall tell the police everything.'

Henry stepped closer. 'I don't reckon you'll be telling anyone much of anything by the time I'm through with you.'

Henry didn't often kill older women. His preference had always been for the young and the pretty when he had the choice, but he made do with the materials that were available to him. He strangled Kate Rich with his bare hands, feeling her papery skin tear beneath his digging fingers. Then he raped her, just the same as he had raped every other woman that he had killed, except the last. After he was finished, he took her out into one of the outbuildings and carved her into pieces, the same way that he had taught Ottis to do. And just like he had shown Ottis, he spent the rest of that night burning each and every one of those pieces until no trace remained, in an old wood-burning stove.

There was little cash in the house when all was said and done, far less than Henry had imagined that rich people kept lying around. And with no means of extracting a signature from the pile of ashes in the outhouses, the chequebook could serve him no purpose either. He set the house back to normal, cleaned away any trace that he had been there, and left quietly in the early hours of the morning, with just enough money to keep his car fuelled as he made his mad dash for freedom.

The luck that had preserved Henry through all of his life was finally starting to run thin. The world had changed while he wasn't looking, and the lifestyle that he was accustomed to had become a thing of the past. Nobody wanted itinerant workers anymore. Technology was booming, cities were growing and everywhere that civilisation blossomed was anathema to a man like Henry, who survived solely by slipping through the cracks. He took on a couple of temporary jobs across the southern states but soon found that he couldn't hold on to them when a simple background check threw all of the details of his officially recognised criminal past up as a barricade. With all of his dreams dead and buried behind him, he turned to the west and rode off for California once more.

The money ran out fast. Henry was drinking a lot to keep his feelings down, and keeping himself in a hazy state of not thinking cost more than keeping the car rolling. Without any work to support him, he thought that he might turn back to petty theft, the way that he had as a teenager, but like all of his other crimes, it seemed to have lost its appeal now. Perhaps, in time, his appetite for destruction and evil would have come back to him, but in the short-term, he still needed to get by.

His family no longer wanted anything to do with him. Stories of his child molestation had spread far and wide, and the cultural shifts of the late 70s and early 80s put far more condemnation on that than before. The things that he considered normal were now abhorrent. Even the squirrel raping half-brothers of his youth now looked down on him with disgust and contempt. All of Viola's children had gotten out of the Virginia woods; they had done their best to make something of themselves, something more than the feral children that their mothers made of them. All of them except Henry—the painful reminder of where they came from, and what they had been.

So, with no safety net left, and just a few stolen dollars left in his pockets, Henry decided to revisit a few old friends. The Smarts were absolutely gobsmacked when they answered the phone and found Henry on the other end. The moment that she realised who was on the line, O'Bere started screaming at him for robbing her mother. She was already on to the third round of expletives when Jack managed to wrestle the phone out of her hand. He clamped one of his hands over her mouth until she stopped flailing, then lifted the phone to his ear. As surprised as he had been to realise Henry had called, it was nothing compared to his surprise that Henry was still on the line after all of that screaming. 'Sorry about that, Henry. Big misunderstanding about that money situation. How are you doing?'

O'Bere was fuming, but it soon dawned on her what her husband was doing, so she kept her mouth shut as he nodded along and made sympathetic noises as Henry spun a tale of woe and abandonment, repeating the same lies over and over, like he was trying to wear through the truth by repetition alone. Eventually, when Henry felt like he was being believed, he asked if they still needed help with their furniture restoration business. He was alone now, and would only require a fraction of the room and board that his little family had required the last time around. He was down on his luck. It would be an act of charity. Jack wasn't enough of a fool to bring Henry to their doorstep. He quickly spun a sad story about their business going under but produced an alternative solution. He had a friend that lived just a little down the road, who was looking for help on his ranch. Would Henry be up for some odd jobs? It was just the bait that was required to reel the man in.

The next day, Henry completed the long drive to California and followed the instructions that he'd jotted dutifully down on a napkin until he arrived at the whitewashed gate of the ranch described. A police car pulled onto the dirt road behind him, flashing its blue and red lights in his rear-view mirror. Henry let out a groan. Jack Smart had set him up.

The Smarts and Henry never interacted the whole time he was

in Hemet. They had made their statements to the police before Henry even arrived, and had now returned home to await whatever results the criminal justice system could dole out. News of Kate's absence had reached them only a few days before Henry arrived, and they did not consider it to be a coincidence that an elderly woman who had been taken advantage of by the man once had now decided to leave town alone in the middle of the night without telling anyone. With some distance from their time together and the opportunity to shake off the charismatic spell he'd laid over them, they now believed that Henry was dangerous. They had presented all of their suspicions to the police, alongside the evidence that they had collected of Henry's petty fraud.

The detective who had investigated the case came to their home twenty-four hours later and sat with them for a while. Henry had been released. There just wasn't sufficient evidence to hold him, and they had no way of corroborating the story that the Smarts had laid out for them when the Texas police were treating the case as nothing more than a matter of some dementia-riddled old woman wandering off. Even the fraud charges lacked sufficient evidence to hold Henry. Despite all of their suspicions and his outright refusal to answer even a single question, there was no legal reason to hold him any longer.

Henry fled from civilisation along the backroads, convinced that he was still under police surveillance, uncomfortably sober for the first time in weeks. He needed somewhere to lay low until this heat died down. He had to find someplace where the police and civilisation didn't encroach. Somewhere that would be called 'off the grid' in modern parlance.

Never one to repeat the same mistake twice, Henry didn't call ahead to the House of Prayer before arriving. The Reverend Ruben Moore was shocked to see the man returning after he'd vanished in the night, but he was even more surprised that Becky wasn't with him. It immediately set alarm bells ringing in his mind. Ruben wasn't an idiot any more than Jack Smart was. He may have been more focused on trying to see the best in people, but he wasn't blind to their faults. You couldn't run a commune that offered housing to drug addicts and career criminals without having some awareness, or you wouldn't live very long. On top of that awareness, he had his finger on the proverbial pulse in the area surrounding his little slice of heaven, constantly taking stock of the opinions being voiced so that he might more easily shelter his little flock from any vengeful souls who blamed them for those who wronged them. He knew all about Henry's dealings with Kate Rich, and he had heard all of the rumours about the old woman's disappearance. She wasn't some drifter that Henry had found at the roadside. She was a pillar of the local community, and when she went missing, she was missed.

While he was loathed to bring the attention of the police to the House of Prayer, his suspicions about Henry did not stop there. He had watched Becky's blind devotion to Henry and the older man's contempt for it. He knew that she would never have parted from him willingly, and when he was pressed, Henry gave up the same story as he'd rolled out before about arguing with her at a truck stop and her taking off with some lorry driver without a backward glance, exactly the way that Henry once had.

Moore found a space for Henry to sleep, promised him shelter from the dangers of the world, and a guarantee of work when there was some. He did exactly what a preacher was meant to do and took all of the man's worries away. Then, the moment that Henry was asleep, Ruben drove into town to find the sheriff.

Ruben Moore had an excellent relationship with local law enforcement, out of necessity, and he really couldn't have the people in his care seeing him betray the trust of any one of them if he hoped to maintain control over them. Having Henry in custody was important to the local police, but not so important that they could overlook the hornet's nest of potential trouble that the House of Prayer could represent if its equilibrium were disrupted. It was agreed that they would keep an eye out for Henry's car about town and perform a traffic stop. All that Ruben had to do now was send the man on an errand.

The next morning, on June 15, 1983, Henry rolled into town and was stopped by a Texas Ranger named Phil Ryan. A cursory inspection of the inside of his vehicle revealed an unregistered handgun. As a felon, it was illegal for Henry to possess such a weapon. They finally had the excuse that they needed to arrest him, and once they had him, there wasn't a chance in hell that he was going to be allowed to walk free until he answered for whatever he had done to Kate Rich.

Anything You Say

The standard operating procedure of the local police seemed to be slightly overlooked when it came to Henry Lee Lucas. He was read his rights during the arrest, but when he tried to invoke them later, he discovered that those invariable rights afforded to every American seemed to vanish in the face of the murder of an old woman. He was stripped down to his undergarments as part of a 'weapon search,' but his clothes were never returned to him. He was deposited in a freezing concrete cell in between bouts of questioning. The police were mysteriously unwilling to fetch him his cigarettes, and when he complained of hunger and thirst, they brushed right past that into more demands for answers. Requesting a lawyer just resulted in him being flung back into the cell to wait for another hour while they 'tried to find one for him'. This was repeated over and over for almost four days, with each new shift of cops coming in and trying their luck.

Everyone knew that Henry had something to do with the disappearance of Kate Rich—they had the previous report of him defrauding her to tie him to an otherwise impregnable case. He was their only lead, and they were going to make him confess, one way or the other. It was only when they changed their tactics as they headed into the second day that they began to get a response from

Henry. They started asking after Becky. Henry almost immediately lost his mind, trying to fling himself bodily over the table to attack the grinning deputy. He had to be restrained and dragged back to his cell to cool off. They had found the lever that they were going to use to pry the case open.

It took a solid hour of questioning before he told them his well-practiced story about Becky running off at a truck stop, and officers were despatched immediately once the timeline of events had been established, to find evidence to the contrary. What they discovered instead was a waitress who remembered Henry and Becky arguing as they left, just as he described. She suspected that she'd seen the girl getting into one of the trucks and driving off, but she couldn't recall for certain. It completely supported Henry's version of events, so the police ignored it. With the very real possibility that it was a dead end, and with Henry having spent another few hours in the freezing cell, they switched back to questioning him about Kate Rich. All that they needed was some small admission of guilt from him and the floodgates would open. Any slight mistake and they could pounce on it. They had him talking now, even if it was just to deny everything, and from there they could tie him to places and dates. They could find the hole in the story and dig through it to the truth, or at least to a plausible enough confession that they could use. Henry still had the same calculating look in his eyes that he'd had from the moment he arrived. Despite everything that had happened, he was still trying to work out how he could turn the situation to his advantage, how he could survive and thrive when all of the rules had been changed.

He took a deep breath and confessed to everything they had accused him of, at least in regards to Rich. He claimed that he couldn't remember where he had burned the old woman's body, but he admitted to strangling her to death, just as he had. As if by magic, a lit cigarette appeared in his hand and his lost clothes were found. A hot meal was fetched in for him, made to order exactly the way he liked it. He went from being lower than the lowest worm to being every cop's favourite person. So, he just went on talking—clumsily providing details that would later be enough to guarantee his conviction—right up until the moment that they came back in with a fresh pack of cigarettes and a typed confession for him to sign. He signed it readily, with only a small handwritten addendum on the last page: 'I am not allowed to contact anyone. I'm in here by myself and still can't talk to a lawyer on this. I have no rights so what can I do to convince you about all this?'

Henry was already in jail by the time that he met his appointed defence lawyer. Ron Ponton took one look at the confession, talked to Henry for all of five minutes, then had it officially recanted. The confession had been extracted under so much duress it would be almost impossible for any court to give it credence. In their rush to convict Henry, they had actually rendered the only real evidence that they had useless. Of course, that wasn't the only front that Ponton had to fight this case on. The sheriff was not running a watertight operation. The police had allowed so much information about the case to leak—including almost every detail of Henry's confession—that any random attention seeker off the street could now walk in and duplicate it. They hadn't just made Henry's confession worthless, they made any confession made by any other suspect worthless, too. The police had been so confident that they had their killer that they had skipped ahead several steps and started to influence the potential jury pool in favour of their case.

Ponton fought fire with fire, unleashing an incendiary statement to the press that turned the whole police department against him for years to come. He described the inhumane treatment that Henry had suffered through, adding that it was 'calculated solely to require my defendant to confess guilt, whether he was innocent or guilty'. The open and shut case had just been blown wide open all over again, and the police were looking to their forensics teams to make up for their failings.

In the wood-burning oven at Kate Rich's house, a single blackened bone fragment was found and confirmed to be human, but because of the heat it had been exposed to, there was no way to extract any more information from it. It could have been Kate's or anyone else's. There was even a marginal chance that it wasn't even a human bone. Henry's countermeasures had done well. Beyond that bone, there were traces of Henry around the Rich house, but it was a matter of record that he had worked there for some time, so there was no way of knowing precisely when those samples originally arrived. Faced with a dead end in that regard, but still certain of Henry's guilt, even if the confession couldn't be used in court, they decided to apply pressure from another angle.

The search for Frieda 'Becky' Powell's body was arduous and slow. They had only the location of the truck stop in Bowie and a vague timeline of the events that took place, but from that, they were able to extrapolate a circle in which it was likely that her body had been dumped. From there they narrowed their search to areas that were more isolated and therefore more likely. Piece by piece, they found the girl's body, and the forensics team painstakingly reassembled it. When they had as much as they could find put together, they could confirm that it was the remains of a girl, likely in her late teens. But beyond that, identification was impossible. Without the missing head, dental records were useless. They couldn't even place the time of death with any accuracy. There was definitely a dead teenager near to where Henry last claimed to have seen Becky, but beyond that, they could be certain of nothing.

Still, the few pieces of circumstantial evidence that they had managed to accrue, accompanied by Henry's now discredited confession, were likely to prove enough to see him convicted of both murders. The specific details that he had let slip about the murder of Rich were too specific to have come from somebody who was not involved, and he was the only one with any motive whatsoever to do harm to young Frieda Powell. It would be enough to convince a jury, and that was all that the prosecutors cared about.

When Henry had his day in court, he pleaded guilty to both of the murders with something resembling pride, rather than allow

Ponton to do his job and fight the case that the state had built. None of this was particularly unusual, but what happened next was much more interesting—at the end of his confession in open court to killing both Frieda Powell and Kate Rich he added, 'And I've killed about a hundred other women, too.' His lawyer nearly lost his mind, but Henry hissed to him. 'If they're going to make me confess to one I didn't do, then I'll confess to everything.'

It was a kind of legal suicide. Henry didn't care about ever being free again. He barely even cared about staying alive. Everything that he had cared about was gone, and he had killed it with his own two hands. He received two life sentences for his crime, which he did nothing to dispute or appeal. Then, he was taken off to Williamson County Jail, where he was meant to live out the remainder of his days. In any sane world, that was where Henry's story would have come to an abrupt end, but his wild claims had already caught the attention of the serial killer obsessed media and the Attorney General of Texas. His confession might have been a bald-faced lie, but it was one that both of those powerful forces could use to their advantage, so they seized on it.

The only person who could have contradicted Henry and put an end to the impending circus was his fellow killer, Ottis Toole. But Ottis had his own problems to contend with at that moment in time. On his arrival back in Jacksonville after leaving Henry and Becky, Ottis had found the police already waiting on the doorstep of his sister's house. He went into custody expecting some follow-up questions about his missing niece, so it is safe to say that he was surprised when the police presented him with not one but two murder by arson charges. Henry's training had protected Ottis from forensics in all of the direct murders that they had conducted since meeting, but when it came to his old hobby of setting buildings alight, his technique hadn't improved since he was fourteen years old. Eyewitnesses put him at the scene of each crime, but the physical evidence required to pin both fires to him was just out of reach for the forensics of the time. His car was impounded for inspection and he was cut loose, with a warning that if he tried to leave town he would be jailed—evidence or not.

For the following year, he lived in a state of limbo, barely scraping by on the sufferance of his family and the few odd dollars he managed to make stripping wrecked cars, just like Henry had taught him. His true passions for murder and mayhem seemed to wither with nobody to share them with, and when science had advanced enough to tie him with certainty to the killings that he was suspected of, he went quietly, with a reserved sadness that nobody might have guessed that the loud and lumbering monster of a man was capable of.

Without Henry, he had no reason to live free, and he had no reason to fight against the charges that were levelled against him. He readily confessed to both of the arson charges and the accompanying murders in a plea deal that kept him out of reach of the electric chair. He was to serve two consecutive life sentences for his crimes, just like Henry. And, just like Henry, he was about to discover the incredible power of telling a lie that everybody wants to believe.

By December of 1983, Henry's story had filtered through to Ottis, even in prison, and he followed his lover's lead gleefully, stopping a passing guard with a flirtatious wink. 'Oh, officer, I've done some real bad things, and I want to talk about them.'

Before Henry had even been deposited in Williamson County Jail, where he was meant to spend the rest of his days, the Texas Rangers had already descended upon him. They formed the 'Lucas Task Force,' taking his confessions of serial murder completely at face value and using him to clear two hundred and thirteen previously unsolved murders through his confessions.

For the first time in his life, Henry was being treated well by other people. More than well, in fact. He was a celebrity, getting preferential treatment everywhere he went. He travelled the country on a private jet, staying in fancy hotels, eating in restaurants and cafés everywhere that he stopped, and generally being treated like royalty. In the police stations where he spent most of his time during each phase of confessions, he was given free rein to wander about, even being granted security codes to open the doors. He wore his own clothes, rarely had to wear handcuffs, and was treated more like a consultant than a convict.

In Huntington, West Virginia, Henry confessed to killing a man whose death had been ruled a suicide. That confession was sufficient to force the insurance company to pay out on his 'victim's' life insurance policy, granting a widow the financial aid that she needed to survive without her husband. The Rangers were delighted—they spent $3,000 dollars throwing Lucas a party in the Holiday Inn, bringing in liquor and prostitutes to celebrate their 'big win.'

Henry's confessions were absolutely perfect, with video and audio recordings of each one, and specific details being offered up that nobody except the investigators and the killer would know. The only problem was, some of them directly contradicted the others. Henry was possessed of a certain animal cunning, and he was a talented manipulator, but he was not an intelligent man by any stretch of the imagination. The dates of several of the murders that he confessed to did coincide, but they would have required some remarkable acts of transportation to make them possible, including a memorable five-thousand-mile cross-country drive in twenty-four hours.

Normal arrangements had been suspended around Henry Lee Lucas, and the end result was that he was gaining access to information about the crimes that he would later confess to ahead of time. He had computer access in some of the police departments that he visited. He was shown pictures of crime scenes ahead of time to 'jog his memory.' He even read through the police's reports while they set up their recording equipment just to 'make sure he got it all straight.'

This was the most comfortable that Henry had ever been, and he was making sure to milk it for all that it was worth. His prison cell in Williamson County was fitted out with all of the modern conveniences, including a television, a proper bed, and a small wardrobe for his clothes, as he was not obliged to wear a prison uniform. When he was on the road, he would often issue orders to the Texas Rangers who were supposed to be guarding him, and local police would marvel as they scampered off to fulfil his every whim. As long as his confessions kept on flowing, he was going to be living the high life, and he conveyed as much through his letters to Ottis, who quickly adopted the same 'tell them what they want to hear' attitude, supporting Henry's narratives where it suited him and contradicting them when he felt like it.

The duo were in frequent telephone contact despite all of the ways that this could taint the evidence that they provided, and at some point they decided that they wanted to create some bigger story out of their crimes and their lies; some grand, American drama played out through the medium of their confessions that would absolve both of them of guilt while still allowing them to reap the harvest of rewards that their confessions brought along with them.

Ottis's childhood provided them with exactly the inspiration that they needed—and so the Hands of Death were born.

Fruit of the Poisoned Tree

Every new confession that Henry gave now came with an introduction, relating to the orders he was issued by the shadowy and mysterious cult known only as the Hands of Death. He claimed that he, Ottis, and many of the other serial killers active in the USA throughout the 70s and 80s were not independent psychopaths as had been previously assumed, but were, in fact, all servants of a Satanic organisation that was using the mayhem that they spread to destabilise America.

It seems like an absolutely ridiculous supposition to the modern reader, but at the time, the 'Satanic Panic' was in full swing. A significant portion of the American people believed that there were devil worshipping cults hiding in plain sight all over the country and that the declining fortunes of America after the boom years following the Second World War could be blamed on infernal influence. As the years of 'flower power' and the hippie counterculture came to an end, all of the abuses of power within the communes and cults of that time period became public knowledge. Combined with some high-profile cases where Satanism was blamed for crimes involving child abuse, this created a surprisingly credulous audience for Henry's stories.

It isn't clear if Ottis ever crossed paths with any Satanists beyond his grandmother, although he would gladly regale you with stories of black masses and cannibal feasts if he was given the opportunity. But the small amount of knowledge he had on the subject still vastly outstretched that of those investigating his claims. As with the false confessions, he and Henry were able to provide just enough real details to make their stories of satanic murder cults seem plausible.

The Florida police were sent out to trawl the Everglades, to search for the Hands of Death cult's secret headquarters, and all the while, Henry and Ottis were still spilling out more salacious details about their crimes in its service. About the girl that they abducted from the roadside and delivered to the Everglades to serve as a meal at the initiation of new members. About the other serial killers that they met who also worked for the advancement of the cult's great objective of destroying America.

With all of the yarns that they were spinning, it was hardly surprising that some of them became a little tangled, and it was even less surprising that eventually one of them was woven into a noose. The 'Orange Socks' case had captured national attention for a short while. It had the whiff of celebrity about it, and now that they had a full confession to the murder, the Texas State Attorney was more than ready to press charges. After consulting the police files, Henry had produced an almost perfect confession to the crime, and there was no evidence that immediately contradicted the idea that it may really have been him, so they pressed ahead with the case. Henry went quite happily into the courtroom, treating it as just another of the many days out that his pseudo-celebrity status in the prison granted him. The jury was shown the video of his confession, which had been heavily edited to remove the coaching and leading questions from the officers in the room at the time of recording. Henry made no attempt to argue with the video, although his lawyer—who had a slightly better grasp on the magnitude of the situation—was quick to contest the veracity of the confession on the basis of that editing, and on the basis that he was able to produce a recorded confession from a completely different murderer that would remove all blame, or at least greatly reduce his client's culpability for his crimes. For the first time, the contradictions that Henry and Ottis had introduced into their shared stories became an advantage—both men claimed to have killed 'Orange Socks,' but only one of them could have committed the act itself.

The jury preferred the evidence on television to the man in a suit who kept talking at them. Henry was convicted of the murder, which he took in his stride. He was coming up on fifty years old. An extended sentence meant nothing to him anymore, which was why he was so gleeful in confessing to every crime under the sun. He was smiling in the courtroom right up until the moment that the judge passed his death sentence. Suddenly, his smile fell away and he started talking in harsh whispers to his lawyer. He was not aware that death was on the table when he started all of this. After he had first been arrested, he was at the lowest point in his life, but now he was living like a king and he didn't want that to stop any time soon. He begged his lawyer to get him out of it, to fix things. So, an appeal was soon set in motion.

Even though he had suffered through that scare, it did nothing to slow Henry's roll when it came to confessions. The Lucas Task Force picked him up again just a few days later to go out and look at some more crime scenes. Unfortunately for Henry and Ottis, by this point, their claims were finally starting to garner some scrutiny. Several officers that the Lucas Task Force had interacted with had noticed the bizarre way that he was being treated, and the completely inappropriate way that he was being given access to case information ahead of his confessions. Enough complaints were filed that the Texas Rangers began to suffer some scrutiny, and as a result, they had to begin running a tighter ship, with a marked reduction in the information that they were feeding to Henry ahead of time. Of course, by this point, Henry was pretty much an expert at manufacturing convincing confessions and in avoiding any potentially contradictory details in his recitals. The lack of solid facts to build on made his confessions a little bit shakier, but no less elaborate.

After Henry confessed to thirteen separate and unrelated murders in Houston, he came to the attention of Dallas detective Linda Erwin. Erwin thought that Henry was a liar from the moment she read the first reports about him, but that last cluster were enough to push her over the edge into taking action. She contacted the Lucas Task Force about a murder that she had on the books, a cold case that sounded like a perfect fit for Lucas's victim profile. She wondered if they might be able to bring Lucas and take a look at it before they left town. Henry looked over the collection of pictures that she had brought from the case, eavesdropped on the conversations that she had with the Texas Rangers outside, and then delivered a confession riddled with enough details to easily convict him of the crime. It would all have been a normal day in the work of the Lucas Task Force if it weren't for the fact that Erwin had fabricated the entire case using old crime scene photos and a little bit of imagination.

She reported this to Phil Ryan in the Texas Rangers, and before long he was repeating the experiment regularly with the Lucas Task Force, feeding them the details of an invented case and watching as they extracted a confession that perfectly matched the case details. By this point, Henry had produced over three thousand separate confessions to crimes so widespread that it was nearing the point of ridiculousness. His devotion to the 'Hands of Death' story just made his claims even more incredulous. But even the idea that he had murdered three thousand people was nothing compared to some of the stories that he made up on the fly. He claimed to have been involved in the assassination of Jimmy Hoffa, through the cult's mob ties. He claimed to have starred in a series of snuff films, filmed in the cult's headquarters in the depths of the Everglades. He even claimed that when Jim Jones decided that the time had come to kill his followers in Jonestown, Henry and Ottis were the ones who had been called on to deliver the poison. If he had confessed to ambushing Neil Armstrong when he first stepped out onto the surface of the moon, it wouldn't have been any more insane than some of the stories that he was already trying to get people to accept. He was rewarded every time that he invented a ridiculous story, so he went on telling ridiculous stories. To the limited intellect of Henry Lee Lucas, no one confession was any more ridiculous than any other. Truth and lie had blended in his mind to the point that he genuinely could not distinguish between them.

No evidence could ever be found of the Hands of Death, despite a frankly ridiculous amount of effort being expended trying to track the satanic cult down and Henry's endless insistence that they definitely existed.

In the midst of all this nonsense, Henry began to recant confessions as and when it suited him, then later confess yet again to the same crimes with altered details. Whether he was trying to make his confessions seem more believable or simply to tangle the web even further for those trying to create actual prosecutions from his claims is unclear, but the end result was that almost nothing that he said was usable in a court of law, if only because his complicated system of confession, recanting, re-confession, and later denial of key details would make things too difficult for a jury to follow.

By 1986, almost every law enforcement agency in the country had learned that Henry's lies could not be trusted, and the jet-setting lifestyle that he was accustomed to had settled into a more comfortable and settled life on death row. The Attorney General for Texas, Jim Mattox, had seen his underlings using Lucas to clear the books of unsolved crimes and was disgusted with their betrayal of the system that they were sworn to uphold. He pushed through a report on the confessions and convictions connected to Henry Lee Lucas, informally known as 'The Lucas Report,' which proved beyond a shadow of a doubt that most, if not all, of his confessions, were provably false.

Working through every single official record from Henry's life, they were able to construct a timeline of his movements throughout the years. There were huge grey areas when he worked cash in hand or drifted throughout the country, but specific confessions were soon easily discounted.

The murder of Curby Reeves in Smith County, Texas, occurred on August 10, 1977. Despite confessing to the crime and providing details that 'only the killer could know,' Henry was working a twelve-hour shift in a mushroom farm in Pennsylvania on that date. Similarly, the 1979 murder of Elaine Tollett in Tulsa, Oklahoma, occurred while Henry was hospitalised in Bluefield, West Virginia. Most pressingly, the murder of 'Orange Socks' in Texas coincided with a roofing job that Henry was recorded to have attended in Florida. It was possible that Henry altered those business records as a forensic counter-measure, or simply to claim wages that he was not entitled to, but the homeowner remembered him specifically. Henry remained adamant about his guilt, but the State of Texas was not prepared to kill a man when the only evidence that he had committed a crime at all was the word of a known liar.

Down in Raiford Prison in Florida, no attempts had been made to construct prosecutions out of Ottis Toole's confessions. Too much of his story was fluid. Too many of his confessions were circumstantially correct at best. Ottis was successfully convicted of a pair of additional murders over the years, but it was never as a result of his confessions, only solid police work, eyewitness testimony, and fresh evidence being uncovered. Two hitchhikers, David Schallart and Ada Johnson, were among his confessions, but DNA evidence on both bodies was what cinched both cases.

More years were added to his sentence, but the death penalty was never sought, not when it was clear that the years of appeals would all prove pointless in the face of Ottis's impending mortality anyway. Instead of making Ottis the centre of attention, the state of Florida let him wither away in darkness, and it took barely any time at all for his steady stream of confessions to run dry with no material reward. He lived a relatively comfortable life in the prison compared to the conditions that many of the other prisoners faced, but he wasn't elevated to a state of royalty like Henry, or Ted Bundy—who slept in the room beside his. The only real pleasure that Ottis seemed to find in his prison life was his weekly telephone call with Henry, where he was often overheard to express his undying love for the other man, even though he knew Henry couldn't return it. Even on their very last phone call, in 1996, when a phone had to be brought to the side of his bed in the medical wing, Henry never told Ottis that he loved him. A lifetime of alcoholism and hard living caught up to Ottis on September 15, 1996, when, at the age of 49, his liver failed. His niece was the only one at his bedside to hear his final words—a deathbed confession that he was the one responsible for the death and decapitation of Adam Walsh, along with the sad story that accompanied it. Nobody came to claim Ottis's body, so he was buried in an unmarked grave in the prison cemetery. If Henry mourned his closest friend's death, he was careful to give no sign of it. Whatever his complicated feelings towards Ottis were, he kept them locked inside, never to be heard by any living soul.

As a result of the Lucas Report findings, in 1998, Governor George W. Bush commuted Henry's death sentence to life in prison—the only time that the future president would ever commute a death penalty in his whole career.

The Williamson County prosecutor, who had devoted no small part of his efforts through the years in trying to secure a conviction for the 'Orange Socks' case, felt simultaneously vindicated and furious about the whole thing. There had been other, far more viable suspects in the case that had now slipped beyond the reach of justice due to Henry's confessions, and there were likely to be thousands of other criminals still walking the streets because of his interference. For every actual serial killer who was annoyed that Henry had taken credit for their work, there were probably a hundred run-of-the-mill murderers delighted to have attention diverted away from them. Convictions based solely on confessions soon became a rarity in the

American criminal justice system because of the actions of Henry Lee Lucas and Ottis Toole.

On March 13, 2001, Henry had been almost entirely forgotten. Even the criminologists and students who used to visit him had stopped after the findings of the Lucas Report proved that any statement he made was worthless. There had been a few crusaders over the years, people with a political interest in seeing Henry as being everything that he said he was, but they were out on the fringe, with no real power to change his life, so he ignored them. He remained in a state of relative comfort within the prison, never having to work for the privileges that other prisoners slaved away for thanks to the deals that he had cut during his rash of confessions. He was tucked up in a real bed, with a real mattress, in a state of comfort that those around him would never experience again, right up until the moment that his heart stopped beating.

The Perfect Liars

If you believed every part of Henry and Ottis's tales without doubt, then the duo were the most prolific and dangerous serial killers in American history. An urban legend come to life: one of them a towering, simpering monster who could only achieve orgasm through killing, the other a one-eyed drifter who exuded a literal miasma of evil.

The truth is a little more complex. Some of the events in this book may not have happened precisely as described. Not just the small details of the specific words that people used, the exact time of day, or the complexities of their motivations, but the actual crimes that formed the centre of Henry and Ottis's stories may not have happened at all. It is almost impossible to separate fact from fiction when it comes to these killers, and it is only by constant comparison between their stories, official records, eyewitness accounts, and every other available source that it is possible to piece together something that seems likely to be the truth.

Both men were devoid of empathy, interested in their own hedonistic pleasure above all else, and devoted to murder as the tool by which they could achieve their goals. They were psychopaths in the purest sense, shaped by biology and circumstance to pursue only their own interests to the exclusion of all else—and then they encountered the system that was meant to keep men like that away from civilisation. The prisons reshaped these crude killing animals into the perfect criminals, giving them the education that they needed to avoid detection for decades and providing them with plain evidence that their lives mattered more than the lives of their victims. Every act of evil that they ever committed was rewarded, both in the pleasure that it brought them and in the comfort that they would later enjoy in prison.

Despite the ridiculousness of their claim that there was some shadowy secret society providing Henry and Ottis with victims and a purpose in life, it turned out to be true. The criminal justice system that was supposed to stop men like them instead empowered them and rewarded them for their crimes.

Both of these men are, undeniably, serial killers—enough evidence has accrued over the years that this one seed of truth beneath the tangled mess of lies cannot be disputed. But beyond that, it all comes down to belief. Either they killed the forty people that criminologists have been able to tie to them with some degree of certainty, or they killed upwards of three thousand people while easily evading detection or capture for decades.

Ultimately, Henry and Ottis's greatest legacy is not their actions, but their stories. Clumsily constructed and blithely told, their tales made legends out of them in their own lifetime. The stuff of nightmares, certainly, but not the kind of nightmares that will readily be forgotten when dawn breaks. The kind that go on preying at your mind and come back to you every time you are lying down to sleep to fill you with dread. They did not kill all of the people that they said they did, but they could have. Anybody could be just as prolific and avoid detection just as easily. And that possibility is more frightening than any cold, hard facts.

BLACK WIDOW

The True Story of Giggling Granny Nannie Doss

Domestic Goddess

Smooth jazz crackled out of the radio on the kitchen windowsill, and Nannie hummed right along with it. Funny to think that just a few years back that kind of music was the province of rebels and teens, when now you could hear it with the turn of a knob. The late afternoon sunlight was still filtering through the trees outside, and though there was sure to be a chill on the air come morning, Nannie was warm in here beside the open door of her warming oven.

There is a fine art to making pie crust that escapes most home cooks, but Nannie had the knack—hard won through years in the kitchen. She'd cut the shortening with flour and salt until it looked like little peas, then she'd snatch in the jug of water that she'd left cooling out in the shadows on the porch and add it all in one go. Her hands moved on their own, without much need for her intervention, just as her lips pursed and whistled along to the music on the radio.

If her mind had been here, in this moment, then maybe she would have been happy. It was as close to idyllic as any moment of her life so far and much better than most of them. If she could turn her thoughts away from the things that might have been—the things that she longed for so desperately—then maybe she could have settled for this moment as her happiest.

The shock of cold on her fingertips brought her back to the moment at hand with a start. When she looked down, there was a fork in one hand, working away at the crust, and her other hand had gone wandering off across the countertop and brushed against the jug from outside. She giggled at her own silliness, then picked up the little cork-stoppered bottle of vinegar to add just a dash, like mother had taught her.

She should have been happy here, in this kitchen, in this house. Her husband heading home from work to eat his dinner across the table from her. Her days filled with the gentle labours of the completely comfortable. The callouses on her hands from years of hard graft had faded. The aches in her joints on cold mornings were soothed by the warmth of this home that she had made. She should have been happy. Why wasn't she happy?

She fumbled the cork, and vinegar spread across the countertop, filling the whole kitchen with its acrid reek. She snatched up a dishcloth and did her best to mop it up, but she could feel tears pricking at the corners of her eyes. Why wasn't she happy? She had everything that she had ever wanted. She had the husband and the home; she had love in her life. Why wasn't she happy? A sob bubbled up her throat, but she caught it before it escaped and turned it into another giggle. 'Silly me.'

No point crying over spilt vinegar, was there? Just another little inconvenience. Hardly worth losing control over. The vinegar hadn't made it far before she righted the bottle and cleaned up. And with a vinegar-soaked cloth, she might as well give the windows a clean when the pie goes into the oven. They didn't need it—sunlight was streaming in—but it was making the best of a bad situation, and that is what Nannie had always been taught to do.

Nannie's hands went back to work on the pie, and she turned inwards again, dreaming of Paris, dreaming of flowers and dancing. Romance had always been her drug of choice, ever since she had been little, and it didn't hurt anybody for her to have a little day-dream. If the man in her dreams didn't look and act exactly like her husband, it wasn't going to hurt anyone. That was the wonderful thing about dreams—you could imagine yourself doing just about anything without ever having to deal with the consequences. You didn't have to think about where you were going to sleep the next day when you'd thrown away your whole life and found yourself cast out into the street. You didn't have to look folk in the eye, knowing that they knew exactly what you had done.

If Nannie could have lived in her dreams, then she would have. What a beautiful life that would be. Breakfast in bed, lunch in some fancy restaurant, carriage rides through the park, bouquets of roses waiting for her behind every closed door, and a single sweet kiss on the lips, just like in the black and white movies that she'd loved ever since the first moment she'd laid eyes on them. True romance. That was what her dreams were made of. There was no sweat dripping in her eyes, there was no grunting or snoring or odious smells, there was just that perfect kiss and then the fade to black.

The fade to black never came. That was the trouble with real life. She had found her husband, he had romanced her, she had melted in his arms and now... nothing. She couldn't just stay melted forever. Life kept on trudging on and wearing her down, and in retrospect, that one perfect moment never quite seemed perfect. She had no shortage of love in her life, but none of it was true. None of it was pure. There was always some ulterior motive, some sordid secret just waiting to be outed. Men were flawed creatures, she understood that—lord, did she understand that—but was it too much to ask for just one of them to truly love her?

She knew love was real, otherwise, how could they have written all those books and songs about it? More than that, though, she knew it was real the same way that she knew there was a sky up above her even when her eyes were closed. Love was a fundamental truth of the universe.

The pie crust was lain out under a clean dishcloth to settle, and her attention was finally turned back to the task at hand. She had a little wicker basket full of apples from the garden, far too sour to eat raw, but sharp and firm, just right for cooking. Her knife danced smoothly through the pale flesh, chopping them into wafer-thin slices that she'd lay across the base and over the top, for texture as much as flavour. A quick dusting of sugar and spice and they were ready.

The prunes were last. Rich and sweet once they were stewed—an old family recipe that her mother and in-laws had all enjoyed, even on their deathbeds. It took more sugar than Nannie would ever admit to get them tasting just right, to be in balance with the apples, but it wasn't like she was going to be eating any of the pie anyway. Her sweet tooth ran in the direction of books and magazines rather than puddings.

Once the prunes were stewing away, Nannie turned her attention to the window panes. She knew that she could be a bit lax when it came to household chores. When her black mood set in it got more and more difficult to find the energy to see to nonsense like scrubbing floors and dusting shelves. Some days it felt like a battle just to get out of bed at all, and her darling husband, the light of her life, would chastise her like she was a spoiled child unwilling to do her share of the chores, even though her share in this house seemed to be every single one of them, while he went slinking off to who knows where with giggling girls half his age. Shameless. He must have thought she was a fool. He must have thought to himself, 'That Nannie is so lost in her daydreams that she won't even notice if I run around on her.'

She had noticed. She noticed everything. She was a dutiful and attentive wife, even when the weight of this miserable life and this horrible little house was pressing down on her like she was pinned in a vice. She knew everything that went on in his life, and he knew not a damned thing about hers, which was exactly the way she liked it.

When he came stomping in, making demands, tossing out her magazines like they were trash instead of treasures, that was when the dark moods came on the strongest. When he left her alone, ran around with teenagers and only slouched in to eat the food that she worked tirelessly to put on his table, it was easier to make believe that everything was going to be okay, that their life together was the true romance of her dreams and not a hollow sham built on a bedrock of lies.

No matter how hard she worked at the windows, she still couldn't see through them clearly. Sunlight should have been streaming right in, but the harder that she tried to see it, the more distant it became. The more that she tried to make it right, the streakier and more opaque the glass became.

Something was burning. The scent of it snapped her out of her furious scrubbing, and she tossed the sour cloth aside into the sink with a grumble. The prunes would be sticking. She stirred at the pot furiously, scraping the wooden spoon across the bottom and hoping that she hadn't wasted a whole tin of prunes on a ruined mess. She stirred and stirred until she was certain that the caramelised fruit was mixed all the way through. She then took a tentative taste. The pie was going to be all right. There was a gristly edge to it that she could taste—a hint that it was burnt and spoiled—but she could pour on more sugar and spice and it would all fade away. Inattention had done that. Something that should have been perfect had almost been spoiled completely just because the one person in the world who was supposed to tend to it had been too busy chasing off after other things. Things that didn't really matter. She could cover it all up, though. She was so very good at covering it all up.

She pulled open the cupboard and let her hands go back to doing things for themselves. Sugar would fix everything. A little more sweetness in their life was exactly what was required. She sprinkled in the white powder and watched with a sigh as it dissolved into the prunes. Just a little more sweetness was all that they needed to make everything come out right.

She set the container of rat poison down beside the sugar packet, then awareness came back to her again, and she giggled at her silliness. She'd forgotten to add the sugar, too. It wouldn't do for that almond flavour to be too bitter. If it was, her husband might not eat enough of the pie. Just one bite wouldn't do. He had to love it so much that he never wanted it to end. He had to guzzle up that pie like it was his last meal on Earth.

Once she was certain of her measurements, Nannie transferred the prunes into the crust and topped it all off with the remaining apple slices and pastry. Once she was satisfied with its perfection, she slipped the pie into the oven and closed the door on it.

Until that moment, the kitchen had remained warm, but now the chill of the evening intruded. That room was the heart of the house, and the heat from her kitchen emanated out to fill the whole space, but with the pie consigned to the oven, there was no longer an excuse to keep on lingering there. Nannie washed off her dishes, threw out the ruined dish-rag and carefully put everything back into its appointed place.

With a sigh, she turned off the radio and headed out into the cold. She wanted the whole house perfect before her husband got home. After all, they'd be getting a mess of visitors soon, and she wouldn't want to shame herself.

Far from Arcadia

Blue Mountain, Alabama, sounds like the kind of place with sweeping fields, scenic vistas, pine forests and hot, humid summers that stretch out long into the latter half of the year, and for the most part that is true. There is some real natural beauty there, but humans have built a legacy of misery right on top of it.

The Hazle farm was far from the idyllic image that most have of rural life. There was more mud than grass and more cursing than praying. James Hazle had inherited it from his parents far younger than he might have expected, and after paying off the loans that they had taken out against future crops that had never even been planted, his inheritance amounted to a few acres of dirt and a few buildings in desperate need of some maintenance. He was alone in the world without a spare penny to hire in help, but, as with so many men, all that he lacked in wealth he made up for in pride. He would have slapped away the hand that offered him charity—not that anyone was ever offering.

His prospects were poor, and the outlook for his future was bleak. No decent woman would marry a man who was certain to lead her into destitution. No bank or seed-loan outfit would front him the cash required to get the farm back in action. He had enough savings and dairy cattle to subsist for a few years, but without a lump sum of money to get things moving his situation was never going to improve.

Lou was in a bad state, too. Try as she might she could not hide her pregnancy from her family any longer, and with no father in the picture, she was destined to be just another one of the many 'ruined women' that Alabama mothers pointed out to their daughters as living warnings about how a sinful life would reward you. Her father took the news about as expected, and if it hadn't been for her mother's rapid intervention he likely would have beaten her until the problem went away. While he was quite content to beat his daughter bloody, he drew the line at hitting his wife. So, with no more recourse to direct violence against Lou for her bad decisions, he switched tactics to the more insidious kind of violence. She was kicked out of the house with no means to support herself—abandoned by her whole extended family until she coughed up the name of the father, so that her father's vicious temper could be turned on him instead and a shotgun wedding could be organised.

Surprising everyone, Lou was resolute in the face of this adversity—whether this was because she genuinely didn't know the identity of the father of her unborn child, or she was so in love with him that she was unwilling to ruin his life the way that he had ruined hers or, most likely, because he was one of the soldiers from the nearby base in Anniston. Whoever fathered her child, she received no financial support from him whatsoever. She scraped by in Blue Mountain by doing odd jobs for a few sympathetic women about town, but the cost of rent on the room that she'd taken was more than she made most weeks.

As she came into the late stages of her pregnancy, Blue Mountain was heading into a fierce winter, and between the cost of wood, the cost of rent, and the minuscule amount of work she was able to do while on the verge of giving birth, Lou ended up in arrears by months with no means to dig herself out of that hole.

Lou's daughter, Nancy, was born out of wedlock on the fourth of November, 1905. She was officially a 'ruined woman' in the eyes of the community, and it was well known by everyone in town that no respectable man would ever have anything to do with her—something that was reported to Lou almost daily by the extended family members who couldn't resist the lure of a cooing new-born baby despite the stigma attached to it.

But Lou just laughed in their faces. No more than a week after the baby had been born, she had received a proposal of marriage from a local farmer. A man with acres to his name, a hardy work ethic, and absolutely no qualms about the fact that Lou had a baby in tow. She was married to James Hazle and settled into her new life on the farm before the end of the year. The town's gossip mill went into overdrive, of course, but it didn't take long before they all settled on the path of least resistance—believing that Nancy Hazle was James' daughter by blood as well as by name and that the timing of events had been the only unfortunate part of their family's story.

If life alone had been hard for Lou, life with James was even harder. She had been starved for even the most basic of human kindness during her pregnancy, and the bare minimum that James had delivered to her then had seemed like a godsend. But now that she was his wife, she was realising with horror that the bare minimum was all that he had to give. James was a dour and miserable man with a mean streak that came out whenever he was put under the least amount of stress.

There was no honeymoon period for Lou. From the moment that she moved into the tiny farmhouse, he started barking orders at her, and when she wasn't pliant or obedient enough for his liking he would lash out with both insults and the cane he used to drive his cattle. Man and wife would be out from dawn working to clear the fields of debris, to plant the crops, to milk the cows. The list of chores that needed doing around the farm was endless, and most nights, they would be up well into the night still trying to get through the tail end of their daily tasks.

Little Nancy, known even then as Nannie, spent most of her

early life completely ignored unless she was screaming, an obstacle for the adults to navigate as they went about the back-breaking work of trying to haul the farm back onto its feet. By the time that she was old enough to walk, she was being set to work. As a small child, there was little around the farm that she could physically achieve, but every small and fiddly task that didn't require brute strength was dumped on her, and she received the same harsh punishment as her grown mother if she couldn't work out how to complete her jobs within the allotted time.

James watched her with the slow cogs of his brain turning, calculating how long it would be until she could clear a field of debris, how long until she could be trusted to fetch things from the storehouse or clean the farmhouse by herself so that Lou could be put to better use. Just as he'd calculate the use of his cattle or any other farm animal, he did the calculations on how long it might be until this little family he had acquired would be yielding the optimal amount of labour, and how much of Lou's labour he was willing to lose if it meant more hands being available further down the line.

One brother and three sisters followed Nannie into the world in rapid succession, all timed carefully so that Lou's pregnancies wouldn't interfere in the harvest.

By the time that Nannie was old enough to retain memories, she knew that she hated her father. As the oldest child, the care of all her brothers and sisters fell to her. She was the one preparing their meals, changing their nappies, and settling their squabbles despite the fact that she was barely more than a child herself. By 1910, when other children her age were heading off to school each morning, Nannie was still trapped at home, taking care of babies and clearing the field of debris ahead of the plough. It was like her life had been put on hold before it even began. Any hopes or dreams that she might have cultivated for the future were ground up and lain as fertiliser for the farm. Despite all of their efforts, the farm rarely did more than break even. Things weren't getting better.

In the winter, when there was less to do around the farm,

Nannie and her older brother were permitted to go to school, hiking two miles in the rain and snow to get there, and the same back again. Even that little escape was a miserable experience for her. She couldn't catch up to the other children academically due to the sheer amount of school time she had missed, and even when she did make some gains, they were wiped out in the springtime when she was dragged back to work on the farm all over again. To make matters worse, the other school children looked down on the Hazle kids, correctly identifying them as poor and picking on them for their odd mannerisms and introverted personalities.

Nannie's formal education would never progress beyond her elementary education, even though she was able to attend school more regularly as her brother and sisters got older and started assuming some of her responsibilities. Despite all of this, she developed a lifelong love of reading. In part, this was because the skill had been so hard won for her, and now she was proud of the achievement, but it was mostly because reading was an escape from her unhappy life. With a book, she could be somewhere else, she could be someone else. It was hardly surprising that it posed a tempting alternative to the reality she was trapped in.

Beyond the hateful schoolchildren, Nannie's social life extended only as far as her family tree. When the weather prevented them from carrying on with work at the farm, the whole family would bundle up and head into town to visit with relatives, and when it seemed that the foul weather would persist for more than a few days, they made plans to go even further afield, taking the train out of Anniston to visit family all over Alabama.

In the spring of 1912, as a storm raked the countryside, the Hazle family set out for another visit, this time intending on taking the train down to spend the weekend with some of James' family in the South. The trip started off as well as usual, with all of the dripping wet children slipping and sliding about the carriage until their father barked at them to sit down before they hurt themselves, then moving on to the quieter and more restive phase of the journey when Lou handed out old magazines from her bag, which then settled them. She gave Nannie a battered old copy of True Romance because she knew that it was her favourite, and even though she had read it a dozen times or more, it only took a moment before Nannie was lost in the stories once more. There wasn't much that Lou could do to make her daughter's life better, but the moment that she had discovered Nannie's love for romantic stories, she had started putting aside all the spare change that she could squirrel away to buy more of the yellowing paperbacks and dusty magazines that could sate that hunger.

Nannie was completely lost in the story when everything abruptly went dark. When she next opened her eyes, it was to a world of pain. Her head felt like it was in a vice, and despite it making it worse, she immediately started sobbing. When she managed to force her eyes open, she found that she was laid out on the ottoman in her uncle's house in southern Alabama. The day-long journey had vanished in the blink of an eye. Her mother rushed in when she heard Nannie sobbing and applied a cold compress to her head that nearly knocked her back into unconsciousness with the amount of pain that it inflicted. It would be hours later before that searing pain calmed down enough for Nannie to hear the story of what had happened to her.

The same storm that had freed them from the farm had been whipping across the whole state, and in its furore, it had managed to down a pine tree right by a bend in the railway track. When the driver spotted it, he had slammed on the brakes, flinging everyone onboard forward, out of their seats. The other children had a few bruises and scraped knees, but Nannie had been seated directly in front of a metal bar. When the brakes went on, she had been flung head-first into it and knocked unconscious for the rest of her journey.

At seven years old, Nannie suffered a concussion so bad it left her with permanent damage to her brain. For the rest of her life, she would experience sharp and sudden headaches that could go on for days at a time, and her once bright and cheerful temperament in the face of adversity seemed to have been knocked clean out of her. She was prone to bouts of severe depression from that point on, depression that exhibited itself most often in 'dark moods' that could last even longer than her headaches, but also in brief bouts of uncontrollable rage before she could regain control of herself.

Forbidden Love

A long period of convalescence was not on the cards for Nannie. The moment that they were back on the farm, she was back to work. Over the year that followed, she suffered from blackouts, severe headaches, and long bouts of depression, to the point that seeing her without tears running down her face was considered an oddity. Through it all, James would not allow Lou to take her to a hospital. They had no money to spare, and he couldn't do without the girl around the farm, even if she wasn't quite working at her usual capacity. If she had been an animal, he would have put her down. If she was his daughter by blood instead of marriage, his attitude might have been different, too. It was during this time that the difference in the way that he treated Nannie became the most apparent. He was still hard with the other children, unrelenting in the face of their complaints or failings, but he recognised that they had limits that couldn't be pushed past. With Nannie, and to a lesser extent Lou, he would go on pushing until they were well past the limit of what even he could endure.

Those long months of pain and misery put her treatment at his hands into sharp perspective, and for the very first time in her life, Nannie started to hate. James had made himself the centre of their little world, isolated in the countryside, miles away from their nearest neighbour and denied even the most basic social life thanks to his never-ending demands. He had made it clear that everything that happened in their lives was under his complete control, so when they were miserable and suffering, who else were they going to blame? He had set himself up as the God of Hazle Farm, and that made Nannie, his enemy, the Devil.

With her new black moods and bouts of fury, she was a good fit for that title. It didn't take long before her siblings realised that even though their father had turned away from her, it wasn't safe for them to treat her badly too. Lou was still fiercely protective of her eldest daughter, and while James had set himself above all of them, he was quite happy for his wife to inflict the discipline he felt was so sorely lacking on the children. More pressingly, this new miserable sister of theirs was more than willing to dole out beatings herself when the fury took her, so they took care not to provoke her. She had no fear of the beatings that James would dole out if she was caught hitting her younger brothers and sisters. She was already in constant pain—what was a little more?

It was like Nannie was seeing her father for the first time. He went from being the centre of her world and the focus of all her efforts to a petty bully. He still held an immense amount of power over her, and she was mindful of that, but her devotion to him was broken. The first man that she had ever loved in her life had let her down in the most brutal way imaginable, showing that he didn't care whether she lived or died. It would be a defining moment in her life.

Where before the accident Nannie had enjoyed her mother's romance magazines and books, they now became her obsession. Love became her obsession, the kind that she had read about rather than the coldness she bore witness to between her parents. Her life was going to be like the women's in the magazines. She was going to love and be loved in return, not sink into a routine of misery and hatred that would just go on repeating until somebody died.

Romance became her dream and her sole ambition, to find

some lover who would take her away from all of this borderline poverty and back-breaking labour and treat her like the lady she deserved to be. Nothing about life on the farm was romantic. Even the few rural romance stories that Nannie read seemed to be talking about an entirely different place, where every hour wasn't filled with manure, sweat, and berating. Riding bareback on a horse with your hair streaming in the wind sounded like the pinnacle of romance, but that was only if you didn't have to muck out the stalls afterwards.

It is hard to sustain a dream when there is no way to move any closer towards it. There were no dances or town fairs for the Hazle girls. No dating or going out at all if there might be men present. Despite both Nannie and Lou having the seamstress skills to make passably pretty dresses, all of the girls were forbidden from wearing anything that James deemed 'attractive.' He was obsessively possessive of his daughters, and he was convinced that the girls would be molested if he let them roam around wearing pretty clothes or makeup. The one time that he caught Nannie trying to fix up her hair like the girls in the magazines, she received a caning. Even as they headed into their teenage years, none of the girls were allowed to go to town without their father or brother there to serve as a chaperone, and many a long night was spent with them staring wistfully out of the window in the direction of whichever barn was hosting that weekend's hootenanny, straining to hear the sounds of music and dancing.

James was obsessed with maintaining their purity, even though it was something he hadn't valued at all in his own wife. Lou couldn't even argue with him because she knew just how badly sex outside of marriage could go, and he used that shame to bludgeon her whenever she tried to speak up for the girls.

All that Nannie could do was wait and wait for her future to arrive, walking on the knife-edge of desperation between wanting a husband—and the escape that he would bring her from her current state of captivity—and fearing all men as the lecherous animals that her father painted them as.

In the end, the assault did not come from strangers on the outside, as the girls had been trained to expect, but from somewhere closer to home. Even as they grew older, the whole family still continued to travel with James and Lou to visit relatives, including no small number of 'family reunions' that basically devolved into getting drunk in a barn. The extended Hazle family was so sprawling that almost anyone could have attended these events, and while James' vicious outbursts and demand for respect at all costs had been intended to make his girls quiet and pliant, it also made them into the perfect victims for the predators that walked among their relatives. When James discovered an uncle or cousin molesting his daughters, he beat them solidly, and the rest of the family closed ranks against them. It didn't take long before the message spread along every twisted branch of the family tree that they were off-limits. Except for Nannie. When James caught one of his cousins trying to force up her skirt behind the barn when she was only twelve years old, it was she who received the punishment and banishment from the social event. When he caught an uncle unbuttoning her dress, it was she who got sent off to her room for being too flirtatious. The same grapevine for perverts carried the message out to anyone who might want to attend—James didn't give a damn what happened to Nannie Hazle.

James railed against her every time that he got her home after one of those incidents, blaming her for the terrible example that she was setting her younger sisters and making strong implications that the apple hadn't fallen far from the tree, as far as her mother was concerned. This fused Nannie's rage at being molested—when she was meant to be safe—and her hatred of her father, into something new and dangerous. It lit a fire in her and drove her into action, where for years she had been complacent.

Her favourite reading material changed. After years spent on the fantasy of romance, she was now fixated on kicking off her own love story. She set aside the romance magazines and picked up her father's discarded newspapers, locking onto the 'Lonely Hearts' and 'Missed Connections' columns and searching through all of the letters that had been sent in for any that might apply to her. If she could not go to the men, then the men would have to come to her. If she couldn't go on a grand adventure to find the man whom she was meant to be with, then she would have to beckon some brave knight errant to her father's doorstep and expect him to fight for her freedom.

She managed to sneak out a few letters over the months, but if she ever got a response it was intercepted by James before she saw it. He never beat her for attempting to contact men, so presumably they went unanswered.

By 1920, Nannie was fifteen years old, completely done with her faltering attempts at school and ready to move on with her life—another of the many things in life that should have been simple and pleasant that was instead transformed into an arduous battle of wills with James. He did not want to let her out of his sight, particularly now that she was old enough and strong enough to start shouldering all of her mother's burdens around the farm. She knew that an emotional appeal to him would always fall on deaf ears, so instead, she had to come at him with a logically constructed argument in favour of setting her free. James had always been fiercely protective of the accounting work around the farm, even though it was something that Nannie could have been handling (even during her periods of bed-ridden migraines). But still, she had managed to gather from hissed conversations that she heard late at night, and their current state of poverty, that the farm was not making enough money. So, she presented him with a simple solution: let her go out to work. He would lose her labour around the farm, and the amount that she could make in an entry-level factory job wouldn't exceed the amount that she could generate doing her chores, but the money from an external source was regular and guaranteed. It would be a buffer during the long months between crops, and a cushion in case of a cow getting sick or a crop turning out poorly. James slept on it, but come morning, he could think of no decent argument to keep her from doing her part to support the family.

She went out looking for work the very next morning, breathing the sweet summer air, and feeling free for the first time in her life.

First Down the Aisle

It didn't take long for Nannie to secure herself a job at the Linen Thread Mill in Blue Mountain and for her little, brown wage packets to start coming home to brighten up her mother's scowl.

For the first time, it seemed like life on the farm was going to start improving. Nannie's escape from her father's clutches served as an incentive for all of the younger children to start planning for the future, too. Until now, it had seemed that they were all doomed to an eternity working the mostly fruitless fields, but she had shown them that there was a way out. If they could prove that leaving brought more money into the family than their staying, they finally had opportunities and options beyond slowly maturing into clones of their miserable parents. Even still, all of that progress and change was just the first stage in Nannie's grander plan.

Nannie was still barred from wearing makeup by her father, but her clothing choices became less bland as a matter of necessity, so that she could fit in with the rest of the girls at the factory, and as a matter of practicality, since the overblown sack-style dresses that her father preferred would have gotten caught up in the machinery. Allowed to dress like every other girl and out from under her father's looming shadow, Nannie became popular; a social butterfly during working hours. She had friends everywhere that she went in the factory, and since she was in town every day, she ended up as the de facto errand runner for the whole farm too. Before long, it was Nannie whom people in Blue Mountain thought of when they heard the Hazle name, instead of her insular father. She was finally living a normal life, and while others wouldn't have found any joy in it, the novelty still hadn't worn off for her. Everyone she met was greeted with a smile; every little bit of help that she could give to others, she gave.

She was the pride of Blue Mountain, and that popularity was not limited to the other women. Older men were cautious in their approach to her—she was still very young, for all that she was pretty, and nobody wanted the reputation of chasing after children. She received no small amount of admiration from the single men about town, but it was always restrained, even though she clearly relished every compliment.

As a prospect for marriage for most of the farming community, she was a shaky proposition, although not nearly as risky as her mother had been. Most women would still have been expected to bring a dowry or the promise of some property along with them when they married, but it was widely known that the Hazle farm was both too small to be portioned up and too poor to provide much in the way of financial incentive. Taking a pretty young thing like Nannie for a bride was considered to be an extravagant luxury that only the wealthy could indulge. Romantic ideas were all well and good, but survival was still the primary concern of most people in rural America, even as late as the 1920s.

Luckily, the old men of Blue Mountain were far from being Nannie's only prospects. The factory itself was packed to bursting with eligible young men, and while their parents may still have had enough influence to steer the majority of them away from the charming young Nannie, some of them were either too stubborn to be steered or lacking in parental guidance.

Nannie took up smoking so as to have an excuse to linger outside the factory with all of the boys, and she was making good enough money at the factory that even her father never bothered to complain about the frivolity of her minor habit. But despite making herself available out in the yard, it was actually in the noisy factory itself that most of them approached her. Out in the yard she held court, but when it came time for the actual advances to be made, the young men wanted the relative privacy that the machine noise could provide.

With her mother's example firmly in mind, Nannie made it clear to all of her suitors that she was only interested in marriage and not a dalliance. That was enough to put off most of the teenagers who had been pursuing her, but certainly not all. One boy in particular, Charley Braggs, was so smitten with her that he almost proposed on the spot.

Charley was seventeen years old, tall and handsome with a head of curly hair and a smile that even managed to melt the heart of the extremely dubious Lou Hazle on the single evening that he was invited home to the farm for dinner. Of all Nannie's potential suitors, he was the only one who managed to win over both Lou and James—Lou with his charm and good looks and James with his uncommon nature. While other boys his age were hanging out in the cafés and gin mills of Anniston, listening to jazz music and cavorting, Charley had a more solitary nature, spending his paycheques on the careful upkeep of his family home and on the care of his sickly mother. Respect for your elders was a constant theme in James' preaching to his children, so it was hardly surprising that this devotion won young Charley some points with the old man.

James clearly didn't care much about the gossip about town and did no prying into the boy's history or family. If he had been worried about those things then he would never have married Lou to begin with, and as far as Nannie was concerned, he felt that beggars could not be choosers. If this boy was willing to take the cost of caring for the rebellious Nannie off his hands permanently, then he was happy for him to do so as soon as possible.

Just four, short months after they began courting, Nannie and Charley walked down the aisle together. She brought nothing with her but a drawer full of home-made clothes and the promise that she would try her best to be a good wife to him.

This was hardly the grand romance that she had always dreamed about. There were no flowers or fancy meals, she wasn't whisked away to an exotic locale or showered with gifts. It barely even contained the level of romance that you might have expected from a usual teenage courtship. Charley spent a little bit of time with her, but with neither of them allowed a social life outside of work hours, that left only the few family meals that he attended in the intervening months, which hardly lent themselves to grand romantic gestures.

From her sporadic diary entries in 1921, we can see that Nannie felt that she was forced into the marriage. She felt as if the great escape that she had been orchestrating had just been undercut entirely by James' compliance and, indeed, delight at the prospect of her marriage. While she had still been testing the waters with other suitors, Charley had pressed his proposal on her through her father, and as a group, the family had railroaded her into it. Instead of being the most wonderful moment in her life, the wedding felt like a transaction taking place, the way that her father would buy or sell a cow.

The ceremony was uninspiring and sparsely attended on Charley's side. His mother was there, and a trio of the guys from work, but he didn't have many friends. His complete absence of a social life didn't leave much time for maintaining relationships, and the majority of the guys at work who were about his age were sore because he'd swooped in on Nannie. Nannie's side of the church was a lot fuller, with her extended family descending like vultures at the first sign that there might be a free meal and some liquor. While she was on good terms with all of the girls at work, she had never developed any particular friends, so her blanket invite had only drawn out a few of the older factory women, who were mostly there to say goodbye to her as they didn't expect she would still be working much after the wedding. They were completely right, of course, she had no intention of working again. That wasn't part of her grand plan.

Despite the specifics of the husband being slightly different from what she might have intended, Nannie planned to be the perfect wife. She would keep the house, raise the babies, cook all of the meals, and excel any expectations that Charley might have had for her. Her love and support would help him to flourish, and out from the controlling whims of her father she might finally find a little bit of enjoyment in her own life. This was her chance to finally break free of controlling parental figures and start living her life, and while he might not have been her first choice, at least she was confident that the quiet and undemanding Charley would be easy enough to manipulate into doing what she wanted, a scenario which was the complete opposite of her obstinate and abusive father.

Mother Knows Best

After the ceremony and the party were over, Nannie was brimming with excitement. She lived on a farm, so she was well aware of the mechanics of sex, and at a young age, she had made the connection between the physical act and the 'marital bliss' that she had read about so widely. Sex was the undercurrent of every romantic story that she had ever read, even if it was forbidden for them to even write about it. It had also served as the primal backdrop for her own life story, too, serving as the motivation behind the amorous overtures of all the young men she had met, the horror story of her mother's extra-marital pregnancy, the drive behind her molestation at the hands of relatives, and now her marriage, where she was allowed, finally, to enjoy this secret pleasure that she had so long been denied.

In the early evening, they arrived at Nannie's new home, the first place that she would ever truly be able to call hers. They would deal with the petty details of squaring away gifts and putting away her little suitcase of clothes in the morning. The young lovers only had eyes for each other. From all accounts, Charley had a perfectly pleasant evening, but for Nannie, the crushing anticlimax of her first intimacy wasn't the perfect end to the day that she'd had. Still, she reasoned that things might get better and less painful with time.

Her own mother had intimated as much during the extremely vague talk that she had given to Nannie about 'wifely duties' at the party. Things were not perfect, as she had always dreamt they would be, but they were not ruined, either.

She still had hope for her future, until she came down the stairs in the morning and found her mother-in-law seated at the kitchen table, glowering at her with a contemptuous sneer on her face. 'Charley will be needing his breakfast before work. Best I go wake him while you see to it.'

Nannie had barely met Mother Braggs before the wedding, in no small part because of the woman's ill health, which had flared up every time a social engagement involving the Hazle family was scheduled. She looked remarkably healthy now as she barked out orders, but Nannie did her best to calm her foul temper. After all, this situation was only temporary; she was surprised that his mother seemed to have stayed over in their house last night without anyone telling her, but at least she wouldn't have to endure the woman's sharp tongue for long.

When Charley came down, he walked right past the plate she had prepared for him to kiss his mother on the cheek before saying 'good morning,' and it took almost the entire time that he was getting ready for work before Nannie managed to corner him and politely ask when his mother would be heading home.

'She is home, silly. She lives here with us.'

Nannie was so stunned that she didn't even have a chance to form any sort of counter-argument before he was out the door and heading off to work. She spent the rest of the day performing household chores under the watchful eye of her new mother-in-law, and while the woman wasn't likely to beat her as James used to, she found fault in absolutely everything that Nannie did. Nothing was up to the standards that she expected in her home, and she expected Nannie to repeat every task until she got it right. In the end, Nannie barely made it through a quarter of the jobs that she had intended to attend to on her first day, and she was exhausted and miserable by the time that Charley came back to take it all in with dismay.

She had traded one slave master for another, and while she felt no qualms about defying her own father, each time she said anything even the slightest bit critical about her new mother-in-law it seemed to physically wound Charley.

She was trapped in a web of social obligation and politeness, more surely than the threats of violence had ever held her. In front of her son, Mother Braggs was nothing but magnanimous with Nannie, barely even correcting her when mistakes were made around the house. Barely speaking loud enough for Charley to hear the litany of his new wife's many faults. Charley's mother had spent a lifetime alternately spoiling and manipulating her son, and she had it down to a fine art.

Mother Bragg was a single parent in much the same way that Nannie's mother had been, but while Lou had been saved from a lifetime of shame and disaster at the last moment, the same could not be said for her counterpart. Charley had been raised in abject poverty until an early inheritance lifted them onto the property ladder, and from an early age, he was groomed to be the man of the house and provider for his mother. What had started as flattery about his maturity had soon been transformed into truth as he was sent out to work, and no small part of his personality had been carefully moulded by his mother to ensure that he would always put her wants and needs first.

Nannie had expected to be able to work her way around Mother Braggs when Charley was home, and she couldn't risk showing her true colours in front of her son, but the older woman had too much experience to be so easily thwarted. If Nannie wanted to go out for a meal with her husband, Mother Braggs would be suffering from a stomach complaint. If she wanted to go to the pictures, Mother would have a dizzy spell and they'd end up sitting around the kitchen table playing Mah-jong yet again. The social life that Nannie had been so desperately craving was held just out of reach once more, and her daily life was just getting more and more miserable.

The fantasy world of romance had been stolen from her by the constant demands on her time. Even though her own chance at a 'happily ever after' had been stripped away from her, she had hoped to at least find some escape in her beloved stories, but Mother Braggs viewed the reading of romances as akin to infidelity and destroyed, on sight, any magazines that Nannie managed to smuggle into the house. For a while, they played cat and mouse, with Nannie seeking out hiding places for her reading materials and the old woman hunting for them, but eventually it came to a head when Mother Braggs laid out in excessive detail, in front of Charley, how pleased that she was to see Nannie wasn't filling her head with such childish nonsense like other, more frivolous girls her age. With the two of them now on the lookout, she abandoned all hope, beyond browsing the racks at the local store.

One by one, her avenues of escape were closed off. Nannie's relationship with her own mother had always been good, even though she viewed Lou as powerless to stop the worst excesses of James' behaviour. She was still an ally against him, though, and she had still been the closest thing to a friend and confidant that Nannie had ever had. Even in married life, she had expected to still see Lou regularly and even intended on baking up fancy afternoon teas for when she came to visit. When Lou did come, she received a frosty reception from Mother Braggs and was always put out of the house immediately after supper, with any suggestion that she might stay the night being immediately torn apart. For his part, Charley seemed to be almost entirely oblivious to the whole situation, as much as he was to everything else going on in his home. Whatever his mother said was the law as far as he was concerned, with there being no point in arguing about it.

With desperation mounting, Nannie started looking for alternate avenues of escape. The smoking habit that she had used as an excuse to step out of work became a ward against Mother Braggs—who detested the smell but couldn't find a way to demand that Nannie quit without sounding unreasonable—and then it became an addiction, with the newlywed puffing her way through forty or more cigarettes a day. Worse still, she turned to the Braggs' liquor cabinet for some relief from the grinding disapproval and disappointment.

Alcohol may have eased the pain briefly, but it didn't take long before messing around with her brain chemistry came back to bite Nannie. The entirely reasonable bouts of depression she was experiencing after seeing her dream snatched away were now accompanied by a constant smog. Her dark moods went from being a rare visitor to a constant companion. There was not a single day that she didn't feel like just curling up in a ball and dying rather than going through the motions of trying to please Mother Braggs all over again. In a strange way, it was actually that antagonistic relationship that saved Nannie's life. She couldn't just lie in bed all day, because that would prove all of Mother's insinuations about her laziness correct. She couldn't just lie down and die, because that would mean letting the old hag win.

The old defiance that had characterised Nannie's relationship with her father came back to the fore, and she powered through each day ignoring every word that Mother had to say and pretending that the old woman wasn't spending every waking moment whispering about her failings into Charley's ear.

After three years of labouring to please her mother-in-law, Nannie put the old woman out of mind, because, ultimately, she had two vital—but related—weapons in her arsenal that Mother Braggs could never hope to match. For the first three years of their marriage, she gave Charley all the sex that he wanted, whenever he wanted it. And when his interest in the carnal began to fade, along with her novelty, she gave him children, binding him to her forever, despite the loathing that she had grown to feel for the spineless runt she had been bullied into marrying.

They had four daughters, one a year between 1923 and 1927, with the eldest named Melvina and the youngest named Florine. In-between her pregnancies, Nannie came to loathe the touch of

Charley. He was still as gormless as ever, completely unaware of her suffering or even the exhaustion that motherhood had brought along with it. She suffered through sex with him only rarely and only when the timing was right to ensure she would become pregnant again. Otherwise, she avoided their marital bed as much as possible, taking to sleeping in the children's room in case they needed her in the night and to her finding comfort elsewhere.

With children in the picture, there was no longer much of a threat that Mother Braggs could do anything to terminate the marriage, and so Nannie's contempt for her grew. All of the complaints and snipes that wounded Nannie in the early days of her marriage now fell on deaf ears, and if Mother went telling tales to Charley, then he never acted on the information.

When either Lou or Mother Braggs could be pressed into service as a babysitter, Nannie would leave her children and head out to the gin mills of Anniston to find men who could make her feel beautiful again, the way she felt when the whole world was courting her. Stories filtered back to Lou about her daughter's harlotry, about the girl roaming bars topless, being fondled in public and going off into back rooms with drunkards. Nannie was trying to wash away all of the pain in a sea of gin and sex, but it was never enough, and in the morning the hangover and black moods would sweep back in, along with the shame.

Neither Charley nor his mother could ever confirm any of the stories that were being told about Nannie's infidelity, and Charley was living in a glass house as far as that was concerned, having struck up several brief but lacklustre affairs with young women in the Linen Thread Mill over the years. Nannie knew all about them and kept notes on them in her diaries so that she could use them against Charley if he ever tried to go against her or end their marriage unfavourably.

When it came to her daughters, Melvina was the apple of Nannie's eye, the girl into whom she poured all of her own hopes and dreams. Melvina was going to go on to live a wonderful life. She was going to have a grand romance and never have to settle for a lesser man. Everything that Nannie had once imagined for herself she promised to Melvina.

Her own life had gone appallingly off track, and every child after Melvina became an even greater burden for her to bear. Suddenly, she wasn't just cooking, cleaning, dressing, and coddling for her husband and his mother, but also for four children under the age of five. Her every waking moment was punctuated by the screams and demands of one of the six, and those brief moments of respite that she had bought herself with liquor, smoking, and escape into the arms of other men became fewer and fewer.

Meanwhile, Charley's own infidelities were becoming more and more obvious to everyone around him. While Nannie had mastered the art of putting on a smile and pretending that everything in her life was perfect around Blue Mountain, he had made his unhappiness abundantly clear to anyone who would listen, and if he ever found a woman with a sympathetic shoulder for him to cry on, it didn't take him long to turn the relationship sexual. He would often disappear for two or three days at a time with his new paramours, abandoning Nannie to deal with everything by herself and providing barely any more support than that, even when he was physically present. It got to the point that the two of them only met by accident—at the dinner table or in the bedroom. They were both alone in the relationship, but while Mother Braggs, along with the many women that he bedded, was there to give Charley an emotional outlet, there was no such comfort for Nannie. Just like in her childhood, she was completely isolated from the community, at large by the controlling parental figure in her life, and for all that she still dreamed of a great romance, nobody was fool enough to actively court her while she was married. She probably would have looked on anyone that tried to do such a thing as despicable.

So, the days rolled on and on, grinding her down a little more with each passing moment. Hangovers and depression clouded her mind and dogged her every step. Unless something drastic happened, Nannie felt certain that she was going to be ground away to nothing.

The Practicalities

Nannie's overwhelming love for her children was apparent to everyone—in the eyes of Mother Braggs it was the girl's only redeeming feature—but they went very rapidly from being the centre of her world because she was so smitten with them, to being the centre of her world because they were so demanding of her attention at all times. She would often go days without sleep because one child or another had an illness, or simply because they weren't tired because their grandmother had decided to put them down for a nap in the middle of the day when she was watching them and Nannie was out running errands.

Even when she was in her darkest moods, Nannie was able to fake a smile for her daughters, but gradually, every single smile that she mustered for them was fake. Whatever joy she had found in becoming a mother was over, and the reality of being a mother for the rest of her life sank in. She tried to keep on going, focusing only on the practicalities, even when she found her love for her children faltering, but as she grew more and more desperate, the practical solution to the problem became more and more apparent. She had too many children to care for.

At almost five years old, Melvina registered in Nannie's mind as another human being and as somebody that she felt she had a strong emotional tie to, even though that connection was currently numbed by her circumstances. The other three were the problem. She could still remember what it felt like to have only one child to care for, back when her husband was still at least partially present and the security that Melvina provided had given her the courage to stand up to her overbearing mother-in-law. There had been no point in her life where she felt as contented or as capable as in that first year of motherhood. She could be an amazing mother when she only had one child to care for, when she could focus her attention entirely on one child's needs and still have enough time left to care for herself.

It was a simple equation in Nannie's mind. She could have four miserable children and live her own life in a constant haze of depression and exhaustion, or she could have one happy and healthy child who would go on to do amazing things with her life. It was no choice at all.

The next time that Charley returned from one of his three-day benders, the whole town of Blue Mountain seemed to be camped out in his house. He had to push through the crowd to get inside, and as hungover and bewildered as he was, he accepted all of the hugs and condolences without any understanding of what had happened at all. When all of the black clothes started to sink into his brain, he immediately panicked, thinking that his mother had died. But before long, he located her in the kitchen, holding court with the other women of a certain age. Charley pushed his way back through to the sitting room, where he finally spotted Nannie at the centre of it all. Her mother was sitting by her side, her father lurking by the window, very deliberately making no comment on where the hell his son-in-law had been. The baby was pressed to her side, snoozing gently, and Melvina sat by her feet, with Nannie gently stroking her hair. The other two were conspicuous in their absence.

'Where are the girls?'

Whispers and mutters started spreading through the crowd as people slowly realised that Charley still didn't know. Morbid curiosity turned all eyes his way. He could feel the weight of their scrutiny, a whole town wondering where he had been, what he had been doing, why he hadn't been here for his family when they needed him the most. Nannie let the tears flow and was enveloped in the comforting arms of her mother and every other woman nearby, and James took Charley firmly by the arm and dragged him away so that nobody could see the boy break.

Florine was still breastfed, and Melvina had eaten nothing but toast on that fateful morning, so whatever had gone wrong with the porridge grain passed her over. But the middle two had eaten their breakfast and went off giggling with the same reckless abandon as had often plagued Nannie's days. By lunchtime, neither one of them could even walk. The doctor had been rushed out and recognised the signs of acute food poisoning, but medical science had no answer to it. If it had been caught immediately then vomiting could have been induced before the sickness set in, but nobody had suspected anything was awry. Even Mother Braggs, usually ready to condemn Nannie in an instant for the tiniest mistake, could find no fault in her actions. Their daughters were dead, and Charley hadn't even been there to say goodbye. For the first time in his life, Charley felt the weight of his mother's disapproval, amplified a thousandfold by the scrutiny of the town.

In the midst of this circus, Nannie sat with huge, unshed tears hanging in her dark eyes, staring out at Charley, her eyes pinned to him everywhere that he went. She didn't say a single word to him. She didn't damn him for his absence nor confide in him about her grief. She didn't seem to care about him one way or the other. Over the coming days, she seemed to silently revel in all of the attention and sympathy that she was receiving, and the girls' death was, at large, treated by the town like some terrible act of God, one that Nannie was deemed as heroic for enduring with such stoicism. Everywhere that Charley went, people were singing Nannie's praises, and even in his own home, in the company of his own mother, his attempts to complain about her were cut off short.

'You'll never understand how a woman loves her babies, so don't you say a word against your wife until all this is settled and done.'

The funeral came almost immediately, with Nannie feigning desperation to get it all over with and the townsfolk more than willing to oblige. There was no delay from the state's side, either—the doctor had observed the children in their last moments and diagnosed the problem on the spot. There was no need for an autopsy—only to throw away the tainted grains that had killed them. There wasn't even a hint that Nannie could have done anything wrong since her house was known to always be spotless and her cooking the envy of husbands everywhere. Despite everything that happened, she still managed to prepare a beautiful spread of food for after the funeral too.

Whispers had dogged Charley's footsteps ever since he came back to find his life in ruins. He had gone from being a liked man to the subject of scorn and contempt. As Nannie's star rose, so his fell. By the time of the funeral, he actually began to seriously consider the possibility that he had done wrong by his wife and family, that he was the source of the unhappiness that had plagued their home since the very beginning. After all, everyone could see how perfect Nannie was. All except him. Even her most stalwart detractor, Mother Braggs, was treating Nannie like a precious angel. But all of that self-loathing and doubt came to an abrupt end when Nannie laid a plate of food down in front of him and gave him a well-practised, sad smile. He hadn't been able to look her in the eye since he'd gotten back into town—shame and dread that she might give him sympathy and crumble his broken heart to pieces had kept him from wanting to—but now he met her dark eyes and was paralyzed with fear. There was nothing in them. She wasn't sad. She wasn't angry. All of the human emotions that you might have expected to find were just absent, and in their place was a dark and fathomless void. One that he had helped to create.

In the dead of night, with two of his children fresh in the ground, Charley packed his bags, grabbed Melvina from her bed and ran for his life. He had no doubt in his mind that Nannie had killed their daughters and even less doubt that now she had a taste for the town's sympathy and adoration she would soon seek to make herself into a widow as well. Florine was nestled in Nannie's arms when Charley made his escape or he would have taken her away too.

The outpouring of sympathy for Nannie redoubled when her husband's treachery was discovered. To begin with, she had tried to treat it as just another one of his binges, but the fact that he had stolen away in the night with Melvina told her that she wasn't so lucky. For a while, she got to live the life that she had wanted, socialising with the people around town, living more or less alone and unbothered in the Braggs' house with only the hint of her mother-in-law still haunting it, but any enjoyment she might have taken in having her wishes fulfilled was tarnished by the loss of Melvina. If she could have rid herself of Florine without suspicion, she probably would have done so, but Melvina had been everything to her.

1927 was the longest year of Nannie's life as she drifted along aimlessly, refusing every offer from her mother to come home and bring the baby with her. The meagre savings of the Braggs family soon dwindled, and she was forced to take up work in a cotton mill to support not only herself and her daughter but her malingering mother-in-law too. At least that last mouth to feed demanded only very little. Mother Braggs had been shocked by her son's actions and begun to decline not long after. Her 'ill health,' which had only previously flared up when she was trying to manipulate her son, had now become a constant and all-too-real presence in her life. She was racked with stomach pains so severe that most days she couldn't get out of bed and was forced to rely on the kindness of Nannie for her survival. Despite all that had happened, Nannie still fed and watered the old woman every day, going so far as to stew prunes for her each day to try and ease her aching guts. It was all for nothing in the end—Mother Braggs expired in the Summer of 1927, with her son still missing and absolutely no doubt on the part of the townsfolk that her death was due to natural causes. After all, she had spent so many years plagued by this illness, it was hardly surprising that it had finally taken her.

Nannie had the whole house to herself, although she could hardly afford a fraction of its upkeep, and legally, Charley remained the sole owner. It was a curious state of limbo, where she had everything that she wanted and nothing at the same time, unable to move on with her life until her errant husband finally re-appeared to release her but dreading it all the same.

As the leaves began to turn and the balmy summer faded into a mild winter, Nannie fought to find her equilibrium. Working full-time and caring for her baby the rest of the time was still a huge relief compared to the workload that she had once faced, but even with only two mouths to feed she found that she struggled without his income, and the house began to slip into disrepair. More importantly, she was intensely lonely once more. Back at home, she had her mother and siblings to distract her from the void in her life where socialising would usually have gone, but no matter how charming and pleasant she was, she lacked the fundamental skills required to form friendships any deeper than the casual acquaintances she'd enjoyed at the Linen Thread Company. Her father had seen to that by isolating her through her formative years. The only relationship that she had ever had that had any substance, was with Melvina, and she had been stolen from her in the night.

In the summer of 1928, Charley came home, arriving unannounced in a taxi from Anniston with Melvina, a strange woman, and a little boy. Nannie stood in the doorway of the house and watched them approaching, fury building in her chest.

Charley had never had trouble attracting members of the opposite sex, and while having a daughter in tow put a slight cramp on his style, it didn't take him long to start using her to his advantage. Realising that he didn't know the first thing about cooking, cleaning, or raising a child himself, he set out to find himself a replacement mother, and before a month was out he had settled into a comfortable enough life with a widow, who had a son about Melvina's age, a few towns over. In theory, his life was just as comfortable as before—even better when you took into account his much more agreeable 'wife'—but something still felt wrong to Charley. He felt like he had been run out of town instead of choosing to leave willingly, and if he was being honest with himself, he had run not because of the judgement of the town but because he was genuinely afraid of Nannie.

There was no logical way to explain it. With her soft curls and rounded face, Nannie looked almost cherubic, and she was so obviously good-natured that her kindness and devotion to her family were the talk of the town. The longer that Charley was away from her, the more that he remembered all of this and wondered what on earth he had been so afraid of. Nannie was a soft, sheltered farm girl. Every time that he paid rent on his new place, he felt resentment bubbling up. Why should he be paying rent while Nannie was living in the lap of luxury in his own home for nothing? When news of his mother's death finally filtered through, and he knew that he would no longer have to face the weight of her disapproval on top of his fears, he became resolute to return home and drive Nannie out.

She stood in the doorway looking just how he remembered her: perfect and pristine with his daughter nestled on her hip. For just one moment he turned back the clock and saw her the way he had first seen her, holding court in the factory yard, men hanging on her every word, rushing to light her cigarette. A hint of glamour amongst the dirt of daily life. A smile tickled at his lips, then he forced it away, chasing off any joy he might have taken in his marriage in the cavalcade of complaints against Nannie, both his mother's and the ones that he had manufactured to reflect them. After all, his mother was always right, and he felt certain that she would have approved of his new girlfriend much more. She was much more respectable, apart from her willingness to shack up with a married man.

They exchanged very few words. Nannie knew that this day would come. She had no illusions that Charley was going to come rushing back and sweep her up in his arms like she had always dreamed. Anything resembling a romantic dream about him had long since withered away in the face of the sad reality that he was just a spoiled, stupid, little boy.

She packed up her clothes, and the children's, took Melvina from his unresisting arms, and walked away from them both. She stole whatever triumph he might have felt at driving her out from under him and left with dignity, despite the fact that the darkest and most murderous mood she had ever experienced in her life had just descended upon her. Nannie's face was arranged into a mask of sadness as she walked by the new Braggs family, and Charley's new wife was overwhelmed with sympathy for her despite all of the horror stories that she had been told. But Charley himself caught another glimpse of the darkness behind Nannie's eyes, and he felt that same bone-chilling terror that had driven him away from home the first time. If he had been alone, he had little doubt that she would have killed him at the first opportunity. Time would prove this assumption to be correct.

Hope Springs Eternal

Nannie returned to the family farm and the constant demands of her father. Lou was delighted to have the grandkids under her roof, but James expected Nannie to immediately resume her duties around the place now that her marriage had failed. The farm was still doing poorly and would continue to do poorly in perpetuity. The divorce papers came through promptly, and Nannie was happy to sign away her marriage so long as the reason listed for the divorce was Charley's infidelity. Given that he was currently living with another woman and a child that referred to him as 'Daddy,' it wasn't exactly hard to swing that addendum. After eight years, her first marriage was dissolved.

With Melvina home at last, Nannie promptly forgot about her obsession with her daughter. She still liked Melvina, loved her even, but the all-consuming fixation on her daughter faded away to nothing in the face of actually having a relationship with the six-year-old. It may have been the most important relationship in Nannie's life, but that didn't mean that it was even slightly fulfilling.

Rather than endure the day-long nagging of her father and, increasingly, her mother, Nannie sought work to get her out of the house and away from them all. Charley had resumed his old entry-level position in the thread mill in Blue Mountain where they had first met, so that avenue was closed off to her. The other mill where she had found work had employed her only as a seasonal worker and dropped her as soon as her divorce became public knowledge, so that offered no recourse either. With no other option, she began looking further afield and finally settled into a job in a cotton mill over in Anniston. The commute was a nuisance, the work was hard, and the conditions in the mill were so hot as to be just barely tolerable. But in addition to paying better than any work she had ever done in Blue Mountain, it also provided her with long periods away from the farm and all of the male attention that she could have asked for.

Four pregnancies and a divorce had done nothing to temper Nannie's natural beauty, and she spent almost every moment at work being admired by the many men that staffed the machinery. She relished this attention, and it did a lot to assuage her wounded ego to have so many men lusting after her, but that did not mean she was ready to jump into bed with one of them again so quickly. She was never going to make the same mistake again, marrying a man just because he was the first to offer, and she would ensure that her parents had no say in any of her future romantic arrangements, just to be on the safe side.

She carefully vetted every one of her suitors at the Anniston mill and found every single one of them wanting. The young ones were still too much in the sway of their parents, and there was nothing that Nannie dreaded more than the idea of inheriting another slave-master along with whatever man she settled for. As for the older ones, men who had worked in the mill all their lives were either sorely lacking in ambition or too badly injured by the mill work to fit in anywhere else. It wasn't that they repulsed Nannie, it was just that there was no possibility of them fulfilling her romantic fantasies, so she immediately discounted them. She was done with settling for anything less than true love, even if that meant that it took her a little longer to find it.

Loneliness had always been the cornerstone of Nannie's

psyche. Her long, isolated childhood followed by her loveless marriage had compounded that feeling into a drive that would persist through the rest of her life. The romance magazines that she hoarded and reread over and over helped to ease the ache for a while, but that couldn't last. She needed to find somebody to fill that void, to make her whole. And so she turned from one of the great comforts of her childhood to the other: the 'Lonely Hearts' columns.

Looking back on the letters she had sent out as a desperate teenager, the now adult Nannie found them equally endearing and naive. Now that she had experienced a sexual relationship, she could recognise the undertones littering the listings. Some of the men she had replied to before had been looking for something very different from what she had offered up, so it was hardly surprising that none of her first batch of replies had gotten a response. With maturity and experience, Nannie was now able to add a whole new layer to her fantasies and reflect those fantasies back to the men that she was in communication with.

She had a photograph taken to send out along with the letters and baked goods that she began to distribute, but it didn't do her any justice. Without the sparkle of life in her eyes and the tiny hint of a smile that came and went from the corner of her mouth, she looked almost average, instead of being instantly recognisable as a woman of distinction. But whatever was lacking in the visual stimulation that she sent along was more than compensated for in other ways. Her baking had always been the pride of the Hazle family, and even Mother Braggs had never been able to find fault in it. So, too, were the few men that she graced with a reply ensnared by her pies. And if the taste of home cooking wasn't enough to win the men over, the letters that she sent out along with those pastries were right on the verge of being lewd.

For several months, this was Nannie's whole life—fastidiously replying to every letter that she received, combing through the newspaper for new contenders for her heart, and feeling for the first time like it was possible that her dream of romance might come to pass. In person, men were always fairly naked in their desires for her, but by letter, they were forced to dress their sordid desires with poetry and prose to win her over. It was like being in one of her romance novels—she was finally being spoken to like she was the star of her own story rather than an afterthought or impediment.

Out of all the many suitors that she considered, there was only one that went beyond an exchanging of letters. In 1929, Nannie received a letter of beautiful verse and a photograph of a man who could have been a film star, with the wavy hair of Grant Withers and the dimpled chin of Clark Gable. Robert Franklin Harrelson, known to one and all as Frank, was a twenty-two-year-old factory worker from nearby Jacksonville. Two years Nannie's junior, he nonetheless impressed his maturity upon her—especially when compared to her ex-husband. He lived alone in a modest apartment in the city, where he had acquired an average social life and a love of jazz music. In reply to his charming letter, Nannie replied with a slice of spice cake, a copy of her photograph, and a letter of her own that was less poetic but carried a powerful subtext.

The day after her reply was sent, there was a knock on the door of Hazle farm. Frank had finished reading her letter and immediately jumped in the car to drive down to see this beauty in person. He was stunned when the real Nannie answered the door. In person, she was vibrant and charming, in a way that no letter or picture could convey. He was utterly smitten with her, and more than ready to just load her into the car and take her home with him on the day. Over the next few weeks he would visit her frequently, showering her with the kind of romantic gifts that she had always dreamed of but learned not to hope for. Flowers, chocolates, lace, and more arrived in carefully wrapped packages with more of Frank's charming poetry attached. A gentleman like that was enough to turn any girl's head, but for Nannie, with her dreams of a grand romance, it was intoxicating beyond anything she had ever experienced before.

He proposed to her only two months after they'd met for the

first time, and she accepted without a second thought. He was a dream made flesh, a larger than life character from out of one of the talkies—how foolish would she have had to be to play coquettish now that her new life was in sight.

Frank had grander dreams than any of the men that she'd dallied with before. He planned to take her away from all of this, to start a new life without the interference of her family or the judging gaze of the people of Blue Mountain. Before the wedding was even planned, he had secured a new job for himself at the Goodyear Textile Mill in Cedartown, Georgia—no great step up from his current role in a Jacksonville factory, but with better prospects for advancement and the added allure of a more exotic locale.

Nannie's second wedding was attended by more people than could fit in the church, with the whole town of Blue Mountain turning out to wish her well and see her off to her new life—one last sign of solidarity with a woman who had suffered so much, so young. The only ones who seemed unhappy with the arrangement were Nannie's parents. They had not been consulted on the marriage in the least, and while Lou had been easily won over by Nannie's doe eyes and fluttering heart, her father was less inclined to take her feelings into account, preferring to judge Frank by his own merits, which he judged to be lacking. No man who was worth a damn would have to use such pretty words to get around folks, after all.

The one point that both of Nannie's parents were in agreement upon was the grandchildren. Since returning home, Melvina and Florine had basically been adopted by Lou, while Nannie was off working all hours and writing letters the rest. And now, without warning, they were going to be ripped from her arms and hauled off across the country where they might never see them again. Of course, all that Nannie had to do to silence any complaints from either one of them was to invoke the name of Charley Braggs.

Despite Lou and James' complaints, Nannie, Frank, and the girls all loaded into the car with suitcases crammed full of all their worldly belongings and set off northeast without a backwards glance towards their new home. Frank had just enough in savings to put down a deposit on a two-bedroom log cabin just outside of Cedartown, a meagre enough place compared to some of the homes Nannie had lived in, but a perfect fulfilment of so many fantasies that romance stories had instilled in her.

With the kids safely stowed away in their bedroom and the night drawing in, the two of them made love by the log fire. It was perfect. This was the end of the story that she had been weaving in her mind throughout her life, when everything would be settled and she would live happily ever after.

But the fade to black never came. The next morning, she woke up in Frank's arms and just went on living, despite the story being over.

The Talk of Cedartown

She kept trying to recapture that same moment of perfect bliss throughout the 'honeymoon period' of their marriage, and she was successful more often than not. Frank remained the consummate gentleman, treating her exactly the way she had always wanted to be treated, relishing every moment with her and complimenting everything that she did. Both of them had their little secrets that they held back from one another, but the parts that were exposed meshed together perfectly. The only slight annoyance on Nannie's part was that Frank seemed to enjoy his whiskey a little too much and a little too frequently for her liking. She had been in the same boat back when she was married and miserable, so she didn't feel entitled to cast any aspersions on his character, but it still made her stop and wonder if he was secretly miserable, the way that she had been. The more that she pushed him to share his feelings, the more closed off he became, so she just tried to accept his words at face value and accept his heavy drinking as just a little personality quirk rather than a sign of some deeper and darker problem. After all, just because her relationship to alcohol had been defined by misery, it didn't mean that his had to be.

Prohibition was in its dying days by the time that Nannie and Frank were wed, and it was little more than a year after they'd settled in Cedartown that he was able to switch from the expensive and illegal moonshine that he had been indulging in to legally purchased whiskey that, out of habit, he continued to pour into a clay jug and hide out in the garden somewhere. But with the ready availability of liquor, Frank's drinking problem became more pronounced. He would spend his time in town after work drinking with his buddies instead of coming home to Nannie.

The beautiful home-cooked meals that she had prepared for him went cold on the table while she sat there glowering at his empty seat dancing in the candlelight. Her old dark moods had never gone far away, and when she was left in isolation it didn't take long for them to flare up. Still, she had known that Frank was a sociable man when she decided to marry him, and she would have to be a real harridan of a wife to deny him a little time with his friends. She suffered in silence, swallowed her feelings, and drifted back to her stories and the dubious social outlet of her children.

She had every reason to be happy. She had the life that she wanted, enough money that they never had to worry about making ends meet, two perfect daughters who were growing into lovely young women, and a home that could have come right out of a storybook. It was only healthy that she missed her husband when he was away. Only normal. But still this sense of doom hung overhead, and Nannie went through the motions of motherhood and housekeeping with a strange sense that all of this was just temporary, that she was just waiting for the other shoe to drop.

One of Frank's friends showed up on her porch with his hat in his hands one night after she had spent another long evening nursing her misery alone. Nannie froze in the doorway, paralyzed with the terrible knowledge that this was it, the doom she had been waiting for was finally coming to pass. But as it turned out, no terrible accident had befallen Frank beyond the one that he'd wilfully inflicted upon himself. He was in the Cedartown Police Department's drunk tank after getting into a brawl in the gutter outside the local bar, and as Nannie would discover when she went to pick him up, this wasn't the first time that he'd found himself in similar circumstances.

Back in Jacksonville, Frank had had a reputation for his drinking and a wicked temper. He had been brought up on charges twice for 'felonious assault' and even served jail time for his actions while under the influence. His family had hoped that a happy marriage and a settled life would be the perfect fresh start for him, that he was heading out of state to get a new start on life rather than running like a coward from the consequences of his actions. It would seem that they, and Nannie, had given Frank too much credit because here he was back in the same position again.

Nannie drove him home in silent fury, caught in between two powerful, but opposing, impulses. One part of her wanted to pretend that this hadn't happened, that their life together could still be the glorious dream that she wanted it to be and that Frank could go on being the perfect husband that she had always longed for but never found. The other part wanted to kill him right now for lying to her, dragging her away from everything that she had ever known. There was no middle ground or compromise for Nannie, no gradual change that she could bring about that would result in the happiness that she desired. Either everything was perfect or everything was a catastrophe, and until she could work out which it was, she was trapped in limbo.

The years rolled by with Nannie still pinned in place by indecision. She tried easing Frank off the drink, resulting in him abandoning her to go on a three-day bender with his buddies. With that failure under her belt, she tried the opposite tactic, going along with Frank when he went out drinking, matching him glass for glass until the two of them were completely smashed.

The two of them went off on one of Frank's benders, dumping the now-teenaged Melvina at a friend's house on the way out of town, but completely forgetting about Florine. The little girl came home from school to find the cabin empty and abandoned. She was there for two days before the police came out and retrieved her, scouring Polk County for Nannie and Frank before eventually turning the little girl over to her father back in Alabama. She spent an awkward weekend in the Braggs household being studiously avoided by both Charley and his new wife until Nannie came by in a blazing fury to snatch her back all over again after a few days. Nannie might not have particularly cared for her younger daughter, but she would rather die than let Charley have her.

After that misadventure, Nannie cut back on her drinking again and decided to just try to endure, to be the good wife that she had always wanted to be and to take the romantic moments as they came, even if they now came only very rarely through Frank's hungover haze. For Frank's part, he managed to hold down the same job at the factory that he had started with despite his frequent absences, but none of the advancement that he had dreamed of ever appeared. His reputation as a drunkard preceded him, and as doors were slammed shut in his face and he was denied what he felt he was entitled to, he turned more and more to the solace of the bottle.

Soured to liquor by her husband's ridiculous antics, Nannie turned to more familiar distractions for comfort. Romance fiction dominated the home, and she poured over every newspaper that came in, never writing to any of the many lonely hearts that caught her eye but always longing to. Always just on the verge of breaking away but never quite making it. Just as her dark moods had always taken her before, now they combined with a steady flow of insults from her 'gentleman' husband to convince her that she was the one at fault. The only common thread between the two 'perfect' men that she had found was her, so she began to assume that somehow she was transforming them into these bestial caricatures of the negligent husband. When Frank began to hit her in his drunken rages, her dark moods told her that she deserved it. When he did the same to her children, she just counted herself lucky that tonight she wouldn't be on the receiving end of his fists.

Despite all of this, Frank would be Nannie's husband for sixteen years in all, with both of her daughters coming to adulthood under his roof. The girls grew up into charming young women. Just as Nannie had overcome her own upbringing to seek love, so did they. Both Melvina and Florine had grown up among their mother's library of romantic fiction, but they understood the fantasy at its core, in a way that their mother had never been able to grasp. They understood that they had to marry to get out from under their father's roof, so they pursued that goal with the same determination that Nannie had, but they weren't expecting perfection or even anything particularly exciting about their husbands. All that they wanted was a better life than Frank and Nannie could provide them with.

Brief Lives

Florine's dating life slipped mostly under Nannie's radar thanks to her continuing disinterest in the girl, but Melvina was a different story. Every potential suitor was vetted by her mother to a far more exacting set of standards than she had ever used to select men of her own, as evidenced by Frank. But out of all the local men that came sniffing around when they heard rumours that the pretty young thing from the edge of the woods was ready to start courting, the only one that passed Nannie's muster was a young man named Mosie Haynes.

Mosie was eighteen years old, just like Melvina. He had a steady job in town, two supportive, but not overly-involved, parents, and a house of his own that he was more than willing to share with one of the most beautiful young women in town. Most important, from Nannie's perspective, was that he seemed to be properly respectful to both her and her daughter. A real gentleman to put right the mistake that Nannie had made with her own husband.

The two of them were wed in 1942 and settled quickly into a comfortable but quiet life, tolerating rare, brief visits from Nannie and Frank but never willingly seeking them out themselves. Nannie did her best not to take offence. She had been young once not so long ago, so she knew what those first few months of romance were like, when the whole world fell away, apart from the one you'd fallen for.

Nannie knew exactly what she'd have been doing if she had a handsome young man like Mosie at her beck and call, and it seemed that her suspicions about her daughter's activities were proven accurate when less than a year into their marriage Melvina announced that she was pregnant. Nannie expressed her happiness to the couple in extravagant terms, promised them all the help that they might need but resisted the natural urge to barge in as the overbearing mother-in-law. Part of this came from a desire to never become anything like the monstrous creature of Mother Braggs that still haunted her nightmares, but an equal part came from a feeling of profound ambivalence about the baby. On the one hand, this was the natural progression of her daughter's life—marriage and motherhood went hand in hand in the 40s—but on the other hand, it was also the end of her life.

Nannie had bitter memories of the way that children had stunted her own womanhood, robbing her of the opportunities to travel and find the great romance of her life, trapping her with a man who grew colder with each mewling mouth to feed. Nannie should have been happy for her daughter, but she could not wipe away the memory of this time in her own life—her dark moods forced her to relive them over and over. Melvina had been her opportunity to escape the same cycle, a chance for her to relive her youth without the same mistakes made again and again. But now her daughter had slipped out of reach, and there was nothing that she could do to avert the inevitable conclusion of this pregnancy. Melvina would have her baby, Mosie's eyes would begin to wander, and they would end up going their separate ways. It was inevitable. Nannie could feel that inevitability like lead lining her bones as she went through the motions of a happy grandmother.

In early 1943, the baby came so easily that Nannie wasn't even called to the hospital in time to hold her daughter's hand. Robert

Lee Haynes was the apple of his mother's eye, just as Melvina had been Nannie's sole fixation. The good memories of her precious baby daughter finally broke through Nannie's deep and abiding depression. The cycle of parenthood might never end, but the cycle of misery might if Melvina had the good sense to stop right there instead of letting that fool Mosie plant baby after baby in her until she was so run-down she would rather die than go on another day.

Nannie offered up her help to her daughter without condition. She wanted nothing more than to lighten the burden that had been placed upon the girl—the burden that men would never see or understand—and the two of them connected again for the first time since Melvina was a toddler, rekindling their close relationship after years of drifting apart.

Florine, ever the afterthought, moved in with her sister to help with childcare until she had settled on a husband of her own. But it is hard to say if Nannie even noticed. The younger girl had never elicited anything more than cool indifference in her mother, so it was hardly surprising that she was ready to take the very first opportunity to get out of the house. Her relationship with Melvina had always been close, with the two of them allied against the deprivations of both sets of terrible parents that they had been born to.

In 1944, as war raged across the world, a new conflict arose in Nannie when Melvina announced that she was pregnant again. It was all of her mother's worst fears realised. Another baby, and so soon after the first. That drooling beast, Mosie, hadn't even given Melvina's precious body time to heal up before he clambered back on top of her again. The baby was going to come and ruin everything. It would even ruin the fresh and tentative friendship that she had finally forged with her daughter through the common bond of motherhood. The worst part was that nobody else could see the nightmare that was about to unfold, and nobody would believe Nannie if she told them the truth about the doom that her daughter carried in her belly. Everything was going to fall apart and there was nothing that she could do to stop it.

Melvina was a small woman, and by the end of her second pregnancy, she could barely walk due to her displaced hips. When labour began for the second time in her life, in July of 1945, she genuinely believed that the pain alone might kill her. Whatever doubts still lingered in the minds of mother and daughter vanished in the heat of the moment. When the agonising contractions began, it was her mother that she cried out for, and it was her mother who answered instantly. Nannie took control of the hospital room, sending Mosie out to fetch fresh towels and glasses of cold water while she stayed by her daughter's bedside, dabbing the sweat from her head, holding her hand, and talking her through every step of the labour. Nannie even ordered the hospital staff around, and they sheepishly obeyed her barked commands. The labour stretched on through the night, but while everyone else was faltering, Nannie remained strong and resolute, getting everyone back into constant action and giving Melvina everything that she needed to push on.

Finally, after many hours, a healthy baby girl was born. Melvina was so exhausted and weakened by her ordeal and the liberal applications of ether that had gotten her through the pain, that she didn't even have the strength to hold her baby when it was all over. The baby was handed off to Nannie, who sat by her daughter's bedside with an artificial smile etched onto her face, presumably to cover her own exhaustion. By the time the doctor returned to the room, the baby was dead. Nannie quickly handed it off to the medical staff the moment that somebody noticed it wasn't breathing, but by then, it was already too late.

After the lengthy childbirth, it seemed likely that the baby had been deprived of oxygen for too long and was unable to survive for itself, but examination showed no clear cause of death. It had to be explained to Melvina over and over before she could understand, and even then she refused to believe it. Her baby couldn't be dead. It couldn't. After all that she had suffered to bring it into the world, there was no way that any loving God would snatch that baby away from her again.

Melvina returned home with Florine and Mosie the next day, still utterly distraught and hazy from exhaustion, blood loss, and the copious ether. But it was only thanks to her shattered state that she was willing to share the nightmare that she had experienced while under the influence of the ether in confidence with her sister. In that nightmare, she had seen her own mother draw a pin from her hat and push it into the soft spot on the baby's head. She had witnessed her baby being murdered by her own mother. Wasn't that a ridiculous dream? Wouldn't her sister give her some assurance that she couldn't possibly have seen what she thought that she had seen? Florine sank down onto her sister's bed in horrified silence. She had been out of the room when the baby died, passing the good news along to Mosie on the seats outside, where he lay after Nannie had chased him out. But when she returned after the baby had been declared dead, she remembered seeing Nannie quite distinctly, still sitting there by her daughter's bedside, her face in a carefully coached expression of grief as she toyed with a hatpin, making it dance between her fingers.

Just the thought of it was enough to send Melvina back into another spiral of despair. Without proof, any accusation that she made would sound like madness. It was madness. Anyone could see how devoted Nannie was to little Robert. The idea that she might have hurt one of her grandchildren was truly insane. So, both of her daughters swallowed their suspicions and tried to keep moving forward.

Mosie couldn't understand what had happened. He was a simple man, resolute in his optimism that everything was going to go his way, and the death of his baby shook his beliefs to the core. With a death that seemed so random, there wasn't even anyone that he could blame, so he gradually shifted his resentment over the tragedy onto Melvina. She made it easy for him. She was completely shattered by her baby's death and completely shut down emotionally. By the time that she had realised that they were drifting apart, it was already too late for the relationship to be salvaged, and she was too far gone to even care. More and more often, she was leaving Robert in her mother's tender loving care, trying to prove to herself again and again that there was no truth to her suspicions about Nannie and the hatpin.

With no sign of a divorce in sight, Melvina started looking for comfort in all the wrong places, actively pursuing a relationship with a soldier stationed back in Anniston, near to her father's house. She spent her weekends back in Blue Mountain, far from all of her troubles, and slept, more often than not, in her new lover's arms rather than in the uncomfortable silence of the Braggs household.

It didn't take long before Nannie caught wind of the burgeoning new relationship, and it took even less time for her to disapprove of it. She could see Melvina making all of the same mistakes that she had made, going off the rails at the very same point that her own life had been knocked off track. Everything that she had tried to avert with one brief thrust of a needle was coming to pass regardless. She cornered Melvina when she came back home after a weekend away smelling like booze, cigarettes, and cheap aftershave. She told her, in no uncertain terms, that she was ruining her life, that there was still time for her to find a new, respectable husband, that she was still young and that people were more understanding than their vitriol suggested.

Either Melvina didn't believe her mother, or she was too far gone to care. The very next Friday, she showed up with little Robert in tow, ready for another weekend-long sleepover. The women had a raging argument over the two-year-old's head. Nannie would not let Melvina leave without hearing her piece, and Melvina refused to listen to a word of it. It was her life, to live as she saw fit, and she'd had more than enough of her mother's interference. If it hadn't been for Nannie, then she would never have married Mosie to begin with. If it hadn't been for Nannie, Melvina could have stayed in Blue Mountain with her father, living together as a family instead of having to endure the insults and slaps of Frank through the years.

All of the bad things that Nannie had blamed on her own parents were now dumped right onto her by the only person in the world that she cared enough about to be hurt by. It was enough to bring Nannie's cavalcade of demands and demeaning to an abrupt halt, and in the shell-shocked silence, Melvina slunk away to her car and drove away.

Nannie's rage did not leave with her daughter. It hung over her throughout the whole day as she went through the motions of caring for her grandson, and once he was settled in the little fold-out bed for the night, it descended on her once more, filling her up until she could remember nothing else. Frank was nowhere to be found, as usual, and the words on the page in front of her seemed to dance and blur, always just beyond her ability to decipher. Everything just made her angrier, and the persistent headache that had started up the moment she set eyes on Melvina did nothing to alleviate her dark mood. She lay there all night, waiting for Frank to return home so that she could take out her frustrations on him, but he never came.

With the dawn, Nannie rose red-eyed and sleepless to tend to little Robert's needs. He was breakfasted, washed, and sent out into the garden to play. Then, Nannie found herself lingering in the kitchen as she always did when she was full of this static-like energy with nowhere to put it. She started to bake, her hands going through the motions that she had learned by her own mother's elbow, without requiring any input from a brain that was too devoted to its own internal chaos to provide her body with anything resembling competent instruction. Little boys loved pastries and sweet treats, and Robert was nothing more or less than the perfectly typical little boy. She could see him dashing around the garden from her kitchen window, swinging a stick around like it was a gun and he was on the front lines in Europe, chattering away in his squeaky little voice, like gunfire had ever been so adorable. Nannie could remember Melvina at that age, before the world had taken her daughter and turned her into a harlot.

How could Melvina do this to her? After all of the planning and high hopes, her life was falling apart just as surely as Nannie's had. She had always been a wilful girl, and Nannie had never been willing to beat that out of her the way that her father had taught her lessons when she was just a girl. She'd been spared the rod for too long. Melvina thought that she could do as she pleased— do whomever she pleased, too—and she was going to run into an abrupt shock if she kept it up. She was going to run right into the harsh reality of a world that Nannie had spent all her days sheltering her from. She had never known real hardship, the stomach-cramping hunger of a failed harvest or the skin-crawling memory of strangers' rough hands sliding over your bare skin. That girl needed a lesson in humility. She needed the kind of hard lesson that the world would be all too soon to give her if she didn't shape up. Something to break her out of this downward spiral that she'd set herself on.

Nannie's tempestuous mind was quick to offer up excuses and justifications for what her hands were already doing, but the truth was that she was angry. She had always been angry. The life that she wanted was perpetually out of reach. Every moment of every day was a constant struggle against her own inherent depression and the minor ordeals that she was forced to suffer through. She was furious that this was her lot in life, and while she couldn't make the people that had caused all of her troubles pay, the little boy playing out in the garden was in easy reach. He was completely innocent, probably the only person in Nannie's life who had never done her any wrong, but she could hurt him. So, she did.

There had always been a problem with rodents out here on the edge of town, just as there had been in the solid farming country where Nannie grew up, so rat poison was a constant companion throughout her life. Arsenic was the poison of choice in those days, sold in little boxes of silvery-white powder. Nannie kept hers in the kitchen on the highest shelf, to make sure nobody ever reached for it by accident. It was no accident at all when she brought it down and added it into the mixture in her bowl. The first set of cookies was ready before lunch, but she made him eat his soup before he was allowed to snack on them, like a good grandmother would. Slowly but surely, she doled out the baked treats that she had made throughout the day, gradually building up the poison inside little Robert until eventually, he was so sluggish and sore that he went to his bed early.

At any time she could have stopped, and the boy might very well have recovered. At any time she could have turned away from the course of action that her rage had set her upon. This was not a second of madness in the heat of the moment; Nannie gradually and meticulously fed poison to a toddler because his mother had failed to obey her.

That night, Nannie slept soundly with a contented smile on her face. She had finally found an outlet for all of her rage, and now she could let it go. By morning, Robert was already cold, but Nannie still went through all the frantic motions of trying to wake him, calling for a doctor and trying desperately to reach her daughter, who was off with her lover instead of staying at the Braggs house as she had promised.

The doctor examined the little boy's body, accounted for his age, and pronounced him dead of 'asphyxia,' essentially saying that the boy had expired of natural causes, in the manner that is now known as cot death. There could be no suspicion put upon Nannie at such an unfortunate turn of events. And the fact that she was so obviously racked with grief eliminated any inkling that the doctor might have had that foul play was afoot. Nannie was known to be a lovely woman, who suffered the misfortune of a bad husband as gracefully as anyone could, and she had no possible motive for killing a little boy, even if she were the kind of person who might be so inclined.

It would be the next day before Melvina came home to the news that both of her children had now died in close proximity to Nannie. All of her suspicions about hatpins came rushing back, but once again Nannie had surrounded herself with a cocoon of sympathetic locals, friends, and family so that she could not be confronted. It was a perfect repeat of her very first murder, down to the real victim that she was trying to spite coming home in shame amidst the aftermath, to face a solid wall of questions about where they had been. Melvina managed to deflect all of that in the short term by following her mother's example and launching into a wild display of grief, but in the back of her mind, some small part of her was still trying to work out if this had been a calculated move on Nannie's part or if it truly was the terrible twist of fate that she and the doctors claimed it was.

At the funeral a few days later, Melvina was back with Mosie. The grief of losing another child had her rushing right back into his comforting arms. The two of them stood alongside Florine by the graveside and watched as Nannie went into fits of hysterical sobbing before finally flinging herself into the mud in a faint. Frank had finally resurfaced from his latest binge, so it fell to him to hoist his wife back to her feet and drag her off home before she did herself an injury, but he returned to drink with his adoptive daughters once Nannie was safely squared away. He startled the girls out of their reverie with a sobering announcement. 'I reckon that I'm next.'

The three of them shared their suspicions, but there was no evidence. They couldn't even fully convince themselves that Nannie was capable of the crimes that she had committed, so how could they convince anyone else? All that they could do was watch her from a safe distance—and wait.

The War at Home

Throughout Nannie's tumultuous marriage with Frank, it may have seemed to her that the rest of the world had ground to a halt outside of her own personal bubble of depression, but sadly this was not the case. By the time of her grandson's death in 1945, the whole world was embroiled in a massive conflict that dwarfed Nannie's minor squabbles and petty cruelties in every way. The Second World War had turned every continent into a battleground, and America was no exception. In 1941, the naval base at Pearl Harbor was bombed by Japanese forces, finally drawing America into the conflict.

While there was a system of conscription in place that might have rid Nannie of her loathed husband, the sheer number of volunteer soldiers in the early days of America's involvement in the war meant that there was a genuine fear that the 'home front' of basic services and matériel production would be halted by every warm body going overseas to fight. An emergency executive order was written into law preventing anyone from the age of eighteen to thirty-seven from volunteering for military service, and before long, the randomised selection of new recruits was replaced with an administrative system to protect anyone who was involved in manufacturing from being sent off to fight.

Frank was protected by the job that he had come to resent from being sent off to die on the frontlines, but he was not protected from the contempt of the community who considered him to be a coward for not putting himself forward before the law was changed. He had lived his entire adult life as the subject of contempt and ridicule thanks to his drinking habit, but this was the first time that he felt any bite in the criticism that he received. For all of his faults, he had always considered himself to have courage, and he attributed his failure to volunteer more to his constant state of inebriation than to any desire to avoid serving his country. Every day through the four years of America's involvement in the war, he would go out drinking as normal, only to find that more of his old drinking buddies had vanished overnight, shipped off to some distant front that German U-boat attacks ensured many of them would never reach.

Every family would receive a letter when a husband or son died, but that news was very rarely conveyed along to the contemptable crowd at the local watering hole. As far as the drinking men of Cedartown knew, every time that one of their numbers went missing, they had gone to their death. Tensions were running high, with the men who were still in the lottery simultaneously excited and horrified at the prospect of their conscription, and the men who were exempted being the constant focus of their nervous energy.

Frank got into more bar-fights throughout the years of conscription than he had ever before in his life, including his wild youth, and it fell to Nannie to come and collect him off the floor every time that he got beaten. Needless to say, his own suffering soon led to his inflicting more of the same violence against Nannie to soothe his own wounded ego.

As the war abroad reached a fever pitch, so too did the indignities that Frank, and in turn Nannie, had to suffer through until finally, it all came to an abrupt and fiery end. On the sixth of August, 1945, less than a month after the funeral of Robert, the United States dropped a nuclear weapon on Hiroshima. On the eighth of August, the Soviet Union invaded Japanese territory, and America dropped a second atomic bomb on the city of Nagasaki. At the direction of the emperor, Japan surrendered unconditionally to the Allied powers, and the war came to an end, with the official announcement of surrender travelling around the world by the fifteenth August. It was a cause for celebration across America. The war was finally over, and all of the survivors were going to get to come home. Almost everyone in Cedartown treated it as a national holiday, with production in the mill grinding to a halt by midday when the frenetic pace of production that they had been pursuing all throughout the war was finally dropped.

Surprising nobody, Frank suggested that his co-workers come out for a drink with him to celebrate their great nation's victory, and for a change, they were actually inclined to go along with him. This would be a chance to clear the air before all of the boys from abroad got back home, to present a united front to the men who were going to need their support. More importantly, it was a chance for them to all feel like they were equal again, instead of half the town having to walk on eggshells while blaming the other half for their misfortune. All of Frank's old drinking buddies who had grown distant were ready to welcome him back with open arms, and the tiny silo of men just like him—who had been growing more isolated and insular as the war raged on—felt like they could breathe again. It was the happiest that Frank could ever remember being. The drinking went on and on through the day and into the night, with every single man in town coming by to buy a round, or so it seemed to the liquor-addled crowd. The camaraderie and goodwill were so bountiful that all of Frank's old sins were forgiven by the men who just a week ago would have punched the grin off his face and left him bleeding in the mud. He was on a high, the likes of which he had never experienced before. So when the bar crowd started to disperse it is hardly surprising that he tried to keep the party going. First, he went back to a friend's house, where they indulged in some of the cheap, local moonshine that had persisted long after the end of prohibition. Then, when all of the hardcore drinkers began to fall away towards dawn, he was forced to call on his wife to come and collect him.

While Nannie had always suffered these night-time trips with quiet dignity in the past, this time she found herself genuinely amused by Frank's overwhelming good cheer. It reminded her of the early days of their marriage, when the two of them still behaved like lovers instead of enemies, and she found herself laughing along with his jokes as if no time had gone by at all. For the duration of that short car ride, Nannie almost forgot all of the pointless cruelties that he had made her suffer. She almost started to think of him as a potential romantic partner again. Almost.

It is unclear whether Frank was so happy that he genuinely believed that his relationship with Nannie was salvageable or if he saw her softening attitude towards him as a sign of weakness, a chink in the impregnable armour of ice that she had formed around herself and their marital bed. But either way, he became increasingly amorous as they approached home until she was forced to pry his hand off her knee so that she could change gears. Once they were in the house, it seemed like any hint of human restraint left Frank entirely. He pushed Nannie up against a wall, smothering her with sloppy kisses and fumbling with her skirt. Up to a point, she reciprocated his advances. This was all so familiar: the smell of rye whiskey on a man's breath, the burn of his stubble on her neck, the pain where his finger dug too deeply into her thighs. It all added up to remind her of finding comfort in the arms of other men, of the teenage dalliances and desperate search for any sort of escape that had characterised her first miserable failure of a marriage. It was too much.

She took hold of his wrists and dragged his grabbing hands away before he could do more than leave some bruises. 'Get off me.'

Frank didn't seem inclined to take no for an answer. He twisted out of her grip, hooked his fingers and started tearing at her blouse. A ragged laugh escaped his lips as she writhed and struggled against him. Her resistance excited him more than her pliant submission ever had. She kicked him in the shins, but the pain barely made it through the haze of liquor. She tried to twist away from him, to deny him free access to the parts of her body that he seemed so intent on twisting until she wept, but that just gave him a better grip on her. He twisted her arm up her back until she could feel the bone creaking inside it and she cried out in pain. 'If you don't listen to me, woman, I ain't going to be here next week.'

Tears were running down her cheeks, and her teeth were gritted together to hold back a scream as he twisted and twisted. Just when she felt sure that her arm was going to snap, he stopped. He held her there at the exact moment of agony for almost a full minute until she whimpered out. 'Fine.'

It was the first time that they had shared their marital bed in years, but whatever passion this place and these motions might have once kindled in her was all burnt away in the raging flames of her fury. She lay there, staring up at the ceiling, tears flooding down her face as Frank flopped around on top of her, grunting and groaning, drawing blood, sweat, and tears from his beloved wife before finally, with one great arch of his back, he was done. He passed out right on top of her, and it took all of her remaining strength to crawl her way out from underneath him and out of the bed before he could rouse himself from his drunken stupor and demand she fulfil her 'wifely duties' all over again.

She sat herself down in the quiet little library she had constructed for herself in her living room, surrounded by all of her precious tales of love and felt her own blood mixed with Frank's foul seed trickling down her leg. She would not sleep that night, just as she had not slept on the night before young Robert's death. That same rage was back, so overwhelming that it was a wonder it didn't seize full control of her body and march her through to the kitchen to draw a knife.

Frank had gotten away with a lot over the years. He had walked all over her, treated her like part of the furniture, and she had just kept her head down and accepted it because she never wanted to admit that there was something fundamentally wrong in her relationship. That was the kind of admission that might lead a person to introspection, the kind of revelation that might make a woman question why she was picking these broken monsters of men. Admitting that there was something wrong with her marriage was tantamount to admitting to some deep, dark flaw in her own psyche, and she had done absolutely everything that she could to avoid that.

Regardless of how she felt about the matter, and regardless of whatever uncomfortable justifications she was going to have to make to herself, the bottom line was that this could not stand. Her tolerance had been taken as an invitation for more cruelty, her kindness had been taken for weakness, and this last gruesome intrusion was the straw that broke the camel's back. Her husband had betrayed her trust in the worst possible way, and now he had to pay the price for that betrayal, for his destruction of her dream of a life full of love with nothing more than the petty evil of a weak-willed man of no consequence. Frank had to die. There was no other option.

But while little Robert had been entirely in her power and easy to snuff out with barely a second thought, the practicalities of killing Frank were a little more complex. If he died, there would be no easy acceptance of 'cot death' or anything like that. There would be questions that needed answers, and Nannie knew that most of those questions would be directed at her. He had to die as cleanly as Robert had, with a reasonable excuse for his death already built in. She had been careless with Robert, and it had only been luck that saved her from scrutiny. She had learned her lessons from that last murder. She couldn't act on rage alone—there had to be planning and finesse when she laid her husband to rest because the whole town already knew how he abused her, and she would be the obvious lightning rod for any suspicion in the air.

Avoiding detection was only a part of the problem. Frank no

longer ate any meals at home, he had always hidden his liquor so that Nannie had no opportunity to pour it away, and after he had sobered up enough to remember what he had done last night his guard was going to be up even more than usual. Poison had always been her weapon of choice—easy to use and hard to detect—but with Frank, she had no opportunity to use it at all. The distance that she had so carefully cultivated to keep herself out of his reach was now protecting him instead.

She stayed well out of his way when he finally woke the following day, listening from her hiding place out in the garden as he bustled and grumbled around the house—her house—like he was entitled to every inch of it when she had earned it with a decade of hard work. Nannie was desperate to burst in and start screaming at him, but she dreaded whatever fresh horror was going to come tumbling out of his mouth next. All it would take would be a single leer and then she didn't think she would be able to control her own actions.

She stayed out in the garden all through the morning, even after Frank had staggered off to work without so much as a backwards glance. The house that she had made into a home over all of these years felt like a prison now, too claustrophobic to tolerate for even a moment. Frank had come sauntering in and ruined that for her, just like he'd ruined every other part of her life. All that she had left that was truly hers was this garden. The flowers that she had planted. The herbs that she had grown. The trees that she had picked apples from. Every part of it had been cultivated and allowed to flourish under her watchful eye. None of her plants had been allowed to grow wild and cause trouble for themselves, or cause trouble for her. None of them ever needed to be torn up from the roots because they were ruining everything else. They were perfectly under her control, and they were perfect as a result.

When she found the patch under her rose bushes that had been dug up, all of the tears that she had been holding back since last night came flooding out. Even this was ruined. Even this had been tainted by the fumbling, useless hands of some man. The one sanctuary that she had left, the one part of her that should never have been violated. And here was the evidence that it had been. She didn't even reach for her trowel—she dug into the earth with her bare hands, scooping the loamy earth away as she sobbed. What could have been so important that it was worth ruining the sanctity of her garden? What in this world was so important to Frank that he would go interfering in a place he had never shown any interest in whatsoever?

Her fingertips scraped over the hard glaze of his moonshine bottle and she froze. Her sobs turned first hysterical and then into joyous, raucous laughter. This was exactly what she needed. This was how she could get to Frank, and nobody would even blink. He'd delivered the perfect and most poetic instrument of vengeance right into her hands.

Taking care not to get mud on herself, Nannie took the bottle over to her compost heap and poured out an inch of the moonshine. She then went into the kitchen and fetched out the rat poison. She topped up the bottle until it was back to the same level, then swished it around, doing a slow and joyful waltz around her garden with the bottle in her arms and a song in her head. Once the arsenic had dissolved into the already-sharp liquor, it was the work of a few minutes to return the bottle to the ground and bury it all over again, hiding any sign that it had ever been disturbed.

As before, all of the rage that had been driving Nannie on through the long, sleepless night left her body in a rush once the act itself was complete. She was almost limp with relief. Inside the house, she barely had time to wash up and hide the evidence of her crime before she fell into a contented nap by the fireplace. She would sleep through until the evening, when she made herself a small dinner and then went to bed early, a smile still haunting her sleeping face.

In the morning, she found her husband's body outside and went to fetch the police. The corpse was practically pickled with liquor when the doctor came to examine it, so full of the local corn whiskey that the scent of it overpowered even decomposition. Frank had not been moved since the violent and painful contortions of the previous night had come to their end, so it was all too easy to construct a story from the scene. There he lay, moonshine in hand, passed out and exposed to all of the elements. Whether his heart gave out, the night's cold got to him, or cirrhosis of the liver finally finished him off, there was no suggestion that any foul play might be afoot.

There was some concern that there had been something wrong with the moonshine that had caused his sudden death—a concern that was quite pressing for the doctor, as he had been known to indulge in a little bit of illicit drinking himself—but there was nothing left in the whiskey jar for them to examine. It seemed, at a glance, that Frank had drunk it to the very last drop, although the truth was that it had been very carefully washed out in the kitchen before being returned to its incriminating position by the side of the body. No post-mortem was performed, and a well-attended funeral was conducted within the week.

While both of Nannie's daughters attended the event, neither of them would go anywhere near their mother. In fact, neither one of them would ever speak to their mother again for the rest of their lives, doing their best to distance themselves from her horrific legacy. With the death of their adoptive father, they saw Nannie's actions all too clearly for the first time. Both girls finally believed that they knew what had happened to their siblings, and Melvina finally felt like she knew the cruel fate that had befallen her children. It was enough. Just enough evidence to support their suspicions. And while they may not have given a damn whether Frank lived or died, they had loved Melvina's children so intensely that even heavy suspicion was an intolerable weight on any sort of relationship with their mother.

In the aftermath of Frank's death, Nannie experienced an unexpected windfall. Early in their marriage, when things had still been going well and Frank's drinking was under control, he had taken out a fairly hefty life insurance policy on himself, to protect Nannie and his newly-acquired daughters. With his unexpected death and no hint of foul play, that policy now paid out. She had never had money before in her life, having survived on subsistence wages, and struggled every single day to stretch the limited cash that her husbands deigned to share with her into enough food to last a month. The idea of having so much money that she didn't have to worry, at a time when she had abruptly had all ties to her dependents cut, was intoxicating. If Frank had been alive, he would have drunk it all. If Charley had still been in the picture, it would have all been spent on returning some of the glitz and glamour that his mother remembered from her youth. For Nannie, the daughter of a farmer and a surprisingly canny businesswoman in her own right, there was only one investment that made sense with that sort of lump sum. She bought land. Ten acres of it on the rural outskirts of Jacksonville, Alabama. In one corner of it, she built herself a little cottage, more a library than a home. It was close enough to the town where she had grown up that she never felt homesick or lost, but far enough from all of her family and history that she no longer felt haunted by her past. Her little plot of land was readily adopted by local share-croppers and worked to its limits, providing her with a regular income to supplement the lump sum of her insurance and the tiny pensions that she had acquired over the years. For the first time in her life, she was completely financially independent, capable of taking care of her own needs without relying on a man to provide for her—along with all of the demands that the simple provision of necessities brought with it.

She was also completely alone with her thoughts for the first time. All of her desires for a better life, all of the dreams that she had harboured for a great love affair in her life, even her dreams of travelling to exotic places—suddenly they were no longer exclusively in the realm of fantasy. She could go anywhere and do anything, without anyone to tell her what to do. There was dreadful loneliness in her time out by Jacksonville. All of her family, even her beloved Melvina, had cut off ties with her in light of the rumours being spread. Her own sisters refused to believe that Nannie could ever hurt a fly, but her mother, Lou, had a better memory of the fire in the young girl whom she had raised and the lengths that she might go to spite her father if given the opportunity. She kept her distance. Nannie corresponded with her sisters by letter, due to the distance that the two of them had travelled, but she shared few details of her real life, instead preferring to regale them with tales of her plans for the future and her hopes for one more chance at love before her life was over.

Roaming Hearts

Idleness had always been the greatest sin imaginable to the Hazle family, so there was no possibility of Nannie just sitting around and wishing for a better future. She began to order newspapers from further afield, to extend the reach of her hunt for a husband into new lonely hearts columns. While her reputation locally was still surprisingly clean, albeit tarnished with associated grief, she did not feel like the dating pool for ladies her age was particularly deep.

For a fresh start and the possibility of a future untethered to her unpleasant past, she needed to cast her net wider, across state lines and around men who had previously been out of her league, as far as the socio-economic class went.

There had never been a formal class structure in the United States, but society had certainly stratified in much the same way that could be found back in old Europe. The aftermath of the war shook that system up. Suddenly, men were coming back from abroad and receiving a free higher education under the GI Bill. Home ownership was becoming available to everyone who had fought in the army, too—it was the birth of America's massive middle-class, and Nannie with her newfound position as a landowner was moving on up along with the rest of her peers, even though her journey was via a slightly more circuitous route.

Making a decision about the quality of the men that she had been approaching to date, Nannie decided that the time had come to look for an upgrade. Even though her education had been minimal, her extensive reading had given her enough of a vocabulary to pass for whichever class background she wanted to mimic. She wrote her very own lonely hearts posting and deployed it to newspapers far and wide. The response that she received was almost overwhelming. The postman began to dread the route that took him past her house because his bag was fit to burst with all of Nannie's correspondence.

Nannie selected the men she wanted to respond to very carefully, drawing out more information from each one before divulging too much herself. She had learned her lessons after her last attempt at this sort of correspondence. A man turning up on her doorstep with another marriage proposal that she felt obliged to accept due to the romance of the gesture was precisely what she was hoping to avoid. As a result, she showed a definite preference for suitors who were from further afield and who seemed contented merely with the letters, photographs, and baked goods that she was willing to dole out.

During the two years between Frank's death and her next great romance, Nannie was very rarely home. She travelled the United States by rail, visiting cities and potential suitors everywhere that she went. There are some partial records of her staying in both Idaho and New York at different times, living the high life on her new personal fortune. In the state of New York, there were some hints from conversations with friends and correspondents of Nannie that she had made a rapid arrangement to marry a man named 'Hendricks,' but no marriage licence has ever been produced to support this claim, and all official biographers of Nannie's life have been forced to set this particular husband and potential victim aside due to the lack of records, just as the police would later do during their own investigations. With the colossal population of

New York at the time and the sheer volume of mysterious deaths that the beleaguered police force had to handle during those boom years, it is hardly surprising that one middle-aged man might slip through the cracks. Whether she wed or not, we do know for certain that she continued to correspond with many of the men who had taken her fancy, stringing each one of them along until she happened to be passing by their town, or possibly just vetting them more extensively than any of her previous matchmakers had bothered to do for her.

One such man was Arlie Lanning. Arlie was a resident of Lexington, North Carolina—a good two states away from Nannie's home base—and his letters were filled with the same sort of language that her romance novels had been teasing her imagination with throughout her life. Born in Alabama himself, he had settled on the East Coast after the war was over, founding a little empire for himself on that distant shore. He had never been married before, although apparently it wasn't for a lack of trying on his part. It didn't take Nannie long to translate his platitudes about 'never finding the right person to settle down with' into the most obvious truth that the man had been a horn-dog chasing after different women all of his life. He was only now realising that if he didn't settle down fast, he was going to be left alone with nobody to keep his bed warm, but even so, he didn't seem to be in any mad rush to put a ring on Nannie's finger. That wasn't enough to dissuade Nannie, of course. She had read enough tales of redemptive love to think that she had good odds of transforming a naughty boy into a good man, even if her personal experience had been the direct opposite. Besides, there was something about Arlie's quiet confidence that really worked for Nannie. He wasn't pushy about meeting her; he was barely even pushy about getting a reply. He was extremely appreciative of the pictures and treats that she sent him, without ever demanding more, and he freely offered up anything that she ever asked for in return. It seemed like another relationship made in heaven, at least on paper.

Almost two years after the end of the war and the death of Frank, Nannie boarded a cross-country train and set out on the next great adventure of her life. She was forty-two years old, once divorced, once widowed, and still as radiant and brimming over with personality as she had been as a teenager. When Arlie met her off the train in Lexington, he was bowled over by her. The pictures that she had sent did no justice to the sight of her in motion. Nannie travelled in a cloud of perfume, her makeup movie-star perfect, her clothes impeccably pressed, her curls carefully coiffed to best accentuate the long line of her neck. She knew that she was still a beauty. She did all that she could to emphasise her own attractiveness, but it was never out of conceit. Part of it was simply her obsession with glamour in all its forms, something that she was finally able to pursue actively now that her impoverished past had fallen by the wayside. Part of it was her ever-active attempts to attract the romance of a lifetime, a whole world of possible suitors that she needed to take notice of her. For the most part though, it was about comfort. Her romance stories had always been the place where she was most happy, so it was hardly surprising that she chose to garb herself in the costuming of them and did all that she could to invoke them into reality by force of will alone.

By the time that Arlie had picked his jaw up off of the railway platform, Nannie had already offered him a hand to kiss and a little package of her home cooked treats for him to enjoy after their dinner that evening. She had booked a room in the finest hotel in Lexington for the next three nights and would return home on the fourth morning. In short, this was an audition. If Arlie could impress her as much with real conversation as he had with his letters, then she would consider letting their dalliance go on. There was no doubt in either of their minds about who was in control of the situation, but the laid-back Arlie seemed to be completely fine with handing the reins to Nannie—the first man in her life who had been quite content to accept his role as a bit-part player in her grand romantic dreams.

In Lexington, Arlie was well-known; a labourer before the war who had gone on to run his own crew after his return. He'd served with distinction in the Navy during the war, earning him the respect of his peers, and while his romantic dalliances of the past would have been a source of scandal out in rural Alabama, here in the city they were barely worthy of notice. He had several family members in the area, including a sister who had fallen on hard times and sought shelter under his wing and a mother whom he had helped to relocate from Alabama just a year back after her husband had expired. The latter fact had been a source of some alarm for Nannie initially, but beyond paying a small stipend for her upkeep, it didn't seem that Arlie doted on his mother too much. That was good—the last thing that Nannie wanted in her life was another overbearing mother-in-law trying to tell her how to live.

The single women of Lexington still considered Arlie to be something of a catch, even if none of them had quite managed to land him yet, and this strange beautiful woman from out of town was something of a fly in the ointment for many of their plans. Despite this initial frosty reception, Nannie soon won the ladies in Arlie's life over with her genuine good humour and kindness. At this moment in her life, her dark moods had been driven off entirely as she launched herself out of obscurity and misery into the person that she had always dreamed of being. As long as she stayed in the fantasy, her old life couldn't intrude—as long as she stayed focused on creating a new Nannie at the centre of a grand romance. Her depression and violent temper were completely suppressed.

Arlie was a perfect gentleman throughout Nannie's stay in town, despite the often outrageous ways that she would flirt with him, and by the end of her visit, her mind was made up about him. She had clearly been chasing the wrong kind of men all her life when by climbing just one rung up the socio-economic ladder, she could have found herself someone like him.

They made arrangements for a wedding immediately after her return home to Alabama, and within a week she was back on a train with her bags packed, ready to start her new life as Nannie Lanning. The wedding was well attended on his side, and the absence of guests on her side of the church was taken as a sign of her mysterious and exciting nature rather than as an indication that there was something wrong with her. After all, how could such a lovely and charming woman be anything but a good person?

The two of them settled into Arlie's comfortable house in town without any issue, and they were soon the very picture of domestic bliss. Nannie had a beautiful meal on the table for him every night when he came home from work. The two of them went out dancing, to the theatre, and even to the cinema on occasion, when there was a particularly romantic film on. From the outside looking in, Nannie had created another perfect marriage for herself. But the seeds of doubt and distrust had been planted in her long ago, and it would not take long before they came to fruition once more. Every moment that she was not in Arlie's company, she was riddled with suspicions about his extra-marital activities. She was not a shrill shrew of a wife, constantly making accusations, but she did establish a solid network of spies amongst the other women about town, and Arlie's movements were noted and conveyed to her daily.

The time that he spent working was actually about half of the time that he was out and about in town each day, with the vast majority of the actual physical labour that his crew undertook requiring only a little bit of guidance on his part before he moved on to bigger and better things. Instead of Frank's rotgut whiskey, the more upscale Arlie drank wines and beers, but the end result was just the same. In the beginning, he kept it under control. He was genuinely quite in love with Nannie, and he knew that his drinking and cavorting with other women was likely to upset her, as it had his many romantic partners in the past, so he did what he considered to be the only honourable thing and lied to her. What she didn't know couldn't hurt her, and as long as he kept his drinking to a reasonable level and didn't get sloppy, he could maintain both facets of his life without any trouble; the happy marriage and the free-wheeling party lifestyle.

Needless to say, it was less than a month later that he 'got sloppy.' He fell asleep at the home of one of the women that he had been having sex with, instead of returning home for his dinner as usual. Initially, this didn't seem like the end of the world—he was only two hours late for dinner. It was the first time he had slipped up in his routine, and Nannie had always been so understanding of the demands of his working life. It might have been the sort of thing that an apology, a lie, and a bunch of flowers could fix. But it wasn't. Nannie was entirely aware of where he had been and what he had been doing. He returned home to a cold and empty house. At first, he was distraught, then frantic. He searched all about town for Nannie in all of her usual haunts, fully intent on apologising and making things right, but once again, she was nowhere to be found. It was almost midnight by the time that he trudged home, some small ember of hope still burning in his heart that she had doubled-back past him, that she would be sitting in her chair by the fire or propped up on her pillows, reading, with her sly smile still plastered on her face. She was not there. But in his haste the first time, he had missed the note that she left behind on the kitchen table, beside his long-cold dinner. It read, quite simply, 'Going on a trip. Be back soon.'

It was a week before she returned. Ostensibly, she had been off checking on her house back in Alabama, ensuring that the business side of the farm was turning over properly and her investments there were safe. Yet the train she rode back into Lexington had come from up north, not the west, and the clothes, hats, and furs that she bought on her travels had all the glitz and glamour of New York lingering about them even here. Arlie didn't dare to pass comment. He was mortified by his own behaviour, horrified that he had been caught and completely contrite when it came time to admit to his faults. He apologised to Nannie unreservedly, swore off alcohol entirely, and swore that he would become the kind of husband that he had promised to be in their letters and on their wedding day.

For a little while, he even managed it. He put in more time with the work crew and brought in more money than either he or his well-off wife could ever reasonably need. His employees were delighted to see more of their boss, particularly when he got hands-on with the work again instead of just rattling off orders and heading to the bar. His sobriety came with some drawbacks however. There was no more slacking or empathy for lateness for his workers. If Arlie was holding himself to a higher standard then he intended to drag everyone else up with him, even if it meant losing his reputation as the most good-natured boss in all of Lexington. It didn't take long before his friends and family realised that he was under some sort of strain, even if they couldn't work out that he was in a deadly battle with his own addiction.

For Nannie's part, she carried on as if nothing had happened at all, presenting herself to the world as the perfect wife and homemaker, lavishing beautiful meals on Arlie every night and tending to his every need, so long as he remained loyal and truthful with her. If he had any sort of support network, then Arlie's story might have been a happy one, rather than a tragedy, but instead, he had a whole town that missed the 'old' Arlie with his good-natured jibes and casual approach to life. It didn't take much effort on the part of his workers to convince him to come out for a drink after work to celebrate a job well done. Just one drink. That was what they said to him. But that one drink was one too many, and he soon discovered that his one drink came in a great many different glasses and lasted long into the night.

He wasn't even surprised when he dragged himself home the next morning and found Nannie long gone. This time, her note was even briefer and her absence even longer. 'Back soon' apparently meant that she would return almost a month later, with the latest fashions in her new suitcases and a complete lack of explanation for her distressed husband. Arlie got back on the wagon, apologised until he was blue in the face, and cut all ties with the men who he felt had led him astray. Once again, Nannie was magnanimous and kind, while still making it perfectly clear that she was not willing to tolerate any nonsense from Arlie. He was so fixated on making things right that it never even occurred to him to question what she had been doing all this time, or who she had been doing it with.

As the years rolled on, the cycle continued. Arlie would slip up, slide into some other woman's bed or pass out in a bar and then Nannie would be off on another grand adventure across country, in the arms of another man, or another, or another. Her eternal desire to be romanced was being fulfilled by a cavalcade of new suitors who did not realise that she was married. Her need for a stable home and husband was being fulfilled by Arlie. To say that she was contented would be to grossly oversimplify the constant fluctuation of her moods and desires, but Arlie's failings gave her sufficient excuse to slink off and relieve the pressure of maintaining her façade of perfection often enough to keep things more or less in balance.

For five years, Nannie and Arlie kept their relationship alive through its ups and downs, but despite all that she did to keep the darkness at bay, it wasn't long before the little slights of a regular marriage began to mount up. All it took was the span of three months, in which Arlie actually managed to maintain his sobriety before Nannie had reached the end of her tether. From the beginning of the long winter of 1951, stretching through to the January of 1952, Arlie stayed home instead of sneaking out with his friends. No small part of this was because a lethal flu virus had hit Lexington, and hale and hearty men were dropping like flies all through the snowy season, but it was also fuelled by his genuine desire to be a better husband—a feat made easier by the removal of invitations to go out and the temptations that came along with them.

As a 'reward' for his good behaviour, Nannie spent almost a full month baking and cooking all of her husband's favourite dishes, lavishing attention on him and performing the wifely duties that she had typically preferred to fulfil outside of their marital bed during her excursions to meet up with other 'lonely hearts' across the states.

When Christmas had rolled by, once again without a single card from any of her family, something just seemed to snap. The house fell gradually into a state of poor cleanliness. The meals became leftovers, then sandwiches, then nothing much at all. Even Nannie's perpetual glamour began to crack under her husband's endless, unintentional scrutiny. She looked unkempt and bedraggled. She didn't bother to put on her makeup some mornings. Her dark moods began to seep out past the mask of kindness that she had always kept held up between her husband and reality. He had seen the real Nannie for the very first time, just a glimpse of who she really was underneath all of the lies, and she could not stand it. Abruptly, she switched back to her usual, perfectly coiffed appearance. She made a great show of setting everything right about the house, and for the first time in their relationship, offered up an apology of her own towards Arlie, even going so far as to promise to make him a special treat to make up for her poor treatment of him—a special pie. One of his favourites. Filled with sweetened, stewed prunes, with an odd, bitter aftertaste that he couldn't quite place but refused to comment on when Nannie had obviously put so much effort into baking it for him.

She called the doctor the next morning, and when he finally made it around to her house after tackling a half dozen other calls of a very similar nature, he declared Arlie Lanning dead on the spot. A passive examination resulted in the cause of death being listed as heart failure, but that was merely the shorthand that people at the time were using to refer to the flu deaths. The medical professionals did not want to spread panic. However, there was no suspicion about what had happened to Arlie, and while the whole town mourned his passing, they banded around poor Nannie in her trying time and did what they could to support the poor widow. It was the same as had happened every time that Nannie instigated a tragedy—she was the immediate recipient of all the benefits that the tragedy brought: the centre of attention, the recipient of charity and gifts. All of the kindness that she had missed out on in her early life was delivered to her in spades every time that she killed someone else. It is hardly surprising that murder soon went from being the means to the end in itself for her.

Arlie's local family took her under their wing, with his mother immediately inviting Nannie to stay with her for as long as she needed, if she wanted to be out of the house where she had lost her husband. Nannie was reluctant to leave the house that she felt she had earned through her polite play-acting over the years, but she couldn't think of a polite way to turn down the invitation and still maintain the appearance of the grieving widow. So, she packed up her mourning clothes in one suitcase and loaded the rest into boxes to be shipped back to Alabama as soon as she found the time. Her time in Lexington was coming to a close, and the sooner that she could put the town behind her, the easier it would be to outrun any stories that might get started about her.

Before Arlie's body was even in the ground, Nannie began to make quiet enquiries about collecting on his insurance policy, and about selling along the house so that she could return to her cottage in Alabama and get sunk back into the lonely hearts columns that she had been neglecting over the past half-decade—plans that were almost immediately derailed by certain arrangements that she had not been made aware of.

The Price of a Life

Arlie's will had not been updated since the wedding with Nannie, and while the majority of his limited wealth passed to her directly, certain items outlined in his old will had other destinations pre-ordained for them. In particular, there was the house where Nannie had lived for the past five years. When Arlie's sister had first moved to Lexington, she was in dire financial straits, supported almost exclusively by her brother, and while her situation was considerably more stable now, the arrangements that he had made for her to receive his house if anything happened to him were still in place. Nannie was going to be left with nothing to show for her marriage, having failed to arrange for a life insurance policy on this husband in-between her many expeditions out of town.

While she was currently living rent-free with her mother-in-law, it was an uncomfortable situation that was continuing to exacerbate the wanderlust that had driven her to kill Arlie in the first place. She felt trapped all over again, pinned in place. And without a substantial windfall to cover her new, more extravagant lifestyle, she wasn't sure how she was going to make her escape. Despite this tension, Nannie wasn't so gauche as to suggest that Arlie's house should go to her rather than his sister, although she did enjoy the extra sympathy that the same suggestion voiced by others garnered her. Poor Nannie. First she lost her husband, and now she was losing her home. Wasn't it terribly cruel?

Arlie's sister seemed strangely resistant to any sort of badgering from friends and family along those lines. She had been through hard times, and she was a survivor. She knew that letting opportunities like this pass you by were how you ended up in trouble further down the line, and without the support of Arlie, she feared that any trouble in the future could ruin her permanently. Paying no heed to the complaints didn't mean that she had no justification for ignoring them; she knew that Nannie had a house back in Alabama and an income from the farming done around it, and she wasn't shy about mentioning it if anyone complained about her 'selfishness.'

As with most things, Nannie was outwardly gracious and internally fuming about the situation, or at least she was until she came across the insurance documents for the home and realised that in case of catastrophe, the payment would come to her rather than any new owner. She had always been exceptionally good at moving quickly once a plan had formed in her mind, and while her sister-in-law was packing up all of her belongings and cancelling her tenancy agreement, Nannie was making some rapid changes of her own.

It was a long month of waiting for Nannie—trapped in the pokey, little house with her mother-in-law, as the local fire department and the insurance company investigated the fire that had gutted Arlie's house. But eventually they gave in. Nobody could prove that the fire that had started in Nannie's beloved kitchen had been an act of arson, even if everyone suspected it and Arlie's sister wouldn't stop shouting about it. None of Nannie's belongings went up in the blaze of course—they had already been shipped back East as she graciously moved aside for her sister-in-law to take the house.

Suspicions began to swirl around Nannie as a result of the fire, and she soon realised that her mother-in-law had moved on from being her caretaker during a trying time to being her jailor, watching her every move and assessing her guilt. Nannie had all that she needed to move away, except for some way to untangle herself from the Lanning family and their expectations of her.

If she had been willing to steal away in the night without a backwards glance or any consideration of the impression that it would leave, then she had everything that she needed to do so. But the very idea that someone might think less of her, that they might suspect her of the wrongdoings that she all too frequently committed, was anathema to her and probably a significant reason why it took so long for her crimes to be discovered at all. Nannie had become an expert in managing public opinion, and she realised early on that the good opinion of Lexington hinged on the report that her mother-in-law gave about her to the local community. Luckily, she had the ideal solution already to hand. After a few days as a guest in her mother-in-law's home, Nannie insisted on helping out around the place, and while the old woman was reluctant to break up her usual routine, she had to admit that Nannie was a far better cook, so she ceded the kitchen to her.

Mrs Lanning had a long bout of illness in the early months of 1952 following her only son's death. Some thought that it was the same influenza virus that had swept through, causing such devastation. Others, such as her daughter, were convinced that it was some sort of cancer of the guts. Ultimately, the doctor took one look at the elderly woman and made his own assumptions about her general health. After idling in bed for months on end, without the strength to so much as chew any food denser than her loving carer Nannie's stewed prunes, she passed away. All of the distance that had plagued the Lanning family since the fire melted away in their grief, and Nannie and her sister-in-law were as close as real sisters again in no time at all. The whole town had seen her kindness, nursing the sickly, old woman even through her own time of grief, and the fact that the old lady's house was going to her daughter, and rendering Nannie homeless all over again, was more than enough to sway the court of public opinion back in her favour.

She lingered in Lexington only long enough to see her mother-in-law buried. Then, amidst declarations of eternal sisterhood and affection, she took a train back to Alabama and her old life, several thousand dollars richer than when she'd started out.

Nannie's return to her old cottage was a bittersweet feeling. She was surrounded once more by all of her home comforts and accompanied by all of the new luxuries that she'd acquired in her travels, but she was, once again, quite painfully alone in the world. She began to pick up her usual correspondence again, getting back into the habit of writing each day before she dove back into the chaos of the lonely hearts columns all over again. But within a few weeks, she had mail back from practically her entire extended family, begging her to go and visit her sister, Dovie, who had taken ill. Notable in its absence from her correspondence was any letter from Dovie.

Usually one of Nannie's regular respondents, she was uncharacteristically silent. Nannie had barely even unpacked her things before she was loading them into a case again and heading off to southern Alabama and her bedridden sister. Dovie had been struck down by some sort of wasting sickness that, by the time that Nannie arrived, had turned her from a pretty woman in her late thirties into something resembling a skeleton draped over with loose skin. She had been trapped in her bed for two weeks with only occasional visits from family members to break up the monotony, and she was exhausted from just the effort of her shaky walks to the bathroom. Nannie immediately took control of the situation, cleaning up the house and her sister, just as she had when the girl was a baby, before settling her back into a clean bed and promising her that she would be with her through it all, to nurse her back to health, however long that took.

It seemed that Nannie's promises extended much further than her patience when it came down to it. She played nursemaid for only a week, feeding her sister by hand and caring for her every need before she came to the decision that Dovie was not going to be getting any better. There had been no marked improvement to her condition in the seven days that Nannie had been watching over her, no regrowth of muscle or change in her terrible pallor. Nannie decided that her sister was dying. Then, shortly afterwards, she decided to ease that journey along as quickly as possible, so that her death wouldn't be such an inconvenience.

She controlled everything about Dovie's life in those final days, from the times that she was helped to the bedpan through to the food and water that was provided to her. It was hardly surprising that stewed prunes were on the menu, as it was a staple of baby food and a sweet treat comparable to apple sauce for those in need of comfort, or those with bowel troubles like Dovie complained of. It was also hardly surprising when Dovie passed away after just a week of her sister's loving care. Her illness had been a topic of great discussion in the church group that she regularly attended, and from there it had spread out through the local, rural community. The funeral was small and sparsely attended, but those who were there took note of sweet Nannie's grace under pressure. Even though she had just lost a sister and a husband, to boot, she was there taking care of everyone else, serving up an impressive spread of food and doing all that she could to make life easier on Dovie's local friends. Neither of her parents were in attendance, even if her brothers made it, and it was only after Nannie had cornered those siblings and layered on the guilt that they crumbled and told her why their parents were not there: James Hazle was dead.

Nannie had very deliberately cultivated a distance between herself and her parents throughout her second and third marriages, aware of how quickly the paper-thin fiction of her life could be torn apart by someone who knew her too well. More importantly, her relationship with her parents had never recovered from her treatment at their hands as a child. With James gone, all of the rage that Nannie had felt towards him now had no outlet or direction. It had provided the baseline of fury that she felt towards all men in every relationship. But now the object of her hatred was gone, she found herself struggling to navigate without that fundamental landmark in her mental geography.

All of her plans for the future seemed to crumble in the face of this sudden change. When she was the agent of massive tectonic shifts in her life, Nannie had no trouble navigating them, but when confronted with something like this—something completely out of her control that nonetheless had a massive impact upon her—she was at a loss.

After Dovie's funeral, she fled back to her cottage in a state of distress, a state that everyone else attributed to being a witness to her sister's early demise. Nothing could have been further from the truth. She had always entertained a fantasy of getting revenge on her father for the way that he had treated her as a child. Alongside her dreams of love, it had been one of the only things to get her through the desolate loneliness of her years on the farm. Now it seemed that yet another of her cherished fantasies had been ripped away by cruel reality. She stewed at home for a few days, unable to concentrate on anything and finding all of her old distractions to be bland and unpalatable. Then, finally, when she realised that only action was going to help, she packed herself an overnight bag and headed home to the Hazle farm, for the first time since she'd fled the state to escape it.

Lou had completely transformed since the death of her husband. Like her daughter, she had finally started to flourish once she was out of his shadow. But while Nannie had escaped decades before, Lou had suffered through a lifetime of his cold indifferent cruelty before finding freedom, and she had no idea what to do with herself without the rigid structure that he had imposed on her life. She was too old now to tend to anything around the farm, and it had never managed to turn any sort of profit throughout her life, at best managing to break even year on year. To make improvements and keep things afloat, James had been in constant debt, and with his death, none of it had been forgiven. The farm would be passing into the bank's hands within a month or so. Any hope of an inheritance that Nannie or the other Hazle children might have hoped for would be vanishing with it, and Lou was facing homelessness for the second time in her life, with no possibility of supporting herself this time around. She would soon fall on the charity of her children, and they were feeling less than charitable. A lifetime in the chilling company of their father had left both of the boys emotionally stunted and interested only in the mechanics of their own survival, they had absolutely no interest in supporting an old woman to whom they felt no particular attachment—particularly when it was well-known that Nannie, her favoured daughter, had plenty of money and space to spare.

While they had fallen out of touch, Lou didn't feel any resentment towards Nannie when she showed up on her doorstep. If anything, her beautiful, glamorous daughter filled her up with pride—after all, she had not only escaped from the nightmarish life that Lou had inadvertently consigned her to, she had made something of herself, even if the thing that she had made of herself was a rich widow.

So it was, that the two widows came to live under one roof, at least for a short while so that Lou could put the last of her affairs around the destitute farm in order and prepare for the move to Nannie's cottage. Once again, Nannie felt like her life was being dragged out of her control, just as she always did when her parents were involved. What she wanted and needed meant nothing in the face of the rules passed down from on high by James, and it seemed like Lou, who had been his messenger so often, had now assumed the mantle of dictator, fully expecting to be obeyed at every turn without question. There was no threat behind any of her demands. Instead, there was something far more insidious—the pressure of expectations and public opinion. What would people think of Nannie if she abandoned her own mother? What would they think of her if she took Lou in and then treated her poorly? Societal expectations lay at her feet like an open bear trap, just waiting to spring shut on her if she failed to give in to whatever her mother wanted. And the fact that Lou seemed to be so apologetic about the whole situation just made Nannie angrier.

This was a woman who had all of the power in the world over her, someone who could have completely changed the course of Nannie's life if she had just had the courage to stand up for herself or her daughter. And now, even now, after the bogeyman of her husband was dead and buried, she was still cowed and weak. For Nannie, this was an even greater affront than any of the indignities she had quietly suffered as a child to make this woman's life easier. It called everything that Nannie knew about her mother into question. It made her wonder if instead of being another victim of James' egomania, her mother had actually been a collaborator, or even instigator, in her hellish childhood.

Nannie's world had already been thrown into chaos by the death of her father, knocked completely off balance by the loss of the pillar around which she had built her long-harboured hatred of male authority figures. But with this slow realisation that the heroic protector in her personal mythology may have been no help at all, one of the other pillars of her worldview was crumbling. Worse yet, all of her plans to get back on the horse and pursue her dreams were going to be ruined if she had an elderly mother to care for. Her entire life was slipping out of her control, so she did the only thing that she could to re-assert her mastery over her own fate, in exactly the same way that she always had.

The kindness of Nannie was the talk of Blue Mountain once more, swooping in from out of nowhere in her mother's hour of need and taking her in. She was so generous with her time, doting on the old woman as she grew sicker and sicker, preparing every meal for her mother even when the old woman ended up bedridden. The whole town turned out for the funeral when the old woman had finally passed away, and even then, as she was awash in sympathy from all sides, Nannie was the pinnacle of good grace, making sure that all of her guests were cared for and barely sparing a moment for her own grief. It was so sad—she had lost a husband, a sister, and a mother, all within just a few years. A real tragedy.

With her mother's death, Nannie became completely untethered from her personal history. Her remaining siblings had no interest in pursuing a relationship with her, her children had fled to escape their suspicions of her, and her romantic partners were all deceased, with the exception of Charley, who had brought so much scandal on himself by betraying his wife in her hour of need that nobody would ever have listened to a word he said about Nannie anyway. She felt like she was free to invent her own history, just as she invented fantasies of her future.

The Diamond Circle Club

As much as Nannie loved to deny reality at every turn, there were certain facts that no amount of tale-spinning could erase. Her dark curls were undeniably turning grey at the temples, her once svelte waist had thickened, and her elegant neckline had manifested a double-chin. When she tried to read her beloved lonely hearts columns now, she required a pair of glasses to make it look like anything more than a blur. Age and too much good food was beginning to have an effect on her attractiveness to men. The young men full of passion, who had always come chasing after her, were now in short supply, so she set her sights on a more mature sort of gentleman, moving on from her old hunting grounds in the lonely hearts columns to a more refined national organisation known as the Diamond Circle Club.

For a not inconsiderable fifteen-dollar fee, members of this club were added to a list of potential suitors, and a list of all available members, and some details about them were circulated each month to see if some romance couldn't be stimulated.

In 1953, Nannie became a member and was soon inundated with offers from across the United States. She had always known how to sell herself. Most of the men pursuing her were not interested in a quick tumble, the way that the majority of the lonely hearts respondents had been. Indeed, sex seemed to be quite low on their list of priorities so late in life. Most were looking for something closer to a maid or housekeeper—a woman to assume the role of the wives that they had lost or the mothers that they had long since outgrown. There were few genuine bachelors among their number—most men had given up on love by that age if they'd had no success before—but one of the letters that Nannie received seemed to have been from a genuine gentleman who was looking for a real romance. He was a believer in love, even if it blossomed late in life, and he was looking for a genuine companion to spend his remaining time on Earth with. He didn't have the skill with poetry that many of Nannie's previous lovers had enticed her with, but without that layer of artistry lain over his letters, they came across as almost painfully genuine, as did his compliments. Nannie didn't even suspect that there was any deception or flattery afoot when he described her as the most beautiful thing that he had ever seen, because he did not seem to be capable of that sort of thing, and because even after all of this time and a good few knocks, her ego was still a force to be reckoned with.

Charmed enough by his sweet letters and accepting that every suitor may not be the most handsome man, Nannie set out to meet Richard Morton a short while before springtime came into full bloom, taking a train northwest to Kansas. The rolling flat fields of the state held her entranced. Nannie had lived all of her life among the hilly forests of Alabama and Georgia, never truly seeing the horizon. But now, for the very first time, she could look out of the window and see the whole world rolled out in front of her like a great, open book. In all of her travels, and even in her fantasies, middle-America had never featured, but now the verdant expanse of Kansas had her enthralled, and her dreams had been furnished with a new backdrop.

Morton met her at the station, and for once it was Nannie who was in for a pleasant surprise. She had known that he was in his sixties, a retired salesman who was now looking to settle down properly in his hometown now that life on the road was behind him, but she had no idea that he was going to be tall, dark, and handsome. With a Native American father, he had inherited hawkish good features, piercing eyes, golden-tanned skin, and thick, dark hair that didn't show even a hint of grey despite his advancing years. Nannie was surprised to find herself quite smitten with him, just as she had been with Kansas. The two of them fell into easy conversation, and Nannie began to fear as the day went on that the spark she had been hoping for just wasn't there. But when it came time to retire to her hotel for the night, Richard swept her up in his arms and kissed her, leaving her to go to bed with a buzz still clinging to her skin and a tiny, brown paper-wrapped parcel containing a beautiful necklace made by a local artist.

The gifts and the toe-curling kisses continued to be lavished on Nannie throughout her stay, and before she could even write home to ask for her things to be sent along, Richard had proposed to her. Within the month, they were wed, and she had moved into his little house out on the prairie. Richard sent a letter in to the Diamond Circle Club, politely requesting that both he and Nannie be removed from their roster of available members, thanking them profusely for making the introductions that had set him on this course and calling Nannie 'the sweetest and most wonderful woman that I have ever known.'

Nannie's new home was isolated from town but idyllic, and she set to living exactly the kind of married life that she had always dreamed of having. She could look out of her window each morning and see nothing but clear, blue skies and the straight line of the horizon beyond the corn fields. She could spend her day in the kitchen or the garden as she pleased, with no children to tend to and a husband who was almost always around to keep her company. Gone were the days when she had to wonder where her husband had gone roaming. All of her fears of betrayal seemed to finally be assuaged. The days were lazy, filled only with the things that she wanted to do, and every night she settled down by the side of her contented husband to relax and watch the television—every bit the image of the American Dream come to life.

The only times that Nannie was left alone with her thoughts were on those few days when Richard had to make a run into town for supplies, and those brief bouts of total silence came as something of a relief to Nannie after the honeymoon period of a few weeks of marital bliss drew to a close. It wasn't that she didn't enjoy Richard's company, it was just that she had become rather accustomed to time alone over the course of her last few marriages. But then, the wait for him to return home started getting longer. He would hop into his truck and head into town in the morning and not return until late afternoon, some days. When she asked him what had taken so long, he would just say that he had 'dawdled.' In the early days of his dawdling, any irritation was soon washed away in the tide of gifts that he brought back to Nannie after every trip into town. She had known from his letters that he was well off, but she had no idea that he would be treating her like a princess every moment of every day, lavishing furs and jewellery on her so consistently that she barely had time to be thrilled with one gift before the next one arrived. After a month, it stopped feeling like the royal treatment and started to feel like a bombardment, as though Richard didn't know how to express affection in any way other than buying things. It hinted at a very transactional approach to romance in his history, and once the excitement of gift-giving had faded, the question of what was taking him so long in town remained.

Nannie's usual network of contacts had never had the opportunity to develop in Kansas, mainly because Richard kept her so isolated, so she had no way of really finding out what was happening when she wasn't around. Her own opportunities to head into town were few and far between, and she always had Richard on her arm when they made the trip together, so there was very little opportunity to learn more about his activities. It was only in the sacred space and brief privacy of the hair salon that she was finally able to pry some details of Richard's life from before her arrival from the local women.

As she suspected, there had been a string of younger women ahead of her, interested only in the things that Richard could buy for them in exchange for their companionship. It would have been enough to induce sympathy for the lonely, old bachelor if it weren't for the fact that some of those same younger women were still in receipt of regular gifts. One girl in particular, who was young enough to be Richard's granddaughter, had been visited by Richard every time that he was in town on one of his dawdling shopping runs, and she had been given presents that were identical in every detail to the ones that Nannie would receive later in the day. The women in the salon were surprised at how well Nannie took the news once she had instilled enough sympathy in them with her stories about her life as a woman isolated by a controlling husband, half a world away from her family. They had expected an emotional breakdown. They had expected the older woman to make a scene, but instead, it was like she swallowed the news down with a single gulp. When Richard came to collect her after her blow-dry, she met him with the same wry smile that she had parted with him on, even as the rest of the salon scowled at him from behind their magazines for tormenting that poor, sweet woman with his infidelities.

Richard had made a terrible mistake when he married Nannie with no intention of being faithful to her. His kindness, combined with fidelity, would likely have brought him a long and happy retirement with Nannie, who was so let down by the other men in her life by this point that she was willing to accept many flaws, except for this one. He may have lied about being faithful only to her, but Nannie was concealing something considerably more dangerous in her own history.

Nannie began writing to a new crop of gentlemen correspondents, making sure to note that she had been recently widowed in Kansas and was open to travel and excitement elsewhere after a lacklustre marriage. She had always been earlier to rise than her new husband, so ensuring that he never intercepted the mail was quite simple. Any letters that were addressed to her were simply slipped inside her blouse until she could find the time to lock herself in the bathroom to pour over them. The spark of romance was back in her life again, even if it was just a fantasy kindled from some crumpled-up letters, but the flames of it would soon rise up to consume the life that she had created here for herself. In amongst the many letters that she concealed about her person there were application forms for several life insurance policies on her husband. She had been caught out once when Arlie died and left everything to his sister, she wasn't planning on having to scrabble about for money again any time soon.

For all that she feared Richard reading her mail, she certainly wasn't shy about opening his while he still dozed away the morning. Bank statements, pension documents, and loan letters piled up alongside her own collected letters, and she quickly constructed a more complete picture of Richard's finances, a better picture than even he would have been capable of articulating. His house had been re-mortgaged, his pensions barely scratched the interest on his debts, and with each passing day, he was making matters worse with his extravagant spending. Even his existing life insurance policies weren't going to be enough to cover his debts when he passed away. Nannie was going to have to dip into the policies that she had taken out just to cover everything. The old fool had intended on ruining her life with his death, so selfish that he didn't care he'd be condemning her to a life of destitution after he shuffled off the mortal coil. It was clear to Nannie that she was going to have to act quickly to stop him from pushing her even further into debt with his outrageous purchases.

Three months into the marriage, Nannie made herself a widow once more. The same recipe of stewed prunes and rat poison was used, this time baked into an apple pie that she claimed was her mother's recipe. Richard went to sleep one night and simply didn't wake up the next morning. He was an old man, so there was nothing to be suspicious about as far as the doctor was concerned, and while the women of town knew about a very good motive for foul play to be afoot, none of them were even slightly inclined to share that view with the police or their husbands. If Nannie had killed her husband, as a few of them suspected, then he had it coming, and she was a local heroine.

She didn't linger for long in Kansas after Richard had died, just long enough for the bank to foreclose on his house and for the various life insurance policies that she had taken out to pay off. When all was said and done, she was up almost two thousand dollars from this marriage, paid out in the form of a half dozen separate insurance policies that she had taken out on Richard immediately after the marriage. In 1953, that amount of money was equivalent to around about twenty thousand dollars today. Not the fortune that she had hoped to make out of the arrangement, but still a substantial amount of money.

The only thing that she took the time and care to tie up before she left Kansas forever was her correspondence, sending out a letter to every man who had been writing to her in the preceding months, to inform them of her new address. She didn't want any hint of her own infidelity being left in her wake. She couldn't bear the thought of anyone anywhere knowing even one fraction of the secrets that she kept.

Wife of a Preacher

The Diamond Circle Club did not regain Nannie as a member. As excited as Richard may have been about his wonderful find amongst their number, Nannie now considered that dating pool to have been contaminated. The quality of the men that they offered—even the nicest looking and kindest men—was clearly being very poorly judged by whoever was in charge, not to mention the fact that they had allowed a murderer into their midst without a second thought. Instead, she continued her campaign of individual correspondence with the few eligible men whom she considered to be worthy of her time, making trips out to meet up with a few of them, but applying a more exacting set of standards to them beyond whether or not they could woo her. It mattered little if a man could make her heart flutter when he was doing the very same to a dozen other women. It mattered little if he was handsome if he was going to plunge her into debt or despair with his drinking and foolishness.

Nannie gradually came to realise the same thing that most older women realise when they try to date: the men who are left in the dating pool after all of the other fish have been caught tend to be the bottom feeders or the sharks. For every meeting that she arranged, Nannie came away more depressed with her lot in life. She was no longer searching for a great romance—she had let that dream die out somewhere in the last few husbands—but she was still on the lookout for a decent man with whom she might live out the rest of her days; the kind of man with solid foundations that she could build a marriage and a life on. They didn't need to set her heart aflame or fill her every moment with delights—she had come to accept that reality would never be a match for her stories and fantasies in that regard. All that she needed was a man who would not betray her trust the way that those that had come before had done. One decent man in all the world. Surely that wasn't too much to ask?

When she made her way to Oklahoma for the first time, she found it quite dull, like a poor copy of Kansas with only a hint of the greenery that she had grown up around in Alabama. Her disappointment did not extend to the man whom she had come there to meet.

Samuel Doss was a sturdily built man, but clean living meant that he didn't show all of his fifty-nine years of age on his face. Combined with a conservative haircut, his looks were more like one of Nannie's old black and white movie stars than any of the men that she had gone chasing in the last decade or more. His manner of dress was equally conservative, with tailored suits giving him the subtle appearance of wealth without any ostentatious displays. Over the course of their time together, Samuel laid out his life before Nannie's eyes with unflinching honesty. He was a state highway inspector, which took him on the road throughout the week, but on Sundays he was a lay preacher at the local church, helping to guide souls to God, as he had been delivered from the dangers of sin when he was but a young man. He never smoked, never drank, had never chased after women in any meaningful way since he was a teenager, gambling was abhorrent to him, and he considered cuss words to be a sign of poor education and breeding. He was a gentleman.

She could tell, after just a few days in his company, that none of the problems that had plagued her previous husbands were going to rear their ugly heads in this relationship, and she thought that simply eliminating all of the things that had gone wrong would be sufficient to ensure that things would go right.

In June of 1953, just a month after she had buried Richard, the wedding took place and she moved into her new home in Tulsa, Oklahoma. Samuel took the time to consider everything in his life carefully, and the swift proposal may have seemed out of character for him were it not for the long correspondence that had preceded it. All that he truly knew about Nannie after years of writing letters, on and off, was that she was a widow, an excellent cook, and a beauty even now in her twilight years. He often advised people in his flock to count their blessings, and he fully intended to follow his own advice. He may not have had any great passion for Nannie, but what did that matter when she seemed like a perfect fit for his lifestyle? He needed someone to cook and clean for him, and to provide him with comfort in his life, and she ticked all of the boxes.

Samuel had none of the bravado of Nannie's previous husbands, none of their alpha male 'king of the house' posturing either. He would help her around the kitchen if she needed it, without a second thought, and while he insisted that the house be kept clean, he was more than willing to lend his efforts to ensure that it remained tidy. He was never threatening or violent if Nannie didn't uphold his standards, only disappointed and occasionally wheedling. The problem was not that she felt threatened or bullied when she didn't uphold his standards, it was that his standards were impossibly high. His penny-pinching attitude extended to every part of his life. Nannie was not allowed to use the electric fan in the house until the temperature was 'unbearable.' When she left a room, the lights were to be switched off and the door closed to keep in the heat. If she wished to read then only the reading lamp was to be used, illuminating a single chair in the otherwise darkened chamber. Every aspect of his life was carefully regimented, with bedtime and dinnertime scheduled for each day and sex planned ahead and marked on the calendar. There was no spontaneity to any of his actions, and now there could be no spontaneity to any of

Nannie's either. All of the joy that she had found in life alone was being stripped away from her until all that she was left with were the cold bones of reality to chew on. There was no room in his budget for treats or luxuries, and Nannie had to justify everything that she purchased as a necessity or suffer through the indignity of having to head back into town to return it as 'frivolous.' Gone were the choice cuts of meat that she once prepared, gone were the fancy clothes and fine wines. Studious mediocrity was Samuel's intention for her final years, all devoted to the cause of living a more holy life. Nannie couldn't abide it.

Three months into the marriage, she made a break for it, heading back to her cottage in Alabama, where she planned to lick her wounds and make plans for the next step in her life. It wasn't clear whether this was a calculated move to prompt some sort of change in Samuel, a desperate bid for freedom from the oppressive living conditions that she had been subjected to, or simply Nannie acting out. But regardless of the motivation, running away from this husband sent her on an emotional journey that she was entirely unprepared for.

On the bus ride home, Nannie felt like a weight was lifting off her shoulders. The presence of Samuel was altogether too familiar, even after all of these years, an older man with a rigid set of rules about what she should be doing with every moment of her day. A man who determined when she was allowed to experience excitement and lust and treated her like a sinful harlot for feeling anything outside of those moments. A man who treated every penny in his pocket as worth more than all of the affection that Nannie had offered up to him freely. The justifications may have changed from a desire to please her father to trying to please Our Father who art in Heaven, but the day-to-day living was identical. Samuel Doss was just another small-town bully, so set in his ways that he'd rather crush all the life out of a woman than hear any dissenting opinion. Escaping him now was like fleeing the Hazle farm all those years ago.

When she arrived at her disused cottage, a letter from Samuel was already there waiting for her. It was not the passionate outcry of a jilted lover—a man like Samuel would have found something like that far too coarse. Instead, it was a carefully reasoned explanation for why Nannie should not leave him. He had a carefully phrased non-apology explaining that he was very set in his ways after years of repetition and that she would soon fall into the same patterns alongside him as they continued their life together. After reading that section, Nannie was incensed. The man clearly understood nothing about the suffering that he had put her through. He was still just as intent on forcing her to do everything his way for the rest of their lives together.

Her father had never apologised, either. He had always been able to present some justification for why things had to be done his way, even when he was clearly in the wrong. Samuel's version of logic seemed entirely too similar to the reasoning of the man who had forced children to work the fields instead of attending school, who had treated her and her siblings as beasts of burden. She'd been a maid and cook to some of her husbands, but it had been out of a desire to please them, not this. Never this.

It took her almost an hour to calm herself enough to go back and finish reading Samuel's letter, and what she saw there just brought all of her rage back up to simmering point. He had followed up his non-apology and none too subtle insinuations about her flighty temperament with a list of some inducements to encourage her to return home to him promptly. He was trying to buy her. Doling out kindness and equality with the same reluctance that he parted with his money. The gist of the offer was quite simple: if Nannie would adopt the same habits as him and follow the regimen that he demanded, then he would place all of his money into a shared account that they could use for household purchases rather than making her come begging to him for money every time that she needed to make a purchase. If he could trust her to behave as he behaved, then he would be willing to give her equal control over the finances, just as he expected to have equal control over their home and her time.

If the wall of frost around him had broken and he had given a genuine apology for the way that he had treated her—a human apology rather than one garbed in the language of holiness—then it is quite possible that things might have turned out differently. But in that letter, Nannie once again saw the face of her father staring back at her and for the first time realised what an opportunity that this might be for her to finally get some closure. Just as James Hazle's death had thrown her into disarray all of those years ago, so now could the murder of Samuel Doss put things right again. She would finally have her opportunity for revenge. She would finally have a chance to kill the man who had ruined her. It was too tempting to pass up. All that she would need to do was wait for a suitable justification. All that Samuel had to do to sign his own death warrant was to break the compact that he was offering in this letter.

She lingered at her cottage for a day to collect some of the belongings that she'd failed to bring along when she first moved to Oklahoma and reply to some of the letters that had accumulated while she was away getting married. There were still a fair few promising suitors waiting tentatively for her reply to their last entreaty, and now that her current relationship was headed towards an early end she felt a renewed need to keep them on the hook. She invented a story about travelling, fed it to all of them, and promised to write back to them as soon as she returned home, stating with some confidence that she would be back in her Alabama cottage before three months were out.

Samuel had no idea that he had so little time left in this world. He was absolutely delighted when Nannie returned to town, and while he was far from flamboyant in his treatment of her when she arrived, there was the briefest crack in his stoic demeanour, the hint of a tear in his eye when he pulled her into his embrace. There was no break from their regularly scheduled marriage that night, despite Nannie's attempts to incite some action, but the next morning, Samuel drove her to the bank and upheld all of his promises regarding her access to his accounts. The bank manager also advised the seemingly happy couple, and Samuel changed the beneficiary of the life insurance policy that he had taken out to ensure that Nannie would be taken care of in the event that something happened to him. He didn't know it, but he had just hammered another nail into his coffin.

Nannie had never killed a husband only for the money. There had always been an emotional component to her murders. When she was entirely rational, it seemed that she could not justify them, so she had to find some point to fixate on, some reason to stoke the flames of her rage until they were sufficient to overcome whatever scruples she had about taking the life of a man who declared his love for her almost daily. If anything, the insurance payouts of her early murders had been a bonus rather than any sort of goal, but now she was falling into the same logical patterns that Samuel insisted guide every decision, and he had just provided the latest in a long line of incentives to kill him as quickly as possible.

Much of what Nannie had brought back with her from Alabama was her personal library of beloved romance books. She displaced many of the leather-bound tomes from Samuel's shelves in the living room and replaced them with her own well-thumbed and yellowing paperbacks—stories that she had read a dozen times over that, nonetheless, still thrilled her and gave her comfort. Almost instantly, all of the magnanimous promises that Samuel had made to Nannie about relaxing his ridiculously high standards evaporated. He did not want those books in his house. When she tried to turn the conversation back on him, to point out that he spent almost every night reading, he shut her down with a snap. The books that he read were for his intellectual and spiritual betterment. They were works of literature, objects of enlightenment, and tools of education, while hers were simply trash, the lowest common denominator entertainment, designed explicitly to induce sinful thoughts and practices. To learn and improve oneself was divine, but to wallow in the filth that she had brought into his home was a guarantee of damnation in itself. She had to cast them aside if she wanted any hope of an afterlife. She had to turn away from the life of sin that had led her to being pathetic and alone in her later years, the life of sin that had rewarded her with nought but a dead husband and an ever-widening waistline. God would reward her if she turned away from that path, and Samuel would be glad to guide her to righteousness. There was no arguing with him. Samuel clearly considered himself to be the mouthpiece of God in this matter, so no matter how she argued, it would come to nothing, because the decision had already been made above Samuel's pay grade.

Nannie had never commented on the fact that Samuel didn't own a television, even though he clearly had the wealth to afford one, assuming that it was just another symptom of his thriftiness, but now she learned it was because he considered everything broadcast to be filth and degeneracy. Television rotted the brain according to Samuel, and he would have no part in the destruction of his own faculties and setting himself on course to the eternal flames of perdition. When he spoke about God, it was the only time that Nannie saw even a spark of the man that Samuel could have been. It was the only time that he raised his voice or spoke with passion, and he wasted it all on chastising her for failing to follow some nonsense rules that he had invented and tacked on to the end of the commandments.

It was safe to say that Nannie was not a religious woman. She probably would have described herself as worldly without flinching, and the idea that something as small as reading the wrong kind of book might have an impact on her immortal soul, when the wholesale slaughter of her husbands, children, grandchildren, and more had not, was laughable to her. Yet there was nothing that she could do to sway Samuel from his religious mania, and there was nothing that he could do to convince her that spiritual life had to be devoid of worldly pleasures and passions. Their worldviews were fundamentally opposed, so Nannie did what she always had when confronted with a difference of opinion with her husband: she fell silent and began laying plans to be rid of him as promptly as possible.

The Last Supper

Ultimately, she needed no greater provocation than Samuel throwing away her books. He may have dreamed of Heaven and the rest and reward that he would find there, but for Nannie, those stained paperbacks were her holy texts, and the world of imagination that they had let her escape to were her salvation from the miseries of life. Without them, she was just as distraught as he would have been if his faith had been taken away, not that he took the time to understand that.

In Samuel Doss, Nannie faced a challenge that was the direct opposite of the one she had encountered with Frank Harrelson. While Frank had never been around to eat the poisoned food that she prepared, Samuel was there every single moment that she was in the kitchen, lingering and loitering. Worse yet, he had little stomach for sweet treats, and without sugar to cover the taste of the arsenic that she had always used, Nannie was at a loss as to how to poison him. Eventually, she resorted to just stirring it into the cup of coffee that he had along with his dinner each night.

By September, this gradual build-up of poison had begun to take its toll. Samuel's appetite and strength dwindled. He shed fifteen pounds of weight and took to his bed for a week, constantly racked throughout all of this time with spasms and stomach cramps. His doctor was stumped, eventually hospitalising Samuel so that his condition could receive around-the-clock care. He was diagnosed with a massive infection of the intestinal tract and started immediately on a course of penicillin, but even with the latest medical knowledge deployed, he still did not seem to recover. He lay in the hospital, attended to by Dr Schwelbein, a gastroenterologist who specialised in cases like his, for twenty-three days before he made a recovery. His dutiful wife Nannie was there by his bedside every single one of those days, impressing everyone with her profound kindness and the deep love that she clearly harboured for Samuel.

While she was enjoying her time alone at home in-between bouts of playacting for the hospital staff, Nannie couldn't relax properly in her new home knowing that soon Samuel would be back to ruin it all over again. Each day, before she caught the bus up to see him, she would have to collect all of the books and magazines that she had been reading and carefully secret them away so that he wouldn't discover them if he happened to be released. It was ridiculous and exhausting. She found herself sticking to Samuel's prescribed bedtime just because she was so out of sorts; she didn't feel like she could enjoy anything. This was the first time that she'd made a mistake like this in her life, and she had been forced into an awkward situation by her misjudgement of the arsenic dose. Samuel was far larger and healthier than her previous husbands had been, having never lived on the borderline of poverty, and the unfamiliar delivery method meant that she couldn't be sure exactly how much was required to get the job done and how much would become noticeable without sugar to hide its distinctive flavour.

On the twenty-third day, Nannie brought her husband home. Samuel was in good spirits when he was finally released from the hospital. He was still shrunken and weak from the experience, but the pain that had been driving him to prayer every few minutes had finally abated, and he felt like life was returning to his body once more. In Nannie, he saw a new hope for the future. He had taken note of how well she cared for him through this adversity, and he believed that this could be a new start for both of them. A chance for him to loosen the reins a little, and for her to flourish as his loving wife and caretaker until death parted them. Keeping that dream alive, he was astonished to find that Nannie had prepared a beautiful spread for his first meal home—a roast of pork with all the trimmings, and a steaming hot cup of coffee, just how he liked it. She told him that the extra expense that she had gone to would not become a regular thing—she knew how much he valued thrifty living—but just this once she wanted to give him a special treat in celebration of his return home. After so long on the extremely limited diet that the doctors had insisted would aid in his recovery, and the long period before that when he had no appetite, Samuel was absolutely ravenous. Only decorum kept him from shovelling handfuls of the delicious food directly into his face. He washed down every mouthful with another swig of coffee, and Nannie, ever attentive, kept his cup topped up. After he had eaten and drunk his fill, Nannie took him through to their shared reading room to rest, settled him in his favourite seat, and placed a new, enlightening book into his hands so that he could fully enjoy the evening while she went back to the kitchen and studiously cleaned everything, taking extra care to scrub out the coffee pot. By the time that she was finished, he was already complaining of pains in his gut once more, but both he and Nannie quickly attributed it to overeating, and he began chastising himself for gluttony as she helped him hobble through to their marriage bed. He settled onto the pillows with a groan, and Nannie calmed him by pressing her lips to his forehead one last time. She returned to her seat in the other room, turned all of the lights on bright and plucked a romance magazine out from under the cushions. Then, she waited, doing her best to ignore the moans of anguish coming from the other room by vanishing into her own world of romance. A smile slowly spread across her face as she sat there in her own little pocket of light, surrounded by night on all sides. She knew that she would find love again. Love was always out there, just waiting for her. It always had been, and it always would be. All that she had to do was take one step outside her front door and it would be hers.

When the ambulance answered her call in the morning, she had done a good job of forcing herself to cry. Samuel's long bout of illness was well-known to his physician, who quickly ascribed the death to the same gastric infection that had been plaguing him. His body was sent off to the hospital morgue, and the town began to rally around the poor widowed Nannie. Everything was going according to plan, even if he had knocked her off schedule a little by refusing to die the first time around. Nannie would have sailed right through the fake grief and the funeral as always and collected her cheque before hopping a train back home to Alabama and the pile of waiting suitors sitting in her mailbox if it hadn't been for one little spanner in the works: Dr Schwelbein.

Schwelbein was a genuine expert in his field, and he had been confused about how resistant Samuel's infection had been to antibiotics during his hospital stay. When he discovered his patient's body in the morgue, just a day after Samuel had been discharged, he immediately knew that something wasn't right. Legally, Schwelbein had no right to conduct an autopsy on the body, even if he had his suspicions about the cause of death. The official report had already been filed. Still, his curiosity and overwhelming suspicions would not relent, so he did the only thing that he could to discover the truth: he approached Nannie directly and asked her for permission to conduct an autopsy on the body.

He had cornered her at home amidst a crowd of mourners and begun talking loudly about the curious death of her husband. The gathered townsfolk were fascinated to hear that, despite outward appearances, Samuel's illness had actually been terribly unusual, possibly the result of some sort of environmental contaminant that he had come into contact with as a result of his work. It could be a public health crisis if it were not investigated properly. While it may cause her some distress to know that Samuel's body was to be examined, surely she could take some comfort in the fact that doing so could save the lives of countless more. If they had been alone, it would have been possible that Nannie could talk her way out of it, but as she was, surrounded by witnesses, there was nothing that she could do but give her consent and sign the damnable doctor's permission slip. The very same appearance of respectability that had always protected Nannie also damned her now that somebody was actually investigating her crimes.

In Samuel Doss' stomach, Schwelbein found almost half of a pork roast with all of the trimmings—barely digested—the remnants of the coffee, and enough cyanide to kill a horse. It was damning evidence that could point to only one suspect.

Mere hours after the autopsy was conducted, the police arrived to take Nannie in for questioning. She denied absolutely everything, of course, but her tone was strange. She kept letting out little strangled, almost hysterical yelps of laughter, as if the idea of her killing her husband was so ridiculous that she didn't even know how to treat it seriously. By the time that they got her to the police station and into an interrogation room, she had gotten herself under control, and those bleating laughs had become a disinterested giggle. She had brought one of her magazines along from home, and she thumbed through it as the police pressed her for answers. She gave them nothing. For hours and hours, the questioning persisted without bearing fruit. The police knew that Nannie had killed Samuel, there was no doubt about it, but as long as she refused to confess to the crime, there was no guarantee of a conviction. By this point in her life, the giggling, old woman was the very image of a sweet, old grandmother, and the police had no doubt that if she were placed in front of a jury she would charm and disarm them just as easily as she kept flummoxing their interrogators.

The Giggling Granny

While the typical suspect would have had the magazine ripped out of their hands and a sturdy beating applied not long afterwards, the investigators couldn't get past the image that Nannie presented, casually deflecting any suspicion, and giggling away at the idea that she could have ever harmed Samuel. After she had spent almost a day in custody, the local police withdrew from the room no closer to a confession, which was when Special Agent Ray Page stepped in. While the local police had worked tirelessly at Nannie and left looking exhausted, she hadn't even begun to wilt under the pressure. Indeed, she seemed to be thriving thanks to all of the attention that she had been receiving. But while they were coming at her over and over again, the investigation had been rolling along out of sight, and Page had now constructed a timeline of Nannie's life. A timeline that was punctuated with mysterious deaths that benefitted her every few years.

She met Page's gaze as he walked into the room, eyes twinkling and smile still dancing over her lips. 'Oh, you are a handsome young man, but if you think I hurt anybody I'm afraid that you're as good looking as you are foolish.'

He had been observing her in-between the many phone calls that he had made that day, and he had come to believe that she was either completely insane and detached from reality or the greatest actress that he had ever seen. But either way, he was going to have to break through the wall that she had built up around herself if he wanted to get to the truth. He carefully removed the magazine from her hands and laid it down in front of him on the table, commanding her attention. 'Do you believe in ghosts, Nannie?'

The question was so out of place that it broke through her veneer of good humour and left her silent. Page pressed on. 'A few years doing my job, you start to believe in them. They don't haunt places, you see, they haunt people. I meet a lot of haunted people, doing my job. People that have done wrong and know that they have done wrong.'

Nannie giggled again. 'I keep telling you boys, I don't know what you're talking about.'

'How many husbands have you buried, Nannie? How many of their ghosts are in this room with us right now?'

The sparkle in her eyes blinked out, and for just one moment, Page could see the black abyss lurking behind her mask of sanity. She heaved a sigh but still said nothing.

'We can do this the hard way, with me running around the country gathering up the evidence of all the folks that you killed. If I have to do that, then I'll be pushing for the death penalty. But if you admit to what you've done, then things will go a little easier on you.'

There was a long moment of silence, then she let out that damnable giggle again. 'All right, all right. I put rat poison in his coffee.'

Beyond the observation window, the whole police station had just fallen deathly silent. Page had done it. He had actually done it. Nannie pressed on. 'He was a miser of a man. He wouldn't let me watch my shows on the television, he wouldn't let me run the fan even on the hottest nights. I mean... what woman could live in circumstances like that?'

Page played along. 'He sounds very cruel, Nannie.'

She let out a breath of air. Then another giggle, like she was a child who'd been caught stealing a cookie instead of a confessed murderer. 'There, you have it. Now my conscience is clear. Can I have my magazine back now?'

'If you'll tell us about your other husbands, I'll be happy to give it back to you.'

'You promise?'

Page nodded. 'I promise. Now tell me about Morton.'

Over the course of another full day, Page was able to tease out confessions from Nannie to the murder of four of her husbands. She outright denied ever doing any harm to her relatives, including her children and grandchildren, and with all of the confessions that Page already had in writing, he didn't push the old woman for total honesty. He and Nannie both knew that she had murdered every single one of the people on his list, but it wasn't like she was ever going to be getting out of prison anyway, so he felt no need to complicate the situation any further.

Nannie was arrested, and the officers fanned out across the country to begin the grisly task of exhuming her victims' bodies. Every one of them was found to be riddled with arsenic on examination. Only the bodies of her children were left undisturbed. The state had more than enough evidence to put her away and no intention of putting anyone through more trauma than was necessary. Reporters swarmed Charley Braggs, the 'one that got away,' and he earned himself a fair bit of money and fame doling out his story to all-comers.

Of course, when the police raked through Nannie's belongings back at her cottage in Alabama, they discovered that Charley was not the 'one' that got away, so much as one of many. Nannie still had a dozen suitors on the hook, ready to be reeled in the moment that she was finished with Samuel Doss. She had a selection of fresh victims just offering themselves up to her, desperate for her lethal attention.

Nannie's own fame was stoked when the reporters finally got a chance to speak to her, and her charming giggling persona stunned the whole nation. They asked her what punishment she believed that she deserved for killing Doss, and she replied, 'Whatever they choose to do to me will be on their conscience.'

A panel of psychiatrists was assembled to examine Nannie in the run-up to her trial date, but try as they might, they could not find grounds to bar her from standing trial on the basis of her mental health. She was sane, and her actions had clearly been calculated and deliberate, not acts of passion. The state only bothered to pursue a conviction for the murder of Samuel Doss, although ample evidence was available in the other cases. Nannie's trial had already turned into a circus, and they had no intention of rewarding her with more attention if they could possibly avoid it. She was due to stand trial on the second of June, 1955, in the Criminal Court of Tulsa, but her lawyers could not come up with any sort of defence for her in all of their deliberations. At their suggestion, she pled guilty on May 17th. After a brief hearing, Judge Elmer Adams sentenced her to life in prison without parole but barred the use of the electric chair due to her sex. He had no desire to deal with the personal backlash of executing a charming, old woman, who could so casually spin a tale of abusive husbands to excuse her own actions.

She was transferred to Oklahoma State Prison, where she lived out the last ten years of her life responding to mail from her many fans, both male and female. Even then, she did not give up all hope of romance in her life, kindling flirtation in many of her correspondents even if she was never likely to see the light of day again. By 1965, Nannie was transferred to the hospital wing of the prison to live out her final days in opiate-doused comfort. Leukaemia killed her in the end. Her heart was still beating as strongly as ever, but the blood that it was pumping had turned to poison. On June 2nd, at the age of fifty-nine, Nannie Doss died, completely alone.

Nannie Doss was not the typical serial killer by any stretch of the imagination. Even if her crimes had been fuelled by a desire for gratification through murder, rather than simply as a way to dispose of unwanted people in her life, the pattern of her killings was so random and unexpected that she likely would have escaped notice regardless.

Many have attributed her murderous behaviour to the head injury that she suffered in her childhood, as though it damaged some 'moral centre' in her brain, but the truth is, of course, considerably more complicated. A family historian quite readily points out that throughout the generations, both sides of Nannie's family tree had violent and angry people on display, and that Nannie's temper had always gotten her into trouble, even before the fateful bump on the head. The truth is that there were two diametrically opposed ideals driving every single one of Nannie's actions. The first was passed down to her by her father: the idea that human life is inherently worthless and that people only have value if they are producing something or can be of use to you—a common enough assertion among sociopaths. The other ideal was passed down to her indirectly from her mother: that true love was the highest of all goals.

Ironically, it was that latter ideal that proved to make her the most lethal in the long run. If she had only been instilled with a contempt for other people then she would most likely have left them well alone, but having been forced to pursue romantic relationships throughout her life, and with her happiness dependent upon the success of those relationships, the dreamy young girl was transformed into an engine of mayhem that would have kept on rolling over the lives of men forever until it was stopped, more by luck than by any sort of intervention.

The society that created Nannie, with its contempt for women as anything other than wives and mothers, also provided the perfect smokescreen for her to operate behind. Nobody could have expected that a weak and simpering woman such as her was behind a brutal series of agonising deaths by poison. The life and times that she had been born into were the perfect disguise for her actions.

To this day, the legacy of 'The Giggling Granny' lives on in public consciousness, recurring over and over in crime fiction—remembered, sometimes a little too late, each time that a wronged wife is set the menial task of preparing a meal for her husband.

ABOUT THE AUTHOR

Ryan Green is a true crime author in his late thirties. He lives in Herefordshire, England with his wife, three children, and two dogs. Outside of writing and spending time with his family, Ryan enjoys walking, reading and windsurfing.

Ryan is fascinated with History, Psychology and True Crime. In 2015, he finally started researching and writing his own work and at the end of the year, he released his first book on Britain's most notorious serial killer, Harold Shipman.

He has since written several books on lesser-known subjects, and taken the unique approach of writing from the killer's perspective. He narrates some of the most chilling scenes you'll encounter in the True Crime genre.

You can sign up to Ryan's newsletter to receive a free book, updates, and the latest releases at:

WWW.RYANGREENBOOKS.COM

MORE BOOKS BY RYAN GREEN

4 books for the price of 2 (save 50%)

Four chilling true crime stories in one collection, from the bestselling author Ryan Green.

Volume 1 contains some of Green's most fascinating accounts of violence, abuse, deception and murder. Within this collection, you'll receive:

- Harold Shipman
- Colombian Killers
- Fred & Rose West
- The Kuřim Case

MORE BOOKS BY RYAN GREEN

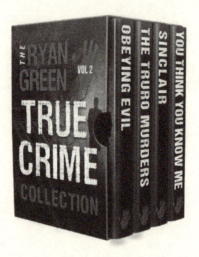

4 books for the price of 2 (save 50%)

Four chilling true crime stories in one collection, from the bestselling author Ryan Green.

Volume 2 contains some of Green's most fascinating accounts of violence, abuse, deception and murder. Within this collection, you'll receive:

- Obeying Evil
- The Truro Murders
- Sinclair
- You Think You Know Me

FREE TRUE CRIME AUDIOBOOK

If you are interested in listening to a chilling True Crime story, follow the link below to download a FREE copy of *Torture Mom*.

WWW.RYANGREENBOOKS.COM/FREE-AUDIOBOOK

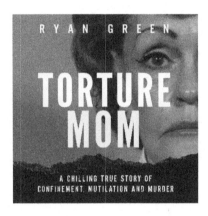

"Ryan Green has produced another excellent book and belongs at the top with true crime writers such as M. William Phelps, Gregg Olsen and Ann Rule" –**B.S. Reid**

"Wow! Chilling, shocking and totally riveting! I'm not going to sleep well after listening to this but the narration was fantastic. Crazy story but highly recommend for any true crime lover!" –**Mandy**

"Graphic, upsetting, but superbly read and written" –**Ray C**

WWW.RYANGREENBOOKS.COM/FREE-AUDIOBOOK

Made in the USA
Las Vegas, NV
24 March 2024